D1593600

MILITARISM AND POLITICS
IN LATIN AMERICA

Recent Titles in
Contributions in Military Studies

MILITARISM AND POLITICS IN LATIN AMERICA

Peru from Sánchez Cerro to *Sendero Luminoso*

Daniel M. Masterson

Contributions in Military Studies, Number 111

Greenwood Press
New York • Westport, Connecticut • London

F
3448
M34
1991

Library of Congress Cataloging-in-Publication Data

Masterson, Daniel M.
    Militarism and politics in Latin America : Peru from Sánchez Cerro
to Sendero Luminoso / Daniel M. Masterson.
        p.   cm.—(Contributions in military studies, ISSN 0883-6884 ;
no. 111)
    Includes bibliographical references and index.
    ISBN 0-313-27213-1 (alk. paper)
    1. Peru—Politics and government—1919-1968. 2. Peru—Armed
Forces—Political activity—History—20th century. 3. Civil—
military relations—Peru—History—20th century.   I. Title.
II. Series.
F3448.M34   1991
322'.5'0985—dc20   90-23010

British Library Cataloguing in Publication Data is available.

Library of Congress Catalog Card Number: 90-23010
ISBN: 0-313-27213-1
ISSN: 0883-6884

First published in 1991

Greenwood Press, 88 Post Road West, Westport, CT 06881
An imprint of Greenwood Publishing Group, Inc.

Printed in the United States of America

The paper used in this book complies with the
Permanent Paper Standard issued by the National
Information Standards Organization (Z39.48-1984).

10 9 8 7 6 5 4 3 2 1

Grateful acknowledgment is given for permission from
Commander Jorge Ortiz to use the photographs from the
Instituto de Estudios Histórico-Marítimos del Perú, Lima.

For my parents
and in memory of
Brian, Les Rout,
and Dave Bailey

Contents

List of Illustrations

Preface

Few Latin American institutions are more controversial, emotion provoking, and less well understood than the region's armed forces establishments. Beginning with the pioneering work of Edwin Lieuwen and John J. Johnson in the early 1960s, scholars have been examining the role of the military in modern Latin American societies. Still, much work is left to be done. While reviewing the state of the literature on Latin American militarism in 1976, Abraham F. Lowenthal appealed for more empirical case studies to further our understanding of the complexities of Latin America's armed institutions. Lowenthal singled out the uniquely reformist military government of General Juan Velasco Alvarado (1968-1975) in Peru as particularly worthy of greater attention. Considered the model of military progressivism in modern Latin America, the Velasco regime has subsequently attracted considerable scholarly inquiry. Yet, aside from the groundbreaking work of Víctor Villanueva Valencia in Spanish, no systematic studies using archival sources in Peru and other nations to trace the historical roots of Velasco's "Revolution from Above" has yet been published. This study seeks to meet this need while encouraging further necessary research on the Peruvian military and the armed forces of the other Latin American nations.

This book is primarily an analysis of the Peruvian armed forces in the context of national politics from the revolution of Lieutenant Colonel Luis M. Sánchez Cerro in 1930 through the first administration of President Fernando Belaúnde Terry (1963-1968). I have concluded this study, however, with an overview of the Velasco regime and the ensuing fifteen years of political and economic turmoil in Peru in the hope of providing a clearer framework for this analysis. My conclusions regarding the

Velasco regime are tentative. Further research is clearly needed, but this must await the availability of military and intelligence records in Peru, the United States, and perhaps even the Soviet Union.

The list of individuals who have aided me in the completion of this book is extensive. The late professors Leslie B. Rout, Jr., and David C. Bailey, who directed my early work at Michigan State University with wisdom and good humor, are owed a debt that I can never repay. Lending assistance in the early stages of this study with research suggestions were Fredrick B. Pike, David Scott Palmer, Allen Gerlach, José García, Jorge Rodríguez Beruff, Liisa North, David Chaplin, and Daniel Sharp. The late Víctor Villanueva Valencia was a guiding influence throughout the first stage of my research in Peru. I have greatly benefited from my conversations with Don Víctor and his valuable insights on my early work. Assisting me in many ways during the final stage of this project has been a Peruvian armed forces officer who must remain anonymous. As a fine historian, this officer made many valuable suggestions for further research. His kindness and that of his family during my two most recent trips to Peru are greatly appreciated. My research in Peru was facilitated by the cooperation of the staffs at the *Sala de Investigaciones* of the *Biblioteca Nacional,* the *Instituto de Estudios Histórico-Marítimos del Perú (IEHMP),* the *Centro de Estudios Histórico Militares del Perú* (CEHMP), and the *Centro de Altos Estudios Militares* (CAEM). I especially want to thank A. Elia Lazarte of the CEHMP and Admiral (R) Federico Salmón de la Jara of *IEHMP* for their continual kindness and assistance over the years. I am also grateful to Major General Alfonso Llosa, subdirector of CAEM, and Admiral Manuel Reyna, director of education and programs at the same institution, for their willingness to share their views with me during my recent visit. I am not able publicly to acknowledge all the Peruvian armed forces officers who have been willing to talk to me during the extended course of my research. I would, however, like to thank retired army generals Edgardo Mercado Jarrín, Jorge Fernández Maldonado Solari, and Francisco Morales Bermúdez Cerrutti, as well as Vice Admiral (R) Luis M. Vargas Caballero for taking the time to express their views to me on the military policies of the Velasco and Morales Bermúdez governments.

Librarians and archivists at many institutions in the United States have given me valuable assistance, most particularly at the National Archives in Washington, D.C.; the Franklin D. Roosevelt Library in Hyde Park, New York; the Lyndon B. Johnson Library in Austin, Texas; the Cornell University Library in Ithaca, New York; and the Nimitz Library of the United States Naval Academy. My views on Peru and the military's societal role were further clarified during two National Endowment for the

Humanities summer institutes, at Stanford University in 1978 and Cornell University in 1990. John J. Johnson, director of the Stanford seminar, Billie Jean Isbell, coordinator of the Cornell institute, and John V. Murra of Cornell offered useful suggestions for my work. Kenneth J. Hagan, the Naval Academy's archivist and professor of history, warrants a *fuerte abrazo* for his constant and often prodding encouragement during the past two years. While Ken was wrestling with Alfred Thayer Mahan, I was doing the same with Juan Velasco Alvarado. I have been exchanging views on Latin America for a much longer time with G. Pope Atkins of the Academy's political science department. Special thanks must also go to my close friend Ted Bogacz of the Academy's history department for aiding my understanding of the Prussian military experience from Jena onward. John Child of American University and Jeffrey Klaiber, S. J. of the *Universidad Católica del Perú* read chapter 10 of this study and offered useful suggestions. While the insights of all these individuals have been extremely valuable, let me emphasize that the interpretations offered in this work are entirely my own.

Two Naval Academy Research Council grants made possible my two most recent visits to Peru, and this financial assistance is appreciated. Connie Grigor and Debby Cutler, who expertly typed the manuscript with my frequent revisions, were a great help to me. I want also to acknowledge the encouragement and patience of Mildred Vasan and Lynn Flint at Greenwood Publishing Group while I was preparing the work for publication. William Cogar of the Academy's History Department and Kathleen Harrod Mach deserve my thanks for their help in the final production phase of this book.

To my parents and my family, whose encouragement and patience helped keep me at this project over the years, I owe my deep gratitude. I especially owe my wife, Deborah, and my children, Katie, Erin, and Andy, much more of my time. For Andy, the trip to Savanna, Illinois, to hunt for Trilobite fossils near the Mississippi River now looks like a good bet.

COLOMBIA

ECUADOR

Río Napo

Tumbes
TUMBES
La Tina
Talara
PIURA
Sullana
Piura
Huancabamba
San
Ignacio
Nazareth

AMAZONAS

Río Pastaza

Río Marañón

LORETO

Iquitos
Amazon

Río Yavari

Río Ucayali

BRAZIL

Chachapoyas
Moyobamba
Yurimaguas

LAMBAYEQUE
Chiclayo
CAJAMARCA
SAN
Cajamarca
Juanjui
MARTÍN
Contamana

Pacasmayo
Santiago
de Chuco
Cartavio
Trujillo
Mollebama
Tayabamba
Pucallpa
Salaverry
Galgada
LA LIBERTAD
Huallance
Chimbote
ANCASH
Huarás
HUÁNUCO

Río Ucayali

Huánuco
Pozuzo
Goyllarisquizga
Cerro
PASCO
Paramonga
de Pasco
Huacho
JUNÍN

Río Urubamba

Río Alto Purús

MADRE
DE DIOS

LIMA
La Oroya
Río Madre di Dios

PACIFIC
Ancón
Callao
Huancayo
Puerto
Maldonado

OCEAN
Lima
Luisiana
HUANCAVELICA
Yauyos
Huadquiña
San Vicente de Cañete
Huancavelica
CUSCO
Cusco
Pisco
Ayacucho
Abancay
APURÍMAC
PUNO

PERU
Ica
ICA
AYACUCHO
Ayaviri

International boundary
Nazca
Juliaca
Lago

Departamento boundary
AREQUIPA
Puno
Titicaca

National capital
Arequipa

Departamento capital
Desaguadero

Railroad
Matarani
Moquegua

Pan American Highway
Mollendo
Toquepala

0   100   200 Miles
Ilo
TACNA

0   100   200 Kilometers
MOQUEGUA
Tacna

CHILE

BOLIVIA

Introduction

Ama Sua, Ama Llulla, Ama Kella (Don't Steal, Don't Loaf, Don't Lie). This famous Quechua slogan painted under the rough likeness of Tupac Amaru II, the leader of a massive eighteenth-century Indian uprising against Spanish rule in highland Peru, greeted those entering the aging sugar mill at the Casa Grande plantation near Trujillo in 1971. Previously owned by the Gildermeister family, one of Peru's wealthiest, the Casa Grande plantation was now administered by a Peruvian army colonel. The officer, a member of the Intelligence Service and a graduate of the United States Army Intelligence School at Fort Meade, Maryland, characterized the attitude of Peru's soldier/reformers to a visiting United States scholar by claiming "The new military man is one who thinks and has social feeling. This is a product of the (Velasco) Revolution. We can no longer be indifferent to the problems of Peru and the deception of its politicians. We have left things to these corrupt politicians long enough."[1]

Confidence in their sense of social justice and contempt for civilian politicians were commonly expressed attitudes of the military progressives dominating the decision making of the government of General Juan Velasco Alvarado (1968-1975). Like no other military regime in Latin American history, these military radicals used their power in a concerted effort to transform Peruvian society during the Velasco regime. Because their efforts fell far short of success, however, Peru today confronts problems as serious as any during its national history.

Those reflecting on the reasons for Peru's social and political torment as it enters the last decade of the twentieth century would do well to turn to the words of José Carlos Mariátegui, the brilliant Marxist intellectual and author of *Seven Interpretive Essays on Peruvian Reality*. Writing in the late

1920s, Mariátegui, in analyzing the geographic and cultural dualism that
has impeded Peruvian national unity, observed:

The Indian race and language, displaced from the coast by the Spaniard and his
language, have fearfully taken refuge in the *sierra*. Therefore, in the *sierra* are
combined all the elements of a region, if not a nationality. The Peru of the coast,
heir of Spain and the conquest, controls the Peru of the *sierra* from Lima; but it
is not demographically and spiritually strong enough to absorb it. Peruvian unity
is still to be accomplished. It is not a question of the communication or
cooperation of former small states or free cities within the boundaries of a single
nation. In Peru the problem of unity goes much deeper. Instead of a single
pluralism of local and regional traditions, what has to be solved is a dualism of
race, language and sentiment, born of the invasion and conquest of indigenous
Peru by a foreign race that has not managed to merge with the Indian race, or
eliminate or absorb it.[2]

More than a half century after Mariátegui noted these deep divisions in
Peruvian society, the economist Hernando De Soto in his book, *The Other
Path: The Invisible Revolution in the Third World*, decried the continuance
of Peru's ruptured social fabric, and wrote, "There is more than one
country within Peru's borders." Noting the persistence of a "mercantilist
economy and the destructive alternatives of terrorist violence and the
impractical exhortations of many progressives," De Soto called for a
solution based upon freeing Peru's poor from the legal restraints of the
modern state and allowing the native genius of the country's innovative
informales to help chart the nation's future course.[3]

De Soto's formula for Peruvian reform represents a complete break with
the highly directive and often authoritarian nature of past efforts to bring
about progressive change. It certainly stands at the opposite pole from
what the Peruvian armed forces tried to accomplish during the government
of General Juan Velasco Alvarado in the seven years after it seized power
on 3 October 1968. The Velasco regime's "Revolution from Above" was
the product of a decades-long process of internal military change and
professional soul-searching by Peru's soldiers and sailors as they labored to
identify and resolve both the nation's fundamental problems and the
military's proper role in solving them.

Now more than two decades have passed since the Velasco government
enacted the most remarkable series of reforms of any Latin American
military regime. These reforms elicited an enormous outpouring of
scholarship seeking to characterize the Velasco government's programs and,
most of all, its motivations. Labeled corporatist, socialist, populist, and
authoritarian nationalist, this military regime still defies precise classification
because the soldiers who took control of the Pizarro Palace in early

October, 1968 were themselves unsure and still unprepared for their intended mission despite their bold self-characterization as innovative nation builders and "permanent vehicles for Peru's modernization."

Velasco's "Revolutionary Government of the Armed Forces" (1968-1975) is regarded as a unique phenomenon in the history of Latin American militarism. Yet, viewed in a broader historical context, it is certainly not without precedent. Armies since the age of Sparta have initiated military and political reform as components of nation building. One of the often-cited examples of soldiers as state builders is the Prussian army. Frederick the Great's axiom, however, that "Prussian expansion can only be done with the sword" could be acted on by Otto Von Bismarck only after the Iron Chancellor's political predecessors, most notably Stein and Scharnhorst, and later Von Moltke, reformed the army after its crushing defeats by Napoleon at Auerstadt and Jena in 1807. Clearly, the Prussian military reforms of the early nineteenth century help lay the foundation for the modern German nation. After their stunning defeat of France in 1871, Prussian soldiers journeyed most notably to Argentina, Chile, and Japan to begin organizing the professional armed forces of these nations. It was not, however, the victorious Prussians that Peru would turn to after its humiliation by Chile in the War of the Pacific (1879-1883) but rather to a rebuilding French army. Arriving in 1896, French army advisers would soon instill in the minds of their Peruvian students the belief that the army must have a role in building a modern nation. This was the belief that Velasco and its activist military colleagues would act upon after the 3 October 1968 revolution.

In an effort to explain the motivations of these military reformers and the ramifications of the failure of their reforms for contemporary Peru, this study will examine the institutional history of the Peruvian armed forces in the four decades prior to the Velasco *coup*. It will also posit tentative conclusions regarding the impact of the Velasco reforms upon the subsequent role of the military in Peruvian society in the troubled years since Velasco's fall from power in 1975. Before this discussion can begin, however, a brief profile of Peru and its people and the evolution of the military within the broader context of Latin American military professional development will help place this study in a clearer perspective.

The Peru that is striving to achieve a national identity is at once a nation of great promise and endemic problems. Four-fifths the size of Alaska, this nation of twenty-two million is both a benefactor and victim of its rugged and diverse geography. Three distinct geographic regions comprise the nation: the *costa*, the *sierra*, and the *montaña*. Stretching for fourteen hundred miles in a narrow band fifty to one hundred miles wide is the arid coastal desert. In this region can be found Peru's five largest cities, including Lima, with a population of nearly six million. Traveling south from Peru's northernmost city of Zarumilla, one encounters more than fifty rivers with their forty oases before reaching the Chilean border at Tacna. These rivers, draining the Andean watershed, supported the Moche and Chimu civilizations before the Incas and today water the rich rice, sugar, and cotton lands of the north coast.[4]

Marine life abounded in the cold Humboldt current off the Peruvian coast and enabled Peru to become one of the world's leading fishing nations in the past thirty years. With the decline in the harvest of anchovies, which were converted into high-protein fish meal, Peru has been forced to turn to other sources for foreign exchange. Unless and until major new reserves of petroleum are discovered in the northeast jungle region, the bulk of Peru's petroleum will be extracted from the north coast and its nearby offshore fields. Peru's main iron ore deposit, the former Marcona mining complex, is also located in the *costa* region at the southern port of Ilo. Finally, the dominance of the coastal region in Peruvian economic life is further demonstrated by the prominence of the Lima-Callao areas in light manufacturing and of the north coast city of Chimbote in steel production and fish-meal processing.[5]

The *sierra*, with many peaks towering above twenty thousand feet, occupies 24 percent of the nation's territory and is home to nearly half the population. Divided into three separate *cordilleras*, the mountainous backbone of Peru offers scarce arable land on the thin soils of the scattered *punas* or *altiplanos* throughout the region.[6] From the rise of the classical civilizations of Tiahuanaco and Huari around A.D. 1000 to the fall of the Inca empire in the early sixteenth century, the *sierra* was the cultural heart of Peru. It still is the pivot upon which Peru's future revolves. Nearly one-third of Peru's population speak only the Indian languages of Quechua and Aymara, and the vast majority of these people reside in the central and southern *sierra*. Exploited from the Spanish conquest until the 1970s under one of the most inequitable land tenure systems in the world, the Indian population of the *sierra* was barred from political participation by its fear of the government and the local *patrón* (landlord). A Spanish literacy requirement prevented Indians from voting until the Velasco era. Many of these problems were addressed by the reforms of the Velasco government but in large measure were not resolved. As a consequence, the *sierra* became a seedbed for the most unified and purposeful guerrilla/terrorist movement in Latin American history: *Sendero Luminoso* (Shining Path).[7]

Realists know that solutions to Peru's problems rest in resolving the land tenure and social integration dilemma of the *sierra* population. Visionaries, however, have traditionally cast their gaze on the *montaña* and its vast resource potential as a "quick fix" for Peru's myriad problems. The eastern Amazon basin, known as the *montaña*, comprises nearly two-thirds of Peru's land mass but less than 10 percent of the population. The *montaña* is composed of two distinct regions. The heavily forested eastern slopes of the *cordillera*, known as the *Ceja de Montaña* (eyebrow of the forest), was the focus of President Fernando Belaúnde Terry's ambitious but ill-fated roadbuilding scheme in the mid-1960s. Peru's vast rain forest is located in the lowland or *Montaña Baja*.[8] The Amazon River port of Iquitos is situated in the heart of this region, which is home to Peru's approximately 150,000 tribal Indians. One of these tribes, the Matses, attests to the nearly impenetrable isolation of much of this rain forest. A primitive hunting and gathering people, the Matses' first contact with the outside world came with the rubber boom in the late nineteenth century. These fiercely independent people violently resisted encroachment by outsiders until the 1970s while they still practiced their ritualistic cannibalism.[9]

Despite the terrain and the resistance of the indigenous population, the *montaña*, like the Brazilian rain forest, has been the target of ambitious colonizing programs since the early twentieth century. But the soils have proven unproductive, and Peru's roadbuilding and colonizing efforts have not matched the pace of those in Brazil. Substantial oil reserves were discovered in this region in the 1970s and further strikes might fuel greater efforts to exploit this immense region.

The people that reside in Peru's diverse lands are only partially defined by statistics. With twenty-two million people (1990), Peru's population will double at its present growth rate (2.5 percent) in the next twenty-eight years. Life expectancy during the troubled 1980s has remained stable at fifty-eight years after a dramatic increase from thirty-seven years since World War II. This lack of progress is in part due to Peru's infant mortality rate, which is one of the highest in Latin America at eighty-eight per one thousand. Like the population of many Third World nations, Peru's population is very young, with 40 percent of Peru's people under the age of fifteen. This youthful nation has come increasingly to reside in its cities as the exodus from rural areas to Lima and other coastal metropolitan areas accelerated dramatically after 1950. As a result, the population of Peru's four largest cities has increased fourfold since the mid-1940s.[10]

Population figures are most misleading regarding Peru's ethnic makeup. Figures for 1989 indicate that Peru's population is 45 percent Indian, 37 percent mestizo, 15 percent white, and 3 percent black and Asiatic. The ethnic distinctions of "Indian" and "mestizo" are, however, as much cultural and economic distinctions as they are accurate characterizations of race or phenotype. Mestizos are defined as persons with some degree of Indian ancestry who have been culturally integrated into the dominant Hispanic culture. Indians, by their language (either Quechua or Aymara), their style of dress, and their general non-Western outlook see themselves and are treated by whites and mestizos as distinctly apart from Peru's dominant Hispanicized culture. At the lower levels of the class structure, transition from Indian to mestizo status is readily accomplished by speaking Spanish and dressing in Western clothing. Financial and professional success, or as the phrase goes throughout Latin America, "money whitens," vastly facilitates the transition from one culture to another.

The "Indian problem" as it is known in Peru is rooted both in social prejudice and in a historic fear of Indian violence. Thomas M. Davies, in his study of Indian integration in Peru, commented on this fear and noted, "The bloody Indian revolt of Túpac Amaru II in 1780 has served for almost two centuries as an example of what could happen. Subsequent, though smaller, revolts merely deepen the fear."[11] *Sendero Luminoso's* efforts to radicalize the Indian population of the *sierra* in the 1980s has intensified this fear to a degree unknown in this century.

This innate fear and the need for labor led to the subjugation of the Indians after the Spanish conquest. The most devastating aspect of this repression has been the alienation of the Indian from his sacred *Pachamama* (motherland). Since the early colonial era in Peru, the land tenure system has rested on two mutually destructive foundations: *latifundia*, large estates demanding substantial Indian labor, and *minifundia*, tiny parcels barely sufficient to feed one family. Within this general framework exists a complexity of labor systems that vary regionally throughout Peru. The one constant in this equation prior to the 1960s was the highly inequitable distribution of land.

The agricultural census of 1961 left no question of the severity of the land tenure problem. Eighty-three percent of Peru's farms occupied less than 6 percent of the land, with one-third of these units being smaller than 2.5 acres. In contrast, less than one-half of 1 percent of the nation's agricultural enterprises occupied 75 percent of the land. Even more troubling, one thousand haciendas larger than forty-two thousand acres accounted for 60 percent of Peru's arable land.[12]

Three primary labor systems supplied the work force on these huge *sierra* haciendas. These systems, evolving slowly since the early colonial period, required local Indians to devote as much as two hundred days per year to the *patron's* field and household. Known as *yanaconaje, aparceria* and *colonaje*, these systems effectively entrapped the Indian and his family in an exploitative relationship with the *hacendado*. This relationship is well characterized by Davies:

Under all the above systems, the *hacendado* requires more of the Indian than just a percentage of his crop and it is these extra services which make the exploitation so extremely onerous. The most widespread form of service is the *pongaje* whereby the Indians and their families are required to work free in the hacienda household as maids, butlers, chauffeurs, cooks, and general handymen. The Indian receives no payment for these services and is even required to travel to the *hacendado*'s urban residence to fulfill his obligation. . . . Since many of these Indians are sons and grandsons of *pongas*, one could argue that they are in fact slaves of the *hacendados*.[13]

The Indians of the *sierra*, striving to maintain their traditional way of life, were able in some areas to resist the encroachment of local haciendas to protect the sanctity of their centuries-old *comunidades*. These communal lands traced their origins to the Inca land-holding system subsumed under the extended family unit known as the *ayllu*. By the late 1950s, however, these *comunidades* were being threatened throughout the central *sierra*. The *comuneros* responded with a massive wave of land invasions throughout the central and southern *sierra*. These seizures and the desperate land tenure problems prompted the Velasco regime to make agrarian reform one of the pillars of its revolutionary program. The inadequacy of Velasco's agrarian policy, nonetheless, raised expectations that government policy failed to meet. Largely unresolved land tenure problems in the department of Ayacucho in the south-central *sierra* allowed the leaders of *Sendero Luminoso*, based at the National University of San Cristóbal de Huamanga, to take advantage of the region's historically exploited Indian population to begin building their revolutionary base in the 1970s.

Peru's problems of geography, ethnic pluralism, and inequitable land distribution provide a tenuous foundation for a national economy that has never realized the potential of its rich and diverse resource base. The observation of the Peruvian historian Jorge Basadre that Peru is a land of missed opportunities most aptly applies to its economic development. The modern Peruvian economy has not been wrapped in the monocultural straitjacket that has made many other Latin American nations acutely dependent upon the whims of the world economy. Like Argentina, with its vast economic potential founded on rich and abundant soils, Peru, with its diversity of mineral resources and productive coastal agriculture, has not been able to translate its wealth into a healthy and stable economy. With substantial petroleum reserves, Peru also boasts significant deposits of iron ore, potash, silver, and gold. When these assets are coupled with its north coast commercial agriculture and an emerging coffee industry, Peru's economic potential makes the dire economic crisis of the late 1980s even more tragic. Underlying Peru's legal economy is, of course, its $1.5 billion annual trade in narcotics. Centered in the Upper Huallaga Valley in north-central Peru, the traffic in cocaine has vastly altered the economic infrastructure of the region. Very much like the peasants in the Guaviare region in Colombia and the Chapare Valley in Bolivia, peasants in this region have now become completely dependent on coca production for their livelihood. Estimates place the numbers of acres in coca production in Peru in 1988 at 270,000. More ominously, the cocaine trade appears to be one of the principal sources of revenue for *Sendero Luminoso's* operations since the mid-1980s. This economic picture must be viewed in the context of Peru's foreign debt obligations, which now total in excess of 20 billion dollars. Because of the García administration's refusal to make payments on the debt in amounts in excess of 10 percent of the value of the nation's exports, Peru's international credit status has been severely impaired. The first months of President Alberto Fujimori's government (which took office in July, 1990) have been characterized by drastic economic austerity measures designed to reestablish a working relationship with the International Monetary Fund (IMF).

It is not within the realm of this study to attempt an analysis of Peru's contemporary economic difficulties. Observations by three noted authorities on Peru's modern economy, however, will help clarify the contemporary economic situation. Rosemary Thorp and Geoffrey Bertram in *Peru, 1890-1977: Growth and Policy in an Open Economy* argue that the geographic and cultural dualism that has been described impeded Peru's economic development since the 1890s. They conclude that economic growth was largely limited to the "modern sector" and concentrated on the coast. Additionally, they discovered that the "dual structure of the economy hardened as the spread of capitalism discriminated among sectors and regions, and as disparities were accentuated by population growth." Commenting on the sharp economic decline that began in the mid-1970s, now continuing more than a decade later, Thorp and Bertram conclude their study with the observation that "no engine of growth other than export earnings emerged to provide the basis for self-sustaining capitalist development; even industrialization, despite its rapid advance in recent decades, has brought new elements of vulnerability and dependence without generating an autonomous economic dynamism."[14]

This analysis raised the question of why the internal market economy in Peru has not grown at the pace of the export sector. One explanation of this phenomenon is offered by De Soto in *The Other Path*. De Soto maintains that Peru's nearly impenetrable governmental and legal bureaucracy has blunted traditional capitalist incentive by presenting a maze of laws and institutional corruption which stand in the way of hardworking but capital-deficient entrepreneurs. These legal and economic conditions have fostered a vast black market or informal economy, largely centered in Lima, that has kept the wheels of the national economy bumping along during the past three decades. According to De Soto, the consequences of the continued legal suppression of the informal economy is the perpetuation of a modern form of mercantilism. De Soto explains:

There are important similarities between the system of mercantilism in Europe and the system of redistributive law in Peru. Both are characterized to a greater or lesser degree by authoritative law-making, an economic system in which the state intervenes directly, obstructive, detailed and *dirigiste* regulation of the economy, poor or non-existent access to enterprise for those who do not have close ties to government, unwieldy bureaucracies and a population which organizes into redistributive combines and powerful professional associations.[15]

De Soto's conclusions are really not surprising. The pattern of bureaucratic economic control has been axiomatic in Spanish America since the conquest. Established in 1521, the Council of the Indies in Seville issued thousands of decrees governing colonial affairs that were never enforced because of unfavorable political conditions in the New World. Viceroys often selectively enforced only those laws that made administrative sense under the rationale *Obedezco pero no cumplo* (I obey but I do not fulfill). A vast smuggling network and thriving local industries attest to the strength of an "informal economy" even during colonial times in Spanish America. But this early type of informalism flourished before the modern governmental and legal apparatus became as pervasive and well entrenched as it is in contemporary Peru. Thus both the roots and the potential solution to Peru's present economic problems rest with its institutional Hispanic heritage. This situation is in some measure also true of the Iberian military legacy.

Two distinct weaves compose the fabric of the Latin American professional armed forces of today: the Hispanic military heritage and the influence of German, French, and United States training in the late nineteenth and early twentieth centuries. Numerous scholars, most notably Americo Castro and Eric Wolf, have suggested that the origins of militarism and *caudillismo* in Spanish America can be traced to the *Reconquista*, the campaign to rid Spain of the Moors. Wolf argues that the Hispanic military heritage "was exemplified most clearly in the armies of

Castile, composed of warlike nobility and a warlike peasantry. . . . The
nobility, partly organized in religious orders of monastic warriors, saw in
warfare a ready source of ego-enhancement and looted wealth."[16] With
the Spanish conquest of the Americas following closely on the heels of the
Reconquista this military tradition was kept alive in the exploits of Cortés,
Pizarro, and their lieutenants. Moreover, as Richard Morse has argued, the
unification of Spain under Ferdinand and Isabella vastly enhanced the
power of the monarch and expanded the authority of Spanish law based
originally on the *Siete Partidas* (Seven Divisions of law) of King Alfonso X,
"The Sage" (1252-1284). This body of laws became the foundation for the
legal and governmental structure of Spain and colonial Spanish authoritarianism.

Thus the roots of authoritarianism exemplified by the ancient Spanish
expression *Del rey abajo ninguno* (After the king, no one is superior to me)
became firmly ingrained in the mentality of Spanish American colonial
leadership. Adding a sophisticated political dimension to this tradition of
authoritarianism, according to Morse, was the "secular Renaissance
counterpart," drawn from Ferdinand's Italian and Navarise campaigns.
Morse concluded that "Isabella presented the unity of spiritually intransigent Christendom to the infidel and pagan. Ferdinand was committed to
the shifting, amoral statecraft of competing Christian princes."[17]

Unquestionably, twentieth-century *caudillos* such as Juan Perón and Fidel
Castro are modern embodiments of this tradition. *Caudillismo* is most
frequently associated with the military elite in Latin America, and scholars
have recognized the link between Spanish medieval warrior castes and the
autonomous power of military elites in the region since the early nineteenth century. Lyle McAlister in his seminal work, *The Fuero Military in
New Spain*, noted the transplantation of medieval military *fueros* (feudal
privileges) nearly intact into the military institutions in colonial Mexico.
McAlister concluded that the *fuero militar*, which accorded special military
privileges to the colonial militia in New Spain, "were important in
promoting praetorian government in Mexico."[18] McAlister applied his conclusions to only that period immediately following the independence epoch
and did not claim that these *fueros* provided the basis for modern Latin
American militarism. His caution is well founded, for while his study does
validate the incorporation of Spanish military tradition in its colonies, it
does not document the creation of a professional military elite that
survived the wars of independence. The only other study of a Spanish
colonial militia, Leon G. Campbell's *The Military and Society in Colonial
Peru, 1750-1810*, suggests that these *fueros* had even less impact upon the

formation of a permanent professional military institution in Peru than in Mexico.

In his well-crafted analysis of eighteenth-century Bourbon military reforms in the viceroyalty of Peru, Campbell examined two hundred *competencias* (legal conflicts) between the military and other "privileged jurisdictions." Unlike McAlister's study, Campbell found that because of the failure of military reform measures and the vitality of other established Peruvian institutions, the army was rarely able to challenge or dominate civilian government. The disparity between McAlister's and Campbell's findings can be partially explained by the inability of the colonial militia in Peru to suppress the massive Indian uprising of 1780-1783 led by José Gabriel Condorconqui (Túpac Amaru II). The report of one departing viceroy in 1801 confirmed the ineptitude of the colonial militia in Peru when he concluded that it was "useless" in the defense of the interior provinces of the viceroyalty.[19] If such a disorganized and undisciplined militia existed at the seat of Spanish power in South America, then it is possible to surmise that no viable professional military institutions manned barracks anywhere on the continent on the eve of independence. The struggle for freedom from Spain, culminating in the Battle of Ayacucho in Peru in 1824, thus left a legacy of *caudillismo* without a commensurate sense of military professionalism for the armies dominating most newly independent Latin American states.

Among the leaders of the independence armies, few boasted more professional military experience than José de San Martín. Bringing more than twenty years of experience to the independence struggle as a soldier in the viceroyalty of Rio de la Plata (modern Argentina), San Martín went on to command successful campaigns in Argentina, Chile, and Peru before turning his back on political opportunity and quietly retiring to Europe in 1823. The model of the modern concept of the professional soldier, San Martín stands in sharp contrast to the ill-trained *caudillos* who dominated the armies and early political life of the Latin American nations. By Samuel Huntington's classic definition of military professionalism, which identifies four consistent components of modern military forces—expertise, responsibility, corporateness, and ideology—the Latin American military establishments of the nineteenth century were woefully amateurish.[20] These armies were certainly lacking in expertise, as many did not found professional training centers until the late nineteenth century. Without a sense of corporate identity built upon tradition, discipline, and institutional self-esteem, Latin American military men lacked a sense of responsibility to their profession and to their nation. Most significantly, these military forces were bereft of individually unique ideologies or a sense of mission that guided the emerging professional armed forces of France, Prussia, England, and the United States.

The major military conflicts of nineteenth-century Latin America—the War of the Triple Alliance, pitting the garrison state of Paraguay against the combined forces of Argentina, Uruguay, and Brazil (1865-1870), and the War of the Pacific with Chile defeating Peru and Bolivia (1879-1883)—left both the victors and the vanquished exhausted and their military forces in disarray. In the three decades following the conclusion of both these conflicts, widespread civil conflicts involving the navies of Chile and Brazil and the Peruvian army splintered the armed forces of these nations.[21] Like the Prussian army's rebuilding process and the French army's reorganization after the military disasters at Sedan and Metz in the Franco-Prussian War, the major South American nations strove to rebuild their military institutions after costly wars.[22] But unlike their European military counterparts, they did not have the rich military tradition of Frederick the Great or Napoleon to build upon. Recognizing this lack and seeking to facilitate the integration of their slowly modernizing economies with those of Western Europe and the United States, civilian and military leaders in Peru, Argentina, Chile, and Brazil quite logically turned to the armies of France and Germany and the navies of England and the United States to help construct the professional military establishments they felt were critical for the development of their countries.

Frederick M. Nunn's carefully researched study, *Yesterday's Soldiers: European Military Professionalism in South America, 1890-1940*, details the influence of Prussian and French military training missions upon the armies of Peru, Argentina, Chile, and Brazil.[23] Nunn's book chronicles how the soldiers who transformed the armies of these South American nations first arrived in Chile in 1885 with the Prussian mission commanded by Colonel Emil Körner. Körner's former colleague, Colonel Alfred Arent, was commissioned by the Argentine government in 1899 for the specific task of reorganizing that nation's Superior War College. Peru, recovering from its humiliation by Chile in the War of the Pacific and just emerging from a bloody civil war that further discredited its army, turned to the French army in 1896 in a desperate effort to rebuild its shattered military institution. Regional bosses (*coronéis*) dominated Brazilian politics during the first decades after the republic was established in 1889, thus delaying until 1919 army modernization and the arrival of a French army mission led by General Maurice Gamelin.

Manned by only a few soldiers but vastly influential within the armies they advised, each of these missions performed similar tasks. In Peru, for instance, as we shall see, French advisers helped initiate new training centers while they established codes for recruitment, justice, promotion, and fiscal policy. The French military liaison with Peru also enabled its army officers to train at specialized military centers in France. Above all else, these missions inculcated an intellectual, almost spiritual affinity for the doctrines of the French and Prussian armies by their South American protégés. As Nunn stresses, this led Peruvian, Argentine, Chilean, and, to a lesser extent, Brazilian army officers to "reject much of their own national and military tradition to adopt the military professionalism of France and Germany. In so doing they adopted a search for an idealized past—a past idealized in Europe but never known in South America."[24]

The Peruvian army's loyalty to the French military tradition can be best affirmed by perusing its military journals, in which evidence of French influence abounds. In particular, a review of the November, 1946 edition of the *Revista Militar*, the army's leading journal, would be most revealing. This issue, commemorating the fiftieth anniversary of the arrival of the French military presence in Peru, was generous in its praise of the French army's contribution to Peruvian military professionalism. The *Revista Militar* made scant mention of the French army's humiliation in June, 1940 while it concentrated on reviewing the history of the mission's activities since 1896. The *Revista Militar* also gave liberal coverage to the elaborate ceremonies conducted to honor the French military delegation.[25] Nunn's conclusions tend to de-emphasize significant professional differences in the professional outlooks of South American armies, but he does call proper attention to the impact of foreign military ideology upon twentieth-century Latin American militarism.

In assessing the influence of European military training in South America one should remember that many nations emulated European military models in fashioning their professional armed forces. The United States army's general staff structure was formulated along the lines of the Prussian army. The United States navy's carrier task force concept of today has its roots in Nelson's victory at Trafalgar and Alfred Thayer Mahan's affinity for the tradition of the Royal navy. But more than counter-balancing these influences has been the native heritage of Yorktown, Gettysburg, Manila Bay, Midway, and the Chosin Reservoir. With very limited battlefield tradition and largely foreign ideological foundations for their modern professional armed forces, the South American nations' soldiers and sailors lacked a clear sense of identity or purpose. Prior to the Malvinas War, for example, the Argentine army conducted battlefield operations only in the Indian Wars of the 1870s following its participation in the War of the Triple Alliance a decade earlier. After more than a century in the barracks the Argentine armed forces were ill prepared in most respects to meet the challenge of the Royal navy and marines.

The only Latin American military institution actually engaged in combat on a broad scale in either world war was the Brazilian army. General Humberto Castelo Branco, a veteran of the Brazilian Expeditionary Force's (FEB) campaign in Italy and later the head of the Brazilian military government that seized power in 1964, credits the experience with erasing the "false optimism" and "irrational nationalism" plaguing the Brazilian army prior to the world conflict. According to another observer, the FEB's experience fighting alongside General Mark Clark's Fifth Army in Italy gave Brazilian soldiers a better perspective on the army's role in underdeveloped nations. Roberto Campos noted:

The FEB had a great impact on Castelo and others. The contact with logistics in an underdeveloped country made them cool and objective. Castelo grasped the difference between the verbalization of power and real power. Castelo was impressed by the complete failure of Italy and Mussolini, a failure which he considered an example of verbalization not backed by real power.[26]

"False optimism" was certainly a trait hampering the Velasco government's reformist program in its early years. This naïveté resulted from the armed forces' lack of awareness of both its capabilities and limitations as an agent of change. In recent years, the conflict with *Sendero Luminoso* has made the Peruvian military even more conscious of its limitations in employing power in a civilian government.

Certainly the armies of the South American nations have been the pivotal institutions in their armed forces in initiating political action and economic change. This fact is reflected in the historical literature, which largely ignores the navy and the air force in its overviews. This omission tends to create an unbalanced picture, especially since the naval forces of Brazil, Chile, and Peru and the Argentine air force have been active participants in the political affairs of their nations. Two significant examples will illustrate this point. First, the Chilean navy's opposition to President Balmaceda in 1891 led to his downfall and the initiation of the long-term "parliamentary republic." Second, in Argentina, navy and air force opponents were instrumental in the terminating of Juan Perón's first regime in 1955. More fundamentally, naval and air force personnel have tended to be a conservative brake on the reformist and populist policies of their army counterparts.[27] This phenomenon was certainly true in Argentina during Perón's two regimes and was decidedly the case during the Velasco regime in Peru.

Equally as much as their counterparts in the army, Latin American naval officers were influenced by foreign advisers. British, United States and, to a lesser extent, French and Italian naval missions fulfilled the role of tutors for modernizing the naval forces of South America. These missions, along with many other aspects of Latin American naval history, are discussed in the only comprehensive study of this topic in English, Robert Scheina's *Latin America: A Naval History, 1810-1987*.[28] In this highly detailed analysis, Scheina discusses the well-known contribution of the former Royal naval officer, Lord Thomas Cochrane, in forging the early navies of Chile and Brazil. He also brings to light the less well-known participation of British and French sailors in the War of the Triple Alliance and the War of the Pacific. The Peruvian vessel *Huascar*, for instance, which fought so valiantly in the campaign against Chile, was manned by a crew composed of 20 percent foreigners.

Despite the heavy foreign involvement in Latin American naval affairs in the nineteenth century, the first formal naval mission was not contracted until 1905, when a small contingent of French officers arrived in Peru. In the years prior to World War I, Chile turned to Great Britain and Brazil turned to the United States for naval advisory teams. After World War I British influence waned as the teachings of Alfred Thayer Mahan and the technical expertise of United States naval advisers became paramount in Latin America. Washington completed negotiations with the Peruvian government of President Augusto Leguía (1919-1930) in September, 1920, establishing a naval bond between the two nations that remains strong to the present day.

The technical expertise made available by these missions was essential for the Latin American navies as the pace of technology raced ahead following the *Dreadnought* revolution after 1905 and the development of naval air and submarine operations during and after the Great War. Once the United States emerged as the world's leading naval power following the Washington Naval Conference of 1921-1922, only Italy, which maintained small training missions in Colombia and Venezuela, offered any challenge to the dominance of United States naval influence in the hemisphere.

With South American armies adhering to French and Prussian military tradition and the navies of these nations looking to Great Britain and the United States for professional inspiration, interservice rivalries were understandably exacerbated. These rivalries surfaced in Argentina with the overthrow of Perón, and they were also quite pronounced throughout the Velasco regime. In many ways the Peruvian navy was ideologically at odds with the army's statist structural reforms from the onset of the Velasco regime. Vice Admiral Luis M. Vargas Caballero, minister of housing and navy minister until his forced resignation in 1974, later expressed a view of the military's role in "nation building" that stood at the opposite pole from that of the military radicals of Velasco's inner circle. In response to a question I posed in 1985 regarding the armed forces' ability to successfully initiate major structural change, Vargas Caballero replied, "The armed forces are not prepared for political action; it should help the government but within its own field." The admiral also confirmed that no naval senior officers were informed or consulted before the Velasco *coup*. Vargas Caballero's position and that of the institution he represented reflected the apolitical outlook of the United States military heritage and contrasted with the activist mind-set of the army still mirroring the developmentalist teaching of its French tutors.[29]

Often closely affiliated with the navy in their conservative outlook, the air forces of the South American nations began to gain institutional independence from war and navy ministries only in the interwar years. Most airmen in South America gained professional competence largely in the post—World War II years, as the students of United States air force instructors. But Peru's fledgling air corps gained its wings in the 1930s as a result of an Italian air mission contracted by President Oscar Benavides (1933-1939). Like the navy, their political differences with army leaders caused considerable interservice tensions. A Peruvian army officer in 1943, for example, was so distressed by President Manuel Prado's favoring of the air force in promotions and pay that he called for the destruction of the air force on the ground in the event of a serious crisis between the two services.[30]

Interservice rivalries were certainly not unique to the South American armed forces, but they added a further negative dimension to military institutions struggling mightily to modernize. What all these institutions sought was a clearer sense of mission that would satisfy both themselves and their countrymen. This meant in South America that military men often had to choose between the role of soldier and the role of politician. Clearly, most soldiers see themselves as warriors, but few armies and even fewer naval institutions boast significant battle experience. In Peru this identity crisis was particularly acute as that nation's military men faced a legacy of defeat dating from the disastrous War of the Pacific that made them suspect in the eyes of their fellow Peruvians. The armed forces thus sought an alternative and meaningful role in national affairs that would mitigate their battlefield failures and unify a badly divided institution. The reforms of the Velasco era represented the military's most active effort to realize this mission.

The search for a mission by Peru's men in arms was made all the more difficult because they were caught up in the maelstrom of national politics as they sought to clarify their corporate identity. Peru's chronic political instability had immensely important and largely negative implications for the military's struggle to professionalize. Accordingly, this study will closely examine civil-military relations in the context of an analysis of the Peruvian military's process of professionalization.

Brian Loveman and Thomas Davies have described the phenomenon of the "politics of anti-politics," in which the Latin American military displayed a powerful disdain for civilian politicians even while military men remained immersed in politics themselves.[31] This concept aptly applies to Peru as soldiers frequently and loudly proclaimed their distrust of civilian politicians and lamented their negative impact on the military's efforts to mold a disciplined and apolitical armed forces establishment. The most powerful civilian counterforce to the military's prominent role in national affairs after 1930 in Peru was the *Alianza Popular Revolucionaria Americana* (American Popular Revolutionary Alliance, *APRA* or *Aprista*) party. The compelling dichotomy of *APRA*'s relationship with the armed forces can be seen in the deaths of military men who fought to defend the party and of those who fought to destroy it. The intricate relationship between *Apristas* and military men has not received adequate attention, and that also is one of the principal objectives of this study.

Fundamentally, however, this book is an analysis of the Peruvian military's campaign to identify a clear professional rationale. As some observers, most notably Víctor Villanueva and Frederick Nunn, have suggested, this quest began to become evident in military literature in the early 1900s and in the policy statements and programs of the armed forces after 1950. Soon after the first French military mission arrived in 1896, Peruvian army officers demonstrated a clear affinity for the French military "colonial school." Most closely identified with this school were its primary theorist, Thomas-Robert Bugeaud, and his more liberal successors, Joseph Simon Gallieni in Tonkin and Hubert Lyautey in Morocco. Both Gallieni's and Lyautey's views will be discussed in greater detail in this study, but it is useful here to note that Lyautey's theories, proposed in two articles in the prestigious *Revue de Deux Mondes*, and his visionary view of colonialism as a "fraternal union between two peoples to vanquish poverty and misery" profoundly influenced the thinking of progressive officers in the Peruvian army from the early twentieth century onward. What is so revealing about Lyautey's campaign in Morocco for the Peruvian military's reformist rationale and particularly the general failure of its reform initiatives after 1968 is that the French colonial general's "hearts and minds" approach was ultimately a failure in the field but a successful publicity endeavor in metropolitan France. As Douglas Porch deftly explained, the economic "centers of attraction" of the French army in Morocco (very similar to *nucleos selváticos* of the Peruvian army in the 1960s) were abandoned after only a few years as the native population resisted pacification. Lyautey then fell back on the only tactic left open to him, the repressive *razzia* (scorched earth) policy. In the French colonial general's words, "We shall hollow out the carcass and leave the shell."[32] Perhaps only with their frustrating campaign against *Sendero Luminoso* in the 1980s have Peruvian army officers begun to appreciate the implications of Lyautey's flawed rationale for development.

That the theories of Lyautey and his tutor Gallieni would form an integral aspect of the Peruvian army's reformist rationale has profound implications. Peru's soldiers were clearly not so much interested in the historical records of the French colonial school's performance in the field as they were in applying these ideas to Peru's unique problems. Moreover, the patriotic zeal of Lyautey and Gallieni appealed to Peruvian army officers who felt that the military must establish a sense of *élan* through an almost single-minded commitment to nation-building.

These progressive officers, few in number at the beginning of the century but comprising the bulk of the officer corps by the 1960s, were concerned about not only managing modernization but also ridding the officer corps of personalism stemming from the well-established tradition of *caudillismo*. Richard Morse, in addressing the issue of *caudillismo* plaguing most Latin American military establishments until the mid-twentieth century, argued that if the *caudillo* is without an heir, then the state often collapses with him. Some would argue that this phenomenon is in fact what nearly happened in Argentina after Perón. The same situation certainly occurred in 19th-century Peru which saw the formative nation-building efforts of Ramón Castilla between 1845 and 1862 destroyed in the debacles of the War of the Pacific and the bloody 1895 civil war. The Peruvian army was unable to rid itself of the "disease" of personalism until it finally abated after the institutional reforms of the 1950s. Prior to this time, three *caudillos*, Luis M. Sánchez Cerro, Oscar Benavides, and Manuel Odría dominated the armed forces in the mid-twentieth century and generally impeded their efforts to professionalize. One of the best examples of the frustration this personalism caused reform-minded junior officers is contained in a manifesto issued by army dissidents in 1945:

A few generals and chiefs who have benefited from the government are not the army; not even a part of it, they are a few individuals and nothing more. They do not have the weight of opinion of the officer corps behind them because they lack professional prestige lost through their dedication to national politics.[33]

The impulse to enact higher professional standards for the army and navy was so strong by the early 1950s that General Odría, the last of Peru's traditional military *caudillos*, was unable to prevent significant institutional reforms.   Along with the establishment of the *Centro de Altos Estudios Militares* (Center of Higher Military Studies, CAEM) and the *Centro de Instrucción Militar del Perú* (Center of Military Instruction, CIMP) the Odría regime decreed military measures that clarified previously ambiguous promotion criteria, modernized a dated military justice system, and stipulated more precise terms governing discipline and retirement.   The *caudillo* also saw the groundwork laid for the creation of a long-delayed armed forces joint command a year after he retired from office.   These reforms served as a lens in bringing the armed forces perspective into clearer focus.   This vision soon led Peru's soldiers to reject the old-style *caudillo* politics of the past for a mission characterized two decades later by General Velasco as "nationalist, independent and humanist."   But the search for such a well-defined professional course would continue to elude the officer corps even after the Velasco regime assumed power.   Significantly, once the Velasco government began faltering badly in 1975, fellow officers deposed the ailing leader while accusing him of "personalism and *caudillo* tendencies."

Thus, the soldiers who deposed President Fernando Belaúnde Terry on 3 October 1968 were products of an institution that labored for decades to define its national mission, limit the intrusion of national politics in the military's internal affairs, rid itself of personalism, and most of all, justify its worth to the nation and themselves.   They were confident in their ability to lead the nation through major social and economic changes.   At the same time they did not appreciate the magnitude of the task nor understand the limitations of their bank of experience as "nation builders." Moreover, these military modernizers would soon discover that reform, whether directed by civilians or military men, is often consumed in the crucible of national politics.

The brash and confident soldiers who occupied the Pizarro Palace in October, 1968, proclaiming their intention to "begin the emancipation of the Fatherland," could never conceive that within two decades the nation they sought to reshape would be on the brink of political and economic collapse.   This study then, while not primarily an analysis of the "new military reformism" of the Velasco years, will offer conclusions regarding the implications of the military's failure to move Peru beyond the racial inequality, bureaucratic inertia, economic dependency, and inequitable land tenure that have impeded social justice and national modernization. While not tempered by time, it is hoped that these conclusions will be useful for students of modern Peru.

NOTES

1. Norman Gall, "Peru: The Master Is Dead," *Dissent*, 18 (1981), pp. 280-320.
2. Jose Carlos Mariátegui, *Seven Interpretative Essays on Peruvian Reality* (Austin, Texas: 1971), pp. 163-164.
3. Hernando De Soto, *The Other Path: The Invisible Revolution in the Third World* (New York: 1989), pp. 231-238.
4. Thomas Ford, *Man and Land in Peru* (Gainesville, Florida: 1960), is the standard source on Peruvian agriculture, land tenure, and geography prior to 1960. A lively but brief introduction to Peruvian geography and society can be found in David Werlich's introduction to his *Peru: A Short History* (Carbondale, Illinois: 1978).
5. Werlich, *Peru*, pp. 1-9.
6. Ibid.
7. *Sendero Luminoso* will be discussed in Chapter 10 of this study.
8. Werlich, *Peru*, pp. 4-5.
9. Peter Gorman, "Visions of the Matses," *Americas*, 41, no. 1 (Spring, 1989), pp. 33-37.
10. An up-to-date statistical profile of Peru and every nation in the world is available on the computer program "PC Globe."
11. Thomas M. Davies, Jr., *Indian Integration in Peru: A Half Century of Experience, 1900-1948* (Lincoln, Nebraska: 1970), p. 4.
12. Werlich, *Peru*, pp. 15-16.
13. Davies, *Indian Integration*, p. 12.
14. Rosemary Thorp and Geoffrey Bertram, *Peru, 1890-1977: Growth and Policy in an Open Economy* (New York: 1978), p. 321.
15. De Soto, *The Other Path*, pp. 208-209.
16. Eric Wolf, *Sons of the Shaking Earth* (Chicago: 1959), p. 157.
17. See Richard Morse's provocative essay, "Political Theory and the *Caudillo*," in Hugh Hamill, Jr., ed., *Dictatorship in Spanish America* (New York: 1967), pp. 52-68.   A useful survey for the early history of Spain is Stanley Payne's two-volume study, *A History of Spain and Portugal* (Madison: 1973). According to Payne, Alfonso X's intention when formulating the *Siete Partidas* was to create a rationalized system of universal justice under the monarchy that would do away with much of common Castillian law and local practices. The *Siete Partidas*, of course, aroused substantial opposition from the regional nobility and was not effectively enforced until the fourteenth century. This body of law did, however, serve as a basis for the legal system of Spain and its colonies after the unification of that nation following the marriage of Ferdinand and Isabella in 1469.

18. Lyle McAlister, *The Fuero Militar in New Spain, 1764-1800* (Gainesville, Florida: 1952), p. 89.

19. Leon G. Campbell, *The Military and Society in Colonial Peru, 1750-1810* (Philadelphia: 1978), p. 216.

20. Samuel P. Huntington, *The Soldier and the State: The Theory and Practice of Civil-Military Relations* (New York: 1957), pp. 7-18. Huntington's definition of military professionalism emphasizes subservience to civilian authority as an important component of military professionalism and is not precisely applicable to the Latin American context.

21. The Chilean navy, supporting the congressional opposition to President José Balmaceda in 1891, led the nation into a civil war, which ended with the defeat and suicide of Balmaceda in September of that year. The year 1891 in Brazil also saw its navy aid in the overthrow of the Old Republic's first president, Marshal Deodoro da Fonseca. Two years later the Brazilian navy again aided the conservative opponents of the government by giving active assistance to a two-year rebellion in the state of Rio Grande do Sul. The Peruvian army, still demoralized after its defeat in the War of the Pacific, suffered another humiliation by the civilian revolutionary militia led by José Nicolás de Piérola in 1895.

22. Students of the Prussian military should consult Gordon A. Craig's classic, *The Politics of the Prussian Army, 1640-1945* (Princeton: 1955). For histories of the French army consult Paul-Marie de la Gorce, *The French Army: A Military Political History* (New York: 1963); John Steward Ambler, *Soldiers Against the State: The French Army in Politics* (Columbus, Ohio: 1968); Maxime Wegrand's fascinating pre-World War II illustrated history, *Histoire de L'Armee Francaise* (Paris: 1938). The history of the French colonial army in Africa is expertly told by Douglas Porch in his two works, *The Conquest of Morocco* (New York: 1982) and *The Conquest of the Sahara* (New York: 1984). Peter Paret, *French Revolutionary Warfare from Indochina to Algeria: The Analysis of Political and Military Doctrine* (New York: 1964) offers a valuable interpretive review of the French army's colonial experience. For a detailed look at French colonial general Hubert Lyautey's role as a soldier/administrator in Morocco from 1921-1925 see Alan Scham, *Lyautey in Morocco: Protectorate Administration 1912-1925* (Berkeley: 1970).

23. Frederick M. Nunn, *Yesterday's Soldiers: European-Military Professionalism in South America, 1890-1940* (Lincoln, Nebraska; 1983), p. 291. Prussian-trained Chilean soldiers would later lead military missions in Ecuador, Colombia, and El Salvador in the early twentieth century.

24. Nunn, *Yesterday's Soldiers*, p. 291. See also George Pope Atkins and Larry V. Thompson, "German Military Influence in Argentina, 1921-1940," *Journal of Latin American Studies*, 4, no. 2 (November, 1972), pp. 257-274.

25. Anonymous, *Revista Militar del Perú*, 43, no. 11 (November, 1946). The entire issue was devoted to the subject of the French army mission.

26. Luigi R. Einaudi and Alfred Stepan, *Latin American Institutional Development: Changing Military Perspectives in Peru and Brazil* (Santa Monica: 1971), p. 109. The FEB experience also drew the Brazilian army closer to its United States counterpart after World War II and presaged the cooperation of the Castelo Branco regime with Washington after the 1964 military revolution.

27. One significant exception was the career of Chilean air force officer Marmaduke Grove Vallejo. This political activist was instrumental in founding Chile's short-lived "Socialist Republic" in June, 1932.

28. Robert Scheina, *Latin America: A Naval History, 1810-1987* (Annapolis: 1987).

29. Personal interview with Vice Admiral (R) Luis M. Vargas Caballero, 6 May 1985, Lima, Peru.

30. First Secretary Jefferson Patterson to the Secretary of State, 27 December 1943, National Archives, Record Group 59, Decimal File Number 823.00/1776. Report of a conversation with an unnamed army officer. State Department documents will hereafter be cited with the author of the document to Sec/State, NA, RG 59, and the file number.

31. Brian Loveman and Thomas M. Davies, Jr., *The Politics of Anti-Politics: The Military in Latin America* (Lincoln, Nebraska: 1989).

32. Douglas Porch, *The Conquest of Morocco*, pp. 289-298.

33. The manifesto of these dissident officers is found in the memorandum of Ambassador White to Sec/State, 2 February 1945, NA, RG 59, 823.00/2-45.

1
Professional Genesis

"Peasant, the landlord will eat no more from your poverty!"[1] This is not the slogan of a radical rural guerrilla, but rather the words of Peruvian Division General Juan Velasco Alvarado as he announced the initiation of one of the most sweeping agrarian reform programs in Latin American history. This program, announced on the national "Day of the Indian," was begun less than six months after General Velasco led a *golpe de estado* on 3 October 1968 against the faltering rule of civilian President Fernando Belaunde Terry. The cornerstone of Velasco's "Revolutionary Government of the Armed Forces," agrarian reform, was only the first of many ambitious, if oftentimes hastily conceived, measures aimed at radically transforming Peruvian society. Observers of the Velasco regime throughout the world were initially both puzzled and intrigued as they sought to understand why a seemingly conservative military establishment could overnight become the architects of a developmentalist policy that prompted even Cuban Premier Fidel Castro to conclude whimsically that the Velasco regime had "started a fire in the firehouse."

Now it is clear that the Velasco-led "revolution" was decades in the making and was not, as many initial analysts suggested, the product of a reformist mentality that began to pervade the officer corps only in the early 1950s. For nearly four decades prior to 1945 Peru's soldiers struggled to define their national mission and overcome a pervasive self-doubt in the utility of their institution. As late as 1945 an army officer felt compelled to defend the army in its leading service journal with an article entitled, "The Army: Is It Unproductive?" Written only four years after Peru's most stunning military victory in its July, 1941 border conflict with Ecuador, this article accurately reflects not this brief moment of military glory but the legacy of previous military defeat as well as civil-military conspiracies and inter-service rivalries that tore the fabric of armed forces unity and prevented the articulation of a precise national mission until the 1960s. Although these problems became more intense after 1930, the origins of the modern Peruvian armed forces in the late nineteenth century were fraught with the same difficulties.

The "fortunate soldiers," as José de San Martín aptly described them, who dominated Peru for most of the seventy years after Spanish power was crushed in 1824 were not military professionals.[2] They frequently displayed tactical military skills, but they rarely sought to formalize standards of professional competence or promote a sense of corporate unity in the amorphous national army under their control.[3] Before the 1890s, the army remained tied to Spanish regulations borrowed from the colonial period but only haphazardly applied.[4] Common soldiers were impressed from the ranks of Peru's poor and illiterate Indians, blacks, and castas (mixed races), with "military necessity" generally being the only determinant of their length of service. Some officers were selected by their performance in battle, but just as frequently family contacts, political patronage, and personal allegiances were equally important in filling command positions.[5]

With the exception of Peru's small nineteenth-century navy, which graduated 70 to 80 percent of its officer corps from the Escuela Naval after the school opened in the early 1800s, Peru lacked adequate facilities for the instruction of cadets and officers.[6] Thus, military expertise was primarily acquired on the battlefield or through individual studies by intellectually curious officers. In short, Peru's army was manned and led by ill-trained military amateurs. Nevertheless, a poorly integrated political system and the authoritarian tradition inherited from Spain's colonial administration enabled military caudillos to dominate the nation as much by their personal charisma as by their soldierly skill.

While the particularly astute caudillo Ramón Castilla dominated Peruvian affairs in the two decades after 1845, the nation enjoyed internal order and economic prosperity. Castilla acquired modern arms, improved military training, and built a navy. Nonetheless, the impact of these reforms was not lasting. Attacking the negative influence of militarism and caudillismo, a civilian, Manuel Pardo, won the presidency in 1872 and promptly set out to subordinate the army to civilian control. Arguing that national security should be based upon negotiated treaties with neighboring nations, Pardo tried to cut the army's manpower and neutralize its influence by strengthening the more reliable Guardia Civil (national police). When a secret pact of mutual military assistance with Bolivia was exposed in 1873, however, Pardo's opponents charged his policies would weaken

Peru in the face of a growing military threat from Chile. Countering that a smaller, better-trained, and apolitical army would be more efficient, the beleaguered president struggled to enact his military program. Numerous insurrections and a deteriorating economy doomed his efforts, however, and Peru's first civilian president acknowledged his failure by supporting General Mariano Ignacio Prado for the presidency in 1876.

Although General Prado was widely recognized as the only man capable of maintaining internal order, a worsening economy and deepening diplomatic crisis with Chile caused his civilian support to evaporate. His unpopular and unprepared government was then plunged into war in April, 1879 when, after Peru refused to disavow its 1873 treaty with Bolivia, Chile seized the Bolivian port of Antofagasta and declared war on both nations.

In the War of the Pacific (1879-1883) the combined forces of Peru and Bolivia were no match for the well-trained and better-equipped Chileans. Yet individual Peruvian commanders fought bravely, and Chile needed to occupy Lima and combat its determined guerrilla resistance for more than two years before wresting peace terms from an exhausted Peru. Impending defeat, however, forced Peru to surrender the nitrate-rich region of Tarapacá while the victors also gained "temporary" possession of the provinces of Tacna and Arica until a plebiscite could be held to determine their future status. In a profound sense, the War of the Pacific established a legacy of defeat that would haunt Peru's soldiers until the army's partial vindication in the 1941 Zarumilla-Marañón conflict with Ecuador. If the war with Chile gave Peru its greatest martyr heroes, it also fostered decades of frustration and demonstrated that *caudillismo* was a poor substitute for military professionalism.[7]

Unfortunately, this lesson was not fully recognized by political leaders vying for power in the aftermath of the war. Consequently, General Andres Cáceres, who had successfully resisted the Chilean occupation with an adroit campaign in central Peru, parlayed his military prestige into a political alliance that enabled him to dominate the nation until 1895. In that year, a civilian revolutionary, José Nicolás de Piérola, unified diverse anti-Cáceres movements, and after a civil war costing hundreds of lives, he restored civilian rule.

Cáceres's defeat meant yet another humiliating reverse for the army. Unlike the Chilean conflict, however, military men could not blame their failure on unpatriotic civilians. Defeat wrought by ill-trained and poorly armed revolutionaries left no glory in its wake. The era of personalist military amateurs was over. Ironically, it was Piérola who fathered Peru's modern armed forces.

Past military failure and a continuing Chilean military buildup under German supervision convinced Piérola of the need to organize a small but efficient standing army to be headed by well-trained and politically subordinate career officers. Toward this end, he turned to France for assistance. Piérola's motives are not precisely known, but it seems clear that his affinity for Catholic and Republican France, his interest in French frontier defense technology, and his unwillingness to deal with the Prussian army then training the Chileans influenced his decision.[8] It should also be remembered that the recent history of the French army paralleled that of Peru's. Stunned by their defeats at Sedan and Metz in 1871, French commanders responded by thoroughly reorganizing the army during the 1880s. Moreover, throughout the troubled first decades of the Third Republic the army remained subordinate to civilian authority. Most French army officers may have been antiliberal, antirepublican, and proclerical, but they also valued obedience as the defining quality of the soldier. Cadets at Saint-Cyr were taught that "the loyalty and devotion of the army to the government must be absolute."[9] To French army officers this obedience was a matter of military honor. Piérola hoped this characteristic would be emulated by a more professional Peruvian army. The French army's principle of political obedience may have been the most important consideration in the establishment of Franco-Peruvian military ties, but other aspects of its "ideological baggage" were more instrumental in the forging of a professional bond between French and Peruvian soldiers that would endure long after the last Gallic officer departed Peruvian soil in 1943.[10]

Despite a military code that accepted ultimate civilian control as a cardinal component of professionalism, eager French army officers found action and power in the colonial service. To a lesser extent these rewards were also available to members of military training missions in Asia and Latin America. As the famed colonial officer and future marshal Louis Hubert Lyautey proclaimed from Indochina in 1894, "Here you won't find a single little lieutenant, responsible for a post and in charge of reconnoitering, who within six months does not develop more initiative, willpower, endurance, and personality than does an officer stationed in France throughout his whole career."[11] The ideas of Lyautey, who only three years before had justified a broad social role for the army officer with his controversial assertion in the Revue Des Deux Mondes that "the officer fights no more, or at least no more frequently than does any other citizen," are applicable to the French experience in Peru.[12]

The French colonial officer served more as an administrator than a combatant. More significantly, he frequently acted independently of Paris and consequently developed administrative competence and a concomitant contempt for remote civilian leaders who failed to comprehend the problems posed by restive indigenous populations in the colonies.[13] Some French officers who served in Peru after 1896 boasted previous colonial service in Tunisia, Algeria, Madagascar, and the Sudan. Although they did not exercise similar political power in Peru, a number assumed all but the very senior army command posts.[14] French officers clearly relished the chance to organize the Peruvian army. For instance, the chief of the first French mission, Colonel (later General) Paul Clément, adopted Peruvian citizenship and later became the army's chief of staff.[15] Other French officers before 1925 served as the army's inspector general and as director of its service academy and general staff college. Significantly, their work was praised even by General Emil Körner, the German chief adviser for the Chilean army, who conceded in 1910, "The excellent members of the French military mission applied the French regulations with great aptitude."[16] Moreover, in 1923 a Lima newspaper praised the "patient and systematic work" of the French officers while noting that "the spirit of the French school has already taken root in the Peruvian army."[17] Thus, the French army "school," enriched by the ideas and experience of its colonial soldier-administrators, became the seedbed for Peruvian military professionalism.

Tracing the work of the French soldiers from their arrival in September, 1896, one can see evidence of their immediate progress in modernizing the Peruvian army. Under the direction of Colonel Clément in 1898, the *Escuela Militar de Chorrillos* was established, replacing the moribund *Escuela Militar de Aplicación*. This service academy graduated its first class of competitively selected cadets in that year. The year 1898 also witnessed the enactment of a more modern military justice code modeled after French military law and legislation creating guidelines for military recruitment and administration. Peruvian males between the ages of twenty-one and twenty-five became subject to an official military draft, and their term and conditions of service were now regulated by law. Besides providing a permanent manpower pool for the army, this legislation established modern norms for promotions, internal administration, fiscal policy, and tactical organization. Piérola left office in 1899, having begun a process of professional development that most of his presidential successors encouraged during the first two decades of the twentieth century.[18]

The years before World War I saw further administrative reforms, more sophisticated training, and the improvement of the military's firepower. With obligatory military service in effect, the army's enlisted ranks swelled from three thousand in 1901 to seven thousand in 1914. At the same time, the officer corps actually declined from 2,345 to 1,239, with 35 percent having graduated from the Escuela Militar de Chorrillos.[19] The smaller officer corps clearly reflected the army's increased professional standards. Understandably, these better-trained officers now sought modern weaponry, and the government responded by acquiring large stocks of small arms, French artillery pieces, and an ammunition factory.[20]

Peru also relied on France to modernize its navy prior to World War I. In May, 1905 Lima contracted a naval mission headed by Commander Paúl de Marguerye of the French navy. This mission was selected because it would be compatible with the French army mission. Before its contract was allowed to expire in 1914, French naval officers improved the Peruvian navy's educational system, established the Naval Academy at its present site in Callao, and provided advanced training for Peruvian naval cadets aboard French vessels. Along with these reforms the Peruvian naval command augmented the core of its fleet. Two cruisers (the Almirante Grau and Colonel Bolgnesi) were purchased from Vickers of Great Britain in 1906, and two French-built submarines, the Ferre and Palacios, were also acquired, with their crews being trained in France. A controversy, however, over the price of an armored cruiser caused a rift between Peru and France and eventually precipitated the cancellation of the French naval mission less than a decade after it was first contracted.[21]

As a framework for these reforms, Peru restructured the Ministry of War and Marine in 1903 for the first time since its establishment in 1821. One year later a general staff school (Escuela Superior de Guerra, ESG) was created. Patterned after the French general staff school founded in 1875, the ESG trained midrank officers for the general staff and soon became the army's center for strategic planning. The French mission attempted to complement the training offered at the ESG by establishing a center for advanced military studies along the lines of their similar prewar institution in France, but World War I intervened.[22] The Peruvian army would wait until 1950 before its own Centro de Altos Estudios Militares opened its doors. Nonetheless, in the intervening years the ESG produced, according to the Peruvian historian Jorge Basadre, "a succession of graduating classes of trained and capable senior officers."[23] It should also be noted that the Diplomados de Estado Mayor (as the ESG graduates were designated) formed the army's most powerful interest group during these years.

With the opening of the ESG came the publication of the military's finest service journal, Boletín del Ministerio de Guerra y Marina (Bulletin of the Ministry of War and Navy, BMGM). Readers of this journal and its successor, the Revista Militar del Perú (RMP), soon found officers articulating, albeit in relatively unsophisticated style, the French military doctrines then being learned both at home and on extended study missions in French military schools.[24] Lyautey's call for French officers to become the "educators of men" under their command was echoed by a Peruvian army lieutenant colonel in one of the first issues of the BMGM. According to Lieutenant Colonel Gabriel Velarde Alvarez, Peru's desperately impover- ished Quechua- and Aymara-speaking peasants clearly offered his colleagues the challenge of a "civilizing mission" as tutors of their illiterate Indian conscripts.[25] With increasing frequency in ensuing decades, the concept of the army as a "civilizing force" reappeared in the pages of Peru's service journals. If these pages mirrored the maturing of Franco-Peruvian military theory, they gave little hint of the political turmoil and resultant military factionalism largely preventing its implementation. Peruvian officers imbued with the "social action" theories of Lyautey and the national defense doctrine of Marshal Joseph Joffre found it very difficult to "exploit all the resources of the nation and all the intelligence of its sons" in the context of Peru's politically unstable and socially fluid society.[26] This lingering inadequacy would become apparent to Peru's men in uniform as early as 1914, a year that marked an important watershed in Peruvian civil-military affairs.

In 1914, after nearly two decades of increased professionalism, the army manifested a newly found sense of institutional pride and corporate identity. Yet when its most prestigious officer, Colonel Oscar R. Benavides, led a February, 1914 golpe against civilian President Guillermo Billinghurst, the army demonstrated it would not become the "obedient and silent servant of the state" envisioned by Piérola. Widely popular for his effective handling of a brief border clash with Colombian troops in 1911, Benavides embodied the best qualities of a career soldier. A member of one of Peru's most influential families, he began his military training at the age of fourteen and graduated first in his class from the ESG in 1906. Thereafter, he studied in France and served on military commissions in Germany and Austria before becoming army chief of staff in 1913. As perhaps the finest example of the professional army officer, Benavides demonstrated that Peru's better-trained soldiers could not remain aloof from the nation's partisan political struggles.[27] Moreover, his golpe showed that a more professional army would enter the political arena once its corporate interests were threatened. When Benavides led troops against Billinghurst, he acted on behalf of both conservative civilian opponents of the reformist president as well as the army. After the president dissolved congress, slashed the military budget, and threatened to arm his working-class supporters, soldiers seized the National Palace.

The Benavides *golpe* presaged the army's role in national political affairs for decades to come. Rapid social change brought on by an accelerated pace of economic development after 1914 prevented the formation of a broad national political consensus. Political instability arising from this situation in large part explains why Peru's more professional army remained immersed in politics despite the influence of its French tutors and their principle of political obedience. More like the Brazilian and the Argentine armies after 1930, Peru's soldiers became the nation's political referees and sometimes its principal players. Benavides and dozens of his army colleagues in future years were called upon to arbitrate the struggles of competing civilian antagonists representing Peru's historically weak political parties. Not surprisingly, this role frequently divided the army as it struggled to professionalize.

Despite leading the army from its barracks in 1914, Benavides clearly had little taste for the old-style *caudillo* politics of the past. He relinquished power to a civilian, José Pardo, after twenty months as provisional president and retired to the political sidelines, where he remained for two decades. For eleven of those years, the remarkably shrewd civilian Augusto B. Leguía autocratically ruled Peru after he enlisted military support to overthrow Pardo, who had repeated Billinghurst's mistakes by reducing military appropriations in a time of social unrest. Leguía dealt with the military much more effectively.

Leguía's eleven-year dictatorship, called the *Oncenio*, was characterized by general economic prosperity made possible chiefly by a significant influx of foreign capital.[28] The armed forces directly benefited from Peru's expanding economy, but military loyalty was primarily maintained by a sophisticated program of political favoritism, repression, and generous attention to the needs of the navy, air force, and *Guardia Civil*. Relying on the experience gained during an earlier term as president (1908-1912), Leguía knew that the backing of key army commanders was crucial for his government's survival. Rather than risk dealing with the existing army establishment, however, the autocrat cunningly built a cadre of army supporters through selective and often unscheduled promotions and transfers. The one constant in his relations with military men was his demand for political loyalty. Thus, the corruption of his army supporters was overlooked, while army opponents were either transferred, exiled, or jailed. As Leguía grew bolder, the list of victims of these purges grew longer and more prestigious. Even the powerful Benavides was exiled in 1921, and, despite his efforts to enlist the support of his army allies to depose Leguía, the politically agile president grew more secure. Against this backdrop it is easy to understand why the army's morale suffered as the problem of political influence descended upon the officer corps. If Leguía had relied solely on military patronage and repression to subordinate the army, it seems likely he would not have ruled longer than any other civilian president in Peru's modern history. Other elements of his military programs further explain his remarkable success.

While Leguía built a core of support in the army, he simultaneously worked to counterbalance its strength. Seeking to enlarge and professionalize the other armed institutions and thereby increase their loyalty, the dictator devoted special governmental attention to the navy, air corps, and *Guardia Civil*. Toward this end a United States naval mission was contracted in June, 1920 and immediately invested with "sweeping powers" to reorganize the entire naval service. The mission chief, Captain Frank Freyer, was named navy chief of staff with orders to "direct and administer" the entire navy. Over the next decade, Freyer and his fellow officer, Captain Charles Davy, used their authority to the fullest, modernizing the navy's educational system and restructuring its command.[29] Another United States naval officer, Lieutenant Commander Harold B. Grow, was given full authority by Leguía to organize Peru's military and civil aviation. After developing a close personal friendship with the president, Grow was appointed inspector general of Peru's Joint Aviation Command (*Cuerpo de Aviación del Perú*) in February, 1928. By the end of the decade, however, Peru's aviators still flew for two separate air services, with the air corps based at Las Palmas and navy airmen operating at Ancon.[30] The restructuring of the navy was completed when plans were made for the establishment of a navy general staff college. The Leguía administration complemented these reforms by modernizing the navy's older vessels, acquiring four new submarines from United States shipyards, and constructing a naval base in Callao harbor.

The *Oncenio* also witnessed the birth and significant professional progress of Peru's small air force. French, British, and, ultimately, United States pilots were hired to train cadets at the aviation school (*Escuela de Aviación Militar de Jorge Chávez*), which was officially opened in 1922. As Leguía calculated, support within the air force, like the navy, remained consistent through the *Oncenio*. Nevertheless, it was not these institutions that the crafty dictator depended upon most heavily to confront a possible challenge from the army. Leguía saw the *Guardia Civil* as his primary base of support.

By heavily arming the national police, contracting a Spanish police mission in 1921, and establishing a police academy in 1922, Leguía sought to create an institution that would both maintain internal order and discourage army opposition to his government. When in 1924 a special

machine-gun unit of the police was organized for the sole duty of guarding
the presidential palace, the ultimate mission of the *Guardia Civil* became
even more apparent. As the United States ambassador noted in 1927:

It is generally believed that President Leguía caused the Spanish police mission to
be brought to Peru to thoroughly reorganize the police force under different lines
[so] that in the event of any attempt by force upon his government in which the
army might become involved, he could have a loyal force, sufficiently strong to
suppress it.[31]

In order to assure that it was "sufficiently strong," the *Guardia Civil's*
manpower was steadily increased until it nearly equaled the army's by
1926. With its modern weapons and thorough training directed by
instructors from Spain's *Benemérita Española*, the *Guardia* became a
formidable ally of Leguía.[32]

Always wary of its potential power, Leguía was unable to ignore the
army in his military modernization program. Both the army's budget and
manpower were substantially increased before 1929, and the government
permitted it to acquire modern small arms and to expand its foreign study
missions.[33] Besides traveling to France, officers journeyed to Belgium,
Germany, Italy, Spain, and the United States for further specialized
training. Many of these "study missions," however, were no more than
thinly disguised terms of military exile. Luis M. Sánchez Cerro, an
ambitious and politically active army officer, for example, was ordered to
Italy, Spain, and France in the 1920s after participating in abortive plots
to oust Leguía in 1919 and 1922.[34] More significantly, the government's
motives in initiating contacts with the United States army were part of
Leguía's attempt to replace the French army mission with a team from the
United States.

The United States army's success in World War I and the effective work
of the navy mission, which, according to the Lima newspaper *La Prensa* in
1923, had shown "proof of devotion to our flag," were important considerations governing this decision.[35] Moreover, Leguía apparently expected
that contacts with United States armaments manufacturers resulting from
a United States army mission would enhance his already close ties with the
North American business community.[36] These efforts, begun in early
1921, were prompted by the dictator's uneasiness regarding the French
officers' relationship with their Peruvian counterparts. Although the
French advisers disdained political intrigue, their neutral posture appears
to have aroused the suspicions of the autocrat, who demanded open
manifestations of loyalty.[37] Thus, the French mission's contract was
allowed to expire in 1925 after the Leguía regime had waged a four-year

campaign to discredit it.[38] Washington refused, however, to send an army advisory team in its place, justifying its position on the grounds that as the chief arbitrator in negotiations then proceeding on the still unresolved Tacna-Arica dispute with Chile, its diplomatic impartiality would be impaired if closer military ties were developed with Peru.[39]

The army was without foreign advisers until 1927, when Leguía secured the services of a German mission commanded by General Wilhem Faupel. A German army expatriate who had previously served as the principal adviser to the Argentine army's inspector general, Faupel left Argentina after his politically tactless behavior alienated influential officers in the army's high command.[40] These same problems recurred in Peru once Leguía named Faupel to the powerful post of army inspector general. The German mission remained in Peru only until 1929, when Leguía asked for Faupel's resignation after repeated army complaints against his excessive influence.[41] In June, 1929, only three months before Faupel resigned, Peruvian army Colonel Carlos A. de la Jara reviewed for a Caracas newspaper the work of both the German and French missions. Barely mentioning the German team, he reserved his praise for the "truly notable" performance of the French officers who were "largely responsible for the reorganization and resurgence of the Peruvian army."[42] Leguía's decision to replace the French advisers unquestionably undermined his support in the army. When the other props supporting Leguía's regime weakened after 1929, his policy of mixing military professionalization with partisan politics cost him the army's support.

Prone to overconfidence because of the economic prosperity and relative political stability between 1925 and 1929, Leguía made uncharacteristic political misjudgments that weakened his regime even before the Depression devastated the Peruvian economy in 1930. His reelection to another five-year term in 1929 led his opponents to believe his regime would go on indefinitely. Furthermore, his controversial settlements of a long-standing border dispute with Colombia in 1927 and the even more unpopular decision to cede the southern province of Arica to Chile as the final settlement of the War of the Pacific angered even his firmest army supporters while arousing a groundswell of civilian nationalist opposition. With his patriotism in question, his continuing political ambition confirmed, and the world prices of Peru's sugar and cotton dropping precipitously, the dictator lost his grip on power.

That Leguía was toppled by a *coup d'état* initiated by an army officer is not surprising. What is more revealing is that his downfall was initiated by a mere lieutenant colonel, Luis Sánchez Cerro, who after the dictator incautiously gave him a battalion command in Arequipa in 1929, enlisted junior and midrank officer support and prominent Arequipa civilian opponents of Leguía for his movement. Particularly demoralized by the partisan army politics of the *Oncenio*, younger officers in garrisons throughout Peru supported the Sánchez Cerro revolt against both Leguía and the *Junta* of army generals that temporarily replaced the deposed dictator. After General Manuel Ponce, army chief of staff, relinquished power to the "upstart lieutenant colonel" on 27 August 1930, no senior officers were subsequently included in his provisional government.[43]

The Sánchez Cerro rebellion confirmed that after more than three decades of professional progress, corporate unity still eluded the armed forces. Repeated use of their support by competing civilian factions coupled with civilian manipulation of the military's internal affairs divided the officer corps and undermined internal discipline. The corporate structures of both the army and the navy suffered even greater strains as a result of the populist politics unleashed by Sánchez Cerro's revolution. The decade of the 1930s would be a period of trauma for the Peruvian military as it became enmeshed in profound civil-military conflict.

NOTES

1. Juan Velasco Alvarado, *La voz de la Revolución: Discursos del General de División Juan Velasco Alvarado*, 1 (Lima: 1972), p. 55.

2. On the historical development of the Peruvian military in the nineteenth century, see Leon G. Campbell, *The Military and Society in Colonial Peru, 1750-1810* (Philadelphia: 1978); Lyle N. McAlister, "Peru," in Lyle McAlister, Anthony P. Maingot, and Robert A. Potash, *The Military in Latin American Socio-Political Evolution: Four Case Studies* (Washington, D.C.: 1970); Liisa North, *Civil-Military Relations in Argentina, Chile and Peru* (Berkeley: 1966). Important works in Spanish are Víctor Villanueva Valencia, *Ejército Peruano: del caudillaje anárquico al militarismo reformista* (Lima: 1973); Luis Humberto Delgado, *El militarismo en el Perú, 1821-1930* (Lima: 1930); Carlos Dellepiane, *Historia militar del Perú*, 2 vols., 5th ed. (Lima: 1964); César García Rosell, *Historia de los cuerpos de tropa del ejército* (Lima: 1951).

3. As indicated previously, Samuel P. Huntington's definition of military professionalism is employed here. See Huntington, *The Soldier and the State* (Cambridge, Massachusetts: 1957), pp. 11-18; and *Political Order in Changing Societies* (New Haven: 1968), pp. 192-198. For a provocative revisionist treatment see Amos Perlmutter, *The Military and Politics in Modern Times* (New Haven: 1977).

4. Campbell, *The Military and Society*, pp. 231-232; Villanueva, *Ejército Peruano*, pp. 11-121 passim.

5. Villanueva, *Ejército Peruano*, pp. 45-47; McAlister, "Peru," p. 24.

6. Jorge Basadre, *Historia de la republica del Perú*, 7 (Lima: 1963), pp. 3148-3152; McAlister, "Peru," p. 24.

7. Admiral Miguel Grau, commander of the Peruvian navy, and Colonel Francisco Bolognesi, defender of Tarapacá, both died gloriously in battle and are particularly venerated members of Peru's pantheon of military heroes.

8. The best study of the French military mission in Peru is Efrain Cobas, *Fuerza armada: Misiones militares y dependencia en el Perú* (Lima: 1982), pp. 27-51. See also Fritz Epstein, "European Military Influence in Latin America" (Washington, D.C.: Unpublished Manuscript, Library of Congress), pp. 159-166; Frederick M. Nunn, "Effects of European Military Training in Latin America: The Origins and Nature of Professional Militarism in Argentina, Brazil, Chile, and Peru, 1890-1940," *Military Affairs*, 39, no. 1 (February, 1975), p. 4, and Nunn's incisive study, *Yesterday's Soldiers. European Military Professionalism in South America, 1890-1940* (Lincoln, Nebraska: 1983).

9. This statement has been attributed to Major Ebner, one of Saint Cyr's most prominent instructors; John Steward Ambler, *The French Army in Politics, 1945-1962*, (Columbus, Ohio: 1966), p. 40.

10. With the exception of periods in the late 1920s and mid-1930s, the army relied on French instructors. Even after the fall of France in 1940 and the subsequent termination of the French government's contract in January, 1941, French army officers remained in Peru as unofficial consultants to the General Staff until 1944; United States army intelligence, G-2 (28 February 1944), Report No. 5940, National Archives, Record Group 319. Hereafter cited as NA, RG 319 with file number and date.

11. Louis Hubert Gonzalve Lyautey, Lettres du Tonkin et de Madagasgar (2d ed.), (Paris: 1921); as quoted in Paul Marie de la Gorce, *The French Army: A Military Political History*, trans. by Kenneth Douglas (New York: 1963), pp. 88-89.

12. Louis Hubert Gonzalve Lyautey, "Du rôle social de l'officier," *Revue Des Deux Mondes*, 104 (15 March 1891), p. 453.

13. On the French army's colonial role see Louis Hubert Gonzalve Lyautey, "Du rôle colonial de l'armee," *Revue Des Deux Mondes*, 57 (15 January 1900), pp. 308-329; Jean Gottman, "Bugeaud, Gallieni, Lyautey: The Development of French Colonial Warfare," in Edward Mead Earle, ed., *Makers of Modern Strategy: Military Thought from Machiavelli to Hitler* (New York: 1966), pp. 234-260, and Kim Munholland, "The Emergence of the Colonial Military in France, 1880-1905," Ph.D. diss., Princeton University, 1964.

14. Epstein, pp. 159-166; Villanueva, p. 126.

15. Poindexter to Hughes, 9 February 1925, 823.20/16, NA, RG 59.

16. Epstein, "European Military," p. 57.

17. This editorial from the Lima newspaper *La Prensa* was reported in a dispatch by the U.S. Ambassador. Poindexter to Hughes, 19 August 1923, 823.20/4, NA, RG 59.

18. General Juan Mendoza Rodríguez, "El Ejército," in José Pareja Paz-Sóldan, ed., *Visión del Perú en el siglo XX*, 2 vols. (Lima: 1962), 1, pp. 296-299; Epstein, "European Military," pp. 159-160; McAlister, "Peru," pp. 24-25.

19. These figures are from Villanueva, *Ejército Peruano*, pp. 144, 410.

20. Mendoza Rodríguez, "El Ejército," p. 301; Comandante José Valdizan Gamio, "La marina de guerra peruana," in Paz-Sóldan, *Visión*, 1, p. 362.

21. Robert L. Scheina, *Latin America: A Naval History 1810-1987* (Annapolis: 1987) pp. 130-131. Scheina's study is the best analysis in English of Latin American navies. See also Jorge Ortíz Sotelo, *Escuela Naval del Perú* (Callao: 1981), pp. 69-80, for a discussion of the French naval mission.

22. Mendoza Rodríguez, "El Ejército," p. 299; Minister in Lima to Bryan, 25 April 1914, 823.20, NA, RG 59. The short-lived *Centre de Hautes Études Militaires* was the model for the French mission.

23. Basadre, *Historia*, 7, p. 3797.

24. Peruvian army officers studied at Saint-Cyr, Saumur, Fontainebleau, and the *Ecole Supérieure de Guerre*.

25. Lieutenant Colonel Gabriel Velarde Alvarez, "Instruccíon civil del soldado," *Boletín de Ministerio de Guerra y Marina*, 1, no. 7 (October, 1904), pp. 843-845, cited in Frederick M. Nunn, "Professional Militarism in Twentieth Century Peru: Historical and Theoretical Background to the *Golpe de Estado* of 1968," *Hispanic American Historical Review*, 59, no. 3 (August, 1979), p. 406.

26. Marshal Joseph Joffre's ideas on national defense received careful attention in Peru. See Mendoza Rodríguez, "El Ejército," p. 303.

27. "Necrología: Mariscal del Perú, Oscar R. Benavides," *Revista Militar del Peru*, 42, no. 7 (July, 1945), pp. ix-xii, hereafter cited as *RMP*. For a detailed discussion of the Benavides *golpe*, see José Zazarte Lescano, *El Mariscal Benavides: Su vida y su obra*, 1 (Lima: 1976), pp. 201-218. This biography was commissioned by the Benavides family and should thus be read with this in mind.

28. A detailed but strongly pro-Leguía study of the *Oncenio* is Manuel Capuney, *Leguía: Vida y obra del constructdor del gran Perú* (Lima: 1951). Two doctoral dissertations offer good coverage of this era. They are Allen Gerlach, "Civil-Military Relations in Peru, 1914-1945," University of New Mexico, 1973, and Howard Karno, "Augusto B. Leguía: The Oligarchy and the Modernization of Peru, 1807-1930," University of California, Los Angeles, 1970.

29. Daniels to Lansing, 16 April 1920, 823,30/17, NA, RG 59, and Gonzales to Hughes (26 January 1921), 823.30/20 NA, RG 59. The navy mission was given such broad powers that one Lima newspaper complained that a "foreign dictatorship was being established."

30. Sharon S. Pope, "Harold B. Grow and the Establishment of Aviation in Peru, 1924-1930," master's thesis, University of West Florida, 1973; José Valdizan Gamio, "La marina de guerra peruana en el siglo XX," in Paz-Sóldan, *Visión*, pp. 268-270; Lieutenant Juan M. Castro, ed., *ORTO: Publicación anual de los cadetes de la Escuela Naval del Perú* (Lima: 1940), p. 21. See also Víctor E. Arce, "La fuerza aérea del Perú en el siglo XX," in Paz-Sóldan, *Visión*, p. 421; McAlister, "Peru," p. 26; Cobas, *Fuerza armada*, pp. 55-58.

31. Poindexter to Kellogg, 3 August 1927, 823.20/25, NA, RG 59.

32. Villanueva, *Ejército Peruano*, pp. 172-173.

33. Mendoza Rodríguez, "El Ejército," pp. 312-313; Poindexter to Hughes, 11 March 1924, 823.24/20, NA, RG 59.

34. Pedro Ugarteche, ed., *Sánchez Cerro: Papeles y recuerdos de un presidente del Perú*, 4 vols. (Lima: 1969), 1, pp. 68-69.

35. Poindexter to Hughes, 21 February 1923, 823.30/21, NA, RG 59.

36. James Carey, *Peru and the United States, 1900-1962* (Notre Dame, Indiana: 1964), pp. 58-59.

37. Epstein, "European Military," p. 161; Poindexter to Hughes, 27 August 1924, 823.20/10, NA, RG 59.

38. Poindexter to Hughes, 26 April 1923, 823.20/2a, NA, RG 59. Juan Leguía, the dictator's son, while on a visit to Washington in 1923 charged members of the French mission with "grafting." The U.S. ambassador in Peru discounted this allegation, however, claiming Leguía was probably just "talking for effect."

39. Poindexter to Hughes, 27 August 1924, 823.20/10, NA, RG 59.

40. Epstein, "European Military," p. 165; Robert Potash, The Army and Politics in Argentina: Yrigoyen to Perón (Stanford: 1969), p. 5; George Pope Atkins and Larry V. Thompson, "German Military Influence in Argentina, 1921-1940," Journal of Latin American Studies, 4, no. 2 (November, 1972), pp. 265-266.

41. Epstein, "European Military," p. 165; Mayer to Stimson, 4 October 1929, 823.20/35, NA, RG 59.

42. Engert (Caracas) to Stimson, 6 June 1929, 823.20/26, NA, RG 59.

43. The New York Times, 29 August 1930, p. 7. Leguía's unsuccessful attempt to flee Peru and his subsequent imprisonment and death in the Bellavista Naval Hospital are carefully discussed in Jorge Ortíz Sotelo, "Sucesos a bordo del B.A.P. Almirante Grau con motivo de la caida de Leguía," Revista de Marina, 374, no. 2, (May-June, 1985), pp. 162-181, and Víctor Villanueva Valencia, Así Cayó Leguía (Lima: 1977), pp. 153-155. For discussions of the details of the Sánchez Cerro golpe, see Villanueva, Así Cayó Leguía, pp. 111-114; Carlos Miró-Quesada Laos, Sánchez Cetro y su tiempo en Perú (Buenos Aires: 1947); Steve Stein, Populism in Peru: The Emergence of the Masses and the Politics of Social Control (Madison: 1980), pp. 86-90; Allen Gerlach "Civil-Military Relations in Peru," pp. 226-249.

2
Populism and Militarism: The 1930s

The economic dislocation caused by the world Depression of the 1930s profoundly altered political and social conditions in Peru and other South American nations. Peru's export-oriented economy, like that of Argentina, Brazil, and Chile, was particularly vulnerable to the decline in world demand following the Wall Street crash of October, 1929. Political instability was the watchword of these bleak economic days as governments throughout the continent toppled in the face of the economic crisis. Underlying the volatile political climate were two primary trends. During the early 1930s Latin America witnessed the formation of new political alliances as emerging middle- and working-class groups gained their first access to political power. The rise of Víctor Raúl Haya de la Torre's APRA party in Peru was reflective of this phenomenon. Chile's particularly acute economic crisis also provided fertile ground for the growth of South America's most viable socialist party, formed by Salvador Allende Gossens and his compatriots in 1933.

A second recognizable outgrowth of the Depression was the evolution of professional military establishments intent upon arbitrating the course of the civilian political process in their nations. The Argentine military was most active in this capacity. After the coup of General José Uriburu ended the presidency of the aging Hipólito Yrigoyen in September, 1930, one freely elected civilian president would not succeed another until the presidency of Carlos Menem began in July, 1989. Similarly, the Brazilian army became active political actors, teaming with Getulio Vargas to bring the Old Republic to an end and the Estado Nôvo to life during the 1930s. Brazilian soldiers would retreat reluctantly to their barracks only in the mid-1980s. With its heavy dependence on copper exports, Chile suffered the worst economic decline of any nation in the world in the early 1930s. These conditions provoked a series of military *coups* and a widespread naval mutiny, badly undermining military discipline and morale. Young Chilean soldiers and sailors beginning their careers in the mid-1930s, lived their entire professional lives with the memory of socialist and communist involvement in these military troubles. Loyal young officers in the navy even witnessed the rise to political prominence of some of the naval personnel involved in the 1931 mutiny. A similar threat to armed forces solidarity during the presidency of Salvador Allende prompted Chilean army commander General Augusto Pinochet Ugarte (who began his army career in 1936) to launch one of the most violent *coups* in Latin American history in September, 1973.

In Peru in the decades after 1930, military men would occupy the presidential palace for fully half this period as they sought to forge their professional identity through a political process they came increasingly to condemn. By the early 1960s Peruvian soldiers saw themselves, like their contemporaries throughout South America, as more capable of administering their nations than were the civilian politicians, whom they perceived as quarrelsome, petty, and lacking in vision. This perception, coupled with the increased threat from the radical left, by the 1960s led South American military establishments either to politically proscribe or to wage open combat with their civilian opponents. Argentina's "Dirty War" during the 1970s, and similar systematic repression by Brazilian, Chilean, Uruguayan, and Paraguayan security forces are tragic examples of this trend in civil-military affairs. Repression during the military *Docenio* (twelve-year government) following the Velasco *coup* of 3 October 1968 was not systematic and far less severe. Nevertheless, this anticivilian bias was reflected in the Velasco regime's unwillingness to engage the masses in Peru in support of its sweeping program of reforms. The Peruvian military's deep distrust of populist politics and of traditional civilian political parties was born during the turbulent 1930s.

The Sánchez Cerro *golpe de estado* of August, 1930 was a major milestone in the course of Peruvian civil-military affairs. The demoralizing partisan politics of the autocrat Leguía that had so badly divided the officer corps was ended. In its place the Sánchez Cerro movement unleashed new political forces that would permanently transform both the armed forces and the civilian body politic. The diminutive lieutenant colonel's Arequipa revolt opened the way for the nation's masses to enter politics for the first time. Aided by the political vacuum brought about by Leguía's near liquidation of Peru's traditional political parties, Sánchez Cerro and Víctor Raúl Haya de la Torre, founder and unquestioned leader of the *APRA* party, waged a titanic struggle for power that would end only after Sánchez Cerro's assassination in April, 1933.

Standing aloof from the intense populist politics and violence of the Sánchez Cerro years was General Oscar R. Benavides. Nevertheless, it would be Benavides, the army's most prestigious officer, who would dominate Peruvian civil-military affairs from Sánchez Cerro's death until the end of the decade. Haya de la Torre and his *Aprista* followers would combat Benavides in the same way as they struggled against Sánchez Cerro: by subverting army and navy personnel in their efforts to seize political power. The breakdown of military discipline, in great measure due to APRA, coupled with the defeat of Peruvian forces in a short engagement with Colombia in 1932-1933, provoked extreme tension and deep frustration within the military. These issues reinforced the Peruvian military man's traditional distrust of civilians and his desire to gain a greater degree of autonomy for his institution.

These severe problems did not prevent some intellectually active army officers from laboring to articulate a mission that would elevate their institution above the *caudillismo* and bloody political strife marking the 1930s. Only a few months after Sánchez Cerro's death and Peru's defeat in its border dispute with Colombia, two army officers confidently espoused an ambitious mission for the army. Writing in the October, 1933 issue of the *Revista Militar*, Lieutenant Colonel Morla Concha noted that Peru's greatest national problem consisted of "forging a national identity from among its diverse peoples." The army would be the agency to resolve this problem and build a modern state, Morla Concha predicted, because military men were the "genuine bearers of a nationalism." The army's "civilizing mission" would be realized through literacy training for Indian conscripts, building transportation and communication facilities, and generally setting a strongly patriotic example for the civilian sector to follow.[1] Morla Concha's ambitious goals were echoed in a more limited fashion two months later in the *Revista Militar* by Lieutenant Mauricio Barbis, who called for the creation of an army battalion charged primarily with the colonization of Peru's remote and lightly inhabited *montaña* region. Barbis argued that such a program would increase agricultural production and generally advance the course of economic development.[2] These two lonely but undaunted voices would be joined occasionally by others throughout the 1930s as a few army officers, ignoring the reality of their institution's plight, clung to a grand vision of their military mission.

Some of this rhetoric may very well have been aimed at undercutting the populist appeal of APRA, which had gained broad-based popular support in Peru after Haya de la Torre founded the organization in Mexico in May, 1924. Born on 22 February 1895 in Trujillo, of middle-class parents, Haya de la Torre, despite never being elected president, was destined to become Peru's dominant political figure until his death in 1979. After briefly attending the University of Trujillo, Víctor Raúl (as his followers came to call him) worked as a secretary to the prefect of the Department of Cuzco. He then entered Lima's San Marcos University, where he quickly became immersed in the politics of the Confederation, and during the next four years the student leader worked tirelessly to construct a coalition of Lima's workers and his fellow university students. His greatest success lay in the creation of "Popular Universities," formed to provide informal educational opportunities for Lima's working class. By 1923 Haya de la Torre had acquired both a national and international reputation due to his student organizing activities. When, however, in May, 1923 he decided to challenge the well-entrenched Leguía political power against the autocrat's decision to consecrate Peru to the Sacred Heart of Jesus, his student demonstration was violently suppressed and Haya de la Torre was first imprisoned and then exiled on 9 October 1923.[3]

Upon settling in Mexico after his exile from Peru, Haya de la Torre announced the formation of APRA in May, 1924. In December of that year he detailed the basic five-point program forming the core of the party's political platform for years to come. These general points included (1) action against Yankee imperialism; (2) the political unity of Latin America; (3) nationalization of lands and industry; (4) internationalization of the Panama Canal; and (5) solidarity of all oppressed peoples of the world. The original objective of APRA was the construction of a broadly based alliance of students, intellectuals, workers, and elements of the middle and peasant classes grouped together in a political front opposing the penetration of foreign, political, and economic interests in Latin America.[4]

Despite limited organizational progress in several Latin American countries during the 1920s, APRA became primarily a Peruvian political party after 1930. Haya de la Torre's desire to attract the widest possible political support during APRA's early years explains his reluctance to detail carefully any specific proposals for political action before 1930. One important exception was his use of the term "Indo-America" for the area commonly referred to as Latin America. This terminology was used as the party attempted to identify with the Indian and mestizo population of Peru and all of Latin America in a bid for their support.

Between 1926 and 1930 the APRA leader traveled and studied extensively in the Soviet Union, Germany, England, Italy, and the United States.[5] During this period he also refined the vague outlines of APRA's ideological program, and carefully separated its objectives from any association with the goals of the international communist movement. By 1928, Haya de la Torre's denunciation of European socialist and communist philosophies helped splinter the small radical leftist element in Peru. When the *APRA* chief attempted in early 1929 unilaterally to launch an armed rebellion against Leguía (after failing to gain support of his own presidential candidacy), Peru's leading Marxist intellectual, José Carlos Mariátegui, severed his relations with Haya de la Torre. The split temporarily undermined *APRA*'s organizational efforts, but by mid-1930 the party was still the most unified representative of Peru's political left.[6]

Although *APRA* made important political gains during 1930, for most of the three months following the fall of Leguía, Sánchez Cerro governed with substantial political support. This shrewd military man stands as one of the most intriguing popular leaders in twentieth-century Peru. Courageous, impetuous, and politically ambitious but apparently never personally corrupt, Sánchez Cerro was born in the northern city of Piura on 12 August 1889. Son of a notary of modest means, he attended public schools in his native city until his decision in 1910 to make the army his career. He enlisted in the army as a private, then a few months later entered the *Escuela Militar de Chorrillos*, from which he graduated as a second lieutenant in 1914. Sánchez Cerro's political ambitions soon became apparent when he took part in the Benavides *golpe* of 1914. Wounded in the fighting, he was rewarded by Benavides with a promotion to captain and a post in Washington, D. C., as Peru's military attaché. Still dissatisfied with his political lot, Sánchez Cerro headed political plots against Leguía in 1919 in Iquitos and then again in Cuzco in 1922. Prior to his 1919 conspiracy, this aggressive military man expressed presidential ambition when he informed a military colleague that he would one day "lead the masses with a piece of bread in one hand and a whip in the other."[7] This statement characterized well Sánchez Cerro's political tactics during his brief tenure as president.

During the first months after the fall of Leguía, Sánchez Cerro's consistent opposition to the Leguía dictatorship and his announced intention to end the corruption left over from the *Oncenio* bolstered his political position.[8] Nevertheless, the *Junta* chief felt compelled quickly to purge senior army, navy, air force, and *Guardia Civil* commanders whose loyalty was suspect. Sánchez Cerro's particular enmity toward the *Guardia Civil* and the navy stemmed from Leguía's close ties to these two institutions. Sanchéz Cerro appointed a new navy chief of staff, divested the United States naval mission of its commands, and turned these posts over to what he deemed loyal Peruvian naval officers. The navy's ships and aircraft were also placed under strict operational control and were required to report their activities frequently.[9]

Military and civilian support for Sánchez Cerro began to evaporate in early December, 1930, however, when it became clear he was planning to seek the presidency without first resigning as head of the governing *Junta*. His intentions were signaled earlier by the adoption of repressive measures against APRA and the Communist Party, which he claimed were responsible for a rash of strikes and student disorders. The lines between the military leader and the APRA became even more clearly drawn when conservative elements of the decades-old *Civilista* party began to support the army colonel's presidential ambitions.[10]

By the first week of January, 1931, a wide range of civilian political groups had demonstrated their open hostility to Sánchez Cerro's plans and voiced their desire for open elections in which only civilian candidates would be allowed to seek the presidency. These demands were backed by many army officers who felt that Sánchez Cerro's affiliation with arch-conservatives had compromised his revolution against Leguía. Nonetheless, in early February the chief executive announced his intention to hold elections at the end of March in which he would be a candidate for president.[11] Within two weeks Peru was in open rebellion. Sánchez Cerro's attempt to calm the opposition by withdrawing his candidacy on 23 February failed, and with the nation on the verge of civil war, he resigned as provisional president on 1 March. Claiming his resignation demonstrated his sense of self-sacrifice necessary for the good of Peru, the outgoing president vowed to return from his self-imposed exile in France to reclaim his rightful place in Peruvian political affairs.[12] After a turbulent ten days, a civilian political leader from Arequipa, David Samanez Ocampo, was named head of a new provisional *Junta*, which ruled Peru from 10 March to 8 December 1931.

The *Junta* represented a broad range of political opinion and boasted the critical support of Lieutenant Colonel Gustavo Jiménez, commander of the important Lima garrison. The government was thus soon able to announce its plans to hold national elections for a new president and a constituent congress in which all parties except the communists would be allowed to participate. In the spirit of this more open political climate, a new electoral law was promulgated on 27 May that instituted the secret ballot and removed property qualifications for voting. These measures, while significantly increasing the size of the electorate, still did not grant the vote to the vast majority of Peru's impoverished Indian population. Most Indians were barred from the ballot box by the law's literacy requirement.[13]

Quickly emerging as the dominant political groups by May, 1931 were the APRA and the faction supporting Sánchez Cerro. APRA leaders registered the party under the title *Partido Aprista Peruano* (PAP) and initiated an effective organizational campaign in Peru's northern departments even while Haya de la Torre still remained in exile. Sánchez Cerro's backers received a temporary setback on 17 May, when the government announced its intention to prevent the army colonel's return to campaign for president. This decision was primarily the work of Lieutenant Colonel Jiménez, who was now Sánchez Cerro's chief political rival.[14] Jiménez viewed his fellow officer's candidacy as a serious threat to the internal stability of the armed forces and for personal as well as ideological reasons favored the PAP in the upcoming elections.

The *Junta* was unable to block Sánchez Cerro's presidential bid because of his substantial popularity and in early June lifted its ban on the military leader's return. Still facing intense opposition from military and civilian opponents, Sánchez Cerro arrived in Peru on 7 July and began his campaign immediately. Ten days later, Haya de la Torre ended nearly nine years of exile with his return to Talara in northern Peru.[15] The stage was now set for the most volatile campaign in Peruvian history. The elections, scheduled for early October, were preceded by a bitter campaign that intensified the already polarized political climate.

Attempting to generate a broader political base, Haya de la Torre moderated radical positions espoused by APRA during the 1920s. The primary target of his campaign messages was the nation's disaffected middle class. While still clinging to the basic tenet of antiimperialism, the APRA chief declared that the middle class represented the "essence" of the nation. This group, he insisted, suffered the most from the engulfing forces of foreign imperialism. The origins of Haya de la Torre's anti-imperialist campaign lay in the displacement of small and medium-size farm operators in the Chicama and Santa Catalina valleys adjacent to the APRA chief's native Trujillo. Large, well-capitalized estates, most notably the Casa Grande sugar enterprise operated by the Grace Corporation, through favorable economic agreements with the government had bankrupted many of their smaller competitors. This process, ongoing since the late nineteenth century, drove displaced farmers as well as rural migrants, merchants, journalists, and labor leaders into *Aprista* ranks. The core of his party's solution to the economic threat of foreign capital was a sweeping political alliance involving the middle class, the emerging urban proletariat, and the exploited Indian masses. Haya de la Torre, however, realized the danger of an uncompromising denunciation of all foreign interests in Peru. He thus qualified his position by stating his party would respect the rights of foreign capital if its role in the national economy were carefully controlled.[16]   Moreover, the APRA leader further softened his political stance in private discussions with the United States ambassador in Peru.   After an interview with Haya de la Torre in early September, Ambassador Frederick Dearing concluded that United States' interests had "nothing to fear" if the APRA candidate were elected president.[17]

During the 1931 campaign APRA experienced little success in gaining significant support from the armed forces. APRA's relationship with the military during 1931 and throughout the time span of this study deserves close scrutiny.   Many of the substantive developments in civil-military relations in Peru to the present day must be viewed in the context of the APRA-military rivalry. Because the ideological orientation of APRA was at odds with the thinking of Peru's military leadership, senior armed forces officers viewed the party as a threat to the viability of the armed forces. What troubled military leaders most about APRA's political program was the party's intent to mobilize middle- and working-class support for its policies. This threat was made even more imposing by the party's rigid organizational framework and strict party unity, which made APRA the most disciplined political force in Peru. The party's internal structure, in fact, closely paralleled that of the armed forces and was an important factor in maintaining party unity during its many years of political proscription after 1931.[18]

When the APRA-Sánchez Cerro rivalry became intense, *Apristas* responded violently. Despite confrontations between *Apristas* and the Sánchez Cerro's military supporters, armed forces officers and enlisted men in significant numbers were still willing to cooperate and conspire with APRA for a variety of personal and political reasons. Ironically, APRA's political power, generated to a large degree by party discipline and the concomitant loyalty of party activists, encouraged dissatisfied and ambitious military men to join forces with APRA. Consequently, APRA's successful subversion of many armed forces personnel added immeasurably to the hostility of loyal military officers who sought to maintain military unity.

In the 1931 presidential campaign Haya de la Torre recognized that his earlier statements criticizing the military and Sánchez Cerro's own popularity among a majority of the armed forces worked against his candidacy. The party leader therefore tried to blunt military opposition. He noted that the bulk of armed forces groups would be the main beneficiaries of APRA's reform programs.[19] Moreover, Haya de la Torre emphasized that the military, with its technically oriented training, could play an active role in civic action projects once he was president. In response to allegations that APRA was intensely antimilitary and sought to replace the national army with its own party militia, APRA leaders pointed to the party membership of a number of army officers in an effort to refute these charges.[20]

Antonio Miró-Quesada, editor of Peru's most influential newspaper, El Comercio, and Sánchez Cerro's most ardent supporter, was primarily responsible for the allegations that APRA was antimilitary. Miró-Quesada and other conservative politicians formed the Partido Union Revolucionaría (Revolutionary Union Party) as the vehicle for Sánchez Cerro's presidential bid shortly after the colonel's return to Peru in July, 1931. The military candidate still hoped to capitalize upon his charismatic image among large segments of the voting population. Vaguely planning to form a political alliance between urban upper-class groups and the rural masses, Sánchez Cerro remained heavily reliant upon the financial and political backing of the nation's elite upper-class elements.[21] Largely because of this support, his political program contained few concrete proposals for economic or social reform. Stressing decentralization, fiscal responsibility, and continued foreign investment, the army colonel made only general references to the need for future land reform. Sánchez Cerro gained popularity among Peru's Indian population, however, with his abolition of Conscripción Vial, a type of forced public works program that exploited Indian labor during Leguía's dictatorship.[22]

With the arrival of national election day on 11 October 1931, a thoroughly polarized political climate existed in Peru. Attempts by moderate centrist groups to have Sánchez Cerro and Haya de la Torre withdraw in favor of a compromise candidate were rejected by both men.[23] Despite fears of possible election day violence, the voting was peaceful. Contrary to Sánchez Cerro's suspicions that the Samanez Ocampo Junta would rig the elections against him, he emerged the victor over Haya de la Torre by a count of 152,148 to 106,088. Not surprisingly, Haya de la Torre's best showing was in the Aprista strongholds of Peru's northern departments, but he did surprisingly well in some voting districts in Lima.[24] Sánchez Cerro triumphed by drawing strong support in the urban centers and among the rural population in Peru's central and southern regions. Although historical opinion is divided regarding the honesty of the 1931 elections, the best assessments portray them as the most honest in Peruvian history up to that time.[25]

Embittered Apristas, convinced that Sánchez Cerro would use his electoral victory to block meaningful reforms and liquidate their party, soon opted for violent revolution to attain national power. Haya de la Torre solicited the help of sympathetic army officers and Guardia Civil personnel in planned civil-military insurrections aimed at blocking the president-

elect's inauguration on 8 December. Due to a lack of coordination among
APRA and dissident army and police units, however, small-scale uprisings
throughout Peru were easily quelled by government troops during the first
week of December.[26]

Almost immediately after donning the presidential sash, Sánchez Cerro
moved to deal with the APRA-subverted military elements. His first target
was the *Guardia Civil*. He shifted regional commanders, made drastic cuts
in personnel, and deprived suspect units of important military equipment.
Command shuffles were also engineered in the navy, and the president
named a civilian supporter as navy minister, better to ensure the loyalty of
that institution.[27]

Most importantly, the chief executive also made changes in the
command assignments of the nation's top army officers. He promoted his
most trusted comrades and eliminated troublesome rivals. The most
prominent victim of these purges was Lieutenant Colonel Jiménez, who was
placed on inactive duty soon after Sánchez Cerro took office.[28] These
measures lowered armed forces morale, and the personal enmity created
between Sánchez Cerro and Jiménez exacerbated existing internal divisions
within the army.

The president also took strong action against his *Aprista* opponents.
After the police invaded APRA party headquarters in Trujillo in late
December, and wounded several party members in the process, measures
were quickly enacted to deal with *Aprista* resistance on the national level.
An emergency law forced through congress in early January 1932
established virtual martial law. By mid-February the president had arrested
and exiled all twenty-three of the *Aprista* deputies elected to congress in
October. Lieutenant Colonel Jiménez was also deported to Chile and
charged with engaging in political subversion.[29]

Political tensions intensified on 6 March when a young *Aprista* wounded
Sánchez Cerro in a Miraflores church in an abortive assassination attempt.
While the wounded president recuperated, orders were issued for the arrest
of Haya de la Torre on charges of subverting public order. The APRA
leader was finally captured on 6 May.

The day following Haya de la Torre's arrest, enlisted men of Peru's two
cruisers, the *Almirante Grau* and the *Colonel Bolognesi*, mutinied in Callao
harbor and arrested their superior officers. The mutiny was quickly
discovered, and the navy's four submarines, remaining units of the fleet,
and planes from the air force base at Ancón soon isolated the two cruisers
and forced the mutineers to surrender. The Sánchez Cerro government
quickly charged that *Apristas* and communists had subverted the mutinous
sailors while the cruisers were in port in Panama. APRA leader Luis

Alberto Sánchez admitted that he had met with *Almirante Grau* and *Colonel Bolognesi* crew members, but he denied inciting them to mutiny. Sánchez countered the government's charges by claiming that the mutiny was precipitated by Sánchez Cerro's poor treatment of the navy, an institution that the military president felt had always opposed him. Sánchez Cerro responded quickly to the mutiny, and claimed it was "of Communist character and surely forms part of a social plan." The government feared the mutineers might try to emulate the Chilean naval mutiny of September, 1931. That massive uprising, involving elements of the Chilean fleet based at Coquimbo and Talcahuano, soon spread to nearby army and air force units. The desperate Chilean government, before the uprising was finally put down, was forced unsuccessfully to request military aid from the United States to suppress the mutineers. Rebellious Peruvian sailors, like their Chilean counterparts, were angry not only over low pay and the working conditions aboard their vessels but also over the broader social inequities within their societies. The Peruvian mutiny was suppressed before the rebels could announce their demands. The Chilean naval insurgents, however, after forming the "Lower Deck Committee," issued a manifesto demanding that "the millionaires of Chile loan 100 million pesos to the government" and that "all uncultivated lands be divided among the workmen." Sánchez Cerro's charge of communist involvement in the Peruvian rebellion mirrored the accusations of the naval high command in Chile. What the military president most feared, however, was *Aprista* involvement in the uprising.[30]   Charged with rebellion, insulting their superiors, and disobedience, thirty-four of these enlisted men were court-martialed on 10 May 1932, and eight were executed by firing squad only an hour after their sentences were read. The tense political climate clearly influenced these extreme penalties, and these executions presaged even greater violence to come.[31] With the failure of the mutiny and with Haya de la Torre confronting an uncertain fate, party members in early May began making preparations for a massive civil-military revolt in Trujillo.

Designated as the chief organizer of the Trujillo revolt in Haya de la Torre's absence was the party leader's brother, Agustín Haya de la Torre.[32] Trujillo was the logical site for the uprising due to the *Aprista* strength in the region and the manpower supplied by the militant sugar workers from the nearby plantations in the Chicama Valley. Original plans called for the sugar workers and other *Aprista* revolutionaries to be trained by army veterans who had joined the party's ranks. Once Trujillo had been taken, Lieutenant Colonel Jiménez was slated to assume command of the revolt as it spread to other parts of Peru. Precise timing was critical to the success of the movement, as the initial operations in Trujillo would be reinforced by simultaneous uprisings in a number of northern towns and Lima itself. Only after initial successes in these areas would Jiménez leave his Chilean exile to take command of operations in the Trujillo region.

Hoping to take advantage of the temporarily undermanned condition at Trujillo's main garrison, an aggressive young *Aprista* mechanic, Manuel Barreto, persuaded Agustín Haya de la Torre to attack on 7 July, well ahead of the scheduled date for the beginning of the revolt. The target of the Trujillo rebels was the O'Donovan military garrison with its stores of arms and ammunition.[33] Barreto's short-term assessment of the military situation proved correct when the garrison fell to the rebels after a sharp four-hour battle. Although the insurgents quickly gained control of the entire city, the premature initiation of the revolt caught other *Aprista* elements by surprise, and supportive movements in other regions quickly faded.

The Trujillo rebels were then forced into a defensive posture within the city as Sánchez Cerro sent overwhelming air, sea, and ground forces to crush the revolt. By the fourth day of hostilities the city was in government hands, and order was restored. Agustín Haya de la Torre and other *Aprista* leaders managed to escape to the interior on 9 July in a futile effort to initiate a new guerilla campaign. But most of the rebels remained to face the government troops that overwhelmed the city on the following two days.[34] After the *Aprista* leadership left the city, thirty-five army and *Guardia Civil* personnel incarcerated in the Trujillo jail were executed in their cells. Five of the bodies were so badly disfigured that they were not identifiable. Responsibility for the massacre has never been accurately fixed, but Sánchez Cerro's troops indulged in massive executions of suspected APRA revolutionaries in the nearby ruins of Chan Chan.[35]

The Trujillo jail massacre had a dramatic impact on APRA-military relations for decades to come. For many years annual military ceremonies were held on 9 July to honor the memory of those armed forces personnel who died at the hands of the Trujillo revolutionaries. Some armed forces officers viewed the massacre as proof that APRA, if given the opportunity, would attempt to liquidate the military.[36] But while these tactics repelled most military men and turned them even more strongly against APRA, they also demonstrated the party's commitment to revolutionary tactics. This commitment was an important factor in the maintenance of the party's radical image during the 1930s and 1940s as it unified *Apristas* during the political repression of that era.[37] APRA's willingness to engage in revolution also had a significant impact on dissident armed forces personnel. It attracted those military men who were willing to forget the excesses of Trujillo in exchange for APRA support for their own causes.

From the suppression of the Trujillo insurrection in July, 1932 until his death at the hands of an *Aprista* assassin in April, 1933, Sánchez Cerro's attention was drawn from internal political affairs to a deepening border crisis with neighboring Colombia. After a contingent of armed Peruvian civilian and military personnel invaded the Colombian-controlled territory of Leticia on 1 September 1932, the president was faced with the dilemma of supporting the action or respecting the terms of the Salomón-Lozano treaty of 1922 granting the area to Colombia. Although the treaty had been ratified by the Peruvian congress in 1927, it had never been popular with large segments of the civilian population or the armed forces.[38]

The initial response of Sánchez Cerro and other political leaders took the form of allegations that APRA had promoted the invasions to create an international crisis.[39] Party leaders rejected these charges and called for negotiations to bring about a settlement of the dispute.[40] Once public reaction to the Peruvian occupation became clearly favorable, the president chose not to repudiate his countrymen's actions but rather to let further developments dictate his policy. Since the government would neither order a withdrawal from Leticia nor reinforce the original invaders, Colombia initiated a successful campaign against Peruvian forces in mid-February, and recaptured most of the disputed territory.

The frustration of Peruvian military on the front was reflected in a secret deposition by Colonel Víctor Ramos to the Ministry of War in 1934. Discussing his role in the military operations against Colombia, he concluded his report by criticizing the government for not supplying sufficient weapons and munitions to Peruvian troops and claiming his "anguish" was shared by the members of the army's general staff.[41] Attempting to reverse the loss of prestige to his regime and the armed forces by the Leticia defeat, Sánchez Cerro tried to generate support for a full-scale war with Colombia. At the end of February, males between twenty-one and twenty-five were ordered drafted into the army. Propaganda campaigns were also launched to convince Peruvians of the need to retaliate with a large-scale military effort against Colombian "aggression."[42]

In the midst of these war preparations, Lieutenant Colonel Jiménez, convinced that Sánchez Cerro was leading Peru into another disastrous defeat, decided to ally with APRA to overthrow the government. Jiménez arrived in northern Peru from Chile and began to organize support for a rebellion among the personnel of the army regiment stationed at Cajamarca. On 11 March, Jiménez led about three hundred men into revolt. But expected *Aprista* support from the surrounding areas failed to materialize, and the rebel leader's forces were swiftly defeated by government troops on the road to Trujillo on 14 March. Rather than surrender, Jiménez shot himself.[43] The insurrection further convinced APRA's military enemies of the party's subversive potential. The Jiménez revolt occurred at a time of national crisis when military discipline should have been strongest. It indicated instead that deep division was created by Sánchez Cerro's decision to press for war without proper military preparations.

Undaunted by the internal military problems caused by his war plans, the president sought in early April to strengthen his position by appointing the highly respected General Benavides (newly arrived from his ambassadorial post in Great Britain and hero of the 1911 conflict with Colombia) as head of a *Junta Defensa Nacional* (National Defense Committee). As chief of the *Junta* Benavides was in charge of all military forces in the campaign against Colombia. The president hoped the prestigious Benavides would lend more legitimacy to his efforts to engineer a national commitment to the war.[44] The government's position was made seemingly more secure when a previously named Constituent Assembly promulgated a new constitution on 9 April 1933, which clearly sanctioned the prominent role of the armed forces in national affairs. Article 213 of the charter read, "The purpose of the armed forces is to secure the rights of the Republic, the fulfillment of the Constitution and the laws, and the preservation of the public order."[45]

Barely three weeks after the constitution went into effect, the Sánchez Cerro era came to a violent end with the president's assassination at the hand of a seventeen-year-old *Aprista* named Abelardo Mendoza Leyva. The assailant was immediately killed by the crowd attending the military rally at which the president was slain. Suspicions arose that a widespread conspiracy, possibly even involving General Benavides, was responsible for Sánchez Cerro's assassination. But the young *Aprista* was subsequently found to have acted alone.[46] Nevertheless, Mendoza Leyva's *Aprista* affiliation added to the party's growing reputation as a violently radical organization, and thus the continued proscription of APRA for nearly all of the period until 1945 was more easily justified by the party's enemies.

Within hours after the assassin struck, the Constituent Assembly met and selected General Benavides as president for the remainder of the slain executive's term. The assembly acted in direct violation of the new constitution, which prohibited active members of the armed forces from assuming the presidency. But because Benavides was Peru's most respected military figure and had demonstrated administrative ability as provisional president in the period 1914-1915, he was the overwhelming choice to lead Peru in its time of crisis.[47]

The most immediate problem confronting the new president was the imminent possibility of renewed hostilities with Colombia. Benavides quickly sought to defuse the situation, and claimed it was imperative that Peru avoid a war it had little chance of winning. Two days after assuming office, negotiations involving the Leticia dispute were begun, involving Benavides and president-elect Alfonso López of Colombia. The men had become close friends during their respective ambassadorial assignments in London, and López was soon invited to Peru to discuss the issue with the Peruvian president. After six days of talks, López returned to Colombia on 21 May, having secured Benavides's acceptance of the League of Nations' proposal to resolve the conflict. With the withdrawal of Peruvian troops from the area in mid-June, war tensions between the two nations were substantially reduced.[48]

Benavides's quick settlement of the Leticia affair promptly alienated many Sánchez-Cerrista war advocates. The president was able to withstand their violent criticism due to his own personal prestige and the support of Apristas who favored the peace efforts that ended a conflict they viewed as an "invention of Sánchez Cerro's."[49] Most military officers backed Benavides, and recognized that Peru's defeat at Tarapacá revealed the nation's shockingly ineffective war potential. Internal factionalism, low morale resulting from repeated command and troop transfers, a lack of adequate arms and ammunition, and poor combat training were the main causes of the defeat. Unquestionably, the Colombian setback greatly undermined the confidence of the nation's young army officers in their commanders.[50] Thus during the next six years the Benavides government improved military training and acquired more modern armaments in an effort to uplift the morale of all the armed services.

Coinciding with Benavides's efforts to end the divisive Leticia dispute was his program aimed at eliminating domestic political strife by reducing political repression. During early May, martial law was lifted, and many political prisoners were released. Within three months amnesty was given to nearly all remaining political internees, including Haya de la Torre. Benavides also announced elections to fill the vacated congressional seats the party had lost in February, 1932, when Sánchez Cerro exiled the Aprista congressman.

As Benavides drew further away from the politics of his predecessor, the Sánchez-Cerristas grew violent. Between May and November, 1933, the president was forced to dissolve his original Sánchez-Cerrista cabinet, suppress an army revolt by the selva garrison in Iquitos and arrest a number of members of the *Partido Union Revolucionaria* for plotting his assassination.[51]

While the government effectively dealt with the new opposition, its announced policy of "peace and concord" still remained tacitly in effect. APRA was allowed to renew its political activity, and in November the party became the dominant member of a newly formed political coalition, the *Alianza Nacional* (National Alliance). The coalition, composed of former supporters of Leguía and Luis Antonio Eguiguren's *Partido Democrático Social* (Social Democratic Party), was represented by Haya de la Torre in direct negotiations with Benavides. The *Alianza* demanded that the president call elections to select an entirely new congress, not simply fill the relatively small number of vacated seats. The demand was rejected by Benavides, who apparently feared that it represented APRA's bid to gain increased national power through domination of the national legislature. In the year following the formation of the *Alianza Nacional*, the government defaulted on its promise to hold congressional elections. Mistrusting APRA and clearly fearing the renewed internal discord that elections might produce, Benavides canceled the elections in early November, 1934 without announcing a new date for the voting.[52]

After a year of frustration, the *Alianza Nacional* collapsed, and APRA leaders once again decided to employ force to attain national power. During the latter part of November and early December, 1934, APRA instigated a series of minor insurrections throughout Peru. For the most part, Benavides's support in the military barracks remained firm, and all the uprisings were suppressed quickly. With the arrest and exile in early December of a small number of army officers and important *Aprista* leaders, including Luis Alberto Sánchez, Carlos Manuel Cox, former army Colonel César Enrique Pardo, and Agustín Haya de la Torre, the uneasy political truce between *Apristas* and the Benavides regime came to an end. Haya de la Torre avoided capture, but continued *Aprista* subversive activity was met by a strengthened National Emergency Law enacted in February, 1935.[53]

Despite continuing internal disorder the government still rejected a program of violent political repression along the lines established by the Sánchez Cerro regime. This position is evidenced by the relatively light jail sentence given to the *Aprista* assassin of *El Comercio* editor Antonio Miró-Quesada and his wife in May, 1935. Under the terms of the Emergency Law, the murderer should have received the death penalty from the military tribunal that tried the case. Instead, the twenty-five year sentence aroused strong anti-Benavides sentiment among the nation's extreme conservative groups.[54] It also embroiled the armed forces' high command in a bitter confrontation between conservative backers of Miró-Quesada and pro-Benavides officers. Strong feelings resulting from the Miró-Quesada incident created a continuing feud involving close military associates of Benavides and the assassinated editor's family until Benavides's death in 1945.[55]

Aided by strengthened police powers and a markedly improved economy, Benavides felt sufficiently secure by early 1936 to begin preparations for national elections to select a new president and National Congress. Nevertheless, the president was still wary of continuing *Aprista* efforts to subvert army and police units. Consequently, in February, 1936, he removed the director of the National Police School and implemented more transfers in army command positions.[56]

By June the presidential campaign was in full swing, with four candidates announcing their intention to seek the office. Representing the nation's right-wing elements were Dr. Manuel Vicente Villaran (a former *Civilista*) and Luis M. Flores of the *Union Revolucionaria* (Revolutionary Union Party). Jorge Prado y Urgarteche, candidate of the *Frente Nacional* (National Front) and longtime associate of Benavides, had the unofficial backing of the government. Haya de la Torre, still in hiding, announced his candidacy in early June and named the exiled former army Colonel Enrique Pardo as his first vice-presidential candidate. This political gesture was aimed at demonstrating that APRA was still not violently antimilitary.

Although APRA presented Haya de la Torre as a candidate, party leaders had little confidence in the government's willingness to conduct honest elections. Therefore, in April, 1936, APRA leader Manuel Seoane made an overture to the Bolivian government for assistance in overthrowing the Benavides regime. Risking a possible insult to his hosts by promoting Bolivian interests during a speech in Asunción, Paraguay, Seoane discussed APRA's position on one of the central issues of the Chaco war then ongoing between Bolivia and Paraguay. In his message Seoane stated, "*Aprista* opinion has always esteemed Paraguayan valor and has criticized official Peruvian policy for being unable to prevent the [Chaco] war [but] when *Aprismo* assumes power it will endeavor to bring about a favorable resolution to Bolivia's right to a port of Pacific."[57]

APRA offered Bolivia support in gaining the port of Arica from Chile in exchange for that country's aid in its revolutionary campaign against Benavides. Bolivian president David Toro's desire to regain a seacoast for his nation (landlocked since Bolivia's defeat in the War of the Pacific) and his close personal relationship with Seoane prompted him to offer a large quantity of arms and ammunition to the *Aprista* cause in August. The Benavides government was quickly made aware of the plot, however, and by exerting strong diplomatic pressure it forced Toro to withdraw his support by 1 September.[58]

Undoubtedly responding to APRA's revolutionary scheme, the National Election Board on 5 September disbarred APRA and Haya de la Torre from participation in the national elections scheduled for 11 October. The board justified its action on the grounds that Article 53 of the constitution, which prohibited international organizations from participation in national elections, disqualified APRA. With the party out of the running, Luis Antonio Eguiguren, candidate of the Frente Democrático, joined the presidential race. Eguiguren quickly exploited the dissatisfaction voters felt toward the other candidates while also gaining the support of Apristas in his presidential bid. APRA viewed Eguiguren as the candidate least likely to continue the conservative policies of Benavides and possibly hoped to dominate his government once he was elected.[59]

With APRA's voting support, Eguiguren moved into an early lead and appeared headed for an electoral victory until Benavides ordered the National Election Board to suspend the vote tabulation on 21 October. One day later the president solidified his political position by naming an all-military cabinet headed by General Ernesto Montagne Markholtz as minister of war.[60] As most Peruvians anticipated, the National Congress then met on 4 November and annulled the election on the basis of illegal Aprista participation in support of Eguiguren. Benavides further justified his action in a speech on 8 December that claimed it was necessary to "maintain internal peace and order." After gaining the assurance of support from most of Lima's senior military officers, on 14 November Benavides had the congress extend his presidential term until 8 December 1939. He thus assumed full dictatorial powers; no congress would serve for the remainder of his term since the elections to replace that body had been voided.

Both APRA and the Sánchez-Cerrista Union Revolucionaría led by Luis Flores attempted to retaliate against the cancellation of the elections. But efforts by Aprista elements and air force personnel to seize a Lima police barracks and the air force base at Ancón in late October again met with failure. A month later, Flores and General Cirilo H. Ortega, once a close friend of Sánchez Cerro, were implicated in an extensive plot to overthrow Benavides. With the arrest and deportation of Flores and eight associates, all effective antigovernmental resistance ended.[61]

Using a program of arrest, imprisonment, and exile employed frequently within the context of his strong executive powers, Benavides ruled until early 1939 without facing any serious challenges to his regime. A continually improving economy contributed to the stability of these years.

National income rose 61 percent between 1935 and 1939, reflecting higher world prices for Peru's mineral exports. Benavides used these resources for an ambitious public works and social welfare program. Additionally, thousands of miles of roads were built and repaired. New irrigation systems brought more than 50,000 hectares of new land under cultivation. Most significantly, a social security system was created and a council of Indian affairs was established to address the many disputed land claims of Peru's long-exploited Indian communities. These measures, coupled with an ambitious public housing construction program, broadened Benavides's public support, although they did not fundamentally alter the continued crushing poverty of the Peruvian masses.[62] The government, while keeping the military budget at about 14 percent of total expenditures, used the increased income to make purchases of new military equipment that modernized many armed forces units. The government also built a new naval hospital and eighteen new army barracks throughout Peru.[63] Benavides also contracted a short-lived German army mission and Italian air force and police training teams in 1937. The regime's affiliation with the German and Italian military institutions prompted charges that Benavides had profascist leanings. But in the case of the Italian air mission at least, it is clear that the government's acceptance of Italian military aid was motivated in large part by pragmatism and the highly competitive nature of the contract bid. Benavides may have also wished to diversify Peru's source of arms supplies in the event of renewed hostilities with Colombia or the possibility of an arms embargo imposed by the United States. The Italian Caproni aircraft company had previously agreed to construct a factory on the outskirts of Lima in early 1937. Moreover, just before the air mission contract was signed, twelve modern Fiat combat planes were sent to perform at the Inter-American Technical Aviation Conference in Lima to influence the government's decision. Evidence that Benavides was motivated as much by the quality of foreign training missions as by his personal politics is reflected in the reinstatement of the large United States naval mission, whose contract was renewed in 1938 after a five-year lapse.[64]

Although the Benavides regime did make significant progress toward improving the professional expertise of the nation's armed forces officers, attempted subversion of individual officers and entire military units by APRA and other civilian political groups never completely abated during the years 1936-1939. In September, 1938, Haya de la Torre claimed that if economic conditions worsened, Benavides would be quickly unseated. In such an instance the APRA leader asserted, "The army will come to me for support, since I have many partisans among the officers, particularly the younger ones."[65]   Events in February 1939, in which *Apristas* and right-wing members of the *Partido Union Revolucionaria* conspired with army General Antonio Rodríguez Ramírez to overthrow Benavides, confirmed the substance of Haya de la Torre's boast.

General Rodríguez was one of the most influential members of the armed forces, and he had parlayed his adept support of Benavides's 1914 *coup* and Sánchez Cerro's 1930 *golpe* into a top army command position. He was promoted to brigadier general in 1934 after serving as army chief of staff during Sánchez Cerro's second regime. The general was then appointed to Benavides's cabinet as minister of government and police in 1935.[66] In early 1939, however, Rodríguez resolved to overthrow his long-time colleague and make himself military president.

In a broad-based conspiracy Rodríguez allied with APRA and its chief political rival, the *Partido Union Revolucionaria*, in his plot against the Benavides regime. *Aprista* leaders joined the conspiracy only after they had failed to convince Colonel Eloy G. Ureta, commander of the Third Army Division in Arequipa, to head a revolutionary movement.[67] The stated goals of the Rodríguez movement were twofold: to restore full participation for all political parties and to guarantee complete amnesty as a prelude to national elections scheduled six months after the general's seizure of power. Upon toppling Benavides, the rebel general planned to establish a provisional government, including elements from nearly all of Peru's major political groups.   Destined to hold the key position as minister of government and police was the *Aprista* Lieutenant Colonel Gerardo Gamara Huerta. General Cirilo H. Ortega, a staunch *Sánchez Cerrista*, was slated for the equally important post of minister of war.[68]

Rodríguez launched his revolt in the early morning hours of 19 February after Benavides had departed for a short holiday at Ica in southern Peru. Support for the movement was spread throughout the three service branches and the police, with twenty-five officers of the army, navy, air force, and *Guardia Civil* taking an active role.[69] During the first hours of the revolt, Rodríguez made a serious tactical error when he attempted to use his post as minister of government and police to secure military control of Lima before making a radio appeal for civilian (mainly *Aprista*) support in other parts of Peru. The resulting confusion within the ranks of both civilian and military insurgents prevented the simultaneous activation of the revolt.   Consequently, most subverted military units did not join Rodríguez at his headquarters in the National Palace, as they believed the uprising had been aborted. Six hours after the instigation of the revolt, the general met Major Luis Rizo Patrón, commander of the Assault Troop Police Regiment, and a number of police and army personnel in the patio of the National Palace. Rodríguez was unaware that Rizo Patrón had not joined the ranks of the rebels, and he was immediately shot and killed by the police captain. In the ensuing gun battle three more persons died and another six were wounded before Rodríguez's supporters were overwhelmed and imprisoned. A supporting movement led by air force Major José Extremadoyro Navarro at Ancón was also rapidly suppressed after the arrest of the major and a small number of his air force associates.[70]

The minister of war, General Ernesto Montagne Marckholtz, was chiefly responsible for suppressing the revolt in Benavides's absence. His order confining most of Lima's army troops to their barracks prevented the spread of the uprising during the morning of 19 February. When Benavides returned to the capital on the evening of the uprising, complete order was restored. Documents found on Rodríguez's body implicated a number of conspirators, who were quickly arrested. On 22 March, twenty-four military men were sentenced to prison terms from one to ten years for participating in the revolt. The Rodríguez conspiracy represented APRA's best chance to overthrow Benavides, but the movement lacked the critical support of junior army officers who had conspired with the party throughout the 1930s. Because of the rebel general's close association with Benavides and Sánchez Cerro, the younger officers were wary of his political motives.[71]

Thus, the Benavides era drew to a close just as the Sánchez Cerro regime had begun, in the midst of civil-military conspiracy and violence. Benavides's strong leadership and his increased spending for the armed forces had not quieted the discontent within the officer corps that had been so virulent throughout the decade. The emergence of mass politics and social class conflict in the early 1930s precipitated much of this turmoil within the military, and Benavides was the target of continuing antagonism as the decade came to a close. Consequently, when he arranged for his longtime civilian political ally, Manuel Prado y Ugarteche, to succeed him as president in 1939, the officer corps did not actively oppose his decision. Nevertheless, the Prado administration would still be plagued by civil-military tension and ideological soul-searching by soldiers seeking a more meaningful national mission.

NOTES

1. Lieutenant Manuel Morla Concha, "Función social del ejército en la organización de la nacionalidad," *Revista Militar del Perú* 10 (October, 1933), pp.

60 Militarism and Politics

843-872, passim. This article has been heavily cited by scholars of the Peruvian military. It is treated at length in Frederick M. Nunn, *Yesterday's Soldiers: European Military Professionalism in South America*, (Lincoln, Nebraska: 1983), pp. 280-281.

2. Lieutenant Mauricio Barbis D., "El ejército y la colonización de la montaña," *RMP* 12 (December, 1933), pp. 1239-1242, passim.

3. Two biographies of Haya de la Torre that should be consulted with their pro-APRA interpretations in mind are Luis Alberto Sánchez, *Haya de la Torre y el APRA* (Santiago: 1955) and Felipe Cossio del Pomar, *Haya de la Torre, el indoamericano*, 2d ed. (Lima: 1946). A provocative biography of Haya de la Torre is Fredrick Pike, *The Politics of the Miraculous in Peru: Haya de la Torre and the Spiritualist Tradition* (Lincoln, Nebraska: 1986). Haya de la Torre touched briefly on his early career during my first interview with him (personal interview with Víctor Raúl Haya de la Torre, 13 July 1974, Lima, Peru). For an analysis of the "Popular Universities" see Jeffrey Klaiber, S.J., "The Popular Universities and the Origins of *Aprismo*," *Hispanic American Historical Review* 55, no. 4 (November, 1975), pp. 693-715.

4. Students of APRA have been hampered by the highly polemical nature of the hundreds of books, articles, and pamphlets devoted to the party's history and ideology. Useful pro-APRA studies are Harry Kantor, *The Ideology and Program of the Peruvian Aprista Party* (Washington, D.C.: 1966) and Cossio del Pomar, *Haya de la Torre*. For works critical of APRA see Víctor Villanueva Valencia, *La sublevación aprista del 48: La tragedia de un pueblo y un partido* (Lima: 1973) and *El APRA en busca del poder* (Lima: 1975); Fredrick B. Pike, *The Modern History of Peru* (New York: 1967); and Eudocio Ravines, *The Yenan Way* (New York: 1951). Of Haya de la Torre's own writings, his *Antiimperialismo y el APRA* (Lima: 1970) is most illuminating in terms of APRA's early ideology. For English translations of most of Haya de la Torre's substantive writings see Robert Alexander, *Aprismo: The Ideas and Writings of Víctor Raúl Haya de la Torre* (Kent, Ohio: 1973). Two extremely valuable studies of APRA's early years are Peter Klarén, *Modernization, Dislocation, and Aprismo: Origins of the Peruvian Aprista Pary, 1870-1932* (Austin, Texas: 1970) and Steve Stein, *Populism in Peru: The Emergence of the Masses and the Politics of Social Control* (Madison: 1980). Thomas M. Davies, Jr., *Indian Integration in Peru, A Half Century of Experience, 1900-1948* (Lincoln, Nebraska: 1973) should also be consulted. For a very useful compilation of Haya de la Torre's writings, see the five-volume *Pensamiento politico de Haya de la Torre* (Lima: 1961).

5. For a valuable analysis of the significance of Haya de la Torre's European travels in shaping the philosophical tenets of *Aprismo*, see Pike, *The Politics of the Miraculous*, pp. 75-149. See also Richard Salisbury, "The Middle American Exile of Víctor Raúl Haya de la Torre," *The Americas*, 40, no. 1 (July, 1983), pp. 1-17. Another source was my personal interview with Víctor Raúl Haya de la Torre, 14 July 1974, Lima, Peru.

6. Klarén, *Modernization*, p. 118; John M. Baines, *Revolution in Peru: Mariátegui and the Myth* (Tuscaloosa, Alabama: 1972), pp. 72-76; personal interview with Haya de la Torre, 14 July 1974, Lima, Peru. The reader should also consult Mariátegui's major work, *Seven Interpretive Essays on Peruvian Reality* (Austin, Texas: 1971).

7. "Autobiografía de Sánchez Cerro" (27 September 1919) in Pedro Ugarteche, *Sánchez Cerro: Papeles y recuerdos de un presidente del Peru*, 1, p. 27, quoted in Stein, *Populism in Peru*, p. 86.

8. Víctor Villanueva Valencia, *Ejército Peruano: Del caudillaje anárquico al militarismo reformista* (Lima: 1973), p. 209, and Stein, *Populism in Peru*, pp. 83-100. For a biography of Sánchez Cerro see Carlos Miró-Quesada Laos, *Sánchez Cerro y su tiempo* (Buenos Aires: 1947).

9. Villanueva, *Ejército Peruano*, p. 202, and Gerlach, *Civil-Military Relations*, pp. 264-267.

10. Klarén, *Modernization*, p. 121, and Stein, *Populism in Peru*, pp. 92-95.

11. Víctor Villanueva Valencia, *100 años del ejército Peruano: Frustraciones y cambios* (Lima: 1971) is highly critical of Sánchez Cerro's politically motivated armed forces policies. APRA leader Ramiro Prialé went so far as to claim that Sánchez Cerro was the "servant of the oligarchy" (personal interview with Ramiro Prialé, 10 May 1985, Lima, Peru).

12. Stein, *Populism in Peru*, pp. 97-100.

13. Sánchez, *Haya de la Torre y el APRA*, pp. 27-274, provides a good review of these organizational efforts.

14. Pike, *The Modern History of Peru*, pp. 252-253.

15. Sánchez, *Haya de la Torre y el APRA*, p. 270; Klarén, *Modernization*, p. 128.

16. Stein, *Populism in Peru*, affords the best analysis of the 1931 elections. See also Davies, *Indian Integration*, pp. 108-111; Villanueva, *El APRA en busca del poder*, pp. 44-45. Klarén and Davies agree that Haya de la Torre attempted to moderate APRA's radical image. Davies states that the APRA leader even sought out officials of foreign-owned corporations in London and New York to assure them that he had substantially softened his view regarding "Yankee imperialism" and nationalization of railroads and industry.

17. Ambassador Frederick Dearing to Sec/State, 7 September 1931, NA, RG 59, 810.43 APRA/102, cited in Davies, *Indian Integration*, p. 111. Dearing concluded that if APRA won the 1931 elections, a "strongly liberal and beneficent administration" could be expected.

18. Villanueva, *Ejército Peruano*, pp. 214-216.

19. Thomas M. Davies, Jr., "The *Indigenismo* of the Peruvian *Aprista* Party," *Hispanic American Historical Review* 51, no. 4 (November, 1971), p. 629; Klarén, *Modernization*, p. 134.

20. Sánchez, *Haya de la Torre y el APRA*, p. 273; Gerlach, "Civil-Military Relations," p. 355. Such officers were Lieutenant Colonel Julio C. Guerrero, Colonel César Enrique Pardo, and Colonel Aurelio García Godos.

21. Stein, *Populism in Peru*, p. 93.

22. Klarén, *Modernization*, p. 131; Davies, *Indian Integration*, p. 99.

23. Klarén, *Modernization*, p. 135.

24. Jorge Basadre, *Historia de la republica del Perú*, 10 (Lima: 1966), pp. 201-203, and Stein, *Populism in Peru*, pp. 196-199.

25. Klarén, *Modernization*, p. 136, calls the elections, "from all appearances the fairest in Peruvian history." Davies, *Indian Integration*, p. 112, agrees and Stein, *Populism in Peru*, p. 198, claims that "the popular sectors and middle sectors had risen to a position of true dominance in Peru's electoral politics." Haya de la Torre claimed "there existed clear manifestations of irregularities in Lima and Cajamarca" (personal interview with Haya de la Torre, 13 July 1974, Lima, Peru). Longtime

APRA leader Ramiro Prialé agrees with Haya de la Torre's assessment (personal interview with Ramiro Prialé, 10 May 1985, Lima, Peru).

26. Klarén, Modernization, pp. 137-138; Villanueva, El APRA en busca del poder, pp. 53-68.

27. Gerlach, "Civil-Military Relations," pp. 383-385.

28. Ibid., p. 386.

29. Sánchez, Haya de la Torre y el APRA, pp. 282-288; Klarén, Modernization, p. 138; Villanueva, El APRA en busca del poder, pp. 93-94.

30. Capitán de Fragata Jorge Ortíz Sotelo, "Actividades politica en la Marina, 1931-1932," master's thesis, Pontificia Universidad Católica del Peru, 1983; Guillermo Thorndike, El año de la barbarie: Perú, 1932 (Lima: 1968), pp. 108-111. Luis Alberto Sánchez's involvement in the mutiny still seems to be the belief of senior naval officers, as this view was expressed by Vice-Admiral (R) Luis Vargas Caballero, the former navy minister during the Velasco regime, in his personal interview with me on 6 May 1985 in Lima, Peru.

31. For a detailed discussion of both mutinies see Robert L. Scheina, Latin America: A Naval History, 1810-1987 (Annapolis: 1987), pp. 107-116. William F. Sater's article, "The Abortive Kronstadt: The Chilean Naval Mutiny of 1931," Hispanic American Historical Review, 60, no. 2 (May, 1980), pp. 239-268, does an admirable job of placing the rebellion in the broader context of Chilean history and world naval affairs.

32. The most balanced account of the Trujillo revolt is Basadre, Historia, 9, pp. 237-238. See also Villanueva, El APRA en busca del poder, pp. 95-116; Gerlach, "Civil-Military Relations," pp. 398-408. Thorndike, El año de la barbarie, pp. 127-254, is an extensive account of the subsequent reprisal. For a good summary of the Aprista version of these events see Sánchez, Haya de la Torre y el APRA, pp. 279-302. An account that clearly confirms Aprista responsibility for the Trujillo jail deaths is Alfredo Rabasa Acosta, Historia de la revolución Trujillo (Trujillo: 1934).

33. Thorndike, El año de la barbarie, pp. 186-187; Gerlach, "Civil-Military Relations," pp. 399-400.

34. Klarén, Modernization, pp. 140-141.

35. There is no consensus on the exact number of military prisoners killed or on whether they were tortured (as alleged) by their Aprista captors. The government's figures, which I have relied upon, place the number killed at fifteen army officers and soldiers and twenty Guardia Civil personnel. The government report makes no mention of torture but states that five Guardia bodies were unidentifiable because of their extensive wounds. See Documentos Relaciones de Trujillo, 1 Division Comandancia General, 23 July 1932, in the Centro de Estudios-Histórico-Militares del Perú. Basadre, Historia, 9, p. 238, cites fourteen army officers and soldiers and twenty Guardia Civil personnel, figures that almost exactly match those of the government. Klarén, Modernization, p. 141, and Pike, The Modern History of Peru, p. 266, place the number of Apristas executed between one thousand and fifteen hundred. Ramiro Prialé claims the figure was actually six thousand (personal interview with Ramiro Prialé, 10 May 1985, Lima, Peru).

36. This belief was still expressed by army officers in 1962 when they acted to overturn the electoral victory of Haya de la Torre in that year's presidential election.

37. For the interpretation that the *Aprista* victims of the Trujillo reprisals were remembered with religious fervor by residents of the surrounding region, see Jeffrey Klaiber, S.J., "Religion and Revolution in Peru, 1920-1945," *The Americas*, 31, no. 3 (January, 1975), p. 308.

38. For the best reviews of the border conflict with Colombia see Bryce Wood, *The United States and the Latin American Wars, 1932-1942* (New York: 1966), pp. 169-255; Colonel José M. Vallejo, *El Conflicto Perú-Colombiano* (Lima: 1934); José Zárate Lescano, *Historia militar del conflicto con Colombia de 1932* (Lima: 1963).

39. Wood, *The United States*, pp. 175-211.

40. Personal interview with Haya de la Torre, 13 July 1974, Lima, Peru.

41. Wood, *The United States*, p. 228; Colonel Víctor Ramos, "Exposición del Colonel Víctor Ramos, sobre las operaciones en el conflicto con Colombia en 1932-1933," (Lima: 1933), p. 10.

42. Gerlach, "Civil-Military Relations," p. 412.

43. Ibid.

44. Wood, *The United States*, p. 228.

45. Russell H. Fitzgibbon, ed., *The Constitutions of the Americas* (Chicago: 1948), pp. 666-667.

46. Among those who have charged Benavides with complicity in Sánchez Cerro's assassination is Haya de la Torre, who claimed that Benavides was "the intellectual author of the death of Sánchez Cerro" (personal interview with Haya de la Torre, 13 July 1974, Lima, Peru). José Zárate Lescano, *El mariscal Benavides: Su Vida y Su Obra*, 2 (Lima: 1976), p. 112, notes only that Sánchez Cerro was killed by a "fanatic."

47. Villanueva, *Ejército Peruano*, p. 225; Zárate Lescano, *El mariscal Benavides*, 1, pp. 115-117.

48. Wood, *The United States*, pp. 228-251; Zárate Lescano, *El mariscal Benavides*, 2, pp. 123-127. The final settlement of the dispute in 1935 involved a return to the terms of the 1922 Salomón-Lozano Treaty or a return to the pre-1932 status quo.

49. Personal interview with Víctor Raúl Haya de la Torre, 13 July 1974, Lima, Peru.

50. Villanueva, *Ejército Peruano*, pp. 217-220, and *100 años*, pp. 91-107.

51. Villanueva, *Ejército Peruano*, pp. 225-226.

52. Zárate Lescano, *El mariscal Benavides*, 2, pp. 137-142; Pike, *The Modern History of Peru*, pp. 269-270.

53. Gerlach, "Civil-Military Relations," pp. 457-458. Haya de la Torre's relative freedom is evidenced by the fact that Benavides never really made a concerted effort to arrest Haya de la Torre during his underground years after 1934. Despite the arrest and deportation of other APRA leaders after 1934, Haya de la Torre remained in Peru and often gave clandestine interviews to foreign journalists and scholars who were not hard put to make contact with him.

54. Pike, *The Modern History of Peru*, p. 273-274; Sánchez, *Haya de la Torre y el APRA*, p. 351.

55. Dearing to Sec/State, 19 February 1936, NA, RG 59, 823.00/1189.

56. Zárate Lescano, *El mariscal Benavides*, 2, pp. 209-214; Gerlach, "Civil-Military Relations," pp. 463-464.

57. Ambassador Findley B. Howard, Asunción, Paraguay, to Sec/State, 24 April 1936, NA, RG 59, 823.00/1203. See also Thomas Davies and Víctor Villanueva,

64 Militarism and Politics

300 Documentos para la historia del APRA, Document 21-36, Archivo Pardo, 17 August 1936, pp. 65-66. This document details the specifics of the potential Bolivian arms deal with the *Apristas*.

58. Ibid.; Zárate Lescano, *El mariscal Benavides*, 2, pp. 206-209.

59. Personal interviews with Haya de la Torre, 13 July 1974, Lima, Peru, and Ramiro Prialé, 10 May 1985, Lima, Peru.

60. Dearing to Sec/State, 23 October 1936, NA, RG 59, 823.00/1223.

61. Dearing to Sec/State, 28 November 1936, NA, RG 59, 823.00/1250.

62. Zárate Lescano, *El mariscal Benavides*, 2, pp. 221-280; Orazio Ciccarelli, "Fascism and Politics in Peru during the Benavides Regime, 1933-1939: The Italian Perspective," *Hispanic American Historical Review*, 70, no. 3 (August, 1990), p. 409.

63. Charge d'Affaires Louis G. Dreyfus to Sec/State, 6 October 1937, NA, RG 59, 823.248/128; Cobas, *Fuerza armada*, p. 57; Jane's, *All the World's Aircraft* (London: 1940), p. 1400.

64. Dreyfus to Sec/State, 8 September 1938, NA, RG 59, 823.00/1315. For a thorough discussion of fascist influence in Peru during the Benavides regime, see Ciccarelli, "Fascism and Politics in Peru," pp. 413-432.

65. *The New York Times*, 20 February 1939, p. 9.

66. Villanueva, *Ejército Peruano*, p. 227.

67. Dreyfus to Sec/State, 25 May 1939, NA, RG 59, 823.00/1363; Villanueva, *La sublevación aprista*, pp. 17-23. Zárate Lescano, *El mariscal Benavides*, 2, pp. 287-290, and Anonymous, *Por la verdad historia: La revolución democrática de Antonio Rodríguez Ramírez* (Lima: 1942). The authors of this pamphlet are listed as "friends" of the deceased general. This pamphlet contains speeches, proclamations, and proposed government personnel in Rodríguez's planned revolutionary *Junta*. In a letter to Colonel César Enrique Pardo, Haya de la Torre claimed to have directed the Rodríguez conspiracy and argued that the most positive step to restore democratic government failed with the collapse of the plot. Donald Henderson and Grace R. Pérez, eds., Literature and Politics in Latin America: *An Annotated Calendar of the Luis Alberto Sánchez Correspondence, 1919-1980* (University Park, Pennsylvania: 1982), Document 1021, p. 232.

68. *La Crónica*, 23 March 1939, p. 14.

69. Ibid., 20 February 1939, p. 15; *The New York Times*, 20 February 1939, p. 1; and Gerlach, "Civil-Military Relations," pp. 473-478.

70. *La Crónica*, 23 March 1939, p. 14.

71. Villanueva, *La sublevación aprista*, pp. 18-20.

3
Battlefield Victories and Barracks Tensions: 1939-1945

As the Benavides administration drew to a close in the wake of the abortive Rodríguez *golpe*, the armed forces' morale remained low. Benavides's increased military spending had not overcome the problems of the poor military discipline, manipulation of internal military affairs for partisan political purposes, and the armed forces' poor combat record. Adding to these problems was the continuing distrust of the capability and commitment of their superiors by the army's junior officers. Within this context Peruvian battlefield victories in a brief border conflict with Ecuador in July, 1941 and a virtual moratorium on civilian subversive activity during the first four years of World War II lessened the violence but not the latent tensions of the nation's civil-military relations during the administration of Benavides's hand-picked successor, Manuel Prado.[1]

As the armed forces entered the era of the world conflict, they totaled approximately seventeen thousand officers and men. The army, with a strength of about thirteen thousand, was by far the most powerful of the three armed services.[2] Headed by Benavides as senior army officer holding the rank of division general, the army officer corps numbered fifteen hundred. Nearly 80 percent of army officers entering the profession during the 1930s were graduates of the Chorrillos Military Academy. This percentage represented an increase of over 10 percent from the 1920s. The ranks of the army's general officers remained small, however, as Benavides was one of only ten generals in 1939. Between 1931 and 1940 only seven officers were promoted to general.[3] This low number of promotions would have an impact on the Prado government's relations with senior officers, as many became impatient for advancement after years of waiting during the Benavides years.

Although most of the Peruvian officers studying overseas were army men serving in France, talented junior officers of the small air force, which operated within the framework of the navy ministry until 1940 (the Ministry of Aviation was created early in 1941), were sent to Italy for advanced training. The largest group of these air force cadets began a three-year course at the aviation academy at Caserta, Italy, in 1939.[4] A number of cadets attending earlier classes at the Italian aviation school performed exceptionally well, impressing air force senior officers with their professional expertise upon returning to Peru.[5]

The United States naval mission had originally been contracted in 1920, and after a five-year hiatus between 1933 and 1938 Benavides renewed its contract as advisers to the Peruvian navy. The president praised the work of this unit in December, 1939, claiming that Peruvian naval officers were benefiting from the North American nation's technically superior naval advisers. As the army's ranking officer, however, the president saved his highest praise for the French army mission, which he asserted was the "most complete" of any foreign training unit ever to serve in Peru. French influence among the senior ranks of the army was profound. Between 1916 and 1940 every officer promoted to the rank of general served some time in France.[6]

As a result of the military programs of the Benavides government the combat efficiency of the active Peruvian army was rated by the United States military attaché on a par with that of neighboring Colombia and significantly superior to the Ecuadoran army soon after Benavides left office. Some Peruvian army commanders were still troubled by the fact that Peru's potential mobilization force of sixty thousand (men aged twenty-one to twenty-five not in the active army) had almost no equipment available for use. They considered this lack a serious problem for the nation's security, which they felt should be based on a "defense in depth," allowing the potential deployment of large numbers of reserves in time of war.[7] As a result, soon after Manuel Prado assumed office, military commanders placed immense pressure upon him to take vigorous measures to correct these deficiencies.

During the last week of March, 1939, Benavides declared that he would leave office as scheduled on 8 December. He also announced that national elections for president and a National Congress would be held in late October.[8] The outgoing chief executive, following the pattern of his previous term as president, was determined to have a civilian succeed him. His choice, Manuel Prado, was the brother of Jorge Prado, who had been Benavides's candidate in the 1936 elections. Manuel Prado belonged to one of the wealthiest and most influential families in Peru. Son of former

President Mariano Ignacio Prado (1876-1879), he was president of one of Peru's largest banks and had extensive holdings in other financial insurance institutions. Benavides and the Prado brothers had conspired to overthrow President Guillermo Billinghurst in 1914, but Manuel Prado was subsequently exiled during the *Oncenio* due to his opposition to Leguía. After Benavides became president in 1933, Manuel Prado remained politically loyal and was named to the cabinet in April, 1939.[9] Benavides then used his substantial influence to advance the formation of the *Concentración Nacional* (National Concentration), a coalition of centrist and conservative groups, to back Prado's candidacy.[10] Additionally, during May the chief executive announced plans to conduct a plebiscite in order to lengthen the presidential term from four to six years and the congressional tenure from five to six.[11] Despite opposition from APRA and some junior army officers, by mid-June the longer terms of office had been approved and Manuel Prado's campaign was in full swing.

The only serious political challenge to Prado came from José Quesada Larrea, who organized the *Frente Patriótico* (Patriotic Front), with the support of Manuel Vicente Villaran and his conservative associates as well as Luis Flores and his wing of the *Partido Union Revolucionaria*. Quesada Larrea, after purchasing the newspaper *La Prensa*, used it as a forum to attack his political opponent and to claim that Prado, as the son of President Mariano Ignacio Prado, who left Peru in the midst of the War of the Pacific, might not be a trustworthy chief executive in a national crisis.[12]

APRA voters played a key role in the election of Prado, despite the presidential candidate's refusal to legalize the party. *Apristas* cast a sizeable number of ballots for Prado. His winning margin of nearly 187,000 votes out of a total of 339,000 cast reflects electoral support well beyond the range of his announced political supporters. Although party chief Haya de la Torre denied the existence of an official party directive to vote for Prado, another APRA leader suggests that rank-and-file *Apristas* may have been unsure of party policy.[13] This indecision explains why some party members, attempting to block Prado's inauguration, initiated an abortive uprising in Trujillo in mid-November. Before the uprising was crushed, Lieutenant Colonel Remigio Morales Bermúdez was killed and two *Apristas* were quickly convicted and executed for their complicity in the murder.

During most of Prado's first twenty months in office many observers speculated that his government would not survive its full six-year term.[14] But due largely to the unifying influence of the border war with Ecuador and World War II, his administration demonstrated greater stability than any civilian government up to that time. Benavides had taken an important step to help ensure stability by increasing the pay of all armed forces officers by an average of 18 percent on 16 November 1939.[15] This increase was deemed necessary by the outgoing president as a sizeable number of army officers were not in favor of Prado's candidacy.[16] After rewarding Benavides with promotion to marshal and an appointment as Peruvian ambassador to Spain in December, 1939, Prado made another bid to gain a more stable political base. He promulgated a political amnesty in June, 1940 that pardoned all political prisoners except those who were "terroristic or connected with any international organization whose doctrines are in violation of Peruvian democratic principles."[17] This clause excluded APRA members from the otherwise general pardon and thus continued the party's political proscription initiated by Sánchez Cerro in 1932 and only briefly lifted by Benavides in the mid-1930s. Haya de la Torre remained in Peru throughout the Prado administration, however, and he was given unofficial freedom to conduct limited party activities.

In spite of Prado's refusal to legalize APRA or free its political prisoners, the party did not mount any serious challenge to his administration before March, 1945. As early as August, 1940, APRA's noncombative attitude toward the government was recognized by the United States ambassador, who noted: "The Aprista party naturally wants to be recognized as a political party in Peru. However, there are few if any indications that it is seeking to cause trouble for the Prado administration."[18] The ambassador also commented that APRA was aware of the danger of its international image if it promoted the overthrow of a "democratically elected government" at the height of Nazi Germany's advances in Europe. Thus he noted that APRA's clandestine journal La Tribuna was continuing to make pleas for "political harmony in Peru and the wholehearted support of Inter-American programs for defense and economic cooperation."[19] Throughout the war Haya de la Torre made a concerted effort to demonstrate his pro-Allied stand. He even proposed the formation of a Latin American division under a joint Inter-American command to engage in military activities aimed at eliminating pro-Axis elements throughout the hemisphere. Haya de la Torre's restraint in openly opposing the Prado administration did not prevent him from bitterly attacking the president in private talks he held with United States Embassy officials throughout World War II. The thrust of his criticism was that Prado was too soft on pro-Axis elements in Peru and that his refusal to legalize APRA was a violation of the democratic principles the Allies were fighting to defend. Apristas openly solicited Washington's aid in pressuring the Prado administration to legalize the party, but the State Department, not wanting to alienate a cooperative ally, rebuffed these repeated pleas.[20]

The Prado administration's support of the Allies, his government's severance of relations with the Axis in January, 1942, and the declaration of war in January, 1945 were in keeping with the public position of the vast majority of Peru's political groups. The support of these political groups was manifested by an almost complete abatement of political conspiracies against the government.

In keeping with the government's rejection of ties with the Axis, the Italian air mission was terminated in March, 1940. Peruvian air force officers also pressured the administration to replace the Italian unit with a United States aviation team.[21] This replacement occurred on 31 July 1940, when the Peruvian government approved the contract for a United States naval aviation mission.[22] With the conclusion of this agreement the United States was operating advisory teams for two of the three branches of the Peruvian armed forces. The aviation mission, coupled with the even larger navy advisory team, substantially increased the influence of the United States in Peruvian military affairs. Still, the French army advisers remained on very close terms with the top army command. Even after the fall of France in the summer of 1940 and the subsequent termination of the French government's contract in January, 1941, French army officers remained in Peru until 1944 as unofficial consultants to the army General Staff. Significantly, while Peru was preparing for hostilities with Ecuador in July, 1941, the army acquired munitions for the impending conflict from the Schneider Munitions Works at St. Chamond, located in unoccupied France.[23] Responding to these continuing contacts with the Vichy government, the United States exerted pressure upon the Peruvian government after 1941 to contract a full-sized army mission to replace the French team. But this objective was not realized until nearly the end of the war. Thus, while United States military influence increased during World War II, senior army officers remained closely tied to their French associates.[24] Few of these Peruvian officers were on personal terms with any United States military representative prior to 1945.

The Prado government's cooperation with the United States navy and the retention of the French army advisers illustrated the president's pragmatic dealings with the armed forces. His initial smooth relations with the army benefited from the fact that high-ranking officers during 1940 and 1941 displayed no overt political ambitions.[25] As 1940 drew to a close, the major concern of the army General Staff was the increasing probability of war with neighboring Ecuador.

Peru and Ecuador had disagreed over their common boundaries since 1829. The specific territory in contention in 1941 involved a small area on the Pacific Ocean and approximately 120,000 square miles in the

Oriente (Eastern Peru and Ecuador) lying between the equator and the Javary River and between the Andes Mountains and Leticia on the Colombian frontier.[26] Following a series of border incidents in late 1940 and early 1941, the Prado administration adopted a rigid stance in negotiations to resolve the dispute. The government's position was in great part dictated by the Prado family's background and intense pressure from the senior officers of the army. Because of President Mariano Ignacio Prado's questionable conduct during the War of the Pacific, his son Manuel Prado was extremely sensitive to allegations regarding his own lack of patriotism. Consequently, it was assumed by most Peruvians that the president had no choice but to act firmly in the Ecuadoran crisis.[27] Furthermore, the armed forces' leadership, given the history of defeat in the War of the Pacific and the Leticia conflict with Colombia in 1933, insisted that the government put the nation on a war footing in preparation for a military solution to the border dispute.

In early 1941 the army demanded that Prado purchase large quantities of small arms and ammunition and indicated that it was willing to obtain them from any source.[28] Military pressure on Prado in 1941 was succinctly described by the United States military attaché:

The army is loyal but needs arms and ammunition and the leaders are demanding that active and immediate steps be taken to get them. The army will not allow a settlement of the border dispute that is not favorable to Peru. The government, aware of these things, is working on a defense program to be financed by a 300 million [soles] internal loan.[29]

The internal loan was negotiated with the Prado family's Banco Popular del Perú and was never publicly announced. It provided immediate funding for war preparations and was used throughout most of the 1940s as a supplement to the official national defense budget.[30] These financial dealings were clearly prompted by pressure from senior army officers, but their younger colleagues shared their complaints about the army's need for more modern equipment and combat training.[31] These complaints took on greater significance as both Peru and Ecuador braced for the imminent conflict during May, 1941.

Border incidents during May led to diplomatic efforts by the United States, Brazil, and Argentina to resolve the dispute. When negotiations in Washington involving Peru, Ecuador, and the three mediating nations broke down in early June, Peruvian forces situated in the Zarumilla-Marañon region along the Ecuadoran frontier were placed on alert.[32] Commanding the Peruvian armed forces in the area was General Eloy G.

Ureta. Born in Chiclayo in northern Peru in 1892, Ureta graduated from the Chorrillos Military Academy in 1913. After serving in Europe to perfect his military training, he was subsequently assigned to the staff at Chorrillos. Upon attaining the rank of colonel, he was named commander of the Third Army Division in Arequipa in 1936. In early 1941, after promotion to general, he assumed command of all military forces in northern Peru.[33] General Ureta was a coolly reserved officer who displayed occasional flashes of humor. He was regarded by his colleagues as one of the most competent officers in the army.

After establishing his headquarters in Piura, Ureta received orders in June only to hold Peru's present positions and repel any Ecuadoran attack.[34] Nevertheless, the general was unwilling to abide by these instructions. Colonel Damasco Arenas Sánchez, the Bolivian military attaché to Peru, claimed Ureta and other senior officers in the army had become extremely sensitive during May and June to accusations that the army was reluctant to take active steps to resolve the border controversy. Arenas went on to report that Ureta then delivered to Prado, during the last week of June, an ultimatum declaring that if he were not allowed to initiate operations against Ecuadoran forces in the Tumbes region, then a military revolt against the government would result. When new border clashes erupted during the first week of July, Ureta went well beyond his original orders by advancing against Ecuadoran positions. These measures were taken as the ranks of the army were augmented by newly drafted recruits who were sent to the front with less than two months' training.[35]

On 5 July, hostilities between Peru and Ecuador commenced on a large scale. Peru charged that Ecuadoran troops garrisoned in the province of El Oro attacked its outposts at Aguas Verdes and La Palma but were driven back. Ecuador countered with the version that Peruvian *Guardia Civil* personnel accompanying farm workers into territory claimed by Ecuador exchanged gunfire with Ecuadoran patrols. In any case, these hostilities precipitated Ureta's initial large-scale operation against enemy positions on 6 July. The operation, however, bogged down, apparently due to incomplete planning. The United States, Brazil, and Argentina once again offered their good offices to mediate the dispute on 9 July. Ecuador, in a precarious military position, quickly accepted the offer, but Peru held back as it sought a more definitive military settlement to the controversy.[36]

After Ureta regrouped his forces during mid-July, he prepared to make a second assault against enemy lines. Employing modern tactics by implementing army, navy, and ground forces simultaneously, the general opened his attack on 22 July after claiming that Ecuadoran soldiers had attacked his units earlier in the day. Operating along a fifty-kilometer front, Peruvian troops advanced quickly against their outnumbered foes.[37] On 28 July, President Prado announced to a huge independence day crowd that Peruvian troops had entered Ecuadoran territory and would not return until Peru's territorial rights were recognized.[38] Three days later General Ureta launched a small blitzkrieg utilizing motorized infantry, air transport troops, and a parachute squad to capture the Ecuadoran towns of Puerto Bolívar, Santa Rosa, and Machala.[39] On 1 August, Brigadier General Antonio Silva Santisteban, commander of the Peruvian army Fifth Division in the *Oriente*, launched another offensive with three battalions totaling 1,845 men. During the first week of August Santisteban's forces occupied considerable Ecuadoran territory, including the towns of Corrientes, Cucaray, and Tarqui, before discontinuing operations.[40]

The Peruvian navy effectively coordinated coastal and riverine operations in support of the army's offensive against Ecuadoran units on both fronts. Its gunboat flotilla captured two small Ecuadoran garrisons at Payana and Matapalo while supplying logistical support for General Santisteban's operations in the *Oriente*. Main elements of the fleet, including the cruisers *Almirante Grau* and *Colonel Bolognesi* and the destroyers *Guise* and *Villar*, "covered the coastal flank" of the Peruvian army's positions between Zorritos and the Jambali Canal.[41]

By mid-August, Ecuadoran resistance on both fronts had completely collapsed. Massive desertions by Ecuadoran officers and troops left Guayaquil and Quito open to Peruvian attack. The swift and overwhelming defeat of the Ecuadoran army was due to a number of factors. Peruvian forces vastly outnumbered their opponents in the main theater north of Tumbes. The Peruvian northern army group totaled 441 officers and 9,386 troops against an estimated three thousand Ecuadoran officers and enlisted men.[42] Peru's effective military leadership provided by Ureta, Silva Santisteban, and Lieutenant Colonel Manuel A. Odría (leader of a particularly impressive attack on 22 July) contrasted greatly with the poor leadership of the Ecuadoran commanders. Additionally, the vanquished nation's troops suffered from a disastrous lack of war matériel and civilian support for the war effort. Very simply, Ecuador was almost totally unprepared to go to war with Peru in 1941.[43]

On the other hand, for the first time in its national history, Peru was able to mount a well-coordinated military campaign that was firmly supported by the government and the general population. The resulting victory helped reverse a tradition of military defeat and raised the morale of the armed forces substantially. APRA, in line with the sweeping civilian support for the military effort, praised General Ureta's actions in its clandestine newspaper *La Tribuna*. The newspaper declared that the military campaign in the boundary dispute was "exceedingly well handled." *Apristas* also took the daring step of visiting Ureta at his military headquarters in late September, 1941 to offer their support for his efforts.[44] Clearly, the party recognized the political necessity of openly backing the nation's most popular and successful military effort in history.

President Prado also attempted to use the military success to his immediate political advantage. During the campaign in late July, the president's wife and daughter visited wounded soldiers at the hospital at Tumbes, and Prado, during his independence day speech, profusely praised the armed forces units engaged in the conflict.[45] Military men killed in the campaign were granted recognition as national heroes, and Prado himself was given an official resolution of gratitude by the congress in 1942 for his contribution to the war effort.[46] By late 1941, the president needed only to have Peru's battlefield victories validated by international recognition of its territorial gains to complete his political success.

Peruvian troops remained in captured Ecuadoran territory until a preliminary settlement of the dispute was hammered out at the Third Meeting of Foreign Ministers of the American States at Rio de Janeiro in late January, 1942. Faced with an unbending stance by Peru regarding any major withdrawal from occupied territories, Ecuador accepted a preliminary boundary agreement that was guaranteed by the United States, Argentina, Chile, and Brazil. The so-called Rio Protocol left Ecuador with a net loss of approximately 13,500 square kilometers, as Peru withdrew its forces by as much as one hundred kilometers from its position in August, 1941. The quick settlement of the dispute reflected the desire of the United States and its close ally Brazil to achieve hemispheric solidarity in the wake of Pearl Harbor. The Department of State was not concerned where the boundary lines were established so long as a formal agreement was reached. This largely unresolved border dispute has continued to cause tensions between Peru and Ecuador, which nearly flared again into open conflict in the early 1980s.[47]

At the Rio conference, Peru attained its diplomatic objectives and also agreed to sever diplomatic relations with the Axis. In 1942, in a further demonstration of solidarity with the United States, the government granted Washington permission to operate an air base at Talara in northern Peru.[48] In the aftermath of the military and diplomatic success attained in the confrontation with Ecuador, President Prado and armed forces senior officers enjoyed their most cordial relations during his entire administration. Nevertheless, General Ureta's prestige among both civilians and military personnel stemming from the Ecuador conflict soon made him a powerful new force that Prado had to watch carefully. Additionally, the govern-

ment's military promotion policies and increasing discontent among army
junior officers soon contributed to renewed armed forces factionalism after
the flush of the battlefield victories in 1941 had diminished.

General Ureta was the main beneficiary of the praise showered upon the
nation's military personnel following the Ecuador conflict.   He was
promoted to division general and was soon named to the powerful post of
inspector general of the army, despite being the army's youngest general.
Also promoted to division general was Antonio Silva Santisteban, who
commanded the army's campaign in the *Oriente*.[49] The congress, which
approved all promotions above the grade of major or its equivalent, also
concurred with the promotions of approximately eighty officers who had
served on the Ecuadoran front under Ureta. The quick action by congress
in approving the promotions in November, 1941 reflected congressional
satisfaction with the military effort as well as a recognition of the political
necessity of rewarding Ureta and his fellow officers.[50] Other officers who
had not served on the northern front and were passed over soon after the
Ecuador conflict were dismayed that a number of their colleagues who
were promoted as a result of the Ecuador conflict had not engaged in
combat but had merely been fortunate enough to have been serving in the
region when hostilities began.[51]

By late 1943 the government's handling of promotions sparked jealousies
among army senior officers as well. During November Prado failed to
supply the yearly list of recommended promotions to the congress for its
approval. At that time six vacancies at the rank of general existed in the
army, and a number of important posts, including the command of two
light divisions, were held by colonels.[52] Prado failed to suggest action on
these vacancies because of a clash with Ureta over the nomination of a
national police general to the Supreme Tribunal of Military Justice. Ureta
and his fellow officers were aware of past attempts to use the national
police as a check on the power of the army. Therefore, they did not favor
any increase in the prestige or power of that institution.[53] The president
was apparently using the army promotions as a bargaining tool to have the
police general placed on the tribunal.

Another element in the promotion issue was Prado's desire to avoid
permanently alienating army officers involved in the controversy.
Originally the president had planned to promote Brigadier General Federico
Hurtado (a former cabinet member under Benavides) to division general.
Strong protests by Brigadier General Yañez, who had powerful allies in the
senate and was furious at being passed over, forced Prado to hold back.
Brigadier General Fausto Figueroa, who, like Yañez, would have been
passed over by the promotion of Hurtado, added his voice to the protests.

Rather than risk an open confrontation with Figueroa and Yañez, the president decided to postpone promotions involving general officers until a less volatile political solution could be reached. Ultimately, no new appointments to the grade of division general were made before Prado left office in July, 1945, and this fact increased the frustrations of the passed-over senior officers.[54]

Although Prado was unable to promote friendly senior army officers, he had more success in the Peruvian air force. In 1942 a close associate of Prado's, General Fernando Melgar, was made minister of aviation. In the previous year the air force had been made independent of the navy ministry, under which it had operated since 1929. Additionally, most of the initial lend-lease equipment obtained from the United States during 1942 and 1943 went to the air force in an effort to modernize that armed service branch. Thirty P-36 fighters, thirteen A-33 bombers, and twenty-five PT-19 trainers were received during these two years.[55] A new air force training school at Las Palmas was also opened in late 1942 in order to expand the pool of active air force pilots.[56] Prado's military budgets reflected the government's support of the air force during its first three years of independent operation. The portion of military expenditures allocated to the air force climbed from 18 to 24 percent between 1942 and 1945. This increase was primarily at the expense of the navy, whose share of the budget dropped from 20 to less than 18 percent during these years.[57]

The special attention given to the air force, while contributing to its expansion and modernization, also created internal problems within the institution and sparked inter-service rivalries as well. The chain of command was often ignored by air force officers, who frequently disregarded orders from superiors and appealed directly to the president himself. This situation resulted in a lack of trust among commanding officers that was compounded by air force officers who used squadron commands for their own personal benefit.[58] Army officers regarded the air force with suspicion and considered it to be closely allied with the president. One army officer in late 1943 claimed that in the event of trouble between the army and Prado, it might be necessary to "destroy the Peruvian air force on the ground."[59] Undoubtedly due in part to Prado's policies, little unity existed among the three service branches throughout the remainder of his administration. Moreover, as the 1945 elections drew near, Ureta and Benavides competed for the support of the army officer corps as a prelude to their presidential candidacies. This competition once again forced military men to choose sides in the political struggles involving senior army officers.

Benavides, after promotion to marshal and appointment as ambassador to Spain in 1939, subsequently was transferred to Peru's embassy in Argentina. Despite his absence from Peru, Benavides's political and military influence remained substantial. Many of his appointees remained in office during the Prado administration not only in the national government but in the departments, provinces, and municipalities as well. Candidates for congress in 1939 were in most cases approved by him, and Senator Carlos Concha, minister of foreign relations during the Benavides regime, was one of the most powerful members of that body.[60] On the other hand, General Ureta, as the military hero of the Ecuador war and inspector general of the army, soon developed his own power base within both the army and civilian political circles.

In 1943 the Miró-Quesada family, owners of the powerful conservative newspaper El Comercio, urged Ureta to seek the presidency in 1945. The Miró-Quesadas wanted a strong military candidate like Ureta to oppose the expected presidential bid of their staunch political enemy, Benavides.[61]

Marshal Benavides, kept closely informed of these events while in Argentina, made overtures in December, 1943 to APRA for support in a possible presidential campaign in 1945. This support was necessary, in part, because President Prado, in spite of his obligations to the marshal, was unwilling to support his presidential ambitions.[62] Prado's reluctance stemmed from his desire to have the constitution amended so that his term of office could be extended beyond July, 1945.[63] This hope faded in 1945, when he was unable to consolidate any support for such a move.

Junior army officers, already disgusted with the system of promotions, watched the political maneuverings of their senior officers with increasing dismay. General Ureta was forced on three occasions to "step down hard upon younger army officers" to dissipate growing discontent with their superiors and the government.[64] Major Víctor Villanueva, writing later about this problem, lamented that the officers of his generation (1930s and 1940s) were testimony to the political influence necessary to reach the rank of lieutenant colonel and above. Villanueva claimed, "Promotions dictated by politics were the norm. The system was detrimental to the efficiency of the army, as politics tended to intervene not only in promotions but also in the assignment of officers and troops."[65] Throughout the final years of the Prado regime unrest among junior army officers resulted in one antigovernment conspiracy and the creation of a clandestine organization of junior army officers dedicated to forcing fundamental military and civilian reforms. With the creation of the Revolutionary Committee of Army Officers (Comité Revolucionario de Oficiales del Ejército, or CROE) in July, 1944, the army officer corps was effectively divided into three factions: the Benavides and Ureta groups and the CROE.

CROE was composed of approximately one hundred army officers from the ranks below colonel. Major Víctor Villanueva, a progressive cavalry officer and former instructor at the Superior War College, was primarily responsible for the creation of this organization. A number of junior officers belonging to CROE had been students of Villanueva's at the war college.[66]

All of these army men had become disenchanted with civilian politicians and the high command after witnessing years of political intrigue, dictatorships, and corruption in both civilian and military circles. They sought fundamental reforms within the armed forces and national politics in order to rectify these ills. A CROE manifesto distributed to hundreds of officers and noncommissioned officers of the army, air force, navy, and national police in early 1945 provides a concise statement of these junior army officers' grievances.

A few generals and chiefs who have benefited from the government are not the army; not even a part of it. They are a few individuals, nothing more. They do not have the weight of opinion of the officer corps behind them because they lack professional prestige, lost through their dedication to national politics. The modern officer has a higher concept of discipline than his superior, a clearer criterion of the national situation as the mass of the army is made up of conscientious officers, non-commissioned officers and soldiers who are united around one idea: To liberate the country from tyranny and tyrants and to make the constitution respected, not mocked. [Thus] the army, which is the same flesh and blood as the people, is united with them.[67]

Specifically the dissident junior officers called for a better-trained army, free from political involvement, which would safeguard the right of the Peruvian people to be governed by authentically representative leaders.[68]

Two aspects of the CROE philosophy illustrate concepts fundamentally important for this study. CROE members, in referring to their "higher concept of discipline," meant that they recognized discipline was both the major criterion of professionalism and, at the same time, the most important characteristic that unequivocally distinguished the armed forces officer from the civilian. This discipline was extremely important to many young army officers as they felt "officers who have frequent and continuing contact with civilians run the risk of corruption, of losing their discipline, and of no longer being sufficiently 'military' in the eyes of their colleagues." Thus, as the CROE manifesto clearly reflects, junior officers—who witnessed the intense political partisanship of civil-military relations during their formative years in the military—looked with contempt upon their officers who "played politics" and consequently impeded the professional development of the armed forces.

Yet CROE members and other armed forces personnel such as General Antonío Rodríguez, who conspired with APRA and other civilian political elements in 1939 for ostensibly "democratic motives," failed to realize that revolution, for whatever reasons, is an inherently political activity. This plain contradiction plagued sincerely progressive armed forces personnel, including members of CROE, who sought during the 1940s to initiate badly needed reforms in the areas of promotions, training, and military justice. Their problem was that only through political activism could they hope to accomplish their objectives. This militancy, of course, undermined the discipline of the institution and exacerbated already existing factionalism within the armed forces. Events in late 1944 clearly demonstrated the dilemma confronting CROE activists.

In 1944, Benavides returned to Peru from his diplomatic post in Argentina in the midst of General Ureta's efforts to generate support for his presidential candidacy.[69] But in Arequipa on 3 June, a coalition of centrist and leftist civilian political leaders formed the *Frente Democrático Nacional* (National Democratic Front, FDN) to select a civilian alternative to these military men.[70] Twenty-six political figures representing a wide variety of political views formed the FDN, which soon expanded from a regional organization to a viable national political movement. APRA was instrumental in the formation of the Arequipa group, which called for the establishment of a genuinely representative and democratically elected regime capable of guaranteeing fundamental freedoms for all Peruvians.[71] APRA supported the FDN, headed by the Arequipa political leader Manuel Bustamante de la Fuente, as party leaders hoped to use the new political coalition as a means to achieve legalization and full political participation. *Apristas* were pessimistic about their future if General Ureta, backed by the intensely anti-APRA Miró-Quesada faction, were elected president. Moreover, Benavides, after making overtures to APRA during late 1943 concerning the party's support for his possible presidential bid, lost interest in continuing his election efforts relatively soon after returning to Peru.

During the last five months of 1944, it became clear to Benavides that his presidential chances were seriously hampered by the growing opposition of junior officers to any military candidate and the commitment of the FDN to backing a civilian for president. Adding to his difficulties were the powerful opposition of the Miró-Quesadas and President Prado's unwillingness to aid his former political mentor. Consequently, on 7 January 1945,

Benavides released a manifesto declaring that he would not be a presidential candidate and urging the election of a civilian government that could achieve national unity. The marshal warned of serious divisions within the armed forces dangerous to the national well-being should a military man be elected president. This warning was aimed directly at General Ureta, who was at the time finalizing his candidacy with the backing of the Miró-Quesadas, elements of the *Partido Union Revolucionaria*, and a number of minor parties.[72]

Benavides's manifesto also signaled the finishing touches on an agreement between himself and APRA that stipulated that both would support the candidate of the FDN and that the marshal would use his influence to guarantee the legalization and political participation of the party. After the manifesto appeared, Haya de la Torre and Benavides exchanged congratulatory messages, and the marshal received telegrams of felicitations from leading *Apristas* in exile.[73] This pact reflected Benavides's strong desire to block the election of his chief military rival and prevent serious divisions in the officer corps. It also was in keeping with his consistent backing of civilian candidates in the elections of 1915, 1936, and 1939.

By the first week of March, Benavides and APRA had offered their support to José Luis Bustamante y Rivero, then Peruvian ambassador to Bolivia, if he would run for president as the choice of the FDN.[74] At the same time, however, Haya de la Torre, allied with the most activist members of the CROE, decided to launch a civil-military uprising aimed at the Prado administration against any attempt to rig the coming elections. CROE members feared the possibility that Prado might attempt to install General Ureta as president, and thus Major Víctor Villanueva laid the groundwork for a civil-military insurrection, involving *Apristas* and army and air force personnel, to be centered in Lima and Ancón.[75] Villanueva's arrest in February did not prevent the plot from proceeding, as most of the preparations had been completed before his seizure.[76] On 17 March, General Ureta made the formal announcement of his presidential candidacy, and in the early morning hours of the following day the plot was activated.[77]

Under the leadership of Sergeant Claudio López Lavalle, approximately twelve noncommissioned air force personnel tried to gain control of the air base at Ancón. But because of divisions within the CROE ranks and the last-minute cancellation of *Aprista* support for the uprising, the Ancón conspirators were isolated and persuaded to surrender after only several hours.[78] Some members of the CROE were opposed to collaboration with APRA, and still others were apparently not willing to engage in an uprising when an electoral pact with the civilian leader Bustamante y Rivero seemed imminent.[79] APRA leader Haya de la Torre called off his party's support for the Ancón uprising when Bustamante y Rivero agreed to accept the backing of the FDN on 17 March. But the subversive elements in Ancón were not informed of these counterorders before they initiated their part of the conspiracy.[80]

As a result of subversive activities during February and March a number of CROE members were transferred to remote garrisons, and eighteen air force and army personnel were court-martialed. Although Haya de la Torre was originally charged with complicity in the abortive revolt, no charges were brought against him because of an agreement between Prado and Bustamante in early April.[81] Bustamante announced his presidential candidacy on 19 March after formally accepting APRA's support in return for a promise of legalization and electoral opportunities for Aprista congressional candidates.

Despite the failure of the Ancón uprising, many APRA sympathizers within the army openly expressed their allegiances to the party during April and May. The Bustamante candidacy freed many young officers to openly support the FDN. These officers had previously feared that any demonstration of solidarity with Apristas would seriously damage their careers.[82] Some CROE members not implicated by the government in previous subversive activities distributed fliers calling for Ureta to renounce his candidacy and avoid following in the footsteps of other ambitious military leaders such as Sánchez Cerro. They also insisted that "only defeated and decadent nations" were under military governments and that Peruvian military leaders should follow the examples of "Pershing, Foch, and MacArthur who did not exploit their military prestige for political gain."[83]

In mid-April Haya de la Torre claimed he was receiving a flood of support from younger army officers. Many of these young officers were sincerely committed to the election of a civilian president under democratic procedures, and they viewed APRA as a key element in realizing these goals. Another very important issue motivating their opposition to Ureta was his leadership of a close-knit group of conservative senior officers opposed to Benavides and APRA and seeking to gain control of the army if Ureta were elected president.[84] Naturally CROE members and other junior officers were alarmed at this prospect and worked actively to prevent it. Benavides, obviously also opposed to the Ureta clique, reacted strongly to his military rival's announced presidential candidacy on 20 March. In a published attack on Ureta's political ambitions, the marshal again warned that the polarization of the military must be avoided at all costs. He also insisted that his renunciation of any presidential ambitions was sincere and should not be interpreted as a political ploy.[85]

General Ureta's presidential hopes suffered a severe jolt on 15 May, when after two months of negotiations the Prado government finally legalized APRA. After registering the party under the title *Partido Aprista Peruano* (Peruvian Aprista Party), leaders were free, following nearly thirteen years of political proscription, to present congressional candidates for national elections scheduled for 10 June.[86] Haya de la Torre did not attempt to seek office, but it was clear to the APRA-Bustamante alliance that the party chief would be influential in the government of the Democratic Front.

Bustamante was not an experienced politician, having served only a short time as a local official in Arequipa during the 1930s and briefly in Sánchez Cerro's cabinet after supporting the 1930 *coup*. He was named ambassador to Bolivia in 1942 and held that post until he was selected as the candidate of the FDN in March, 1945.[87] A lawyer by profession, this rather shy, religious, and scholarly man was not well suited for the rigors of high-level Peruvian politics. Haya de la Torre years later described Bustamante as a "very innocent man." But Bustamante's sincerity prompted the APRA leader to comment that he was favorably impressed with the FDN candidate after their first meeting in late 1944.[88] Bustamante also accepted Haya de la Torre as the leader of a party that had come to reject the "extremes" marking the first fifteen years of APRA's participation in Peruvian politics.[89] Despite these initial impressions, both men entered the political alliance with some suspicions of the other's ultimate intentions.

In the initial negotiations Bustamante imposed the condition on APRA that he would reserve the right to "gradualize" the reforms initiated by the party during his administration. Moreover, prior to the legalization of APRA on 15 May, there were disagreements between the party and Bustamante regarding the number of *Aprista* congressional candidates allowed to seek office in the June elections.[90] Bustamante, apparently fearing the domination of the new congress by APRA, sought to keep the party's candidacy below 40 percent of the number of available seats. APRA leaders resisted this restriction strenuously, and Bustamante dropped his efforts and allowed the party to present a full slate of candidates.[91]

In the 1945 election Haya de la Torre tried to encourage the widest possible support for APRA candidates. Paralleling his attempt to present a more moderate image during the 1931 presidential election, APRA sought to allay fears of its radicalism during and immediately following the election campaign. Speaking at a huge rally on 20 May 1945 only a few yards away from the exclusive upper-class *Club Nacional,* Haya de la Torre reassured wealthy Peruvians: "It is not necessary to seize the wealth of those who possess it but rather new wealth should be created for those who do not have it."[92] This clear effort to soften his public hard-line anticapitalism was coupled with a rejection of the antimilitary image of APRA. He insisted that the army and the *Partido del Pueblo* were united in defending the best interests of the nation.[93] This comment was in keeping with the APRA tactic of rejecting any direct attack on General Ureta's candidacy so as to avoid arousing new antagonisms within the army leadership against APRA. In July, Haya de la Torre also demonstrated a desire to head off any foreign business opposition to APRA. Speaking with a United States correspondent, he claimed he was not in favor of the expropriation or division of private property. He also encouraged foreign capital investment because "large capital does not exist in Peru."[94]

The moderate stance of APRA in the 1945 campaign corresponded to the cautious and rather vague political platform of Bustamante. Bustamante made only a brief reference to the armed forces and pledged to upgrade its equipment. He also proposed the expropriation of uncultivated estates (with compensation), which were then to be distributed among small landholders. Other tax and social welfare reforms, in addition to guarantees for the protection of civil liberties, comprised the remaining significant provisions of the platform.[95]

Ureta's campaign principles were even more vague than those of his political opponent. As the candidate of the *Union Nacional Democrática* (National Democratic Union) he made only general references to the need for national unity and the protection of such basic institutions as the church and the family.[96] Despite heated exchanges between the supporters of Ureta and Bustamante in the nation's newspapers, the candidates themselves did not engage in vitriolic campaign rhetoric.

Voting was conducted in an open and legal manner on 10 June. Bustamante, with the support of APRA and most of the nation's centrist and leftist groups, garnered 305,590 votes as opposed to Ureta's total of 150,720.[97] Bustamante's resounding victory resulted from the critical support of APRA and Benavides as well as the serious divisions within the armed forces, which weakened Ureta's candidacy. A less tangible factor seems to have been the attitude of many voters that Peru, in electing a military president, would not be in keeping with the democratic trends fostered by World War II and the defeat of the Axis. In the spirit of this atmosphere Ureta did not contest Bustamante's victory and took the highly unusual step of personally congratulating the victor.[98]

Elected with Bustamante were thirty-five senators and seventy-three deputies running under the banner of the Democratic Front. Within the group were eighteen *Aprista* senators and forty-six deputies from a total of forty-six senators and 101 seats in the Chamber of Deputies.[99] Although APRA lacked a voting majority in either chamber, it represented the largest single voting bloc in the congress. This showing prompted members of Lima's upper class to hold a lavish dinner party in Haya de la Torre's honor at the home of Pedro de Osma Gildermeister (a member of one of the wealthiest families in Peru) in late June. Few Peruvians questioned the likelihood of Haya de la Torre's assuming a powerful role in national politics, and Lima's leading blue bloods were no exception.[100]

On 28 July 1945, Manuel Prado transferred the reins of government to José Bustamante y Rivero. Marshal Benavides, who had been instrumental in the election of the president, did not witness the culmination of his labors, as he died of a heart attack on 5 July.[101] The armed forces, following his lead and that of General Ureta, accepted the constitutional transfer of the presidency without protest.

The dual traumas of the Depression and World War II added new dimensions to military professionalism in Peru and throughout South America. In Argentina, Juan Perón, in a far more innovative and charismatic manner, built a populist alliance of working-class and army supporters that eluded Sánchez Cerro in Peru and Carlos Ibañez in Chile. The Brazilian army, fresh from a highly successful campaign with Allied forces in Italy, quickly ended Getulio Vargas's *Estado Nôvo* and embarked on a caretaker role in national politics as it developed an intimate relationship with the United States military. Many junior officers in Peru saw the Allied victory as a signal to push for internal military reforms they felt were ignored during the Prado regime. *Apristas*, allying with some of these junior officers and enlisted men, made ready to use their newly won congressional power to challenge Bustamante for control of national affairs.

NOTES

1. Useful discussions of the key civil-military issues of the Prado administration are found in Víctor Villanueva Valencia, *Ejército Peruano: Del caudillaje anárquico al militarismo reformista* (Lima: 1973), pp. 231-244, and *El APRA y el ejército, 1940-1950* (Lima: 1977), pp. 21-63; Bryce Wood, *The United States and Latin American Wars, 1932-1942* (New York: 1966), pp. 255-345; David H. Zook, Jr., *Zarumilla-Marañón: The Ecuador-Peru Border Dispute* (New York: 1964); Luis Alberto Sánchez, *Haya de la Torre y el APRA*, pp. 365-385.

2. See G-2 Report No. 202039, 27 August 1945, NA, RG 319. This highly significant report summarizes a Peruvian army General Staff study done in late 1944 entitled (United States military attaché's translation) "Exposition of the Army on the War Strength Organization." Extensive information on the General Staff's analysis of the army's military capabilities, basic weaknesses, and future requirements is provided. The document was listed as "secret" by the Peruvians in 1943, but the U.S. military attaché was able to obtain a copy in mid-1945. The social action aspects of this report will be discussed in Chapter 4.

3. Perú, Ministerio de Guerra, *Escalafón General del Ejército*, 1939, p. 116 (hereafter cited as *Escalafón* with year and page number). These are army officer staff lists. Villanueva, *Ejército Peruano*, p. 408.

4. Report of the United States naval attaché (unsigned), 23 June 1939, NA, RG 59, 823.248/188.

5. Ibid.

6. Chargé d'Affaires Louis G. Dreyfus, Jr., to Sec/State, 19 December 1939, NA, RG 59, 823.00/78; Villanueva, *Ejército Peruano*, p. 132. As many as 30 percent of the army's general officers in the early 1960s were products of French military training.

7. Report of the United States military attaché Captain Uzal G. Ent, 23 February 1940, NA, RG 59, 823.20 M.I.D./5.

8. *El Comercio*, 28 March 1939, p. 1.

9. *The New York Times*, 20 April 1939, p. 3; *Peruvian Times*, 23 March 1945, p. 2.

10. Dreyfus to Sec/State, 20 October 1939, NA, RG 59, 823.00/1361.

11. Enrique Chirinos Soto, *El Perú frente a junio de 1962* (Lima: 1962), p. 54. This is one of the most valuable general reviews of twentieth-century Peruvian politics.

12. Dreyfus to Sec/State, 20 October 1939, NA, RG 59, 823.00/36; Sánchez, *Haya de la Torre y el APRA*, pp. 366-367. For a detailed documentary review of the political intrigue leading up to the 1939 elections, see Thomas M. Davies, Jr., and Víctor Villanueva Valencia, eds., *Secretos electorales del APRA: Correspondencia y documentos de 1939* (Lima: 1983).

13. Sánchez, *Haya de la Torre y el APRA*, pp. 367-368, concedes that confusion over party directives may have led to a large number of *Aprista* votes for Prado. Haya de la Torre insisted that the 1939 election was a "fake" and that there was no formal support for the winning candidate by APRA (interview with Víctor Raúl Haya de la Torre, 13 July 1974, Lima, Peru).

14. Ambassador Henry Norweb to Sec/State, 4 June 1940, NA, RG 59, 823.00/1433.

15. Ibid.

16. G-2 Report no. 4040, 14 June 1940, U.S. military attaché to War Department, NA, RG 319.

17. Perú, Ministerio de Guerra, *Legislación Militar*, 1940, pp. 254-255 (hereafter cited as *Legislación Militar*, with year and page number); Norweb to Sec/State, 26 June 1940, NA, RG 59, 823.00/1427.

18. Norweb to Sec/State, 14 August 1940, NA, RG 59, 823.00/1433.

19. Ibid. It should be noted, however, that APRA leaders tried to gain legality for the party by appealing for support from U.S. embassy officials. Haya de la Torre, in particular, claimed that APRA was the leading pro-Allied element in

Peru and that the Prado regime was undemocratic and not truly pro-U.S. See my "The Changing Focus of *Aprismo:* Haya de la Torre, Alan García and the Anti-Imperialist Tradition in Peru," *Journal of Third World Studies* (Fall, 1990); personal interview with Ambassador Norweb, 27 July 1980, Cleveland, Ohio.

20. Butler to Sec/State, 14 January 1943, NA, RG 59, 823.00/1625. For Haya de la Torre's pro-Allied stance see his *La defensa continental,* 4th ed. (Lima: 1967); personal interview with Ambassador R. Henry Norweb, 27 July 1980, Cleveland, Ohio. Ambassador Norweb stated flatly that if Haya de la Torre and APRA had engaged in subversive activity during the Prado regime, "he [Haya de la Torre] would have been ridden out of Peru on a rail." Details of the talks between *Apristas* and the U.S. Embassy officials are provided in Masterson, "Changing Focus of *Aprismo.*"

21. Norweb to Sec/State, 14 March 1940, NA, RG 59, 823.248/243; "Naval Aviation Mission: Agreement between the United States of America and Peru," *Executive Agreement Series,* no. 178 (Washington, D.C.: 1940).

22. Ibid.

23. G-2 Report no. 5940, 28 February 1944, NA, RG 319; *The Harry Hopkins Papers,* Box 143, Franklin D. Roosevelt Library.

24. On the fifteenth anniversary of the arrival of the first French mission in November, 1946, the army celebrated the occasion with festivities for visiting French army personnel. See *Revista Militar del Perú* (11 November 1946). The entire issue is devoted to honoring the French mission. The Peruvian army's views on this occasion will be discussed in Chapter 4.

25. G-2 Report no. 4040, 14 June 1940, U.S. military attaché to War Department, NA, RG 319.

26. Wood, *The United States,* p. 255. As with the Leticia conflict, Wood's discussion of the diplomatic aspects of the Peru-Ecuador border controversy is quite comprehensive.

27. Numerous scholars have noted that Prado's family background was an important factor in determining the government's position during the controversy. See particularly Wood, *The United States,* p. 295; Sánchez, *Haya de la Torre y el APRA,* p. 368.

28. G-2 Report no. 4190, 3 January 1941, U.S. military attaché to War Department, NA, RG 319.

29. Ibid.

30. Ibid.; G-2 Report no. 385333, 30 June 1947, U.S. military attaché to War Department, NA, RG 319.

31. G-2 Report no. 4324, 30 June 1941, U.S. military attaché to War Department, NA, RG 165.

32. *Peruvian Times,* 13 June 1941, p. 18.

33. Ibid., 13 April 1945, p. 2.

34. Eloy G. Ureta, *Apuntes sobre una campaña, 1941* (Madrid: 1953), p. 34.

35. G-2 Report no. 4336, 14 July 1941, U.S. military attaché to War Department, NA, RG 165.

36. Wood, *The United States,* pp. 278-279. For the best discussion of the military aspects of the conflict see Zook, *Zarumilla-Marañón.* A valuable series of official documents dealing with the Ecuador conflict is Colección Documental de la Guerra con Ecuador, 4 vols., (Lima: N.D.) found in *Centro de Estudios Histórico-Militares del Perú.* Other useful works are Luis Humberto Delgado, *Las guerras del Peru:*

Campaña del Ecuador, batalla del Zarumilla (Lima: 1944); General E. P. Felipe de la Barra, *El conflicto Peruano-Ecuatoriano y la victoriosa campaña de 1941 en las fronteras de Zarumilla y nor oriente* (Lima: 1969). For the Ecuadoran version of these events see Luis A. Rodríguez, *La agresión peruana: La campaña del Zarumilla documentada* (Quito: 1955).

37. Zook, *Zarumilla-Marañón*, p. 177.

38. *El Comercio*, 28 July 1941, p. 19.

39. Zook, *Zarumilla-Marañón*, p. 183.

40. Ibid., p. 188.

41. Rear Admiral (R) Jorge Camino de la Torre, "La Marina de guerra del Perú en el conflicto peruano-ecuatoriano de 1941," *Revista de Marina del Perú*, 361, no. 9 (July, August, 1979), pp. 103-116.

42. De la Barra, *El conflicto Peruano-Ecuatoriano*, p. 51.

43. Zook, *Zarumilla-Marañón*, pp. 184-185.

44. Norweb to Sec/State, 1 October 1941, NA, RG 59, 823.00/1472, and 7 October 1941, 823.00/1475.

45. *El Comercio*, 27 July 1941, p. 5, and 28 July 1941, p. 19.

46. The relatively limited scale of the conflict is reflected in the low number of casualties suffered by both Peru and Ecuador. Ecuador suffered an estimated four hundred killed and wounded while Peru lost 107 army, air force, and *Guardia Civil* personnel killed. Zook, *Zarumilla-Marañón*, p. 186; "Relación nominal de los oficales, clases y soldados muertos en las acciones de armas en la fronteras del norte y nororiente en el conflicto con el Ecuador en 1941," *Centro de Estudios Histórico-Militares del Perú*. This is a mimeographed list of individual armed forces members killed in the Ecuador conflict. Despite government recognition of returning war veterans, according to John V. Murra, some wounded soldiers were left with poorly treated injuries (eyewitness account by John Murra, personal interview with Murra, 31 July 1990, Ithaca, New York).

47. Wood, *The United States*, p. 338; Zook, *Zarumilla-Marañón*, p. 203. A useful discussion of the border dispute from an international legal perspective is George Maier, "The Boundary Dispute Between Ecuador and Peru," *American Journal of International Law* 63, no. 1 (January 1968), pp. 28-47.

48. James C. Carey, *Peru and the United States, 1900-1962* (Notre Dame, Indiana: 1964), p. 108.

49. *Escalafón*, 1941, p. 21.

50. Ibid., pp. 21-69 passim; Ambassador John Campbell White to Sec/State, 3 April 1945, NA, RG 59, 823.00/4-345. Special promotions were granted during November, 1941 (regularly promotions were scheduled for February) for approximately eighty-five officers serving in the areas of the Ecuador conflict. From 1939 to 1941 the number of yearly promotions in the army was approximately seventy.

51. Letter from Víctor Villanueva, 3 May 1975, to the author.

52. G-2 Report no. 5857, 31 December 1943, U.S. military attaché to War Department, NA, RG 319.

53. Ibid., Report no. 5911, 25 June 1944.

54. Ibid.

55. U.S. Department of State, *Papers Relating to the Foreign Relations of the United States, 1944*, 7, p. 1508.

56. G-2 Report no. 352, 1 April 1944, U.S. military attaché to War Department, NA, RG 319. Entrance into the flight school at Las Palmas was largely based upon political contacts as each cadet was obliged to have a "sponsor" before being admitted. The military attaché concluded that the majority of officers entering the school were "upper class" and there was a very low number of *cholo* (mestizo) pilots. As late as 1990, "*Aspirantes,*" as first-year cadets at Peru's service academies are known, were required to pay a substantial entrance fee to cover the cost of uniforms and other essentials during their initial year of study. This fee has discouraged poorer applicants from applying to the academies.

57. Perú, Ministerio de Hacienda y Comercio, Dirección Nacional de Estadística, *Anuario Estadístico del Perú: 1945-1949,* pp. 710-711. Hereafter cited as *Anuario Estadístico,* with year and page number.

58. G-2 Report no. 9210, 27 February 1943, U.S. military attaché to War Department, NA, RG 319.

59. First Secretary Jefferson Patterson to Sec/State, 27 December 1943, NA RG 59, 823.00/1726. Report of conversation with an unnamed army officer.

60. Norweb to Sec/State, 4 June 1940, NA, RG 59, 823.00/1433.

61. Norweb to Sec/State, 29 July 1943, NA, RG 59, 823.00/1666. The Miró-Quesadas' opposition to Benavides was a manifestation of the continuing feud begun with the former president in 1935 after the assassination of Antonio Miró-Quesada and his wife by an *Aprista.* See Chapter 2.

62. Patterson to Sec/State, 18 December 1943, NA, RG 59, 823.00/1726.

63. Ibid.

64. Patterson to Sec/State, 27 December 1943, NA, RG 59, 823.00/1726.

65. Víctor Villanueva Valencia, *La sublevación aprista del 48: Tragedia de pueblo y un partido* (Lima: 1973), p. 30.

66. Personal interview with Víctor Villanueva, 27 July 1974, Lima, Peru.

67. White to Sec/State, 2 February 1945, NA, RG 59, 823.00/2-245.

68. Personal interview with Víctor Villanueva, 27 July 1974, Lima, Peru; "Programa de acción de C.R.O.E.," in Villanueva, *La sublevación aprista,* pp. 191-192.

69. *Peruvian Times,* 8 July 1945, p. l.

70. First Secretary George Butler to Sec/State, 13 June 1944, NA, RG 59, 823.00/1780½. There were twenty-six individuals listed as founders of the FDN in its first political flier released in early June in Arequipa. Listed as the president of the coalition was Manuel Bustamante de la Fuente, as vice president Julio Ernesto Portugal, and as secretaries Jorge Vasquez Salas and Jaime Rey de Castro.

71. Butler to Sec/State, 13 June 1944, NA, RG 59, 823.00/1780½.

72. *El Callao,* 7 January 1945, p. 8, and Chirinos Soto, *El Perú frente,* p. 61. The manifesto is presented in Zárate Lescano, *El mariscal Benavides: Su vida y su obra* (Lima: 1976), 2, pp. 373-374.

73. White to Sec/State, 13 January 1945, NA, RG 59, 823.00/1-1345.

74. Counselor of Embassy Edward G. Trueblood to Sec/State, 6 March 1945, NA, RG 59, 823.00/3-645. Trueblood indicated that if Bustamante refused the offer, Haya de la Torre was prepared to explore the possibility of presenting his own candidacy.

75. Ibid.; Personal interview with Víctor Villanueva, 27 July 1974, Lima, Peru. Trueblood reported that an *Aprista* informant close to Haya de la Torre told him during the first week of March that if the coming elections were "rigged," then

"APRA would attempt to carry out a *coup* designed to place in power a *junta* which would have the sole purpose of guaranteeing fair and uncontrolled elections." The informant indicated that steps were already in progress to prepare for this contingency. The Villanueva plot clearly fits the informant's description of APRA's contingency plans.

76. Villanueva interview, 27 July 1974.

77. *El Comercio*, 17 March 1945, p. 2; Villanueva, *La sublevación aprista*, p. 26.

78. *El Comercio*, 17 March 1945, p. 2; Villanueva, *La sublevación aprista*, pp. 26-27, and Villanueva interview, 27 July 1974.

79. Villanueva interview, 27 July 1974. Bustamante agreed to run as the presidential candidate of the FDN as the Ancón rising was being activated.

80. Villanueva, *La sublevación aprista*, pp. 26-27.

81. White to Sec/State, 19 April 1945, NA, RG 59, 823.00/4-1945; *La Crónica*, 23 March 1945, pp. 3, 5; *Escalafón*, 1945, p. 85.

82. White to Sec/State, 19 April 1945, NA, RG 59, 823.00/4-1945. The U.S. ambassador reported that Haya de la Torre informed one of his colleagues that he had the support of some "70 percent of the entire young officer element in the army." Even while discounting what he considered an exaggerated claim by Haya de la Torre, the ambassador acknowledged evidence of sizeable support for APRA among junior army officers.

83. Anonymous, "Patriotas, Civiles y Militares; Carta abierta al General Eloy G. Ureta," *Colección de Volantes*, April, 1945 folder.

84. See White to Sec/State, 19 April 1945, NA, RG 59, 823.00/4-1945, and 3 April 1945, 823.00/5-345. This group belonged to a military lodge called "Mariscal La Mar."

85. *El Callao*, 20 March 1945, p. 3.

86. Ibid., 16 May 1945, p. 3; *Peruvian Times*, 18 May 1945, p. 1.

87. Fredrick Pike, *The Modern History of Peru*, (New York: 1967), p. 280.

88. Personal interview with Víctor Raúl Haya de la Torre, 13 July 1974, Lima, Peru.

89. José Luis Bustamante y Rivero, *Tres años de la lucha por la democracía en el Perú*, (Buenos Aires: 1949), pp. 18-22. This is Bustamante's account of his three years as president and is a valuable source for his version of the controversial events of these years.

90. Ibid., p. 22; White to Sec/State, 11 May 1945, NA, RG 59, 823.00/5-1145.

91. White to Sec/State, 11 May 1945, NA, RG 59, 823.00/5-1145.

92. *El Callao*, 21 May 1945, p. 3; Villanueva, *La sublevación aprista*, p. 29.

93. *El Callao*, 22 May 1945, p. 3.

94. *Peruvian Times*, 6 July 1945, p. 2.

95. Bustamante, *Tres años*, pp. 23-25; White to Sec/State, 19 April 1945, NA, RG 59, 823.00/4-1945.

96. *El Comercio*, 17 March 1945, p. 3.

97. *Peruvian Times*, 20 July 1945, p. 1.

98. Bustamante, *Tres años*, p. 29; Trueblood to Sec/State, 29 July 1945, NA, RG 59, 823.00/6-2945.

99. *Peruvian Times*, 3 August 1945, p. 1.

100. Trueblood to Sec/State, 29 June 1945, NA, RG 59, 823.00/6-2945.

101. *Peruvian Times*, 6 July 1945, p. 1; Zárate Lescano, *El mariscal Benavides*, 2, pp. 396-397.

4
Prelude to Rebellion: 1945-1948

During the first eighteen months of the Bustamante regime the political bipartisanship characterizing the formation of the *Frente Democrático* collapsed as a result of a number of developments. Rightist civilian and military opponents of APRA opposed the party's efforts to dominate the government. This opposition prompted street violence and political terrorism by *Apristas* and their opponents as the political crisis deepened. Contributing to the continuing division of the officer corps were APRA efforts to gain military support through the manipulation of promotions and salaries. Finally, when efforts of progressive young officers to initiate institutional reforms and further clarify the postwar role of the armed forces in national affairs met with little success, their distrust of their superiors grew deeper, leading some of the more radical officers to begin planning to overthrow the government.

The armed forces emerged from the Prado years with a different institutional makeup and professional outlook. The army, after relying on French military advisers for most of the years since 1896, severed its ties with the French and turned to the United States for technical training assistance. By the beginning of the Bustamante administration all three of the armed services were under contract to United States. Besides the long-standing naval mission first established in 1920, the army began working with a sixteen-man United States army team in July, 1944. On 7 October 1946 the naval aviation mission, that had previously trained Peruvian air force pilots, was replaced by a much larger United States air force team.[1] The policy of sending young armed forces personnel to the United States and its overseas bases for advanced schooling begun during World War II was expanded in the two years following the end of the world conflict. On one such visit in August, 1947 thirty-five naval officers and 263 enlisted men traveled to the United States and returned with nine vessels sold to Peru by Washington.[2] Despite this reorientation toward the United States military establishment, many senior officers still retained their allegiance to their former French tutors and the theories taught in French military institutions. For example, in late 1946 the army celebrated the fiftieth anniversary of the founding of the French military mission by holding a series of ceremonies in Lima. Marshal Ureta gave the keynote address for these ceremonies at the Circulo Militar and argued that French and Peruvian soldiers should recall "the glory of Napoleon, Foch and De Gaulle" and not the "treason" of Pétain. And Lieutenant Colonel César Pando Esgusquiza, in another address praising the French military adviser's role in the years before World War II, concluded, "An army without tradition and memory is an army without origins and without direction. The French army during the last two World Wars has acted with bravery and glory."[3] Other older officers and a number of younger military men recognized that these theories would have to be reexamined, however, in light of the sharply altered structure of world military power after 1945.

Prior to World War II, a very few of the best Peruvian officers received training in Peru and overseas that placed their preparation on a par with that of United States and European military men. Moreover, with the advent of the nuclear age and a new world order dominated by the United States and the Soviet Union, Peruvian officers were forced to acknowledge that their national security was intimately tied to the immense military might of the United States. As a result, Peruvian generals and admirals, handicapped by their limited conventional means of making war, could not consider themselves as equals with their United States counterparts during discussions of mutual security. Some of the shrewdest Peruvian military leaders recognized that this new power structure meant that Peru's professional military development would be restricted by its dependence on the United States and by its limited conventional military capability. Consequently these few armed forces leaders sought to redefine the role of their institution within the context of this new reality.

Following the Ecuador conflict army Chief of Staff General Felipe de la Barra and fellow members of the General Staff worked on a comprehensive program of national defense planning. Seeking to use the strategic lessons of the Ecuador engagement and the "total war" concepts learned from World War II as a basis for Peru's national defense scheme, these army leaders detailed their findings in a report entitled "Exposition of the Army on the War Strength Organization." Completed in mid-1944, the study designated the army as the most important element in the nation's defense.

The General Staff recognized, however, that divisions existed among the three armed services, and thus the report stressed the need for the creation of a centralized armed forces high command designed to bridge these divisions and facilitate a more coordinated framework for national defense.[4]

The primary recommendations of this highly significant study are important as precedents for postwar national defense policy. They also give evidence of the forward-looking concerns of some army leaders long before most of their suggestions were implemented. The most important conclusions of this study were (1) the army, as the predominant institution of the armed services, has the primary duty to study the nature of modern combat and make adjustments in Peru's military training techniques; (2) the national conscription law must be reformed because it discriminated against the nation's "impoverished and humble" Indian population, who were often in bad health and were consequently not fit for military service; (3) the military promotion law, which gave the congress control over promotions above the rank of major or its equivalent, must be reviewed to remove politics from this vital internal military matter; (4) improvement of recruitment and the rate of reenlistment (only 5 percent at the time of the study) must be encouraged; (5) education programs for illiterate Indians to prepare them better for military service and to help raise their basic living standard must be initiated; and (6) the enactment of a national defense law "assuring the full contribution of all elements within the nation in times of war mobilization" was also urged at the earliest possible date.[5]

The final recommendation of this study was the key statement of the report. The necessity of developing a strategy of full-scale mobilization was a reflection of the General Staff's understanding of the concept of total war so graphically demonstrated during the world conflict. Moreover, the document reflects the pervasive influence of French military theory among members of the General Staff. General Raymond Laurent served as chief of the French army mission from 1941 to 1943 and adviser to the General Staff during this entire period.[6] Laurent regularly attended staff conferences, and his influence is evident in the creation of this defense plan. The army document, calling for full national mobilization in time of war and the enactment of a national defense law to facilitate such mobilization, closely mirrors similar measures enacted in France in 1938. In France, legislation titled the "Organization of the Nation in Time of War" was passed in that year; it created the framework for a centralized organization headed by a Ministry of Defense.[7] But civilian fears of centralized military authority and resistance by air force and navy commanders blocked the implementation of these measures before the French military disasters of 1940.[8] These same pressures prevented the implementation of the

Peruvian army's defense plan during the last year of the Prado regime. But the campaign to implement a broad national defense plan occupied the attention of far-sighted army officers during the Bustamante years and beyond.

After 1945 the social aspect of national defense planning reflected in the recommendations of the 1944 General Staff study calling for the education of the "impoverished" Indian population took on much greater importance. The writings of army officers reflected both their acceptance of the growing social implications of a comprehensive national defense plan as well as their willingness to defend the role of the army, partly on the basis of its social contributions to Peruvian society. As we have seen, these concepts had been articulated in relatively unsophisticated conceptual frameworks prior to World War II. In the postwar decade, they became closely interwoven with national defense strategy.

Writing again for the *Revista Militar* in August, 1946, Lieutenant Colonel Pando Esgusquiza, in an article entitled "The Army, Is It Unproductive?", argued that for national defense purposes the army will always be needed because "the guarantee of national tranquility and liberty does not have a price."[9] Although providing few specific examples, Pando also stressed that the army had been traditionally involved in social projects that, while not falling strictly within the realm of military operations, did contribute to the national welfare and represented a positive contribution to the nation. He made references to the limited colonization and road-building projects undertaken by the army to populate remote areas along Peru's contested frontiers during the Benavides administration. Such projects contributed to national development as well as national defense, according to Pando.[10]

Along this same line Pando insisted that all Peruvians must be cognizant of their responsibility to contribute to the defense of the nation. He alluded to the defeat of France in 1940 and claimed that the lack of civilian support for the French army's national defense plan was largely responsible for the collapse of its war machine. The lesson for Peru, according to Pando, was that wartime victories are determined by peacetime preparation.[11] In arguing that the army performed valuable social as well as military functions for the state, Lieutenant Colonel Pando referred to Lieutenant Colonel Manuel Morla Concha's 1933 article on the army's social role. Pando and Morla Concha were struggling to define a "nation-building" mission for the army, which had been the goal of military intellectuals since the early twentieth century.[12]

Among these intellectuals was General Oscar R. Torres, who would later become Bustamante's first minister of war in 1945. Speaking before an audience of San Marcos University professors, Torres insisted that the mission of the military man was not incompatible with that of the civilian educator and that the social function of the army should not be over-looked by other professionals. Torres took his argument further, claiming that national defense was the responsibility not only of the military but of civilian politicians, economists, and other professionals who must be aware that the ability of the armed forces to ensure national security is dependent upon the support given the military by the civilian sector. These views and Torres's argument that advanced education is an integral aspect of the "complete" military professional presaged doctrines espoused by Peruvian military educators beginning in the 1950s at the newly formed *Centro de Altos Estudios Militares* (Center for Higher Military Studies, CAEM). In spite of Pando's and Torres's assertions regarding the army's civic action record, the Prado and Bustamante administrations ignored the armed forces in the implementation of their limited colonizing projects. The more active of the two presidents, Prado initiated the Puno-Tambopata Indian colonization project near Lake Titicaca in 1942. Bypassing the army, Prado delegated the program to the Bureau of Indian Affairs, which eventually developed several cooperatives in the region by April, 1945. Prado's policy once again demonstrated that the distance between rhetoric and reality regarding the army's "civilizing mission" remained substantial.[13]

As Bustamante's minister of war in 1945, however, General Torres was confronted with less abstract and more politically volatile issues. The newly legalized APRA's efforts to gain a stronger allegiance among the army's junior officers and enlisted men presented Torres with his major challenge as the leading military cabinet minister during the early years of the Bustamante administration.

Although APRA was not represented in Bustamante's first cabinet, party leaders planned to exert sufficient political power in the national congress to direct government policy. APRA's position against its congressional opponents was strengthened by party discipline, which was ensured by the *Aprista* congressmen's undated resignations, held by Haya de la Torre.[14] Thus APRA was able to enact a substantial amount of its legislative proposals before July, 1947. Adding to the party's congressional strength was its support in the labor movement, the universities, and local government agencies. *Apristas* lost no time in exerting their political power. When congress first convened on 28 July 1945, party representa-tives engineered the repeal of the constitutional amendments passed in June, 1939, that expanded the power of the president in relation to congress.[15] This repeal opened the way for a measure that allowed congress to override a presidential veto by a simple majority vote. On the same eventful day the emergency laws passed by the Benavides and Prado governments were also repealed, and a general amnesty for all military and civilian prisoners sentenced by military court-martial was enacted.[16]

The amnesty provoked immediate controversy within the armed forces due to its stipulation that military men sentenced for political crimes were to be reinstated as active members of the armed forces and returned to the regular promotion process.[17] This clause affected a significant number of officers who had been involved in past *Aprista* subversive activity. An incident emanating from senate debates concerning the amnesty illustrates the intense emotions generated by this measure. APRA Senator and army Colonel (R) César Enrique Pardo, in a senate speech, praised those members of the armed forces who had resisted the "dictatorships" that had controlled Peru since 1930. These men, according to Pardo, were the ones who had remained most true to the principles and "high moral code" of their profession. These comments provoked an immediate reaction from General Federico Hurtado, inspector general of the army. Hurtado, who had served in both the Benavides and Prado governments, was enraged by Pardo's statements and challenged the senator to a duel. After contesting with pistols, both men remarkably emerged from the duel without injury. Pardo was later to confront strong verbal challenges from Senator and General (R) Ernesto Montagne Marckholtz, who also vehemently opposed the APRA legislation.[18] During these debates Haya de la Torre insisted that Pardo was speaking for "himself alone," but few opponents of the amnesty accepted this interpretation.[19]

During March, 1946 General Hurtado, Colonel Luis A. Solari, and Admirals Carlos Rotolde, Enrique Moral, and Roque A. Saldías became incensed over *Aprista* interference in the military promotion process. Hurtado and Solari had been denied promotion to division general and brigadier general, respectively, by the vote of APRA representatives in congress. The three navy admirals threatened to resign in protest over *Aprista* attempts to reinstate Captain Pablo Ontaneda to active service and promote him to the rank of rear admiral. Ontaneda was known for his pro-*Aprista* sympathies during the Benavides administration but had been court-martialed on charges of incompetence. Thus the political amnesty of July, 1945 did not clearly apply to his case.[20] This liberal interpretation of the amnesty law prompted the vehement objections of the naval officers.

By May, 1946 more senior officers of the armed forces joined to resist APRA's handling of internal military issues. By then, *Apristas* had completed the draft of a congressional proposal that would have caused the immediate retirement of 240 older officers, including eighteen generals, by lowering the retirement age. The bill would have increased the rank and salaries of junior officers at the same time. United States Chargé d'Affaires Walter J. Donnelly commented that the obvious purpose of this proposed legislation was to gain the allegiance of junior officers while at the same time removing some of the most troublesome anti-APRA elements from the senior ranks.[21] The bill did not progress very far, but it marked one of the boldest attempts by Apristas to manipulate the power structure of the officer corps. This measure helped create new and powerful enemies for APRA in the armed forces.

Disenchantment with APRA tactics also spurred Lieutenant Colonel Alfonso Llosa, who had been actively involved in political intrigue throughout the early 1940s, to organize support among anti-APRA army officers for his political ally Luis A. Flores. Both Llosa and Flores were leading members of the rightist Partido Unión Revolucionaria, and the latter hoped to gain support for his own candidacy for a senate seat in special congressional elections scheduled for 30 June 1946.[22] Llosa, an impetuous officer who drank heavily, continued to exploit anti-Aprista sentiments in the military throughout the Bustamante regime. In September, 1947 he led a small group of army officers in an assault on the office of the APRA newspaper La Tribuna as a prelude to more ambitious revolutionary activities in mid 1948.[23]

While some senior officers were becoming increasingly hostile to APRA during the first two years of the Bustamante regime, other junior army officers sought the aid of the party in promoting the institutional reforms they favored. A group of junior army officers (many of whom were members of CROE) led by Major Víctor Villanueva met with Haya de la Torre in early 1946 to discuss his party's possible support for their program. Minister of War Torres, after being informed of these discussions, reprimanded Villanueva for dealing with APRA and refused to meet with the delegation of junior officers to listen to the suggestions they had presented to Haya de la Torre.[24] Interestingly, the proposals of the Villanueva group were similar to a congressional measure enacted in late 1945 creating a mixed commission of armed forces officers and civilians designed to study possible administrative reforms for the military. Specifically, the mixed commission was mandated to deal with the reorganization of the high command of the armed forces, writing new military legislation, and the revision of existing law, regarding the organization of the army.[25] The panel began its work in early 1946, but as with less ambitious proposals for internal military reform during the Prado administration, political partisanship and the resistance of influential senior officers prevented the passage of any substantive legislation. While these issues were being discussed in congress, Major Villanueva and fifty junior army officers and thirty police officers demonstrated their support for the proposed military legislation in the congressional chambers. The minister of war, General Torres, reacted to this demonstration by transferring many of the men involved to remote garrisons. A number of these officers were members of CROE, and this action effectively ended the organized activity of the group. Villanueva was sent to the United States on an arms-purchasing mission. He did not return until mid-November, 1947.[26]

Frustration among junior officers that stemmed from the failure of the military reform initiative added to the general unrest created by Aprista-inspired violence designed to intimidate the political opposition. Consequently, as Bustamante entered his second year in office, the political climate was extremely tense.

President Bustamante was ill-prepared to deal with increasing disorder during the first eighteen months of his administration. Unlike his immediate presidential predecessors, he did not immediately employ secret police to deal with political subversion. The Social Brigade of the Division of Investigations of the national police was abandoned during his first month in office. Also disbanded was the effective informer (soplóneria) system that had aided both Benavides and Prado.[27] As a result, the government was not well prepared to deal with the organized violence carried out by Aprista activists against their political opponents. At an anti-APRA rally on 7 December 1945 demonstrators, protesting the party's attempts to pass a press censorship bill aimed at curtailing conservative criticism of its tactics, were attacked by Apristas, who used dynamite to destroy the speaker's platform and break up the rally.[28] APRA leader Manuel Seoane, in two interviews with U.S. embassy official, Edward G. Trueblood, following the riots in December, claimed that the disorders reflected the growing opinion among Apristas that Bustamante was moving too slowly in allowing the party to assert greater political power. Moreover, Seoane claimed that the APRA violence brought the party new respect from some members of the armed forces who considered Apristas "soft and effeminate." Seoane claimed he had received numerous visits from military men as a result of APRA's tactics.[29]

Bolstered by their success in December, Apristas stormed the offices of La Prensa and El Comercio in early April, 1946 after the two newspapers attacked the party's campaign of violence. In the aftermath of these actions, the minister of government and police, General Manuel Rodríguez, an avowed anti-Aprista, fired the Lima prefect of police and ordered the arrest of policemen who failed to defend the newspaper offices.[30] After Bustamante vigorously denounced APRA's tactics in a national radio broadcast on 30 April, high-ranking army officers assured him of their unqualified support in his stand against the *Apristas*.[31] In an attempt to prevent any further violence, the president then assigned the armed forces the task of supervising the upcoming congressional by-elections scheduled for 30 June.[32]

"Wealthy and influential reactionaries" who were convinced that the *Apristas* would win a majority of the four senate and fifteen Chamber of Deputies seats at stake in the elections offered their support to General Rodríguez if he would lead a *coup d'état* against the Bustamante government in June.[33] But Rodríguez remained loyal to the government, and the elections were conducted without any major incidents. *Apristas* won nine seats in the Chamber of Deputies and two in the senate, and thus strengthened their position in congress. This success did not quiet the violence, however, as in early December an assassination attempt was made against Rodríguez by terrorists who tried to bomb his home in the Lima suburb of San Isidro. APRA claimed that its political enemies were responsible for the act, because they sought to instigate government repression against *Apristas*. APRA's claim was supported by an anonymous, non-*Aprista* army lieutenant colonel who told the United States military attaché that Communist Party terrorists, who were fiercely at odds with APRA, were responsible for the attempted bombing.[34]

The APRA-communist rivalry, which centered primarily on the control of the Peruvian labor movement, was encouraged by conservative opponents of APRA, because they preferred the more manageable communists in positions of trade union leadership.[35] The Peruvian Communist Party, which numbered only two thousand members in 1942, had grown to approximately twenty-five thousand by December, 1946.[36] Haya de la Torre attempted to use the issue of growing communist influence and increasingly close ties of communists with right-wing opponents of APRA as a tool to gain stronger support for his party from Washington.

Apristas, in their effort to gain support from the United States, supplied information about communist activities in Peru during late 1946 and 1947. During a conversation with a United States Embassy representative on 29 October 1947, Haya de la Torre claimed that rightist elements under the banner of the *Alianza Nacional* (National Alliance) had close ties with Eudocio Ravines, whom the APRA leader claimed was the "No. 1 Moscow representative in Peru." He also insisted that communists had gained a strong foothold within the Bustamante government and suggested that the United States government find a way of expressing to members of the Bustamante regime "its concern at the drift away from democratic methods and at the similarity of the communist line with that of the *Alianza Nacional* which now appears to dominate the government."[37] Seemingly as a show of good faith concerning APRA's anti-communist position, Haya de la Torre claimed that he would like to reestablish the liaison that he had previously held with the United States Federal Bureau of Investigation. The APRA chief also stated that he wished a similar relationship could be set up with a representative of the embassy who could, by maintaining contact with leading *Apristas*, follow up the frequent communist "leads" that the party uncovered in its regular activities.[38]

Haya de la Torre's bold effort to seek the support of the United States in 1947 by stressing APRA's anticommunism was in part a reaction to the growing strength of the civilian and military opposition to APRA. During the next twelve months this opposition would solidify as a controversial foreign petroleum contract, the assassination of a prominent and outspoken critic of APRA, and intensified political unrest all contributed to the unification of anti-APRA elements.

In early 1946 President Bustamante, seeking to increase the nation's petroleum production in the midst of serious economic difficulties, signed a contract with the International Petroleum Company (IPC), a subsidiary of Standard Oil, for an exploration concession in the Sechura desert in northern Peru.[39] IPC, which produced the vast majority of Peru's petroleum and natural gas, had been the subject of nationalist controversy ever since its initial operations in the 1920s. During mid-1946 both wealthy capitalists and economic nationalists denounced the Sechura contract as a "giveaway."[40] Nevertheless, the contract was approved by the Chamber of Deputies on 8 June 1946 with the wholehearted support of APRA. Referring to the contract, Haya de la Torre stated that expanded IPC operations would "facilitate social and economic betterment" in Peru.[41]

Final congressional approval of the petroleum contract was blocked, however, by the refusal of conservative senators to pass the measure in the upper chamber. Debate over this issue continued throughout 1946, while APRA became the target of increasingly harsh criticism from the two conservative newspapers, which portrayed the party as the betrayer of the national interest.[42]

In the forefront of the attacks on APRA was conservative businessman and associate editor of *La Prensa*, Francisco Graña Garland. On the night of 7 January 1947 Graña Garland was assassinated as he was leaving his pharmaceutical firm in downtown Lima. The crime touched off an immediate political crisis, and Bustamante's entire cabinet, including three APRA ministers who had served since January, 1946, quickly resigned.[43] Despite the denials by APRA leaders that their party was involved in any way with the Graña murder, the opposition immediately linked *Apristas* to the crime. Bustamante, facing the most crucial test of his presidential tenure, responded to the crisis by naming powerful military figures to his new cabinet on 12 January.

Named as minister of government and police and placed in charge of the Graña investigation was General Manuel A. Odría, who was one of the staunchest anti-*APRA* officers in the army. Odría was born in Tarma, in central Peru, on 26 November 1897 into a relatively prosperous family. His grandfather was an officer in the Peruvian army who distinguished himself in a brief confrontation with invading Spanish forces in May, 1866. Following in the footsteps of his grandfather, Odría entered the Chorrillos Military Academy in 1915 and graduated at the head of his class. After serving as an instructor at the academy, he attended the *Escuela Superior de Guerra Naval* and was eventually promoted to lieutenant colonel in 1936. He then assumed command of the First Light Division in northern Peru, where he emerged as one of the heroes of the brief border war with Ecuador in 1941. Before being named to Bustamante's cabinet in January, 1947, he was promoted to colonel and then to brigadier general while serving as an instructor at the *Escuela Superior de Guerra Naval*.[44]

Odría was shrewd, politically tough, and a good judge of personalities. Before 1947 he used his close association with General Federico Hurtado (the inspector general of the army and an equally strong anti-*APRA* force in the army) to increase his influence in the high command.[45] His well-known aversion to *Aprista* policies helped Odría emerge as one of the leading spokesmen of the anti-*APRA* element among senior officers. After Bustamante selected Odría to help guide his government through the political crisis, an observer correctly suggested that the president "took upon himself a dangerous counselor, and perhaps his master."[46]

Acting as a counterforce to Odría's influence in the new cabinet was General José del Carmen Marín, who was appointed minister of war. Del Carmen Marín, like Odría, had demonstrated leadership qualities early in his career. He was born in San Miguel de Guayabamba on 2 March 1899 and at the age of eighteen entered the School of Infantry at Chorrillos, where he graduated first in his class. As an army second lieutenant Del Carmen Marín was trained as an engineer. Between 1921 and 1939 he spent two training periods in France, studied engineering, and graduated with honors from the Superior War College in Paris in 1939. During the early 1940s he attained a reputation as one of the leading intellectuals in the army and was also a "recognized mathematician and engineering authority."[47] In late 1943 Del Carmen Marín was named director of the military preparatory school, the *Colegio Militar Leoncio Prado*, and in

October, 1945 he assumed the directorship of the *Escuela Militar de Chorrillos*.[48] As head of these two institutions Del Carmen Marín might have gained substantial prestige among the younger officers of the army. But the United States military attaché reported in 1944 that Del Carmen Marín as "probably the purest-blooded Indian in the Peruvian army," tended to be noncommittal to his colleagues, "from whom he has undoubtedly received social slights in the past."[49] As minister of war in January, 1947, Del Carmen Marín, who was inclined toward moderating tough measures against APRA, represented the party's only hope to check Odría.

Notwithstanding Haya de la Torre's claim that General Del Carmen Marín was one of the party's best friends in the cabinet, Bustamante appeared to be accepting the counsel of Odría and other anti-APRA political elements in the six months following the Graña murder.[50] After replacing the civilian prefect of Arequipa with army Colonel Benjamin Chiarliza Vasquez in early January, the president then received pressure from Odría to remove *Apristas* from other government positions.[51] In the face of this threat to his party, Haya de la Torre still remained confident that the anti-APRA officers would be unable to force the complete repression of the party. He reasoned that such a campaign by anti-APRA senior army officers would be opposed by junior officers who were largely pro-*Aprista*. Additionally, the party chief declared that any attempted *coup* directed against APRA would ignite a civil war since "the great mass of the people would not submit to such a government."[52]

In spite of the APRA leader's confidence, Bustamante clearly indicated the more authoritative stance of his government in a speech on 12 April 1947. He insisted that his administration was ending the "period of appeasement in dealing with disruptive political forces." And in a direct reference to APRA he stated that the prevailing political agitation was due to attempts by political groups to achieve an "unwise and even exclusive predominance in the direction of the national affairs.[53] Bustamante also called upon the armed forces to adopt a nonpolitical position regarding the solution of the Graña murder and related political controversy.[54] But the actions of senior officers in the month following his address illustrated the unrealistic nature of this request.

Three days after the president's speech a delegation of high-ranking officers of the three armed services, along with the director general of the national police, met with Bustamante to express their support for the firm tone of his address.[55] But General Odría was still not satisfied that the government was taking strong enough measures to deal with APRA. Consequently, during the first week in May he threatened to resign his cabinet post if he were not allowed to have a free hand in purging *Apristas* from their positions as prefects and subprefects in a number of departments throughout Peru. Bustamante bent to the pressure from his minister of government, and Gerardo Bedoya, the *Aprista* prefect of the department of Junin, was quickly replaced. Plans were then made to appoint army officers to the prefect posts at Callao, Trujillo, and Puno and a naval officer to the prefecture at Ica.[56] Meanwhile Haya de la Torre responded to these measures by attempting to remove some of the most troublesome army opponents of APRA who were immediate threats to his party.

Exploiting his good relations with the United States diplomatic delegation in Peru, Haya de la Torre, during an interview with Maurice J. Broderick, third secretary of the United States Embassy, requested that the United States invite General Alejandro Villalobos, commanding general of the Armored Division, Colonel César Pando Esgusquiza, and Lieutenant Colonel Alfonso Llosa on a training mission to the United States along with ten other army officers.[57] Haya de la Torre's stated purpose for this request was that he hoped these officers would benefit from viewing "democratic processes" at work in the United States. Broderick, however, suggested that the political expediency of removing these officers from Peru for an extended period of time was clearly at the root of APRA's request. The United States diplomat also indicated that a dangerous precedent might be established if his government granted this favor.[58]

The six-month investigation of the Graña killing culminated in mid-June with the arrest of two *Apristas*, Alfredo Tello Salavarria (a member of the Chamber of Deputies) and Hector Pretell Cobosmalon, who were charged with assassinating Graña.[59] As with many other cases of political terrorism attributed to APRA before 1947, party leaders denied the validity of the government's charges. Tello, in an open letter to Bustamante, insisted upon his innocence and charged the police were intent upon persecuting *Apristas*.[60] Tello and Pretell were never brought to trial during the Bustamante regime and were eventually found guilty only after a protracted legal process that ended in December, 1949 with their being sentenced to long prison terms.[61] Following the arrest of the two *Apristas*, civilian political opposition to APRA united under the leadership of Pedro Beltrán, editor of *La Prensa*, and Hector Boza, a conservative leader in the senate. These two men were the most influential members of the *Alianza Nacional*, a coalition of rightist groups and other political opponents of APRA, formed during early 1947.

As the strength of the *Alianza Nacional* grew, a United States official observed in late June, 1947 that there was "little doubt that the more intransigent among the conservatives favor turning the government over to a military group which would ruthlessly attempt to destroy the *Aprista* party."[62] But it was in the senate, under Boza's leadership, that conservatives launched their first coordinated effort to undermine the political power base of *APRA*.

Boza, as the leader of a bloc of twenty-two conservative senators opposed to APRA, organized a boycott of the senate session beginning on 28 July 1947. According to the Peruvian constitution, the senate could not conduct a legislative session until its executive officers had been elected. For this election to occur, two-thirds of the senate membership had to be in attendance. The government charter prohibited the Chamber of Deputies from conducting business without a simultaneous session of the senate. Thus Boza and his twenty-one colleagues prevented the nineteen *Aprista* senators and their five *Frente Democrático Nacional* sympathizers from convening the congress, because a quorum could not be achieved to elect senate officers.[63] The conservative senators were, of course, aiming to use the senate boycott to cripple the principal source of APRA's national power. This tactic proved effective, but it plunged the Bustamante regime into a political crisis from which it never recovered.

At first, APRA leaders tried negotiation and legal arguments to end the political impasse. On 14 August, APRA senator Ramiro Prialé approached Boza in an effort to arrive at a compromise solution with the dissenting members.[64] During the same week the minister of war, General Del Carmen Marín, arranged a meeting at the French Embassy between Haya de la Torre and Pedro Beltrán.[65] Del Carmen Marín also made an appeal for armed forces support for the Bustamante regime at the same time. But these efforts at mediation proved fruitless. APRA leaders then charged that the senate boycott was clearly in violation of the constitution and that the dissident senators were breaking the law by their calculated absence from the senate chamber.[66] When these arguments also proved to be of no avail, party leaders turned to direct action to force the hand of their conservative opponents.

On 28 August, APRA leaders called a general strike in Lima and Callao, which was implemented by the *Aprista*-dominated Workers Syndical Union.[67] The strike was organized in an effort to break the stalemate in congress and force the resignation of the Bustamante cabinet dominated by General Odría. On 1 September, after serious student rioting in Lima, the president suspended civil liberties for thirty days.[68] Bustamante, elected on a political platform that most heavily emphasized his commitment to defend basic human rights, was pressured to take this firm step by General Odría.[69]

The tense climate promoted by the general strike and the suspension of constitutional guarantees contributed to a serious confrontation between navy enlisted men and army troops aiding municipal police in Callao during the last week of September. Instigated by a clash between a sailor and a policeman over a streetcar fare, a riot involving naval enlisted men stationed at the port city of Callao against elements of the Thirty-ninth Infantry Regiment broke out on 21 September.[70] The incident reflected the tensions building in the navy and the armed forces in general regarding the worsening political situation and the political polarization of the nation's military leadership.[71]

During the last three months of 1947 the officer corps, mirroring the divisions in the civilian body politic, became further divided over the issue of Bustamante's increasing reliance on rightist military and civilian supporters. Leading anti-*Apristas* were army generals Manuel Odría, Federico Hurtado, Alejandro Villalobos, Zenon Noriega, and Armando Artola. In the navy, Admiral Roque A. Saldías (who had earlier clashed with APRA on the promotion issue) was the primary anti-APRA figure.[72] Although General Juan de Dios Cuadros, who commanded the Second Light Division in Lima, was the only general officer in the army who was willing to cooperate with APRA against the officers who sought the party's destruction.[73] Although General Del Carmen Marín was not willing to commit himself regarding support for the party during his tenure as minister of war, he was later to contact party leaders regarding an antigovernment revolutionary movement.

On 18 October 1947, anti-APRA senior officers, disturbed by continuing labor strife and the unwillingness of the president to take even stronger measures against APRA, demanded a meeting with Bustamante. With Generals Odría and Hurtado and Admiral Saldías as their leading spokesmen, the delegation issued a virtual ultimatum to the president either to assume a stronger role as chief executive or to step down and turn the government over to a military *Junta*. Bustamante's only response was that he needed more time to work out a solution for the problems besetting the nation.[74] Within two weeks, the president reorganized his cabinet, which had served since the week following the Graña assassination.[75] Saldías was named the president of the new cabinet and replaced Admiral José R. Alzamora. General Odría was retained as minister of government and police and his anti-APRA colleague, General Armando Artola, was designated minister of justice and labor. General Del Carmen Marín, who was still assuming a cautious political stance, was renamed to his post as head of the Ministry of War.[76]

By mid-November, 1947 APRA leaders, facing a primarily hostile cabinet, a congressional impasse that effectively negated their national political power, and the prospect of President Bustamante's ruling by decree in the absence of a functioning legislature, began laying plans for the overthrow of the president. Haya de la Torre adopted a flexible approach toward the revolutionary preparations. He allowed militant civilian and military activists within the party to prepare the groundwork for a widespread popular insurrection. At the same time he sought the support of a few senior officers in the army for a simple *coup d'état* aimed at deposing the president in order that new elections could be held in which APRA hoped to gain a more firm hold on national power.[77] The APRA leader's hope for a simple *coup* rested with the ability of Generals Del Carmen Marín and Cuadros to organize support for the plot among the high command. But meanwhile, party militants were progressing much more rapidly in organizing popular support for their cause.

Soon after Major Víctor Villanueva returned from the United States on 15 November 1947, he began organizational work with civilian and military APRA adherents in an effort to raise money, acquire arms, and coordinate plans for a popular revolt.[78] During the last two months of 1946, Villanueva and other APRA militants sought out the support of the rank-and-file of the armed forces in addition to that of the traditionally politically active junior officers. But, in contrast to the high degree of support for APRA and its proposed revolutionary effort among junior army officers, the rank-and-file soldier viewed revolutionary politics with indifference.

The vast majority of army troops were Indian conscripts from the *sierra* who had been drafted into the army with little formal education or interest in national political issues. Since the nineteenth century, Indians had been forcibly conscripted into the army, often by simply loading those without proper identification on army trucks and transporting them to the local barracks. This practice was the primary method of recruitment during the Ecuador war and would continue through the 1970s. The disruption of families and the harsh treatment these Indian recruits suffered at the hands of their officers created a legacy of fear and resentment toward the army that was only partially overcome by the vocational and literacy training that a two-year stint in the army offered *sierra campesinos*.[79] Most of these army recruits thus lacked the political commitment to become involved in a revolutionary campaign.[80] It is understandable that these soldiers would lack the militancy of other armed forces personnel who were more acutely attuned to fundamental political, social, and professional issues. APRA leaders nevertheless attempted to gain the support of some army enlisted men by sponsoring legislation aimed at improving their economic condition. One such example of this legislation was a bill introduced during a January, 1947 session of congress that proposed the establishment of a series of grades for army mechanics that would have raised the pay of top mechanics to the level of an army second lieutenant.[81] Measures such as these, however, directly affected only a very small number of soldiers and seemed to have little impact on the political allegiance of these men. *Apristas* had greater success in gaining adherents among the air force and police ranks, while the greatest number of converts came from among the ranks of navy enlisted men.

The Peruvian navy, numbering 443 officers and 4,370 enlisted men in June, 1947, remained relatively free from political subversion during the twentieth century.[82] The important exception to this trend was the *Aprista*-inspired mutiny of noncommissioned officers of the cruisers *Almirante Grau* and *Colonel Bolognesi* in May, 1932. Thirteen years later in August, 1945, APRA leaders had the remains of the eight sailors executed by the Sánchez Cerro regime moved from their original graves on the prison island of San Lorenzo for reburial in a Lima cemetery.[83] The accompanying ceremony hailed the sailors as "martyrs" to the APRA cause and signaled the party's willingness to acknowledge publicly the support of navy enlisted men in party revolutionary activities. It also angered military leaders who felt the government should not have allowed a demonstration that glorified *Aprista* success in subverting military personnel.[84]

The August, 1945 ceremony indicated that APRA recognized the sharp divisions existing in the navy between officers and enlisted men and was intent upon exploiting this schism. The factors contributing to this polarization were both social and professional. Most of the officers in the navy were from financially secure families, and family ties were often an important qualification for admittance into the *Escuela Naval*. In contrast to the naval officer class, most of the navy enlisted men were ill-educated draftees. A lack of adequate funding for the proper technical training of navy enlisted men also served to lower their morale and further alienate them from their officers.[85] The confrontation with army troops and police involving navy enlisted men in Callao during late September illustrated the belligerent mood of the sailors at the time APRA was making its appeal for revolutionary support. The party would enjoy its greatest organizational success among the disaffected naval enlisted men during the next eight months.

Aiding Major Villanueva with his organizational efforts during the last two months of 1947 were militant party activists called *Defensistas*. These men had served in the party's "Defense Brigades" as shock troops during the years of *Aprista* revolutionary activity after 1930. Most of the *Defensistas* were veterans of a number of insurrections, and the vast majority had suffered imprisonment and torture during the years before 1945.[86] Principal figures among the *Defensistas* were Luis Chanduvi, Carlos Collantes, Víctor Colina, Amadeo Varillas, and Julio Luzquinos, all of whom worked closely with Villanueva to organize a cadre of approximately five hundred civilian followers.[87]

The party leadership viewed the *Defensistas* as a necessary but potentially volatile element in APRA quest for power. Party discipline, which was strictly maintained throughout the years of APRA's illegality, demanded that these militants remain completely subservient to the orders of Haya de la Torre and the party's Executive Committee. But as Haya de la Torre vacillated during late 1947 regarding the course that the party should take in terminating the Bustamante regime, relations between the militant wing of the APRA and the party leadership began to become severely strained.

During the last three days of 1947, Haya de la Torre added to the growing tension between the party leadership and the *Defensistas* by ordering Luis Barrios Llona (the APRA chief's aide) to organize a civil-military insurrection in Arequipa aimed at toppling Bustamante. Very little organizational work had been done in that southern Peruvian city by party activists, and the possibility of gaining recruits for an antigovernment revolt was small. Nevertheless, Haya de la Torre stressed the symbolic impact of beginning a revolution in Bustamante's native city and claimed the conduct of the revolt would be easy. After only a few days in Arequipa, Barrios sent a coded message to APRA leaders in Lima that conditions did not exist for a successful revolution to be initiated in that city.[88] Villanueva and other party activists, although deeply troubled by the lack of coordination between their operations and the overall objectives of the party leadership, went ahead with plans to launch a widespread civil-military revolt during the first two months of 1948.

Thus, less than eighteen months after President Bustamante had assumed the presidency with APRA support and the approval of the nation's armed forces, political factionalism within the military and civilian body politic rendered his civilian regime politically impotent and ripe for forceful overthrow. The first ten months of 1948 would witness the violent culmination of these struggles with the most serious armed forces discipline crisis since the early 1930s.

NOTES

1. *Peruvian Times*, 16 February, 1947, p. 29.
2. Ibid., 8 August 1947, cover page.
3. Revista Militar del Perú, 43, no. 2 (November, 1946). This entire issue of the RMP was devoted to commemorating the French mission.
4. G-2 Report no. 202039, 27 August 1945, U.S. military attaché to War Department, NA, RG 319. Full information on this document is given in note 2 in Chapter 3.
5. Ibid.
6. G-2 Report no. 5940, 28 February 1944, U.S. military attaché to War Department, NA, RG 165.
7. John Steward Ambler, *The French Army in Politics, 1945-1962* (Columbus, Ohio: 1966), p. 57.
8. Ibid.
9. Lieutenant Colonel César A. Pando Esguisquiza, "¿El ejército, es improductivo?" *RMP*, 43, no. 8 (August, 1946), p. 387.
10. Ibid.
11. Ibid., p. 391.
12. See Lieutenant Colonel Manuel Morla Concha, "La función social del ejército peruano en la organización de la nacionalidad," *RMP*, 30, no. 10 (October, 1933), pp. 843-872. In 1904 the role of the military man as an educator was discussed by Lieutenant Colonel Gabriel Velarde Alvarez in an article in the *Boletín del Ministerio de Guerra y Marina* entitled, "Instrucción civil del soldado," BMGM, 1 (October, 1904), pp. 843-845. Subsequent articles dealing with the social aspects of the military career appeared intermittently during the following three decades. These articles are analyzed in Frederick M. Nunn, *Yesterday's Soldiers: European Military Professionalism in South America, 1890-1940* (Lincoln, Nebraska: 1983), pp. 276-284.
13. Oscar N. Torres, "La instrucción militar en las universidades y las escuelas superiores," *RMP* 37, no. 7 (July, 1940), pp. 369-402. For a discussion of Prado's Indian program see Thomas M. Davies, Jr., *Indian Integration in Peru: A Half Century of Experience, 1900-1948* (Lincoln, Nebraska: 1974), pp. 136-137.
14. Chirinos Soto, *El Perú frente a junio de 1962* (Lima: 1962), p. 65.
15. Ibid.; and *Peruvian Times*, 3 August 1945, p. 1.
16. *Legislación Militar del Perú*, August, 1945, pp. 87-88.
17. Ibid.
18. Ambassador William D. Pawley to Sec/State, 27 October 1945, NA, RG 59, 823.00/10-2745.
19. Ibid.
20. Pawley to Sec/State, 20 March 1946, NA, RG 59, 823.00/3-2046.
21. Charge d'Affaires Walter J. Donnelly to Sec/State, 16 April 1946, NA, RG 59, 823.00/4-1646.
22. Pawley to Sec/State, 20 March 1946, NA, RG 59, 823.00/3-2046.
23. Ackerson to Sec/State, 2 October 1947, NA, RG 59, 823.00/10-247.
24. Víctor Villanueva Valencia, *La sublevación aprista del 48: Tragedia de pueblo y un partido* (Lima: 1973), pp. 33-35. Major Villanueva was released from prison under the terms of the general amnesty of July, 1945.

25. Legislación Militar del Perú, August, 1946, pp. 19-20; Víctor Villanueva Valencia, El CAEM y la revolución de la fuerza Armada (Lima: 1973), pp. 28-29. A ley orgánico del ejército, or basic organizational law of the army, did not exist in 1945, and the commission was charged with writing such a law. Also the law of obligatory military service was written in 1895 and was badly outmoded.

26. Villanueva, La sublevación aprista, p. 35.

27. G-2 Report no. 36812, 8 May 1947, U.S. military attaché to Department of the Army, NA, RG 319.

28. Pawley to Sec/State, 11 December 1945, NA, RG 59, 823.00/12-1145.

29. Counselor of the Embassy Edward G. Trueblood to Sec/State, 7 December 1945, NA, RG 59, 823.00/12-745.

30. Pawley to Sec/State, 16 April 1946, NA, RG 59, 823.00/4-1646.

31. Peruvian Times, 10 May 1946, p. 2; Pawley to Sec/State, 6 May 1946, NA, RG 59, 823.00/5-646.

32. Donnelly to Sec/State, 21 June 1946, NA, RG 59, 823.00/6-2146.

33. Ibid., 25 June 1946, NA, RG 59, 823.00/6-2546.

34. La Tribuna, 3 July 1946, p. 1; The New York Times, 30 December 1946, p. 5; Ambassador Prentice Cooper to Sec/State, 9 August 1946, NA, RG 59, 823.00/8-946. APRA now controlled sixty-five of the 132 seats in the Chamber of Deputies and twenty of the forty-seven seats in the Senate.

35. See Grant Hilliker, The Politics of Reform in Peru: The Aprista and Other Mass Parties of Latin America (Baltimore: 1971), pp. 117-118.

36. The New York Times, 30 December 1946, p. 5.

37. Cooper to Sec/State, 11 November 1947, NA, RG 59, 823.00/11-347. Ambassador Cooper was reporting on the content of a conversation between Haya de la Torre and embassy official Maurice J. Broderick.

38. Ibid.

39. Peruvian Times, 15 March 1946, p. 2, and José Luis Bustamante Rivero, Tres años de la lucha por la demócracia en el Perú, (Buenos Aires: 1949) pp. 89-107 passim.

40. Fredrick Pike, The Modern History of Peru (New York: 1967), p. 285.

41. Peruvian Times, 15 March 1947, p. 1; The New York Times, 30 October 1946, p. 15.

42. See the political flier, "El gran negociado petróleo de Sechura," Colección de Volantes, 1947 folder, for charges that APRA was in league with United States business interests to betray the country's just claim to its natural resources. The ebb and flow of the senate debates concerning the Sechura contract can be followed in the Diario de los Debates del Senado Legislativo Extraordinario de 1946, 2, pp. 813-969 and 1355-1380.

43. El Comercio, 9 January 1947, p. 3; Chirinos Soto, El Perú frente, p. 73; "Retiro sus ministros el Aprismo," Colección de Volantes, 8 January 1947.

44. Anonymous, "El General de Brigada D. Manuel A. Odría, Presidente de la Junta Militar de Gobierno," RMP, 45, no. 10 (October, 1948), pp. 5-8.

45. Cooper to Sec/State, 30 October 1947, NA, RG 59, 823.00/10-3047.

46. Ibid., 16 September 1947, NA, RG 59, 823.00/9-1647.

47. G-2 Report no. 353, 2 February 1944, U.S. military attaché to War Department, NA, RG 319; anonymous, "General D. José del Carmen Marín, Nuevo Ministro de Guerra," RMP, 41, no. 1 (January, 1947), pp. 1-4.

48. Ibid.

49. G-2 Report no. 353, 2 February 1944, U.S. military attaché to War Department, NA, RG 319.

50. Cooper to Sec/State, 2 February 1947, NA, RG 59, 823.00/2-247. Haya de la Torre also warned the U.S. ambassador that Odría was capable of engineering a *coup* against Bustamante in the near future.

51. *The New York Times*, 13 January 1947, p. 4; Cooper to Sec/State, 12 May 1947, NA, RG 59, 823.00/5-1247.

52. Donnelly to Sec/State, 3 February 1947, NA, RG 59, 823.00/2-347.

53. *Peruvian Times*, 18 April 1947, p. 1.

54. Ibid.

55. Ibid.; Cooper to Sec/State, 18 April 1947, NA, RG 59, 823.00/4-1847.

56. Cooper to Sec/State, 19 May 1947, NA, RG 59, 823.00/5-1947.

57. Third Secretary Maurice J. Broderick to Sec/State, 23 May 1947, NA, RG 59, 823.00/5-2347.

58. Ibid.

59. *The New York Times*, 21 June 1947, p. 6.

60. "Carta abierta del Diputado Tello al Presidente de la Republica," *Colección de Volantes*, 17 June 1947. See also Luis Alberto Sánchez, *Haya de la Torre y el Apra*, (Santiago: 1955) pp. 422-426.

61. *The New York Times*, 7 December 1949, p. 16.

62. Ackerman to Sec/State, 23 June 1947, NA, RG 59, 823.00/6-2347.

63. *Peruvian Times*, 15 August 1947, p. 1.

64. Ibid.

65. Cooper to Sec/State, 18 August 1947, NA, RG 59, 823.00/8-1847.

66. See Célula Parlamentaria Aprista, *La Constitución del Estado y el Receso de las Camaras Legislativas* (Lima: 1947) for the APRA position on the senate boycott.

67. *Peruvian Times*, 5 September 1947, p. l.

68. Cooper to Sec/State, 19 May 1947, NA, RG 59, 823.00/5-1947.

69. Cooper to Sec/State, 16 September 1947, NA, RG 59, 823.00/9-1647. Ambassador Cooper reported that Odría and other "ultra-conservative" political elements led by the former Peruvian ambassador to the United States, Pedro Beltrán, pushed Bustamante to take this action.

70. *Peruvian Times*, 26 September 1947, Supplement 1; Cooper to Sec/State, 25 September 1947, NA, RG 59, 823.00/9-2547.

71. *Peruvian Times*, 26 September 1947, Supplement 1.

72. Villanueva, *La sublevación aprista*, p. 48; Cooper to Sec/State, 30 October 1947, NA, RG 59, 823.00/10-3047.

73. Villanueva, *La sublevación aprista*, pp. 46-47.

74. Cooper to Sec/State, 30 October 1947, NA, RG 59, 823.00/10-3047.

75. *Peruvian Times*, 2 November 1947, p. 2; *The New York Times*, 1 November 1947, p. 8.

76. *Peruvian Times*, 2 November 1947, p. 2.

77. Villanueva, La sublevación aprista, pp. 39-47. This is Major Villanueva's personal account of his revolutionary activities during the 1940s, and it provides some invaluable insights into the relationship of military and civilian revolutionaries with the APRA leadership.

78. Ibid., pp. 52-56.

79. G-2 Report no. 202039, 27 August 1945, U.S. military attaché to War Department, NA, RG 319; Villanueva, *La sublevación aprista*, p. 56; the Harry

Hopkins Papers, Box 143, Franklin D. Roosevelt Library; personal interview with Father Robert Hoffman, Chicago, Illinois, 10 June 1989. Father Hoffman, a Maryknoll priest who served in the southern *sierra* near Puno for nine years in the late 1970s and early 1980s, commented on the army's forcible recruitment practices and claimed that local Indians would often seek sanctuary in churches from the army's "press gangs."

80. Personal interview with Víctor Villanueva Valencia, 27 July 1974, Lima, Peru.

81. Cooper to Sec/State, 3 February 1947, NA, RG 59, 823.00/2-347.

82. G-2 Report no. 385333, 30 June 1947, U.S. military attaché to Department of the Army, NA, RG 319.

83. *Peruvian Times*, 7 September 1945, Supplement 1.

84. Víctor Villanueva Valencia, *100 años del ejército peruano: Frustraciones y cambios* (Lima: 1971), pp. 129-130.

85. G-2 Report no. 385333, 30 June 1947, U.S. military attaché to Department of the Army, NA, RG 319.

86. Personal interview with Víctor Villanueva Valencia, 27 July 1974, Lima, Peru; Villanueva, *La sublevación aprista*, p. 44.

87. Villanueva, *La sublevación aprista*, p. 44.

88. Ibid., pp. 67-68.

5
Rebellion and Reaction: 1948

The first ten months of 1948 witnessed the most intense political unrest since the Sánchez Cerro era. During this period one conspiracy and two abortive revolts severely undermined President Bustamante's remaining support and opened the way for the *coup d'état* of General Manuel Odría in late October. The violence and political tension of these months resulted from *Aprista* success in subverting both senior army officers and naval personnel as part of the party's campaign to seize complete political control of the nation. Also contributing to the political instability were the efforts of rightist civilians and anti-APRA armed forces officers to combat these *Aprista* tactics and ultimately to topple Bustamante so they could completely crush the APRA. The most active militants during this ten-month period were Major Víctor Villanueva and his *Defensista* allies who were involved in two of the four civil-military movements.

Throughout January, 1948, dissident armed forces personnel and *Aprista* militants led by Villanueva consolidated support for a proposed civil-military insurrection they hoped would ignite a popular revolution against the Bustamante government. Villanueva and his *Defensista* allies managed to subvert a large number of naval enlisted personnel and, to a lesser extent, police and junior air force officers stationed at the Las Palmas air field near Lima.[1] In late January, before leaving on a lecture tour in the United States, APRA chief Haya de la Torre gave Villanueva his approval to finalize plans for the revolt. Leading figures in the conspiracy, besides Villanueva, were General Juan de Dios Cuadros, air force Colonel José Extremadoyro Navarro, and the APRA's Action Committee, led by Ramiro Prialé, Carlos Manuel Cox, and Jorge Idiáquez.[2]

The general plan for the insurrection called for naval, air force, and police units to seize strategic military and communications facilities in the Lima and Callao area, while APRA rebels aided in the neutralization of the army's armored units headed by the anti-*Aprista* Colonel Alejandro Villalobos. Once these objectives had been accomplished, it was expected that Bustamante, deprived of his critical military support in Lima, would capitulate. The conspirators then planned to establish a transitional revolutionary *Junta* to be headed by General Cuadros. He would be given the primary task of calling new elections aimed at giving APRA full claim to national political power.[3]

On 31 January Villanueva reported to members of the Action Committee that the civil-military units under his command were ready to initiate the revolt. But General Cuadros and APRA leaders Luis Alberto Sánchez and Manuel Seoane voiced their opposition to the timing of the insurrection. Seoane and Sánchez maintained that since the Bustamante government was in the throes of an economic crisis, prompted by acute food shortages and serious inflation, the revolt should be postponed until these economic problems reached a "climax." Cuadros also insisted that the military situation was not yet favorable for the launching of the insurrection. Thus, APRA leaders rejected Villanueva's argument that the revolt had to be launched within a week if it were to have any chance of success.[4]

After being rebuffed by the APRA leadership, the conspirators decided to lead the revolt on their own. Contributing heavily to this decision was the fact that many of the subverted armed forces personnel scheduled to play key roles in the movement would be shifted from their posts due to the general transfers scheduled to take place in February.[5] On the night of 6 February the planned revolt was initiated, but almost immediately APRA leaders learned of the move and issued counterorders temporarily immobilizing key rebel units. The inspector general of the army and the minister of war quickly reacted to the rebel activity by confining all troops to their barracks and ordering the occupation of the strategic Central Telephone Exchange in downtown Lima. The insurrection was thus quickly aborted in its initial stage with no loss of life and few arrests.[6]

Apparently hoping to avoid worsening tensions within the military at the time of the abortive insurrection, armed forces leaders adopted a restrained approach to their handling of the identified conspirators. No public acknowledgement of the movement was made until 12 February, when the newspaper *El Callao* carried a general account of the insurrection and the subsequent arrest of nine air force officers, along with an army captain and a police lieutenant. Major Villanueva and Colonel Extremadoyro were also mentioned in connection with the plot.[7] Neither officer was detained by the police, however, and Minister of War Del Carmen Marín issued a communiqué that labeled the El Callao story "absolutely false and tendentious." He claimed that it was not the armed institutions that were responsible for the grave political crisis of that present moment, but that on the contrary it was the "meritorious and patriotic attitude" of the military that stood in opposition to those who disrupted public order.[8] On the same day the communiqué was released, Jornada reported on the conspiracy but claimed it was of "only minor importance" and involved a "disorderly scandal promoted by discredited persons."[9]

Despite the failure of the 6 February conspiracy and the resulting discouragement among Aprista military and civilian activists, the party continued its violent anti-government tactics. On 16 February, the civilian prefect of Cerro de Pasco, Francisco Tovar Belmont, was assassinated by a mob led by APRA party members Mercedes Aguero, Atilio Leon, and Pablo Chavez.[10] The minister of government, Odría, immediately placed the blame for the murder on the APRA party leadership and ordered army Colonel Emilio Pereyra to assume military control of the Cerro de Pasco district. Immediately after the Tovar Belmont assassination, Odría and Admiral Rocque Saldías demanded that President Bustamante outlaw APRA. When Bustamante refused to accede to the anti-APRA officers' demands, a serious cabinet crisis ensued.

Although Bustamante remained firm in his refusal to declare APRA illegal, the anti-APRA faction of the armed forces leadership unquestionably dominated a new all-military cabinet named by the president on 27 February. Minister of War Del Carmen Marín, who failed to take decisive action against the military personnel in the abortive revolt in early February, was replaced by Odría's close associate, General Armando Artola. Odría was retained as minister of government and police, and Admiral Saldías was named prime minister in a government now almost totally dominated by rightist armed forces officers.[11] In addition to the cabinet shuffle, the transfer of General Cuadros from the command of the strategically important Second Light Division in Lima to the Superior Council of the Army in late February deprived APRA of its most prominent potential ally in the army. Cuadros lost his troop command to General Zenon Noriega, who later supported Odría's seizure of power in late October. With the shift of Del Carmen Marín and Cuadros from influential command positions to relatively powerless advisory roles (Del Carmen Marín was slated to become director of the proposed Center of Higher Military Studies), the anti-APRA armed forces faction now dominated the cabinet as well as the key military command positions in the Lima regions.   Colonel Alejandro Villalobos held both the post of minister of justice and the command of the army's armored division.[12] Thus the abortive revolt of 6 February, while evoking a relatively mild response by the armed forces hierarchy, did have important repercussions after the anti-APRA clique asserted its power.   Moreover, the indecision of the APRA leadership's attitude toward the party's militant wing foreshadowed deep divisions within Aprista ranks that would doom a more concerted revolutionary movement in October, 1948.

Reflecting the pressure from his new cabinet to take a firmer line against APRA, Bustamante lashed out during a national radio broadcast of 29 February against the "irresponsible" tactics employed by Aprista leaders to foster "discontent."   One week later the president abolished the local municipal councils that had been established at the beginning of his term and had come under the control of APRA in many areas throughout the nation.[13]   As a result, the political situation by 1 April found APRA isolated and the government dominated by Odría and Saldías, with Bustamante desperately holding on to power.[14]   Still, the chief executive, who had lost most of his power through his increasing dependence upon conservative armed forces officers, refused to make the final break with APRA by declaring the party illegal.   This refusal may be explained by Bustamante's strong commitment to constitutional government and his continued hope that APRA would moderate its policies in the face of increased pressure from the military.

Undaunted by Bustamante's refusal, between the beginning of April and mid-June, Saldías and Odría intensified their demands that the president proscribe APRA in order to end the party's continuing subversive activities within the armed forces officer corps.   The two men may have been aware that General Del Carmen Marín, soon after he was removed from his post as minister of war, approached APRA leaders and offered his services in support of their efforts to overthrow Bustamante.[15]   Although the sincerity of Del Carmen Marín's offer was questioned by many Apristas, including Major Villanueva, Haya de la Torre considered the former minister of war to be a valuable check against the anti-APRA campaign of the Odría-Saldías clique.[16]

On 17 June, after Bustamante once again rejected the proposal by a majority of his ministers that APRA be outlawed, the entire cabinet resigned.   General Odría was then replaced as minister of government and police by Dr. Julio Cesar Villegas and Saldías relinquished his post to air force General Armando Revorado.[17]

Soon after General Odría lost the showdown with Bustamante over the question of outlawing APRA, he made plans to lead a revolt and establish a military government with himself as provisional president. Lieutenant Colonel Alfonso Llosa, commander of the army garrison at Juliaca in southern Peru, was selected to initiate the movement by seizing the army posts at Cuzco, Juliaca, and Puno. Llosa had been involved in numerous conspiracies throughout his military career and was labeled "the longtime bad boy of the army."[18] As a bitter foe of APRA, Llosa had been transferred to the Juliaca region after his armed attack on the office of the party newspaper, *La Tribuna*, in September, 1947.[19] Also involved in the conspiracy to oust Bustamante were Colonel Alejandro Villalobos, still in command of the armored division in Lima; General Zenon Noriega, chief of the Second Light Division in the capital; Colonel Felix Huaman, who headed the Chorrillos Military School; eight army officers stationed in the Juliaca and Puno regions; and the Miró-Quesada family, which backed the movement with the expectation that the resulting military government would liquidate APRA.[20]

The general plan of the revolt called for Llosa to gain control of the Cuzco, Juliaca, and Puno garrisons and arrange for the capture of the commander of the Third Military Region in Arequipa, General Eduardo Castro Rios. In Lima, General Odría would lead the *Guardia Republicana*, *Cuerpo Asalto* of the police force, and elements of the Second Light Division into rebellion. Colonel Felix Hauman's role was to assure that the cadets in the Chorrillos Military School did not oppose Odría's forces. Much the same task was assigned to the armored division commander, Colonel Villalobos. His units were to be used only if *Apristas* took to the streets against Odría. The signal for military action to be initiated in Lima would be the spread of the uprising from Juliaca and Puno and the capture of General Castro Rios.[21]

The plans of the conspirators went awry, however, when Llosa launched his phase of the revolt prematurely on the night of 4 July in Juliaca and Puno. After failing to gain any support from other army garrisons, by the afternoon of 6 July Llosa's movement collapsed. Faced with a hopeless situation, Llosa and seven fellow officers involved in the revolt in Juliaca fled to the Bolivian border town of Puerto Acosta on the morning of 7 July. The Bolivian authorities granted the rebel officers political asylum in La Paz.[22] With the flight of these officers the most serious military challenge to the Bustamante government up to that time ended.

Other than Llosa's immediate supporters in the Juliaca and Puno garrisons, the only officer involved in the conspiracy against whom the government took action was Colonel Villalobos. He was replaced in mid-July as chief of the armored division by Colonel José M. Tamayo. General Odría, who applied for retirement from the army in the wake of his resignation from the government in June, continued living quietly at his residence in Lima while he renewed his efforts to organize another anti-government uprising.[23]   In the aftermath of the Llosa uprising, he reportedly claimed: "I do not support revolutions, I start them. Llosa acted prematurely."[24]   After the events of early July, Odría's political influence still remained substantial, a fact made clear when the editor of the newspaper *Vanguardia*, Eudocio Ravines, was arrested after publishing a report that Bustamante's minister of government and police, Julio Cesar Villegas, ordered Odría's detention after the Llosa revolt.[25]

Despite the failure of Llosa's revolt and his apparent effort to upstage Odría and other senior officers involved in the conspiracy, the rebel leader remained in contact with his fellow conspirators from his place of exile in La Paz.   Consequently, between mid-July and the end of October, the threat to Bustamante from the rightist officers who had failed to depose him on 4 July gathered renewed strength.

In the wake of the Llosa revolt, three clearly identifiable elements within the armed forces emerged, all of which were determined to end Bustamante's ineffectual rule. The Odría faction, allied with intensely anti-APRA civilians led by the Miró-Quesada clan, confronted radical junior officers and enlisted men under the leadership of Major Villanueva and navy commander Enrique Aguila Pardo. In the middle ground, General Del Carmen Marín headed a small group of army senior officers who, while favoring the overthrow of the president, advocated a peaceful *golpe de estado* aimed at establishing only a short-term military government.

During early August, Del Carmen Marín approached Haya de la Torre with the plan that if the APRA leadership would cooperate with him and Generals Cuadros and Noriega in a simple *golpe de estado* to depose Bustamante, then *Apristas* would be allowed to participate in the free elections that Del Carmen Marín claimed would subsequently be held.[26] The APRA chief was clearly attracted by Del Carmen Marín's proposal as it seemed to him to represent a less risky path to national power than a broad-based revolutionary movement. Also, Haya de la Torre may have been prompted to welcome the proposed support of the generals because Bustamante had announced his intention to call a convention to revise the constitution as a means of breaking the political impasse created by the continuing senate boycott.   If this tactic were successful, it would strengthen Bustamante's political position, a result that the APRA leader wanted to avoid.[27]

Upon hearing of Del Carmen Marín's overtures to Haya de la Torre, Major Víctor Villanueva and Aguila Pardo expressed doubt about Del Carmen Marín's sincerity. They questioned why he approached APRA only after he was removed as minister of war, when it was exactly that position that would have enabled him to wield the military and political power necessary to depose the president. When August and most of September passed without any action being taken by Del Carmen Marín, APRA militants and disloyal military units decided to initiate the long-postponed revolution that had been in preparation for almost one year.

During the last week of September, army Colonel (R) César Enrique Pardo joined his nephew, navy commander Enrique Aguila Pardo, and Major Víctor Villanueva as leaders of the planned insurrection. The decision was also made not to inform the APRA leadership of the details of the uprising.[28] It is important to note that Haya de la Torre was aware of most activities of the party's militant wing. But because of his reluctance to sanction a full-scale revolt and his apparent willingness to back Del Carmen Marín's plans, the revolt's leaders feared Haya de la Torre or other party leaders might sabotage the insurrection.[29] Undoubtedly, Haya de la Torre hoped to hold the APRA activists in reserve in case his plans with Del Carmen Marín fell through and a full-scale uprising was the party's only means of achieving power. But pressure to act from the revolutionary cells within the ranks of navy enlisted men and the refusal of the revolt's leaders to accept the strategy of Haya de la Torre set the stage for the rebellion, which centered in Lima's port city of Callao on 3 October.[30]

The basic plan called for rebellious naval units to begin the action in the early morning hours of 3 October. Sailors aboard the cruiser *Almirante Grau*, under the command of Aguila Pardo, would initiate the attack by shelling the barracks of the army's Thirty-ninth Infantry Battalion in Callao. The main targets of the rebels were the Chorrillos Military Academy, the Naval Academy and Naval Arsenal in Callao, the fortress and arsenal of *Real Felipe*, and the Central Telephone Exchange in downtown Lima. Designated to lead the action in Callao, along with commander Aguila Pardo, were navy lieutenants Juan F. Ontaneda and Víctor Romero, who were specifically ordered to take the Chorrillos Military Academy. Navy commander José Mosto's task was to capture the Naval Arsenal.[31] Air force major Luis Contero, with other subverted pilots from the air force base at Las Palmas, was ordered to fly support for the rebellious units against the military academy and bomb the building if necessary. *Aprista Defensistas* would aid the naval units in the capture of the key targets in Callao, and rebel leader Luis Chanduvi was ordered to take the strategic Central Telephone Exchange, which controlled most of the communications for the Lima metropolitan area.

Most vital for the success of the revolt was the support of *Aprista* revolutionaries, who were ordered to block the movement of government troops from Lima during the first crucial hours of the revolt to assure that rebel operations in Callao and Chorrillos would not be overwhelmed before their military objectives could be accomplished. The rebels would thus have to prevent units from the army's Thirty-third and Nineteenth Infantry Battalions, as well as tanks from the armored division, from reinforcing the Thirty-ninth Battalion, which the rebels hoped to isolate and destroy.[32] The revolt would surely fail unless the APRA leadership decided to throw the full support of the party to the rebel cause. *Apristas* would have to take to the streets by the hundreds not only to initiate appropriate military action but also to create the impression that the revolt was very broadly based. This massive show of force would be the only way to convince both government and armed forces leaders to capitulate to the rebels. Such was the situation when the guns of the cruiser *Almirante Grau* commenced firing at military targets in Callao at 2 A.M. on 3 October.

During the first hours of the revolt the rebels achieved most of their military objectives but failed to neutralize the vitally important Thirty-ninth Infantry Battalion. Rebel sailors gained control of the cruisers *Almirante Grau* and *Colonel Bolognesi* (which was undergoing repairs at the Naval Arsenal), the frigates *Ferre* and *Teniente Palacios*, and the destroyer *Contralmirante Villar*, as well as the Naval Academy at La Punta.[33]

The general success of the rebel efforts in Callao was more than counterbalanced by setbacks in Lima and at the air force base in Las Palmas. Major Conterno and his supporters were unable to gain control of the base, and after dawn, loyal pilots flew a number of sorties against the rebellious ships. This action, coupled with hostile fire from loyal vessels in Callao Harbor, forced the rebels to abandon their attack positions.[34] In Lima, Generals Noriega and Hurtado were quickly informed of the rebellion and took steps to suppress the uprising. At midnight, from a person who was later identified as an *Aprista*, General Hurtado received a telephone warning that a revolt was imminent. He then issued orders that confined all army troops to their barracks until they received direct orders from him to act. Four hours after the revolt began, the government brought troops from the Military Academy (which had resisted a light rebel assault), Artillery Groups Two and Seven, a tank battalion, the Assault Battalion of the national police, and Infantry Battalions Thirty-nine, Thirty-three, and Nineteen into the battle against the rebels. The fighting continued until the early afternoon at the Real Felipe Fortress until it fell to government troops at 2:45 P.M. While this fighting was occurring, cadets from the Chorrillos Military Academy, with the assistance of naval cadets, recaptured the Naval Academy at La Punta and took 150 rebel sailors prisoner. Navy captain Pedro Vargas Prada led the government's operations against the Naval Arsenal, with the bulk of the fighting carried on by the Assault Battalion of the *Guardia Nacional* and the Thirty-third Infantry Battalion. In the midst of these counterattacks against the rebels, loyal submarine forces led by Captain José Torres Matos threatened the less mobile mutinous vessels in Callao Harbor and forced them to surrender. When the Naval Arsenal was finally taken at 8 P.M., the Callao revolt effectively ended.[35]

From the initiation of the revolt at 2 A.M. until government reinforcements effectively isolated the rebels in the Callao area four hours later, it is conceivable that the uprising might have succeeded if the *Aprista* leadership had decided to support the rebellion. Major Villanueva, who by 5 A.M. recognized that the rebel military situation was desperate, vainly sought to open a second front in Lima manned by *Aprista* street fighters. He hoped this action would engage the troops that were being sent to put down the rebellion in Callao.[36] But the APRA leaders, having failed to persuade Generals Del Carmen Marín and Cuadros to initiate their proposed movement in conjunction with the Callao uprising, withheld their support for the revolt.[37] APRA leader Manuel Seoane, shortly after the Callao revolt, claimed that the rebellion was not authorized or supported by the party and represented the work of "hotheads" within the organization's ranks. The party leadership's lack of support for the movement was also recognized by United States ambassador Harold Tittman, who reported on 14 October that "the Callao affair, while probably not unknown to the APRA directorship beforehand, was not officially ordered or supported by the party."[38] The division between the APRA leadership and the militant wing of the party during the crucial stages of the revolt ended any chance of success for the rebels.

By the morning of 4 October all fighting had ceased, and government troops were in complete control of Lima and Callao. The most serious insurrection in Peru since the Trujillo revolt of July, 1932 cost the lives of approximately sixty government and rebel troops and 175 civilians.[39] Since the rebellion had not spread to other areas of the nation, government troops and police concentrated their roundup of suspected insurgents in the Lima metropolitan area. Although only about five hundred naval personnel and approximately one hundred civilians actively participated in the revolt, on 4 October over one thousand persons were arrested and charged with complicity in the rebellion.[40]

Claiming that the APRA "proposed and directed the revolutionary movement in Callao on 3 October, costing numerous lives, attacking the stability of the constitutional institutions and destroying important elements of national defense," President Bustamante finally outlawed the party on 4 October.[41] The *Casa del Pueblo*, the APRA party headquarters, and the offices of the party newspaper, *La Tribuna*, were occupied by government troops in the immediate aftermath of the revolt. APRA leaders either went into hiding or sought asylum in foreign embassies to avoid arrest.[42] By 14 October, the government issued indictments against ninety-four *Aprista* party leaders, including Haya de la Torre, in connection with the Callao revolt. Minister of Government and Police Julio César Villegas also announced on 14 October that police at the APRA headquarters had seized a letter written by Commander Aguila Pardo to Haya de la Torre in April that "proved" the party leader's complicity in the rebellion.[43]

Despite the arrest of a large number of *Apristas* and the deportation of party leaders Manuel Seoane and Luis Alberto Sánchez to Chile on 13 October, Haya de la Torre named Major Luis Contero to "reorganize the *Aprista* military forces."[44] Attempts were made to raise money to finance a second movement, but the distrust generated within APRA ranks as a result of the party leadership's failure to back the Callao revolutionaries doomed these efforts to failure. Nevertheless, *Aprista* student leaders at the University of San Marcos and the University of Trujillo staged protest demonstrations that were suppressed only after strong government action.[45] These protests contributed to the continuing political tension throughout the first three weeks of October and helped erode President Bustamante's last remaining support within the armed forces.

The Callao uprising and the continuing conspiracies in its aftermath had a profound impact upon the armed forces. Over eight hundred of the navy's forty-eight hundred officers and enlisted men were arrested and interrogated.[46] A few months after the revolt, navy junior officers and cadets in the Naval Academy openly blamed the navy leadership for the revolt. Many young officers felt the low pay and the need for administrative reform had caused the discontent among the ranks of the enlisted men. Forced into early retirement after the revolt were Admiral Víctor Barrios, chief of the navy's General Staff; Admiral Heriberto Magueña Suero, commander of the fleet; and Admiral Manuel R. Neito, director of the Naval Academy at La Punta. Significantly, Admiral Neito was replaced as director of the Naval Academy by United States navy captain Gordon A. MacLean, only the second United States naval officer to hold that important position. Moreover, Admiral Rocque Saldías, the Peruvian navy's senior officer, appointed United States navy lieutenant commander Jack Roudebush to administer the Naval War College as soon as he arrived

in Peru in January, 1949. Other members of the United States naval
mission were named to key positions in the Peruvian navy during the two
years following the Callao revolt.[47]

In the other branches of the armed services the effect of *Aprista*
subversive efforts was also dramatic.   Scores of air force and police
personnel sympathized with the APRA cause but had not joined the
movement because of the indecision of the party's leadership at the time
of the revolt.   In outlawing APRA, Bustamante alluded to the party's
subversive activities and claimed that the Callao revolt was the
"culmination" of its efforts to subvert members of the nation's military.[48]
Most of all, the Callao revolt convinced many armed forces officers that
APRA, as the most serious threat to the discipline and corporate unity of
the officer corps, must be dealt with far more harshly than President
Bustamante was capable of doing. This development strengthened the
position of the staunch anti-APRA faction led by General Odría and
established the setting for still another military plot aimed at deposing
Bustamante and destroying the last vestiges of APRA's political power in
Peru.

President Bustamante's failure effectively to eliminate APRA-related
subversive activity after 3 October led to the nearly complete evaporation
of his military support during the last three weeks of his presidency.
General Noriega, having participated personally in the quelling of the
Callao uprising, now demanded that the president completely suppress
APRA. Noriega and other military leaders went to the National Palace on
8 October to pledge their support for the president, but General Odría,
Admiral Saldías, and Marshal Eloy Ureta did not join them.[49] Thus, three
of the most influential armed forces leaders had pointedly displayed their
disapproval of the president's handling of the Callao crisis. Additionally,
Generals Del Carmen Marín and Hector Martínez were forced publicly to
deny reports in the Lima press that they were involved in the Callao affair.
These allegations placed both of these officers on the defensive and made
other officers even more distressed over the public airing of the worst
armed forces discipline crisis in decades.[50]

The failure of the Bustamante regime to apprehend most of the key
APRA chiefs and leaders of the Callao revolt was the main source of
discord between the president and the armed forces senior officers. Nearly
all of the APRA leadership, including Haya de la Torre, avoided arrest
until after Bustamante was deposed. Majors Villanueva and Conterno, as
well as a number of the *Defensista* leaders, also remained free during this
period.[51]

Consequently, at the end of October the armed forces leadership was now more inclined to back Odría's anti-APRA campaign than it had been when Lieutenant Colonel Llosa attempted his *coup* in July. The Callao revolt had clearly tipped the balance against Bustamante by the end of October. The economic crisis that gripped the nation in the last month of Bustamante's regime, which saw massive food shortages and a high rate of inflation, further convinced military leaders that Bustamante had to be deposed. Finally, student disorders in Lima underscored Bustamante's lack of control of the political situation. On 25 October, in the midst of this tense political climate, General Odría arrived in Arequipa to begin the military movement that would oust the president.[52]

Odría's revolutionary plan was much the same as that of Lieutenant Colonel Llosa in that he hoped to gain control of Arequipa and persuade other important garrisons in central and southern Peru, including Cusco, Juliaca, and Puno, to join his rebellion. The general would then rely on his support among officers in the high command in Lima as he assumed that they would not risk a divided military in order to save the discredited Bustamante regime. Odría's key fellow conspirators in Arequipa were Colonel Daniel Meza Cuadra, Captain José Vargas Mata, *Guardia Civil* lieutenant colonel Isidoro Ortega Cáceres, and Majors Oswaldo Berrocal and José Caitan López. Major Alejandro Izaguirre Valverde, who had participated in the Llosa uprising, returned from Bolivia to render valuable service to the revolutionary cause in the border garrison of Juliaca when Odría launched his uprising on 27 October.[53]

The Arequipa revolt began at 7 P.M. on the twenty-seventh when the conspirators seized the central plaza, the prefecture, and local mail and telephone offices in the city. The main radio stations and the airport were also quickly taken, and the leading political figures affiliated with the Bustamante regime were arrested.[54] Among those detained were the president's brothers Miguel, Guillermo, and Ricardo Bustamante y Rivero, and the prefect of Arequipa, General Figueroa San Miguel. Colonel Meza Cuadra was named *Jefe Político* of Arequipa by Odría soon after the city was in the rebels' hands. Once Odría was completely assured of the allegiance of the personnel of the five army regiments stationed in the Arequipa region, he broadcast a radio appeal for the other military garrisons throughout Peru to join his movement.

On 28 October the Arequipa uprising spread to Cuzco, Juliaca, and Puno, but military leaders in Lima still remained undecided whether or not to support Odría. The issue was resolved the following day when twenty-five armed forces leaders met in a stormy three-hour session to decide Bustamante's fate. Most of the air force leaders and the inspector general of the army, Federico Hurtado, supported the president, but Hurtado was unwilling to commit large numbers of troops to suppress Odría's uprising in the south. Marshal Ureta, the most prestigious member of the group, cast an important vote for Bustamante's removal, and General Noriega, commander of the strategically vital Second Light Division in Lima, ended the debate when he decided he would not use his troops against Odría. Bustamante was then ordered by the armed forces commanders to submit his resignation. He refused, but at 11:40 P.M. on 29 October, he was escorted from the National Palace and placed aboard an airplane bound for Argentina in the company of Colonel Alejandro Cuadra Ravines.[55] Odría's *coup d'état* triumphed without a single shot being fired by the conspirators.

The revolt was supported by the extreme right, and the conservative *La Prensa* hailed the *coup* with headlines proclaiming, "The patriotic movement of the army has triumphed." The Miró-Quesada family, having backed the abortive Llosa uprising, was also clearly in agreement with the strongly anti-APRA directive of what Odría called his "Restoration Movement of Arequipa." A further link between the Llosa conspiracy and the Odría *coup* was Llosa's appointment to the rebel general's first cabinet as minister of development. Moreover, by a decree of 14 December 1948, the Odría government appropriated the sum of 138,000 soles to "cover the expenses occasioned in connection with the revolutionary movement in Juliaca" in July, 1948.[56] This bold public move gave proof of Odría's support for Bustamante's overthrow several months before Odría's campaign was initiated.

General Ernesto Montagne Marckholtz, a prominent retired army leader and senator, in characterizing the Odría movement, claimed that "Odría's rebellion was proposed one year before by a group of capitalists, supported by some political professionals and executed by ambitious military figures."[57] Bustamante's evaluation of the 27 October revolt was, of course, highly critical. From Buenos Aires on 31 October, he defended his actions as president and claimed that there had been "no justification" for his overthrow.[58] Odría and the staunchly anti-APRA military and civilian figures who engineered the president's ouster immediately set out to refute Bustamante's allegations.

Odría arrived in Lima on 30 October to assume the post as provisional president of the revolutionary government, which he promised would "only remain in power long enough to call a new election in the name of democracy and freedom."[59] During a speech at Limatambo Airport before a receptive crowd, the general vigorously attacked APRA and justified his seizure of power by asserting that the violently partisan politics of the Bustamante regime had "poisoned the hearts of the people and sickened

124 Militarism and Politics

their minds."[60] Despite Odría's promise of free elections, few Peruvians expected that, in the aftermath of the swift collapse of democratic institutions under Bustamante, any measure of civil liberties would be quickly granted by the new military regime. Armed forces leaders, for the most part, also gave little credence to their colleague's remarks concerning free elections. Their main concern was the re-establishment of discipline and morale within the officer corps after the massive breach of discipline inspired by *Apristas* during the three years of the Bustamante government. They were thus anticipating tough authoritarian measures from the new president that would be aimed at eliminating remaining subversive cells within the armed forces. These measures were quickly forthcoming.

NOTES

1. Personal interview with Víctor Villanueva Valencia, 27 July 1974, Lima, Peru; Víctor Villanueva Valencia, *La sublevación aprista del 48: Tragedia de pueblo y un partido* (Lima: 1973), pp. 78-79.

2. Personal interview with Víctor Villanueva Valencia, 27 July 1974, Lima, Peru; Villanueva, *La sublevación aprista*, pp. 75-76.

3. Personal interview with Víctor Villanueva Valencia, 27 July 1974, Lima, Peru; Villanueva, *La sublevación aprista*, pp. 73-90 passim.

4. Villanueva, *La sublevación aprista*, p. 82.

5. Personal interview with Víctor Villanueva Valencia, 27 July 1974, Lima, Peru.

6. Villanueva, *La sublevación aprista*, pp. 73-90; *El Callao*, 12 February 1948, p. 1.

7. *El Callao*, 12 February 1948, p. 1.

8. *Peruvian Times*, 13 February 1948, p. 1.

9. *Jornada*, 13 February 1948, p. 1.

10. *Peruvian Times*, 20 February 1948, p. 1; *El Comercio*, 18 February 1948, p. 3. Víctor Villanueva claims that Tovar Belmont's assassination was "probably ordered by the Party" (letter to the author from Víctor Villanueva Valencia, 17 October 1976, Lima, Peru).

11. *Peruvian Times*, 27 February 1948, p. 2.

12. G-2 Report no. 446306, 9 March 1948, U.S. military attaché to Department of the Army, NA, RG 319.

13. Ibid. no. 454624, 1 April 1948; *Peruvian Times*, 2 April 1948, p. 1.

14. Villanueva, *La sublevación aprista*, p. 104.

15. Ibid.

16. Ibid. General Del Carmen Marín's affiliation with APRA leadership was not a well-kept secret. In October, 1948, U.S. Ambassador Harold Tittman claimed that Del Carmen Marín "has been suspected of being APRA's chief spokesman within the army." See U.S. Ambassador Harold Tittman to Sec/State, 15 October 1948, filed under G-2 Report no. 500943, NA, RG 319.

17. *Peruvian Times*, 18 June 1948, p. 1.

18. G-2 Report no. 476531, 7 July 1948, U.S. military attaché to Department of the Army, NA, RG 319.

19. See Chapter 4 for a brief discussion of this episode.

20. G-2 Report no. 483966, 5 August 1948, U.S. military attaché to Department of the Army, NA, RG 319.

21. Ibid.

22. The officers who fled to Bolivia with Llosa were Major Alejandro Yzaguirre Valverde, Lieutenant Colonel Reynaldo Rubio, Major Belisario Bustios Pimental, Major Oscar Zamalloa Obregoso, Major Reuben Aguilar Astete, Captain Alberto Otero Roldon, and Lieutenant Rafael Aerranos.

23. G-2 Report no. 483966, 5 August 1948, U.S. military attaché to Department of the Army, NA, RG 319; José Luis Bustamante y Rivero, *Tres años de la lucha par la democracía en el Perú* (Buenos Aires: 1949), pp. 248-252.

24. Tad Szulc, *Twilight of the Tyrants* (New York: 1959), p. 178. This is a colorful, journalistic account of the careers of Odría and four other authoritarian political leaders in Latin America during the 1950s.

25. *Peruvian Times*, 16 July 1948, p. 1.

26. Villanueva, *La sublevación aprista*, pp. 114-117.

27. Bustamante, *Tres años*, p. 168.

28. Villanueva, *La sublevación aprista*, pp. 120-126; Tittman to Sec/State, 14 October 1948, filed under G-2 Report no. 500373, NA, RG 319. It should be noted that neither Villanueva nor Colonel César Enrique Pardo and his nephew were APRA party members; they merely sympathized with the party's objectives.

29. Villanueva, *La sublevación aprista*, pp. 120-126; Tittman to Sec/State, 14 October 1948, filed under G-2 Report no. 500373, NA, RG 319.

30. Villanueva, *La sublevación aprista*, pp. 120-126; Tittman to Sec/State, 14 October 1948, filed under G-2 Report no. 500373, NA, RG 319.

31. Commander Mosto graduated first in his class from the *Escuela Naval del Perú* (Naval Academy) in 1926. For years after the Callao revolt his name was deleted from the list of honor graduates. (Personal interview with Capitán de Fragata Jorge Ortíz Sotelo, La Molina, Peru, May, 1985). See also Jorge Ortíz Sotelo, *Escuela Naval del Perú (Historia Ilustrada)* (Callao: 1981).

32. Villanueva, *La sublevación aprista*, pp. 127-128. Major Villanueva's specific task was to neutralize the tanks of the armored division.

33. Detailed accounts of the revolt have recently been declassified by the Peruvian Ministry of the Navy. Particularly informative sources for understanding the ebb and flow of the revolt are "Movimiento revolucionario informe sobre," 16 October 1948, by Capitán de Corbeta Fernando Rojas Guerrero (commander of the Naval Arsenal) and a series of reports by Capitán de Navio Felix Vargas Prada to the inspector general of the army and the chief of the navy's General Staff, dated 5-15 October 1948, Archivo Histórico de Marina del Perú, 1988. These reports will hereafter be cited with the author and date and Archivo Histórico de Marina. Other useful sources for the Callao rebellion are *La Prensa*, 4 October 1948, p. 1; *El Comercio*, 4 October 1948, p. 1; Bustamante, *Tres años*, p. 179; letter to the author from Víctor Villanueva Valencia, 17 October 1976, Lima, Peru.

34. Vargas Prada, 5 October 1948, Archivo Histórico de Marina, *La Prensa*, p. 1. For an account of the capture of the Naval Academy see Ortíz Sotelo, *Escuela Naval*, p. 127-128.

126 Militarism and Politics

35. Vargas Prada, 6-8 October 1948, Archivo Histórico de Marina; Ortíz Sotelo, *Escuela Naval*, p. 128; Bustamante, *Tres años*, p. 179; G-2 Report no. 504530, 27 October 1948, U.S. military attaché to Department of the Army, NA, RG 319; Villanueva, *La sublevación aprista*, p. 155. Bustamante charged that General Noriega was "negligent" in not immediately placing all of his forces on alert after General Hurtado received the information that the rebellion was about to begin. Villanueva offers a slightly different version of these events and claims an *Aprista* called the office of the prefect of Lima at 12:00 A.M. and said, "The Party of the People (APRA) has nothing to do with the Callao revolt." Since the uprising had not yet begun, this call provided a warning to government authorities.

36. Vargas Prada, 6-8 October 1948, Archivo Histórico de Marina; Ortíz Sotelo, *Escuela Naval*, pp. 128-129; Bustamante, *Tres años*, p. 179; G-2 Report no. 504530, 27 October 1948, U.S. military attaché to Department of the Army, NA, RG 319; *La sublevación aprista*, pp. 142-143.

37. Personal interview with Víctor Villanueva Valencia, 27 July 1974, Lima, Peru.

38. Tittman to Sec/State, 7 October 1948, filed under G-2 Report no. 500213, NA, RG 319. As of July 1974, Haya de la Torre denied that the APRA leadership was connected with the Callao revolt. He claimed that the rebels were affiliated with General Odría, who wished to create a state of civil disorder so as to promote the conditions necessary for his own movement to triumph. (Personal interview with Víctor Raúl Haya de la Torre, 13 July 1974, Lima, Peru).

39. *La Prensa*, 4 October 1948, p. 4; *Peruvian Times*, 8 October 1948, p. 1.

40. Tittman to Sec/State, G-2 Report no. 500213, NA, RG 319.

41. Villanueva, *La sublevación aprista*, p. 143; G-2 Report no. 536711, 10 February 1949, U.S. military attaché to Department of the Army, NA, RG 319; G-2 Report no. 497953, 5 October 1948, NA, RG 319.

42. *Peruvian Times*, 8 October 1948, p. 1; *Legislación Militar del Perú*, 1948, p. 28.

43. *Peruvian Times*, 14 October 1948, p. 2.

44. Villanueva, *La sublevación aprista*, p. 169.

45. *Peruvian Times*, 22 October 1948, p. 2; Bustamante, *Tres años*, p. 186.

46. G-2 Report no. 536711, 10 February 1949, U.S. military attaché to Department of the Army, NA, RG 319. The judicial proceedings involving the alleged conspirators will be discussed in more detail in Chapter 6. It should be noted that the Peruvian navy as of February, 1991, is releasing documents dealing with the Callao revolt's judicial proceedings. These documents will be available under the title Archivo Histórico de Marina, Estado Mayor General de Marina/Jefe de la Zona Judicial de Marina. Ortíz Sotelo, *Escuela Naval*, p. 128; telephone interview with U.S. navy captain (R) Jack Roudebush, Monterey, California, 18 November 1989.

47. Telephone interview with Captain (R) Jack Roudebush, 18 November 1989.

48. *Peruvian Times*, 8 October 1948, filed under G-2 Report no. 500373, NA, RG 319.

49. Tittman to Sec/State, 14 October 1948, filed under G-2 Report no. 500373, NA, RG 319.

50. G-2 Report no. 599043, 15 October 1948, NA, RG 319.

51. Villanueva, *La sublevación aprista*, pp. 166-180.

52. *La Prensa*, 31 October 1948, p. 4.

53. Ibid.

54. Ibid.; Bustamante, *Tres años*, pp. 253-255.

55. G-2 Report no. 507002, 4 November 1948, U.S. military attaché to Department of the Army, NA, RG 319; *The New York Times*, 30 October 1948, p. 1; *La Prensa*, 30 October 1948, p. 1.

56. Anonymous, "La Revolución del Sur," *Revista Militar del Perú*, 45, no. 10 (October, 1948), pp. 150-155; Bustamante, *Tres años*, pp. 256-260. A probable factor in the bloodless *coup d'etat* was the fact that the Odría revolt was very likely financed by a "kitty" of eight million soles raised by a group headed by the Gildermeister family, Pedro Beltrán, and former president Manuel Prado y Ugarteche. Only three million soles were actually expended, almost all of which were dispersed in Arequipa. Reportedly the money used to assure support for the revolt was dispersed at one hundred soles per soldier and as much as ten thousand soles for an army major. No figures were given for the Lima region, nor was there an explanation of what happened to the remaining five million soles. See Tittman to Sec/State, 9 November 1948, NA, RG 319.

57. Ernesto Montagne Markholtz, *Memorias del General de Brigada E.P. Ernesto Montagne Markholtz* (Callao: 1962), p. 218.

58. *The New York Times*, 1 November 1948, p. 7.

59. *La Prensa*, 31 October 1948, p. 1.

60. Ibid. The crowd greeting Odría was very likely swelled by the active efforts of his supporters. See the flier calling for a warm reception for Odría upon his arrival at the Limatambo Airport: Anonymous, "Manuel A. Odría, Es un deber patriotico de todo Peruanos. Rendir homenaje al salvador de la patria," *Colección de Volantes*, 30 October 1948, 1948 folder.

6
The Odría Era: 1948-1956

General Manuel Odría's *coup* did not represent a departure from the historical pattern of twentieth-century civil-military relations in Peru; rather it followed closely the trends of the Benavides and Sánchez Cerro *coups* of 1914 and 1930, respectively. Most armed forces officers sympathized with the anti-*APRA* motivations of the 27 October movement because they considered *Aprista* subversion in 1948 the greatest threat to the corporate unity of the officer corps since the 1930s. Yet many officers not directly linked to any of the conspiracies or revolutionary movements resented still another incursion into national politics by colleagues who they felt were supporting the personal ambitions of an old-style *caudillo*. This feeling was particularly strong among navy junior officers not involved in the Callao revolt and a few army senior officers who resented Odría's seizure of power. As the armed forces' discontent with Odría's continued rule increased after 1953, key army commanders and Odría's former rightist civilian allies worked actively to end his regime. Meanwhile, other progressive officers during the early 1950s moved beyond criticism of Odría's *caudillismo* to articulate a more comprehensive mission for the armed forces, with broader implications than the simple guardianship role dictated by the military president. Ironically, these pressures forced Odría to introduce some military reforms that made the officer class more conscious of its modernizing mission and far less tolerant of Odría's limited vision of the armed forces' role. None of these currents of resistance to Odría coalesced, however, until the *caudillo* solidified his hold on political power during the first two years of his regime.

General Odría ruled as president of the military *Junta* until he was able to engineer his own election as constitutional president in June, 1950.

During this period he consolidated his political position by jailing and deporting civilian and military opponents of his regime. The primary targets of the government were *Apristas*, hundreds of whom were arrested in the two months following Odría's seizure of power. At the same time he solicited the support of the Lima working class by launching a series of public works projects, employing thousands of unskilled laborers in the capital.

Firmly supporting Odría's initial policies were the right-wing, anti-APRA officers comprising the general's first cabinet. Most were young, the majority were in their forties, and only two of the army officers held the rank of general.[1] General Zenón Noriega and Admiral Roque A. Saldías (as war and navy ministers, respectively) demonstrated their solidarity with Odría during his tenure in Bustamante's government and the subsequent *coup*. Some other members of the all-military cabinet traced their connection to the *Junta* leader to a comradeship forged during the military campaign against Ecuador.[2] The ministers, particularly Lieutenant Colonel Alfonso Llosa, backed the campaign to crush APRA as a political force, and this resolve was enthusiastically seconded by conservative civilians who encouraged the overthrow of Bustamante.

Odría's leading civilian supporters, Oscar and Carlos Miró- Quesada, Pedro Beltrán, and Ramón Aspillaga, were openly supportive when, during early November, the government extended the state of siege originally imposed by Bustamante on 4 October. The government soon employed its sweeping powers to arrest nearly one thousand *Apristas*. Party leaders Ramiro Prialé and Armando Villanueva were captured, but Haya de la Torre eluded the dragnet.[3] The government also outlawed the Communist Party on 2 November, charging communists and *Apristas* with joint responsibility for antigovernment subversion against Bustamante.[4]

Stern measures aimed at preventing organized military opposition to the *Junta* were adopted during November. Throughout the first days of the Odría regime, police raided the homes of suspect military personnel and interrogated them at length before jailing them in the Lima penitentiary.[5] Of all those imprisoned, the sailors involved in the Callao revolt received the worst treatment.[6] A number of Odría's military opponents were also subsequently deported, including Major Víctor Villanueva Valencia, who was exiled to Venezuela after serving eighteen months in the Lima penitentiary. In July, 1949 a small group of these deportees voiced their sentiments from Panama concerning Odría's *coup*. Claiming that the military government had "profaned" the name of the armed forces by allowing partisan politics totally to dictate the conduct of military affairs, the group insisted that they spoke for the majority of Peru's junior officers when they declared:

We seek only to return the institution to its former level of professional prestige and remove the armed forces from the political involvement which provides a painful spectacle to the Peruvian people. Our resolution is sacred and pure: the return of peace and constitutionality to Peru. We know this feeling is shared among the rank and file of the armed forces of today.[7]

Although the appeals of these disaffected officers went unanswered, Odría was well aware of the potential threat to his regime posed by officers who shared these views. Consequently, he balanced the numerous arrests and deportations of suspect military men with measures designed to placate disenchanted junior officers. On 11 March 1949, pay raises ranging from 15 to 25 percent were ordered for army officers and police. Significantly, the biggest pay boosts were granted to the grades below major in the army and to all grades in the police.[8]

While ordering pay raises, the government also modified the promotion law of the army to clarify the minimum time of service each officer above the rank of major would have to serve before promotion to the next grade.[9] Prior to this law, political influence rather than seniority was frequently more important for promotion to lieutenant colonel and above. Odría thus appeared to be courting junior army officers by addressing the promotion problems prevalent during the civilian regimes of Prado and Bustamante. In practice, however, the paternalistic general used promotions as a political tool throughout most of his regime after 1950. The government also moved to show its concern for the social welfare of military personnel by ordering the construction of a modern military hospital in Lima during December, 1948.[10] Overall, Odría expanded the military budget 45 percent during his first year in office.[11]

The military president further sought to assure the allegiance of the Lima working class by enacting a number of social welfare measures. Only three weeks after taking office, the president greatly expanded social security coverage for the nation's workers.[12] On 30 April 1949, the government institutionalized its labor programs by creating a new Ministry of Labor and Indian Affairs.[13] An extensive public works program was also begun during 1949, which provided large numbers of jobs in the construction of public buildings in Lima and irrigation systems in Peru's arid coastal regions. At the end of 1949, Odría followed the salary increases ordered for the military in March by granting a 20 percent increase in the pay of government employees. At the same time, the chief executive suggested that private employers follow the government's example.[14]

Odría's public works program and his later policy of encouraging the growth of squatter settlements in Lima's environs reflected the dictator's goal of creating a populist base for his regime in an attempt to free himself from total dependence upon the conservative military and civilian elements that supported his *coup d'état*. Very likely inspired by the success of Juan Perón in Argentina, Odría and his wife María Delgado de Odría, in the words of David Collier, "sought to build the idea that the poor enjoyed a special relationship with him." This was part of Odría's attempt to establish a dependent, paternalistic relationship between the president and the poor. As Steve Stein has also noted, one important additional motive for these policies was to undermine the popularity of APRA and gain control of Peru's burgeoning labor movement.[15] Hernando de Soto credits Odría with allowing Peru's informal economy to take root during his regime. Peru's informal housing settlements, or *barriadas*, began to appear on the outskirts of Lima, as the capital, like most major cities throughout Latin America, experienced explosive population growth as a result of heavy migration from rural areas. Commenting on Odría's policy, De Soto notes:

Through its relations and dealings with the popular classes, the Odría regime was able to offer to the formal society the apparent loyalty of the informal settle- ments—the government was in a position to assist the settlers by helping in the acquisition of land and the provision of services—and at the same time, to reduce political unrest by allowing poor people to put up their own homes without major cost to the national treasury. Each time he provided assistance, Odría won a little more political support, or at least neutrality, from the pragmatic settlement dwellers.[16]

After 1968 the Velasco regime would take its cue from the success of Odría's policy by giving formal government sanction to these squatters' settlements. The Velasco government renamed them *pueblos jóvenes* (new towns) and made an effort to mobilize the residents of these settlements to support government reforms.

The Odría regime was able to finance these programs without incurring major budget deficits due to an economic policy that stressed increased foreign investment and the elimination of trade-restrictive foreign exchange rates. Increased demand for Peruvian exports created by the Korean War enabled the government to expand its public works and social welfare projects throughout the next four years. The economic prosperity of these years contributed significantly to the president's popularity among the working classes of Lima, who benefited directly from these extensive public projects. But despite growing economic prosperity during 1949 and 1950, Odría refused to loosen the tight restrictions on individual liberties imposed during his first year in power.

In a New Year's Day address in 1949 Odría justified his campaign against the APRA by insisting that the party was dominated by Marxists who were engaging in a continuing campaign of antigovernment subversion.[17] Most important APRA leaders at this time, however, were either in exile or in prison, and on 3 January, party chief Haya de la Torre finally despaired of further resistance and sought diplomatic asylum in the Colombian Embassy in Lima.[18] The government's refusal to allow the APRA leader safe conduct to leave the country initiated one of the most bizarre episodes in Peruvian history. For the next five years, Haya de la Torre remained a prisoner in the Colombian Embassy, surrounded by trenches and machine-gun positions erected soon after his presence was made known to the Odría government. Efforts by the Colombian government and the International Court of Justice at The Hague to resolve the political asylum issue failed until the party chief was finally allowed to leave Peru in April, 1954.[19] With Haya de la Torre's isolation, APRA was deprived of its most important leader. The party continued underground activity, however, and Manuel Seoane and Luis Alberto Sánchez worked to hold APRA together by organizing a committee of APRA members in exile.[20]

Between January and July, 1949, Odría tried to suppress remaining resistance to his regime by enacting tough new measures to deal with acts of political subversion. In late March the penal code was modified, sanctioning the death penalty for political terrorism.[21] In mid-April, the government announced that it had aborted a plot by fugitive Apristas and a small number of armed forces and police personnel to assassinate Odría and other members of the military Junta.[22] The arrest and imprisonment of the alleged plotters was followed on 5 July by the declaration of the comprehensive Internal Security Law. This law, which remained in force throughout Odría's rule, granted government agents sweeping powers of search and seizure, in addition to suspending the right of habeas corpus for persons suspected of committing political crimes.[23] APRA was the immediate target of this measure, but it was soon used to deal with all forms of political opposition. In response to these measures APRA exiles began an antigovernment propaganda campaign in a number of Latin American countries in an effort to discredit Odría.[24]

The president used his Independence Day speech of 28 July to justify the necessity of the Internal Security Law and to outline his proposals for further military spending. Insisting that the fundamental reason for the existence of his military government was the elimination of the APRA "menace," Odría claimed that the security law was a needed tool for dealing with the party most responsible for the violence and political unrest of the past eighteen years in Peru.[25] On the subject of the armed forces' morale, the general maintained that the navy had recovered from the crisis of the Callao mutiny.

Odría's claim concerning the navy was definitely false. In the wake of the Callao revolt, navy junior officers expressed the belief that the blame for the mutiny rested mainly with the poor leadership provided by their institution's senior officers. They felt that the 3 October 1948 uprising had disgraced the navy, and the junior officers pushed for a reorganization of the navy command and internal structure "from top to bottom." Most importantly, the discontented younger officers felt that their own superiors were incapable of conducting these reforms and suggested that substantive changes should be made under guidelines provided by the United States naval mission. No action was taken on these demands during the Odría regime, and naval morale remained low for most of his tenure as president. Odría did promise in 1949, however, to upgrade the quality of the navy's equipment and coastal defenses along with the plans to renovate army and air force installations at Pisco, Juliaca, and Cuzco.[26]

Although the Odría government fulfilled its initial promises to improve the financial and material condition of the armed forces, military resistance to his regime continued throughout his first eighteen months in office. An army officer, risking contacts with APRA, explained to a party representative in November, 1949 that many young army officers deplored the government's suppression of civil liberties. Echoing the sentiments of the army exiles in Panama, he charged that Odría was not qualified to run the government. The new generation of officers and soldiers, he further claimed, were completely dedicated to their profession, and the institution's involve ment in national politics had created a sense of uneasiness concerning the Peruvian people's attitude toward the military's professional mission.[27]

Among senior officers of the army, there also prevailed opposition to Odría's policies. Within the membership of the Superior Council of the Army, Generals Juan de Dios Cuadros and José del Carmen Marín were Odría's chief critics. Del Carmen Marín, apparently because of his personal prestige, was not purged from the army leadership, although his position on the Superior Council was relatively powerless.[28] Cuadros, however, after openly ridiculing the Odría regime in late 1949, was replaced by General José Vasquez Benavides and placed on inactive duty.[29] In addition to the vocal opposition of Generals Del Carmen Marín and Cuadros, one of Odría's former colleagues in the Ecuador campaign, Colonel Miguel Monteza Tafur, spoke out openly against the government in February, 1950. Angered at what he termed Odría's diplomatic exile of General Ureta to Spain and perhaps further motivated by being passed over for promotion, Colonel Monteza claimed that "things are going very badly and there are some disreputable people in office." Hinting at a possible *coup*, he was reported to have told the former Peruvian ambassador to Ecuador, Juan Ignacio Elgenero, that "you may be quite confident that this state of affairs is not going to last."[30] Colonel Monteza was eventually arrested in April, 1954 for plotting against Odría.

Adding to the internal tensions within the armed forces was the trial of the military personnel and civilians charged in the Callao revolt. The proceedings, begun in January, 1950, aroused uneasiness in the navy concerning the possibility of death sentences that might be imposed by the tribunal headed by Vice Admiral Carlos Rotalde.[31] But when 238 of the original 248 defendants were convicted and the sentences read on 21 March, the relative lack of severity apparently reflected a desire on the part of the tribunal to avoid exacerbating naval morale problems resulting from the Callao mutiny. Of the 248 military and fifty civilian defendants, only one noncommissioned navy officer, Domingo Castañan Rivera, who was convicted of murdering a superior officer, was given the death sentence. Petty Officers Ricardo Olaya Mogollon and Francisco Davila Manrique were the only two receiving life prison terms. Other sentences ranged from one to fourteen years, with navy commander José Mosto given the stiffest sentence among this group.[32]

The tribunal charged APRA with inspiring and planning the revolt and sentenced party members Ramiro Prialé, Carlos Manuel Cox, Luis Heysen, Armando Villanueva del Campo, and air force major José Extremadoyro to from three to seven years at hard labor. The panel also cited fifty-three civilians, including Haya de la Torre, Manuel Seoane, and Luis Alberto Sánchez (most of the remaining APRA leadership), as fugitives from justice. Odría wanted stiffer penalties, but as he was preparing his presidential campaign for national elections scheduled for June, 1950, he apparently wished to avoid creating a major issue of the tribunal's decision; thus he let the sentences stand.[33]

In early January, 1950, the chief executive announced plans to hold elections for president and a National Congress on 2 July. Odría soon established the electoral framework for his almost certain election. The electoral statute was issued by the *Junta Militar*, which he controlled, and the National Election Jury, which monitored the balloting, was hand-picked by the general and included two of his relatives.[34] Moreover, the Internal Security Law could be used by the government to limit severely the political activities of opposition candidates. Despite his nomination for president by a coalition of six minor conservative parties under the title *Partido Union Democrática* (Democratic Union Party), Odría refused to make formal his candidacy until 19 May.[35]

Five weeks before the *Junta* chief announced his intention to run, another political coalition calling itself the *Liga Nacional Democrática* (National Democratic League) organized a campaign to present an alternative candidate. During the first week of May the *Liga* named army general (R) Ernesto Montagne Marckholtz and Dr. Francisco Mostajo presidential and vice-presidential candidates, respectively.[36] The *caudillo*, however, fearing any substantive opposition, had the National Election Jury invalidate General Montagne's candidacy. Odría's opponents then rebelled in protest in Arequipa in mid-June. The military leader had Montagne arrested and deported to Argentina, and the uprising was quickly put down.[37]

After suppressing the Arequipa rebellion, Odría felt secure enough on 2 July to proceed with the formality of holding national elections as scheduled. Without opposition, he was "elected" as constitutional president for a six-year term, along with a subservient congress containing some token opposition members from the Socialist Party.[38] The circumstances surrounding Odría's election further alienated officers who questioned his seizure of power in 1948. During the next six years, Odría gradually lost his grip on the armed forces, which had not seriously challenged him during his first nineteen months in office. Odría's reduced control enabled more forward-looking officers and their progressive ideas to gain acceptance by an officer class that was separating itself from the dictator's autocratic leadership.

As had been illustrated by the discussion of the writings of army officers since the early twentieth century, it is clear that military men constantly advocated a modernizing mission for the armed forces.[39] But despite the limited road-building, public education, and similar civic projects that the army engaged in before the Odría administration, the military took little effective action to deal with underdevelopment. A primary reason for this inaction was the lack of a clearly defined rationale for the armed forces to deal with projects beyond the realm of its traditional concept of national defense. Despite the writings in service journals, the military's mission was defined officially as the protection of Peru's frontiers from external military threats and the suppression of internal disorder. Although the 1944 General Staff study, entitled "Exposition of the Army on the War Strength

Organization," cautiously proposed a broader definition of national defense that included some references to army-sponsored social reforms, no significant action was taken on the study's recommendations during the 1940s.

In large measure because of the lack of action on the suggestions of the General Staff document and also because of the concern of a few army senior officers that the *Escuela Superior de Guerra* did not prepare the army's high command with the means of formulating a modern national defense strategy, progressive officers argued that a new military studies center should be created. This center would be dedicated primarily to formulating new theories of national defense based on the "realities" of Peru's national potential and military capabilities. Such a center would also play a key role in preparing armed forces officers for important command positions upon their graduation from the institution.

The first appeal calling for the creation of a specialized military training center was made by General Oscar N. Torres in 1945.[40] The general declared that a *Centro de Altos Estudios Militares* (Center of Higher Military Studies) should be formed to prepare army officers for the command of strategically important military units.[41] But for three years his proposal was not acted upon despite the creation of a mixed commission charged with writing the Organic Law of National Defense in 1945.[42] Only five months before Odría's *coup*, Colonel (R) César Enrique Pardo, the *Aprista* senator from Lima, presented to the Second National Congress of his party a proposal calling for the creation of a military studies center to improve the quality of military professional training.[43] Pardo's proposal reflected his recognition of the growing desire among armed forces officers for a government commitment to act on this project.

When Odría took office, he bowed to this pressure and soon named a commission to study ways of upgrading the quality of Peru's armed forces. Among the measures the commission advocated were the organization of the three armed services under a joint command and the establishment of a higher military studies center for the armed forces.[44] Nevertheless, resistance by navy chiefs to a joint command, which would have assuredly been dominated by the army, undermined both that project and the proposal for a studies center.[45]

Undaunted, army officers supporting General José del Carmen Marín, who was a member of the armed forces commission, finally succeeded in securing the establishment of the *Centro de Altos Estudios del Ejército* (Center of Higher Military Studies of the Army) in July, 1950. Three months later the institution's name was changed to the *Centro de Altos Estudios Militares* (CAEM).[46] Outlined as the original objectives of the

CAEM were (1) to define a national war doctrine; (2) to incorporate the basic principles of this doctrine into the training of army officers destined for high command positions; (3) to study the fundamental questions of national defense and its relation to basic national problems; (4) to develop systems of education and instruction for the army; and (5) to supervise the instruction of army colonels as a means of preparing them for promotion to brigadier general.[47] These functions were in line with those of similar studies centers in Argentina, Brazil, France, and the United States. The National War College, founded in Washington, D.C., in 1947, and, in particular, a center for advanced military studies created in France during the 1920s provided the best working models for the architects of the Peruvian institution.[48]

Named as the first director of the CAEM was General José Del Carmen Marín. He was an accomplished mathematician and engineer and was considered one of the leading intellectuals in the army.[49] But because of General Del Carmen Marín's association with APRA during 1948, Odría used the post of CAEM director to isolate Del Carmen Marín from a position of power in the army.[50] Although Del Carmen Marín had been slated to assume the post as director of a future studies center as early as March, 1948, Odría's influence did apparently prevent the center from becoming a focal point of prestige and influence within the military during its first years of operation.[51] Two commentators on the CAEM's role during the Odría administration claim that the president sought to downgrade its importance:

During the first years there was a widespread feeling, at least within the army, that the CAEM was a junkyard designed to dump officers unwanted by those in command or who were politically unreliable to the Odría regime. Consequently many colonels resorted to influence and political-military contacts to avoid assignment there.[52]

The makeup of the first class of colonels at the CAEM in 1951 substantiated its ancillary role in the army's power structure. Seven of the ten colonels attending the center's first program retired the following year. And one of the other colonels, Miguel Monteza Tafur, as has been discussed, was a consistent opponent of Odría's policies until his arrest in 1954. Nearly all these men lacked potential for top command positions in the army. Thus Odría undermined CAEM's mandate for the preparation of candidates for leadership roles in the armed forces during its first years.

Despite the handicaps imposed by Odría, General Del Carmen Marín demonstrated a determination to make the center an important source of military theory and influence within the armed forces. In an address delivered at the opening of the CAEM in 1951 Del Carmen Marín insisted that the center would play an integral role in developing an ever-broadening concept of national defense. It would then become the duty of the armed forces high command to translate this concept into positive actions designed to promote the nation's well-being, he concluded.[53] For the most part, the military leadership under Odría ignored the work being done at the CAEM during its first three years. But as the president became increasingly occupied with growing civil-military opposition to his regime after 1953, the prestige of the center increased concomitantly. This prestige was partly due to a growing recognition among armed forces officers that CAEM's reformist doctrine was a far more acceptable alternative than the autocratic paternalism of the Odría regime.[54]

In the four years following his 1950 election as "constitutional" president, Odría responded to increasing resistance to his regime by repeated implementation of the Internal Security Law. During the 1950 electoral campaign the government's tactics and the violent suppression of the Arequipa uprising alienated civilian leaders who had supported Odría during his tenure as president of the *Junta Militar*. Pedro Beltrán, the editor of the newspaper *La Prensa* and a strong supporter of Odría in 1948, became estranged from the president because he believed that Odría was no longer responsive to the views of the civilians who had backed the general's original *coup*.[55]

Odría responded to civilian pressures for a greater voice in his government by naming six civilians to the twelve cabinet posts, but the position of minister of war remained in the hands of General Noriega, and Admiral Rogue A. Saldías was retained as minister of the navy.[56] Furthermore, the president served notice that his "constitutional" leadership would follow the same pattern as his earlier rule when he ordered that the six hundred decrees issued by the *Junta Militar* be declared constitutional laws of the Republic.[57]

For the next three years the government centered its financial priorities on military programs and various social welfare and public works projects. During late 1950 additional pay raises were ordered for public employees and military officers serving in foreign countries as attachés and trainees. Ambitious road-building and irrigation projects were also announced, along with a proposal calling for the creation of a national health and social welfare fund.[58] Increases in the value of Peruvian exports and loans for development programs sponsored by the Export-Import Bank and the International Bank for Research and Development supplied the initial funding for these projects.[59]

The Eisenhower administration looked with favor on the Odría regime because of its public anticommunist stance, and the dictator was even decorated by the United States for his contributions to hemispheric defense. As a result of these close ties, a bilateral military assistance pact between the United States and Peru was signed on 22 February 1952, giving a substantial boost to Odría's military programs. The agreement, signed under the auspices of the Mutual Security Act of 1951, formalized a United States military presence in Peru that had become increasingly important since the end of World War II.[60] At the time of the treaty, the United States army mission in Peru was assigned a number of important advisory roles. Colonel James Cole, chief of the mission, was attached to the Ministry of War and the inspector general of the army. The deputy chief, Colonel Andrew J. Adams, worked with the commanding general of the armored division, and Colonel Adrian L. Hoebeke served as an adviser to the CAEM.[61] The United States Defense Department was also continuing its policy, begun during World War II, of sponsoring study missions and goodwill visits of Peruvian officers to United States military installations. During the early 1950s, such officers as General Zenón Noriega, air force general Ernesto Bernales, and Admiral Roque A. Saldías were given extensive tours of such establishments as Fort Benning, Georgia; Fort Bragg, North Carolina; and the army General Staff School at Fort Leavenworth, Kansas.[62]

Under the military assistance agreement, United States military aid (grants and loans) increased from only $100,000 in 1952 to $9.1 million at the end of the Odría regime in 1956.[63] This assistance provided the government with part of the funds for some of its major equipment purchases, including three World War II vintage United States destroyer escorts, two new submarines, and a squadron (twenty-five) of P-47 pursuit planes.[64] These additions apparently reflected Odría's recognition of the navy's continuing complaints that it was traditionally shorted in the military budgets since the early 1940s and clearly helped improve navy morale.[65]

Regarding domestic affairs, relative economic prosperity before 1953 did not prevent the continuation of protests against the government's restriction of civil liberties. Antigovernment student strikes in Arequipa during September, 1952 were so serious that the prefect of Arequipa, Daniel Camino Brent, was replaced by army colonel Ricardo Pérez Godoy, who formerly commanded the Third Light Division in that southern Peruvian city.[66] Students were then joined by textile workers in a series of strikes in 1953 that reflected rising unemployment as Peru's economy began to suffer from declining world prices of sugar and cotton. Suddenly faced with an unfavorable trade balance that reached seventy million dollars in 1953, Odría adopted a tougher stance toward labor union agitation. After a general strike immobilized Arequipa in January, 1953, police arrested members of the Communist Party, thirty-nine of whom were subsequently imprisoned under the provisions of the Internal Security Law. These arrests signaled the abandonment of Odría's policy of encouraging limited communist penetration of the labor movement in an effort to offset APRA's influence among Peruvian workers.[67]

The depressed economy also forced Odría to make cutbacks in military spending and curtail his program of public works and social welfare projects during 1954.[68] The uneven nature of his public assistance programs was soon made apparent as little effort was made to extend government aid beyond Lima and a few other coastal areas. As had been the case with all government leaders throughout modern Peruvian history, Odría did little to alleviate the crushing poverty of the Indian population. The government's inaction in this regard was at odds with the thinking of the military strategists at the CAEM and some progressive armed forces officers who viewed the plight of the Indian as a serious national problem having important implications for national defense.

As we have seen, concern for the economic and social isolation of the Indian had been a recurring theme in the writings of armed forces officers for decades. But a young army officer, writing in the *Revista Militar* in 1955, complained bitterly that deficiencies in education and literacy among the Indian population seriously undermined the capabilities of Peru's soldiers. Pointing out that the army's basic manpower was drawn from the Indian population, the officer insisted that the education of the Indian and his resultant integration into Peru's social and political mainstream would not only strengthen the armed forces but also help develop a true national consciousness.[69] The problem of the Indian and land tenure in the *sierra* will be discussed in greater detail later, but it is important to note here that army officers in the mid-1950s were beginning to recognize the tremendous tensions building among Indian *comuneros* in the *sierra* departments of Cuzco, Puno, Apurimac, Ayacucho, and Huancavelica. These areas would witness massive land invasions by *comuneros* in the years after 1958. These same locales would be the focal points for the guerrilla campaigns of 1965 and for *Sendero Luminoso's* initial offensive in the 1980s.

The concept of Indian integration was one component of an increasingly sophisticated national defense rationale then being articulated at the CAEM during its first years of operation. By 1953, largely through the efforts of General Del Carmen Marín, the center had been able to overcome its initial stigma as a "junkyard" for unreliable armed forces officers. The CAEM's growing prestige as an important source of military theory and as a key training institution for officers with high command potential attracted topflight army officers in increasing numbers by the mid-1950s. Attending the 1953 class was Colonel Alejandro Cuadra Ravines, destined to be become the youngest brigadier general in the army in 1955 and named minister of war in 1956.[70] In 1954, Colonels Marcial Romero Pardo and Marcial Merino Pereyra (a former minister in Odría's first cabinet) enrolled at the CAEM. Colonel Romero Pardo soon replaced General Del Carmen Marín as director of the center, and Colonel Merino Pereyra assumed command of the army's *selva* division, headquartered in Iquitos, after being promoted to general in 1955.[71] At the CAEM these officers had been prepared for their command posts after a careful "introduction into the realities of the state and its national potential."[72]

The CAEM's interpretation of national defense included social and economic development as a mandatory component of national security.[73] In essence, the center's doctrine was that a dependent and underdeveloped nation such as Peru was extremely vulnerable to threats of internal disorder, as well as attack from external enemies. National development and national defense were thus considered closely interwoven concepts. The instruction offered at the CAEM for senior armed forces officers was aimed at defining the military's relationship to Peru's basic problems of underdevelopment. During the early 1950s the CAEM became the most important agency for the clarification of the military's growing commitment to development. But it must be kept in mind that the center was not the exclusive proponent of a modernizing mission for the armed forces. As will be illustrated in the following chapter, after 1956 army officers without any links with the CAEM were increasingly advocating an expanded role for the armed forces in resolving Peru's basic national problems.

These ideologies voiced within the armed forces during the Odría regime were formulated with minimal influence from APRA, Peru's only viable political party. During the party's first twenty years of political activity, its progressive ideology favorably influenced reformist military men. But during Odría's first seven years in office, the APRA leadership was scattered in exile or imprisoned, while its party chief, Haya de la Torre, remained confined in the Colombian Embassy. Moreover, the party's image as a revolutionary force for change in Peru had been undermined by the failure of APRA leaders to back the Callao revolt. Consequently, many more defections from the party's ranks occurred during the period of the underground activity under Odría than during the earlier era of the party's illegality before 1945.

In a conversation with H. Gerald Smith of the United States Embassy in Santiago, Chile, APRA leader Manual Seoane summarized the state of the party's internal dissension and his own dissatisfaction with Haya de la Torre's autocratic style of leadership. Talking with Smith in November, 1951, Seoane claimed APRA was then split into three factions, with a small group of about 5 percent of the membership disaffected from the party because of a "lack of confidence in the party leadership" as a result of the Callao revolt. Seoane called this group "extremists" and "all-out revolutionaries." A second faction, representing 20 percent of the party, remained completely loyal to Haya de la Torre as the "*Jefe Maximo*" and "mystical leader of the party." Clearly seeking to bolster his own leadership image in the party, Seoane concluded that the remaining 75 percent of the party remained loyal to him as the APRA's designated leader in exile. Reflecting the strains of his relationship with Haya de la Torre, Seoane concluded his discussion by arguing that APRA required a thorough organizational reform to make it more "democratic," and he suggested that Haya de la Torre's leadership powers be substantially reduced.[74]

At the Party Congress of APRA Exiles in Guatemala in 1952, four *Apristas* apparently representing the extremist faction referred to by Seoane denounced the party leadership. These dissidents charged that the APRA leaders abandoned the party's policy of anti-imperialism and thus created unnecessary divisions in the working classes. They also claimed that the problems of the Indian and related agrarian reform had been largely ignored by the party chiefs.[75] Much of the bitterness of these particular critics stemmed from their conviction that the failure of the Callao revolt signaled the end of APRA's commitment to revolution. They insisted that because APRA leaders had resorted to political opportunism in denying their affiliation with the revolt, the party had lost a great deal of prestige as one of Latin America's leading representatives of the working class and the peasantry.[76] *Aprista* feminist leader Magda Portal went even further. She not only decried the party leadership's loss of courage, but also bitterly denounced the useless sacrifice of APRA militants by the party's hierarchy. "Always martyrs from the working class, never from among the leaders," she complained as she explained her reasons for renouncing her APRA membership in the aftermath of the abortive Callao insurrection.[77]

The accusations by party dissidents that the APRA leadership had moved to the right during the early 1950s were valid. When the Odría government finally allowed Haya de la Torre to leave Peru on 6 April 1954, one of his first statements to the press indicated his intention to present a moderate party image.[78] In Mexico City during late April he stated: "I believe democracy and capitalism offer the surest road toward a solution of world problems even though capitalism has its faults." In a subsequent press interview in Rio de Janeiro in June, 1954, Haya de la Torre also sought to renew his pre-1948 favorable relationship with Washington by declaring that the United States was the "*maestro* nation of the continent."[79]   The APRA leader also continued to deny an involvement of the party leadership in the Callao revolt.[80]

Fredrick B. Pike views Haya de la Torre's enforced five-year "retreat" in the Colombian Embassy as a critical interlude of relaxed contemplation and personal growth. Free from the physical and "psychic" terrors of his earlier underground years, the APRA leader, armed with the writings of Arnold Toynbee, carefully assessed APRA's future course. Continued revolutionary activism seemed out of the question given the massive repression following the Callao revolt and the defection of many party militants after October, 1948. Instead, the Cold War provided APRA the opportunity to continue its shift from anti-imperialism to anticommunism begun during the Bustamante regime, while even more aggressively soliciting Washington's aid for the *Aprista* cause. As Pike notes, "Haya looked to Washington as a well-nigh indispensable agency for shielding APRA from persecution, and thereby providing its members with the access to power that was essential to prevent the party from withering away."[81] During early 1956 this policy was given its first test as Odría's opposition to APRA began to soften in the wake of growing attacks on his government from both rightist politicians and senior army officers.

In the final two years of Odría's regime, opposition from conservative political leaders and army commanders reached it peak. The minister of war, General Zenón Noriega, led the first serious attempted military *coup* in August, 1954. Fearing that Odría would not step down as president after his constitutional mandate expired in July, 1956, Noriega made plans with army units in Lima to depose him. Working mainly with General Ernesto Ráez Cisneros and the Seventh Artillery Unit in Lima, Noriega planned to seize strategic points in the capital and broadcast appeals for support from armed forces units throughout the nation.[82] The plot was activated at 2:30 A.M. on 10 August when rebellious army units seized the Central Telephone Exchange and Radio Magdalena in Lima. Simultaneously, General Ráez Cisneros and Lieutenant Colonel Walker Alexander Osores, commander of the Seventh Artillery Unit, attempted to deploy their forces throughout the city.[83] Despite his seemingly powerful role as minister of war, Noriega's movement had no active support beyond the confines of Lima, and within a few hours government troops and police had recaptured the city's main communications facilities. Odría, after communicating directly with leaders of the subverted artillery unit, convinced the rebels to surrender.[84]

Among the thirteen army officers implicated in the conspiracy (in addition to Noriega, Ráez Cisneros, and Alexander Osores) were Colonel Juan Baretto Saavedra, commander of the Lima garrison, and Lieutenant Colonel Romulo Vasquez Zapata, chief of the armored group Mariscal Castilla.[85] Very likely hoping to avoid the problems of court-martialing his supposedly closest military and political ally, Odría had General Noriega quickly deported aboard a navy destroyer on 11 August. Upon his arrival in San Francisco on 26 August, the former minister of war did not deny his role in the plot but justified his actions on the grounds that Odría had no plans in 1956 to hold elections in order to elect a successor.[86]

Noriega's failure to oust Odría and his subsequent deportation did not end his efforts to topple his former army comrade in the months immediately following his expulsion from Peru. After traveling from the United States to Argentina, he continued his subversive activities.

The second plot by Noriega met with even less success than the first. He planned to instigate a revolt in Arequipa, but the arrest of one of the conspirators on 19 December led to the government's breakup of the conspiracy. One of the civilian plotters, Wilfred Pfluker, was seized with documents implicating Noriega and his civilian allies. Following up the investigation, government agents arrested the other leading conspirators, and by the third week of January, Noriega's intrigues were ended. The prime motivation for his continued plotting can be attributed to his own presidential ambitions. As the number two man in the Odría government for six years (and provisional president for a brief period in 1950), the general apparently felt he should succeed Odría in 1956.[87] When his prospects appeared uncertain in August, 1954, he began planning his attempted *coup*.

In response to the threats against his regime during the latter half of 1954, Odría continued to employ the Internal Security Law vigorously during all of the following year. At the same time, the president made the first public announcements of his intentions to retire from the presidency when his term expired. In mid-April, 1955, Odría claimed that he was prepared to step down and insisted that Peruvians should trust him because "the people know I do not talk nonsense."[88]

Most of his countrymen, however, were not convinced. In July, Pedro Beltrán, the editor of *La Prensa*, who had become increasingly alienated from Odría since the 1950 elections, initiated a campaign to prevent any continuation of the regime past July, 1956. Publishing a front-page manifesto signed by a number of opponents of the government on 20 July, the newspaper editor and his colleagues demanded repeal of the Internal Security Law, free elections, and the declaration of general political amnesty.[89] Soon after the publication of the manifesto, Beltrán's colleague, Pedro Rosello, formed the *Coalición Nacional* (National Coalition, based on the single policy of opposition to the Odría government). Throughout the remainder of 1955 the group continued to press the administration to ease political controls and to guarantee free elections.

In early November the government did announce that elections for all national offices were scheduled for 3 June 1956.[90] Moreover, on 3 December a political amnesty for all political prisoners except *Apristas* and Communist Party members was decreed by the regime.[91] Some APRA exiles, however, were permitted to return to Peru during December, 1955 without fear of arrest as Odría demonstrated his first sign of conciliation toward his avowed political enemies.[92]

Civilian pressure for Odría to honor the constitutional process was also supported by important elements within the armed forces. Many officers continually questioned the military's support for Odría, and their role in the enforcement of the Internal Security Law disturbed many of them. In late 1955, opposition to Odría's attempt to remain in power or name his successor was forming in the army's senior ranks.[93] Odría attempted to deal with this issue in an Army Day speech on 9 December and asserted that his government had been marked by a lack of personal ambition in its attention to the needs of his countrymen and the armed forces in particular.[94] On this theme he emphasized the administrative reforms in the armed forces promulgated during his presidency. The most comprehensive of these, the *Ley de Situación Militar de Oficiales de Ejército, Marina y Fuerza Aerea* (Law governing the Military Condition of the Officers of the Army, Navy, and Air Force), was being formulated during late 1955. This reform further clarified conditions for such important military matters as promotion and retirement.[95] Despite these measures and Odría's assurances, some top army commanders remained intensely suspicious of the president's political ambitions.

One of these officers was General Marcial Merino Pereyra, who after graduating from the CAEM in 1954, took command of the army's *selva* division, headquartered in Iquitos. There on 16 February 1956, Merino rose against the government and seized the prefecture and other important buildings. The general then broadcast his revolutionary manifesto over Radio Loreto and proclaimed that his revolt was aimed at assuring that free and open elections would be held as scheduled on 3 June. He also charged that Odría was attempting to convert the army into an instrument of terror (a reference to the army's role in the enforcement of the Internal

Security Law) in order to impose his own electoral process upon the citizens.[96] In Lima the government responded immediately to the crisis by declaring martial law and arresting leading members of the *Coalición Nacional*, who were charged with complicity in the Merino revolt. On 17 February, Pedro Beltrán was imprisoned in Peru's maximum security installation of *El Frontón*.[97]

General Merino was unable to enlist the support of other regional commanders from his relatively isolated jungle headquarters. His forces did hold out for ten days as government planes dropped leaflets on Iquitos's central plaza and threatened the city with bombardment if the rebels failed to surrender. General Julio Humberto Luna Ferracio, sent by Odría to force Merino's surrender, succeeded in capturing the city on 26 February.[98] Casualties were light, and General Merino, after failing to gain asylum in the Brazilian consulate in Iquitos, turned himself over to Luna Ferracio. In a rambling radio message before his surrender, the rebel leader reiterated his charge that Odría planned to rig the coming elections and emphasized that his movement's overall objective was to achieve a clearer understanding with the Peruvian people concerning the good intentions of the armed forces.[99]

By the first week of April order had been restored, and civilians jailed during the first days of the Merino revolt were released. Pedro Beltrán's imprisonment prompted severe international criticism of the Odría government and led many Peruvians to doubt that elections would be held as scheduled.[100] Odría, even as he lashed out at his conservative political opponents, announced that the elections would be held as originally announced. Odría claimed that "the forces of the right had lost the political game to the left" because of their hostility to his regime in the last year.[101] This statement seemed to be in reference to the new policy adopted by Odría of enlisting APRA's aid in the election of a presidential candidate acceptable to him. The government had already allowed the party to convene its Third National Congress in Lima during March, thus granting the APRA de facto legality. But as the president hesitated in his endorsement of his own presidential choice, APRA leaders began negotiations with the leading candidates to obtain a commitment for the legalization of the party after the June elections.[102]

Three candidates remained in contention for the presidency by 5 May. On 19 April, Odría gave his endorsement of Hernando de Lavalle, a conservative lawyer of little political appeal, who was running as the candidate of the *Unificación Nacional* (National Unification Party). Fernando Belaúnde Terry, a forty-four-year-old architect and professor, sought the presidency as the head of the politically heterogeneous *Frente*

Nacional de Juventudes Democráticas, (National Front of Democratic Youth). Finally, former President Manuel Prado y Ugarteche, after spending most of the Odría era in Paris, ran as the standard-bearer of the well-financed *Movimiento Democrático Pradista*, (Pradist Democratic Movement).[103] These three political leaders realized that APRA support would be the critical factor in deciding the national elections. Despite the party's proscription during the first seven years of Odría's rule, it still claimed the largest single following of any political group in Peru. APRA needed rebuilding, however, after years of repression and party defections. APRA secretary-general Ramiro Prialé sought a guarantee of political legality as the price of support for a presidential candidate. Prialé held talks with the candidates and President Odría only months after being released from the Lima penitentiary.[104] Justifying his dealing with the party's former enemy, the secretary-general offered the explanation that his most important mandate was to rebuild the party. He added that APRA leaders had a great capacity to forget past injustices.[105]

Notwithstanding Odría's newly conciliatory attitude toward APRA, his hand-picked candidate, Hernando de Lavalle, was unable to gain the party's backing. Lavalle's failure can be attributed to his unwillingness to make a firm public promise that APRA could legally function during his presidency. This reluctance is understandable in light of the long tradition of conservative opposition to the party and his apparent uncertainty of Odría's real position toward APRA. But Lavalle's indecision and the unpopularity of his association with the administration prevented him from gaining any substantial following, and his candidacy faded badly by mid-May.[106]

Fernando Belaúnde Terry, although from a distinguished family (his father, Rafael, was President Bustamante's first prime minister, and his uncle Víctor Andrés Belaúnde was Peru's leading scholar-diplomat), had only limited political experience as a deputy in the National Congress from 1945 to 1947. The young architect's political organization was composed largely of students and middle-class professionals who ranged from moderate to Marxist in political orientation.[107] Belaúnde's political strength was uncertain until Odría made the tactical error of ordering the National Election jury to invalidate his electoral petitions—the same procedure he employed against General Montagne in 1950. This time the strategy backfired as the aggressive Belaúnde challenged Odría to reinstate his candidacy or face violent resistance. The president backed down, and the jury reversed its decision on 1 June. One week later in Lima, Belaúnde drew one of the largest crowds at a political rally in Peru.[108] Haya de la Torre, apparently recognizing a possible threat to his leadership by the now clearly popular Belaúnde and motivated further by his personal animosity toward the young architect, balked at making a deal with the candidate seemingly closest to the party's political philosophy.[109] The still-lingering possibility that Odría might not accept Belaúnde's election and thus undermine any electoral agreement APRA might make with Belaúnde was another reason in the decision not to support his candidacy.

The postponement of elections from 3 June to 16 June allowed Ramiro Prialé more time to reach an accommodation with Manuel Prado. The former president refused to legalize APRA during his first regime, but he was ready to accept a policy of *convivencia* (coexistence) to assure his election in 1956. Only one day before the election he signaled an agreement with APRA by declaring in a public address: "One of the first acts of my government will be to convoke ample political amnesty; to abrogate the laws of political exception; to eliminate all dispositions foreign to the precepts of our constitution. In this way Peruvians will be able to enjoy fully their civil rights."[110]

With this announcement, Prado satisfied APRA leaders of his commitment to legalize APRA, and instructions were given to the party's followers to vote for the sixty-seven-year-old representative of Peru's conservative upper-class interests. Odría accepted the deal because he knew his own candidate would lose, and he sought assurances, which Prado was willing to give, that investigations of some of the corrupt practices of his regime would not be pursued.[111]

Relying on this unlikely coalition, Prado was elected to a second term as president. With women voting for the first time, Prado polled 568,057 or 45 percent of the vote. Belaúnde made a very impressive showing with 458,248 or 36 percent, identifying him as a definite future political force. Lavalle, whom Odría had all but abandoned in his last-minute dealings with Prado and APRA, trailed badly with 222, 618 votes.[112] Although Prado was declared president on 13 July, many Peruvians still expected a last-minute effort by Odría to extend his presidential rule. But the general, ailing from an injured hip suffered in a fall soon after the elections, lacked the support for any such move. The armed forces accepted Prado because he was a better alternative to Odría's continuation in power. Very few officers were willing to back the discredited Odría beyond the constitutional limits of his regime. Moreover, Prado had pledged to continue the military housing, health, and pension programs begun under Odría. He also promised to make purchases of necessary military equipment, and most importantly, he vowed not to interfere (as he had done during his first regime) with military promotions or other primarily internal military matters.[113]

The Odría era closed quietly when the former military strongman left Peru practically unnoticed a day before Prado's inauguration on 28 July 1956. As Odría departed for the United States, few of the military men who composed his movement of October, 1948 remained his close comrades. The armed forces that he had led no longer identified with many of his views regarding the military's role in national affairs. But just as significant, the officer corps was not badly divided after his eight-year dictatorship. Lacking the charisma, ambition, and perhaps most importantly, a dynamic partner like Eva Perón, Odría could not mobilize Peru's masses nearly as successfully as Juan Perón was able to do with Argentina's *descamisados* (shirtless ones). A byproduct of the Argentine leader's populist politics, however, was the polarization of the Argentine army; the two major army factions, the *colorados* and the *azules*, were fighting each other in the streets seven years after Perón's ouster in 1955. As a leader of the armed forces, Odría, in contrast to Perón, was more a caretaker than a powerfully directive *caudillo*. His regime was thus a bridge between the traditional *caudillismo* of Peru's premodern military and a more unified and professional armed forces. As a result, Peru's military establishment was better prepared to initiate major reforms during the Velasco era, while the Argentine military, like the society it mirrored, remained badly divided.

NOTES

1. Anonymous, "La junta militar del gobierno, *Revista Militar del Perú*, 45, no. 10 (October, 1948), pp. 154-160.
2. Ibid. These included Minister of Housing and Commerce Colonel Luis Ramírez Ortíz, Minister of Public Health Colonel Alberto López Flores, and Minister of Agriculture Carlos Miñano Mendicilla.
3. Ibid.; *Peruvian Times*, 11 November 1948, p. 1.
4. *Legisiación Militar del Perú*, 1 November 1948, p. 1.
5. "Manifesto a los institutos armados y el pueblo del Perú," signed by Major Jorge Tejada Lapoint, Captain German Guerrero, Major Carlos Meza Navarro, and Captain Jorge Rosas Burgos in Panama during July, 1949. *Colección de Volantes*, 1949 folder.
6. Ibid.
7. Ibid.
8. Perú, Ministerio de Guerra, *Ordenes Generales del Ejército*, 11 March 1949, p. 71.
9. Ibid. General officers (brigadier general and above) received the minimum pay raises of 15 percent.
10. *Legislación Militar*, 9 December 1949, p. 69.

11. Perú, Ministerio de Hacienda y Comercio, *Anuario Estadístico del Perú: 1948-1949*, pp. 710-711.

12. *The New York Times*, 17 November 1949, p. 12.

13. *El Comercio*, 1 May 1949, p. 1.

14. *Peruvian Times*, 25 November 1949, p. 2. For a review of Odría's early public works programs see Colonel Ricardo Zegarre de la Flor, *El gobierno del presidente constitucional de la republica, General de División, Don Manuel A. Odría y el progreso del Perú* (Lima: 1952).

15. David Collier, *Squatters and Oligarchs: Authoritarian Rule and Policy Change in Peru* (Baltimore: 1976), p. 110.

16. Hernando De Soto, *The Other Path: The Invisible Revolution in the Third World* (New York: 1989), p. 40.

17. *El Comercio*, 1 January 1949, p. 1.

18. *Peruvian Times*, 7 January 1949, p. 1.

19. For Haya de la Torre's description of his ordeal see "My Five-Year Exile in My Own Country," *Life Magazine*, 3 May 1954, pp. 154-162. Extensive documentation regarding Haya de la Torre's efforts to gain political asylum in Colombia is located in serial file 723.00 (Peruvian International Political Affairs), 1950-1954, Department of State Records, RG 59, U.S. National Archives.

20. Broderick to Sec/State, 11 November 1951, NA, RG 59, 723.00/11-951.

21. *El Comercio*, 26 March 1949, p. 2.

22. *Peruvian Times*, 22 April 1949, p. 2.

23. Perú, Ministerio de Gobierno y Policía, *Ordenes Generales de la Guardia Civil y Policía*, 5 July 1949, p. 2.

24. *Partido Aprista Peruano*, Comité Nacional de Acción, *Secretaria Nacional de Prensa y Propaganda*, "Directiva Nacional #1," 1 July 1949. *Colección de Volantes*. This flier claimed that exiled *Aprista* committees were publishing newspapers and bulletins in Uruguay, Ecuador, Colombia, Panama, Mexico, Guatemala, and Costa Rica.

25. General Manual A. Odría, "Mensaje a la Nación del Señor Presidente de la Junta Militar del Gobierno, General de Brigada, Manuel A. Odría" (Lima: 1949), p. 6.

26. Ibid., pp. 60-115, passim.

27. Anonymous, "Juventud Aprista Peruano," *Colección de Volantes*, November, 1949, p. 5. The officer, unidentified for obvious reasons, was described as "young and prestigious" by the APRA representative.

28. G-2 Report no. 655428, U.S. military attaché to Department of the Army, NA, RG 319, 31 March 1950.

29. Ibid.; *Escalafón General del Ejército*, 1950, p. 18.

30. Tittman to Sec/State, NA, RG 59, 723.00/2-650, 6 February 1950.

31. Ibid., Report no. 622042, NA, RG 59, 23 December 1949.

32. Ibid., Report no. 643333, NA, RG 59, 4 April 1950, Archivo Histórico de Marina, Jefe de Zona Judicial (detailed reports summarizing the judicial proceedings) will be available February, 1991. *El Comercio*, 22 March 1950, pp. 1-10. Castañan Rivera was not subsequently executed. Personal interview with Capitán de Fragata Jorge Ortíz Sotelo, 3 May 1985, La Molina, Peru, and Tittman to Sec/State, NA, RG, 723.00/3-330501, 30 March 1950.

33. See note 32.

34. Enrique Chirinos Soto, *El Perú frente a junio de 1962* (Lima: 1962), p. 87.

35. *El Comercio*, 20 May 1950, p. 2.

36. *Peruvian Times*, 10 May 1950, p. 1; Anonymous, "Los Hechos Hablan," *Colección de Volantes*, May, 1950.   This handbill called for signatures for Montagne's election petitions.

37. For Montagne's version of these events see Ernesto Montagne Marckholtz, *Memorias del general de Brigada, E.P. Ernesto Montagne Marckholtz* (Callao: 1962), pp. 220-240. U.S. Ambassador Harold Tittman claimed "communists and *Apristas* were involved in the revolt." See Tittman to Sec/State, NA, RG 723.0016/1750, 17 June 1950.

38. *Peruvian Times*, 21 July 1950, p. 1; Fredrick Pike, *The Modern History of Peru*, (New York: 1967), p. 291. Odría received 550,779 votes, slightly more than his vice-presidential running mate, Hector Boza.

39. See previously cited articles in the *Revista Militar del Perú* and Frederick M. Nunn, *Yesterday's Soldiers: European Military Professionalism in South America, 1890-1940* (Lincoln, Nebraska: 1983), for a discussion of these writings prior to 1940.

40. Víctor Villanueva Valencia, *El CAEM y la revolución de la fuerza armada* (Lima: 1973), p. 28.

41. Ibid.

42. See Chapter 4 for a discussion of this commission.

43. Villanueva, *El CAEM*, p. 29.

44. Ibid., pp. 30-32.

45. G-2 Report no. 667591, 17 May 1950, U.S. military attaché to Department of the Army, NA, RG 319.

46. The center was included as a provision of the *Ley Orgánico del Ejército* (Organic Law of the Army) of 14 July 1950.   See Colonel Armando Cueto Zevallos, "El CAEM, escuela de la defensa nacional," *Revista Diplomatica Peruano Internacional*, 5, no. 36 (January-February-March, 1972), pp. 10-11, 62.

47. Villanueva, *El CAEM*, pp. 32-33.

48. Villanueva, *El CAEM*, p. 37 cites the impact of the National War College.

49. A U.S. military attaché commented on Del Carmen Marín's intellectual ability as early as 1944, claiming he was "a man to be reckoned with." See G-2 Report no. 353, 2 February 1944, U.S. military attaché to War Department, NA, RG 319.

50. Ibid., G-2 Report no. 446306, 9 March 1948, NA, RG 59, U.S. military attaché to Department of the Army.

51. Luis Valdez Pallete, "Antecedentes de la nueva orientación de las fuerzas armadas en el Perú," *Aportes* 10, no. 17 (January, 1971), p. 177.

52. Carlos A. Astiz and José Z. García, "The Peruvian Military: Achievement Orientation, Training and Political Tendencies," *Western Political Quarterly*, 25, no. 4 (December, 1972), p. 674.   Rear Admiral Federico Salmón de la Jara concurs with this interpretation (personal interview with Admiral Salmón de la Jara, 4 May 1985, Lima, Peru).

53. Villanueva, *El CAEM*, pp. 40-41; G-2 Report no. 642900, 3 March 1950, NA, RG 319, U.S. military attaché to Department of the Army.

54. Villanueva, *El CAEM*, pp. 41-42. For an insightful analysis of CAEM's role in the formation of the armed forces' ideology see Jorge Rodríguez Beruff, *Los militares y el poder: Un ensayo sobre la doctrina militar en el Perú, 1948-1968* (Lima: 1983).

55. Víctor Villanueva Valencia, *Ejército Peruano: Del caudillaje anarquico al militarismo reformista* (Lima: 1973), p. 259.

56. *Peruvian Times*, 4 August 1950, p. 4.

57. Villanueva, *Ejército Peruano*, p. 259.

58. *Legislación Militar*, 11 November 1950, p. 86.

59. *Peruvian Times*, 6 January 1952, p. 1.

60. *The New York Times*, 20 June 1952, p. 7.

61. *Peruvian Times*, 29 February 1952; Federico Gil, *Latin American-United States Relations* (New York: 1971), p. 215.

62. *Ordenes Generales del Ejército*, 22 February 1952, pp. 5-6

63. *United States Congressional Record, Senate*, "U.S. Foreign Assistance and Loan Obligations," (Washington, D.C.: 1962), p. 15443.

64. *Peruvian Times*, 29 February 1952, p. 2, and 27 March 1953, p. 1.

65. The three destroyers were named the *Aguirre*, the *Castilla*, and the *Rodríguez* and were first built for the U.S. navy in 1943. The submarines, built by the Electric Boat Co., were named *Tiburon* and *Lobo* and were the first new vessels purchased by the Peruvian navy since the 1920s. *Jane's Fighting Ships, 1954-1955* (London: 1955), pp. 281-283. These ship purchases were seen as essential to the professionalization of the navy, particularly by its younger officers. Personal interview with Vice Admiral (R) Luis Vargas Caballero, 6 May 1985, Lima, Peru.

66. Federación Universitaria de Arequipa, Comité Ejécutivo de Huelga, "Comunicado #1," 5 September 1952, *Colección de Volantes*; *The New York Times*, 5 October 1952, p. 25.

67. *The New York Times*, 4 February 1953, p. 7.

68. *Anuario Estadístico del Perú: 1953-1954*, pp. 710-711. Government spending, which had been rising sharply since 1948, declined by 3.5 percent in 1954 over the preceding year.

69. Captain Marcial Figueroa Arévalo, "El oficial del ejército y la integración del indigena a la nacionalidad," *RMP*, 52, no. 621 (September, 1955), pp. 104-109.

70. *Escalafón General del Ejército*, 1955, p. 18; Villanueva, *El CAEM*, p. 221.

71. *Escalafón General del Ejército*, 1955, p. 10.

72. Colonel Edgardo Mercado Jarrín, "El ejército de hoy y proyección en nuestra sociedad en periodo de transición, *RMP*, 59, no. 685 (November-December, 1964), pp. 1-20.

73. Ibid., p. 16.

74. Broderick to Sec/State, 9 November 1951, NA, RG 59, 723.00/11-951.

75. Víctor Cárdenas, Laureano Checa, Hector Guevara, and Orestes Romero Toledo, *El Apra y la revolución: Tesis para un replanteamiento revolucionario* (Buenos Aires: 1952), pp. 5-9.

76. See Víctor Villanueva Valencia, *La sublevación aprista del 48: Tragedia de pueblo y un partido* (Lima: 1973) for the best statement of the dissidents' sense of betrayal.

77. Magda Portal, *¿Quienes traicionaron al pueblo?: A los Apristas* (Lima: 1950), p. 28, quoted in Fredrick Pike, *The Politics of the Miraculous in Peru: Haya de la Torre and the Spiritualist Tradition* (Lincoln, Nebraska: 1986), p. 238.

78. Haya de la Torre interview, *Life Magazine*, 3 May 1954, p. 164; Tittman to Sec/State, NA, RG 723.00/6-2254, 22 June 1954.

79. Haya de la Torre traveled widely in North and South America soon after leaving Peru.

80. Haya de la Torre continued to deny the party leadership's involvement in the Callao revolt as late as 1974 (personal interview with Víctor Raúl Haya de la Torre, 13 July 1974, Lima, Peru).

81. Pike, *The Politics of the Miraculous*, p. 242. For a discussion of interparty tensions during Haya's five-year exile see Edward Epstein, "Motivational Bases of Loyalty in the Peruvian *Aprista* Party," Ph.D. diss., University of Illinois, 1970, p. 55.

82. *El Comercio*, 11 August 1954, p. 2.

83. Ibid.

84. *Peruvian Times*, 13 August 1954, p. 2.

85. Ordenes Generales del Ejército, 21 August 1954, pp. 81-90. Other officers implicated were Lieutenant Colonel Gustavo Conterno Fraysinet, Lieutenant Colonel Teodoro Villavicencio Castañeda, and Lieutenant Colonel José Matallana Moran.

86. *Peruvian Times*, 13 August 1954, p. 2; *The New York Times*, 27 August 1954, p. 3; Tittman to Sec/State, NA, RG 723.00/8-1354, 13 August 1954.

87. The largely political motivations of these subversive efforts apparently deterred many officers from supporting what appeared to be only a simple power play against Odría.

88. *The New York Times*, 14 April 1955, p. 12. This comment was made to correspondent Herbert Matthews.

89. *La Prensa*, 20 July 1955, p. 1. The political persuasions of the signers were extremely varied, ranging from the extreme rightist Luis Flores to moderate reformers Luis Bedoya Reyes and Fernando Belaúnde Terry.

90. *Legislación Militar*, 2 November 1955, p. 172.

91. *Peruvian Times*, 10 February 1956, p. 2.

92. Arnold Payne, *The Peruvian Coup d'etat of 1962: The Overthrow of Manuel Prado* (Washington: 1965), p. 47.

93. César Martín, *El preludio de la democracia* (Lima: 1956), pp. 64-66.

94. General Manuel A. Odría, Principios y postulados del movemiento restaurador de Arequipa: Extractos de discursos y mensajes del General Don Manuel A. Odría (Lima: 1956), p. 149.

95. *Legislación Militar*, 2 July 1956, p. 11.

96. *Peruvian Times*, 17 February 1956, p. 2.

97. Ibid., 19 February 1956, p. 3. In the process of arresting members of the *Coalición*, government police raided the exclusive *Club Nacional* in Lima. This raid further alienated many wealthy Peruvians from the Odría government.

98. *El Comercio*, 26 February 1956, p. 2.

99. *Peruvian Times*, 2 March 1956, p. 2. The government announced fourteen casualties in the suppression of the revolt.

100. *The New York Times*, 27 February 1956, p. 8; and 28 February 1956, p. 20.

101. Ibid., 5 April 1956, p. 14.

102. For the best discussions of the APRA leader's preelection negotiations see Chirinos Soto, *El Perú frente*, pp. 11-126; François Bourricaud, *Power and Society in Contemporary Peru* (New York: 1970), pp. 272-278; Carlos A. Astiz, *Pressure Groups and Power Elites in Peruvian Politics* (Ithaca, New York: 1969), pp. 99-103.

103. Chirinos Soto, *El Perú frente*, pp. 119-126.

104. Bourricaud, *Power and Society*, p. 81; *The New York Times*, 7 April 1956, p. 6; personal interview with Ramiro Prialé, 10 May 1985, Lima, Peru.

105. Bourricaud, *Power and Society*, p. 81; *The New York Times*, 7 April 1956, p. 6; personal interview with Ramiro Prialé, 10 May 1985, Lima, Peru.

106. Chirinos Soto, *El Perú frente*, p. 124.

107. Bourricaud, *Power and Society*, p. 91.

108. Chirinos Soto, *El Perú frente*, pp. 121-122.

109. In a letter to Luis Alberto Sánchez in June, 1956, Haya de la Torre referred to Belaúnde as an "enemy" of APRA and a "tool" of Admiral Rocque Saldías and Pedro Beltrán. This letter signaled a long feud between Haya de la Torre and Belaúnde that would reach its zenith during Belaúnde's first presidency (1963-1968). Donald C. Henderson and Grace R. Peréz, *Literature and Politics in Latin America: An Annotated Calendar of Luis Alberto Sánchez Correspondence, 1919-1980* (University Park, Pennsylvania: 1982), Document 1098, p. 270.

110. *El Comercio*, 16 June 1956, p. 9; personal interview with Ramero Prialé, 10 May 1985, Lima, Peru.

111. Pike, *The Modern History of Peru*, p. 295; Villanueva, *Ejército Peruano*, p. 255.

112. *El Comercio*, 15 July 1956, p. 2.

113. Ibid., p. 9.

1. Colonel Luis Miguel Sánchez Cerro as he appeared for his official presidential photograph in 1933. *Source:* Instituto de Estudios Histórico-Marítimos del Perú (I.E.H.M.P.).

2. General Oscar R. Benavides presiding at graduation ceremonies at Peru's Naval Academy during his second presidential administration. *Source:* I.E.H.M.P.

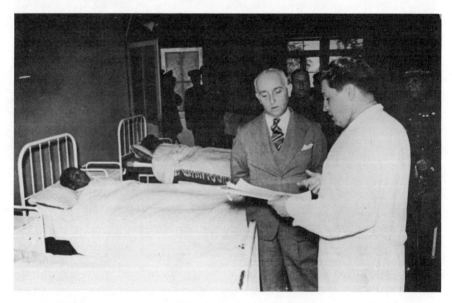

3. President Manuel Prado y Ugarteche visiting wounded soldiers at a military hospital during the July 1941 border conflict with Ecuador. *Source:* I.E.H.M.P.

4. President José Luis Bustamante y Rivero (front row, third from the left) and his assembled cabinet, July 1947. General Manuel A. Odría, who would overthrow Bustamante in late October 1948, is standing in the front row on the extreme left. *Source:* I.E.H.M.P.

5. General Manuel A. Odría hosting a reception in September 1950, shortly after his "election" to a six-year term as Peru's president.

6. The young architect/politician, Fernando Belaúnde Terry being carried on the shoulders of his enthusiastic supporters during his unsuccessful 1956 presidential campaign. *Source:* I.E.H.M.P.

7. General Juan Velasco Alvarado delivering an emotional address on the third anniversary of his October 3, 1968 *golpe de estado*. *Source:* I.E.H.M.P.

8. *APRA's Jefe Máximo* Víctor Raúl Haya de la Torre as he appeared near the end of his long career in Peruvian political affairs. *Source:* Biblioteca Nacional del Perú.

9. A Perúvian army "ranger" unit on parade during the July 28, 1974 Independence Day celebration. *Source:* Author's photograph.

10. A brand new Soviet-made medium tank on display for the first time during the July 28, 1974 parade. These tanks were the first in a series of major weapons purchases by the Peruvian armed forces from the Soviet Union during the 1970s and early 1980s. *Source:* Author's photograph.

7
Prado and the
Military Modernizers: 1956-1962

The second Prado administration was a critical period for the further clarification of the military's changing professional outlook. The military's perception of its mission as a disciplined agent of national development was a key motive prompting its decision to overthrow President Prado in July, 1962 and cancel the national elections of that year. These actions were taken mainly because Fernando Belaúnde Terry, the candidate favored by most members of the officer corps due to his technocratic orientation, failed in his presidential bid. Notwithstanding the ouster of Prado only ten days before the end of his presidential term, his tenure was relatively free of civil-military conspiracies. This relative lack of civil-military unrest freed armed forces officers from much of the political bickering of the past and allowed them to turn more of their attention to the clarification of their long-perceived "nation-building mission." From an institutional viewpoint, the CAEM became the focus for the refinement of the military's moderniz-ing mission, but this perception was also held by officers who were never directly affiliated with the CAEM. Moreover, the need to modernize the armed forces' corporate structure was advocated by the officer corps as a unit, not just by a select group of progressive officers as in the past.

One of the army's most prominent theoreticians, General Edgardo Mercado Jarrín, reasoned that four main ideological precepts formed the core of the armed forces' evolving professional orientation. General Mercado Jarrín argued that the army, primarily as a result of its increasing professionalism and social consciousness, became a more confident and independent-minded institution following the border conflict with Ecuador in 1941. Contributing to this evolution after 1950, according to Mercado

Jarrín, were (1) the reorganization of the military's command and internal structure, (2) the "affirmation" of a new concept of national defense, (3) the influences of modern technology upon military thinking, and (4) the effort to develop an effective strategy to respond to the emerging threat of internal subversion.[1]

Most of the armed forces' structural reforms that Mercado Jarrín considered so important occurred during the second Prado administration. When it was enacted in 1956, the Ley de Situación Militar provided a badly overdue revision of regulations governing promotions, retirements, military justice, and discipline for the three armed services. The establishment of the Comando Conjunto (joint command) of the armed forces in February, 1957 created a unified command structure for the first time.[2] Navy commanders, after an "exhaustive study," submitted their own Ley de la Marina (Organic Law of the Navy), which was finally approved by the National Congress in December, 1960.[3] This law was followed by a detailed navy promotion law passed in August, 1961, modernizing the "archaic" promotion regulations that had been in effect since 1934. These two laws represented the first attempts by the navy for administrative reform since the disastrously divisive Callao revolt of October, 1948. In addition to these measures, the Naval War College was reestablished by mid-1961 as a vital training center, reflecting the reformist concerns of naval leaders.[4]

Meanwhile, a significant number of armed forces officers were attending command and staff schools in the United States during the 1950s. These experiences led some of them to reevaluate the relative quality of their own Escuela Superior de Guerra (ESG) upon their return. In a 1958 article in the Revista de Escuela Superior de Guerra, Mercado Jarrín offered a detailed comparison of the training offered at the United States army's Command and Staff School at Fort Leavenworth, Kansas, and the instruction at the ESG in Peru. Mercado Jarrín concluded that Peruvian officers could benefit from such schooling at Fort Leavenworth, but they should also recognize that such training would not completely prepare officers for the army's high command.[5] Mercado Jarrín was alluding to the concept, increasingly recognized by a growing number of progressive-minded military men, that hemispheric security depended upon the United States' nuclear deterrent capabilities. Moreover, he reasoned that nations like Peru possessed limited conventional warfare capabilities. Mercado Jarrín was certainly not suggesting the abdication of the armed forces' external defense mission, but he was insisting that counterinsurgency was fast becoming the armed forces' paramount function. Inseparably joined with this internal security role in the minds of officers like Mercado Jarrín was the military's parallel mission as an agent of national development. Mercado Jarrín was becoming increasingly unhappy with command training, both in Peru and overseas, that emphasized conventional military axioms as the principal preparation for promotion to the high command. CAEM attendance therefore met a very real professional need for these officers; in fact, the CAEM was the sole agency teaching nonconventional military doctrine in Peru until the opening of the army's Intelligence School in June, 1959.

The center served another valuable function after air force colonels and navy captains began attending in the late 1950s. According to Vice Admiral Luis M. Vargas Caballero, a 1962 graduate of the CAEM and a member of General Juan Velasco Alvardo's "Revolutionary Government of the Armed Forces," the CAEM provided a valuable opportunity for officers of the three armed services to become acquainted with one another's views. The admiral stressed that very few of these opportunities existed before the CAEM opened its doors.[6]

While keeping in mind the increasingly vital role of the CAEM within the armed forces, it must be recognized that it was not the only vehicle for the clarification of the military's national defense mission. As has been amply demonstrated, armed forces officers using the avenue of their professional journals were striving to do this for decades prior to the opening of the CAEM. Even while the center grew in prestige after the mid-1950s, army officers never affiliated with the CAEM accelerated these efforts. For example, Captain Mario Lozada Uribe authored a pamphlet in 1959 arguing that the armed forces should adopt a more intensified role in the national development process. Captain Lozado insisted that the military should devote at least 30 percent of its time and resources to "social action" projects and the remainder to its traditional duties. In Captain Lozada's view, the army should lead the way in developing civic action projects designed to raise the standard of living of the poverty-stricken Indian masses.[7]

The writings of two other army officers are particularly illustrative of the reformist orientation of non-CAEM personnel. In 1956, Lieutenant Colonel Alejandro Medina argued that the armed forces should carefully examine the potential of atomic energy for its possible future use in agriculture, industry, and transportation. Civic action programs, including road building and irrigation in Peru's remote regions, were also carefully detailed and praised by Lieutenant Colonel Artemio García Vargas in Peru's leading military journal in 1962.[8] These articles and a significant number of other writings by officers unaffiliated with the CAEM give evidence of the increasingly widespread nature of the modernizing perspective throughout the officer corps during the Prado years.[9] It is clear, then, that the significance of the CAEM is not so much that it exclusively introduced such thinking to armed forces officers, but rather that it served as a catalyst to crystallize this outlook for the officer corps as a whole. The new CAEM director in 1956, General Marcial Romero Pardo, was the man most responsible for this accomplishment.

General Romero Pardo has been called the chief ideologist of the CAEM. His training and career focus closely paralleled those of the first director, General Del Carmen Marín. Romero Pardo was influenced by his early training in France, particularly at the Superior War College in Paris. There he observed that French political leaders, economists, and government bureaucrats closely interacted with the military leadership to chart long-range plans for national defense.[10]

Under Romero Pardo's command, the CAEM continued to increase in prestige. Between 1956 and 1961 twenty-four graduates of the CAEM went on to become government ministers in the Prado, Belaúnde, and Velasco Alvardo administrations. Among these graduates were civilians who had begun to attend the CAEM in 1955, and who enrolled in the institution in increasing numbers after 1956.[11] For colonels (or officers of equal rank in the other armed services) the CAEM apparently became an increasingly important step toward promotion to general. Between 1952 and 1962, 213 army officers were promoted to colonel, of whom approximately 60 percent had attended the CAEM. Of those attending the CAEM, 70 percent were eventually promoted to general, while only 29 percent of the non-CAEM students reached that rank. For armed forces officers, appointment to the CAEM was made by the commander-in-chief of the three armed services and the police.[12] Unquestionably, as the CAEM grew in ideological importance, its political significance within the armed forces commensurately increased.

By 1959 the CAEM course had evolved into three separate four-month terms. In the first term students studied such diverse subjects as climatology, budgetary analysis, statistics, demography, sociology, linear programming, geopolitics, agricultural development, national income accounting, and banking. During the next two terms officers were asked to create military strategies that related national development theory to hypothetical wartime situations. These students were required to demonstrate a methodology that would "exploit all of Peru's national resources in a wartime effort."[13]

Further evidence of the growing recognition of the armed forces' nation-building role and the importance of the CAEM is provided in comments made to United States ambassador James I. Loeb by navy minister Vice

Admiral Guillermo Tirado Lamb in February, 1962. Although Admiral Tirado never attended the CAEM, he succinctly expressed many of the key ideological precepts of that institution's philosophy in his comments to Loeb. Tirado claimed that the military was fully conscious of its dominant role as a "disciplined and intellectually prepared force which has studied the national problems in a sincere effort to find the best solutions." After this obvious reference to the CAEM programs, Tirado claimed that "in underdeveloped countries the armed forces represent the most organized and coherent sector" for gaining an "accurate vision of the national realities." The admiral concluded that after several years of careful study of national problems, the military finds itself at the "center of gravity" of those groups charged with the responsibility for dealing with these national issues.[14] These comments reflected acceptance of developmental theory among even conservative members of the high command by 1962. Nevertheless, the Prado regime was still not willing to listen to the CAEM strategists regarding national development policy.

In 1958, for example, the CAEM proposed a development project for the central *selva* region. The proposal represented the first systematic military attempt to present financial estimates for such a program. Moreover, the CAEM project proposed exclusive military administration of this large geographic area in order that a controlled experiment in agricultural and industrial development could be conducted. The ultraconservative prime minister in Prado's government, Pedro Beltrán, opposed the project and was able to substitute a far less comprehensive program prepared by the A.D. Little Corporation of Cambridge, Massachusetts.[15]

The frustration caused by the government's rejection of the CAEM project, compounded by Prado's inability to finance the purchase of military equipment that armed forces officers felt was badly needed for the modernization of their institution, forced Peru to seek large-scale military assistance from the United States. Although Peru's military men recognized that they could never be competitive with the world's leading military powers, their desire to modernize their outdated conventional equipment was a logical component of their sharpened professional consciousness. Thus, they sought foreign military assistance to accomplish this objective, with Washington as the primary source.

Continuing its military aid from the Odría years, the United States gave military aid of all types (including deliveries of excess stocks) that totaled over seventy million dollars.[16] This sum ranks as one of the highest in Latin America. A sizeable share of the military acquisitions was allocated to the navy. Three destroyers, two submarines, and a floating dry dock were obtained from the United States in the late 1950s. These purchases did not completely fulfill the navy's requirements, as two more modern British cruisers were purchased in 1959 to replace the obsolete flagships the *Almirante Grau* and the *Coronel Bolognesi*.[17]

Washington's interest in promoting civic action programs after 1960 caused a sizeable amount of this military aid to be channeled into road-building and other development projects. In 1961 the Sixth Engineer Combat Battalion, numbering over eight hundred men, was supplied with five million dollars worth of equipment for road clearing and construction projects in the Peruvian *sierra*.[18]

Major credit for the initiation of United States-sponsored civic action projects in Peru must be given to General Juan Mendoza Rodríguez. As head of the Peruvian delegation to the Inter-American Defense Board, General Mendoza Rodríguez presented a resolution calling for the board to facilitate vocational training for Latin American armed forces recruits for their employment in construction and colonization projects. This resolution resulted in a 1960 statement recommending such activities.[19] Point four of this resolution succinctly states the guiding theory of the civic action programs:

The General Military Plan for the Defense of the American Continent recognizes the desirability of doing everything possible to raise the standards of living of the peoples, with the object of effectively combatting Communist propaganda, which tries to exploit the ignorance and poverty of the underdeveloped areas.[20]

In the context of the Peruvian military's defense rationale, General Mendoza's proposal was best articulated by General Mercado Jarrín. Other than the obvious developmental value of the army's involvement in "nation-building" projects, Mercado Jarrín called the technically proficient Peruvian soldier a "permanent vehicle for Peru's modernization." He insisted that the army was one of the key agents for change as it best understood the strategy of modernization and most acutely appreciated Peru's array of social and economic problems. Consequently, Mercado Jarrín argued that the illiterate *campesino*, upon being drafted into the army and given adequate technical training, could return after his two-year stint in the military and be ready to use his technical expertise for the Indian community's benefit.[21] Mercado Jarrín clearly overstated the positive influence of military service upon the socialization of Indian conscripts. But one study, which will be discussed in detail in Chapter 10, did conclude that the political awareness of Indian recruits was heightened by military service.[22]

The primary motivation for the United States-initiated civic action programs was the perceived threat posed by Fidel Castro's Cuba. In the case of Peru, it is also possible to characterize the military's markedly increased commitment to an internal development strategy as predicated largely on the basis of its increasing fear of internal insurgency. Although other issues were also instrumental in stimulating the reformist conscious-ness of the armed forces, bloody confrontations between *campesinos* and *Guardia Civil* units throughout Peru after 1958 dramatized to the armed forces the discontent of the rural population. In addition, the destruction of the regular army in Cuba and its replacement by a popular militia starkly demonstrated the potential threat of successful guerrilla movements to the very existence of regular armed forces throughout Latin America. The concepts of counterinsurgency warfare were not new to many army officers, as their training in French military doctrine included some exposure to guerrilla warfare theory. As we have seen, Peruvian army leaders were familiar with the thinking of two famous French colonial generals, Hubert Lyautey and Joseph Gallieni, who stressed in their nineteenth-century writings strategies based upon winning the confidence of the local population and increasing the economic prosperity in the zones of pacification.[23]

Subsequent failures by the French army to defeat popular insurgent forces in Indochina and Algeria undoubtedly had an impact upon the Peruvian officers' perception of the armed forces' role in counterinsurgency after 1956. These officers demonstrated in their writings and training programs an awareness of the difficulties in combating guerrilla forces. Writing in 1956, Major Romulo Zanabria Zamudio outlined what were then recognized as the basic tenets of guerrilla campaign tactics. He stressed the need of the armed forces to be able to combat the "highly mobile, cold-blooded and tightly disciplined" actions of the typical guerrilla fighter. Major Zanabria concluded that to deal effectively with a guerrilla threat, special counterinsurgency units should be organized and an efficient military intelligence organization should be created.[24] Indeed, in June, 1959, the army established an Intelligence School, later to be followed by the creation of a special antiguerrilla Ranger unit in the early 1960s.[25]

The army's treatment and training of Indian conscripts also reflected a desire to counteract the growth of Indian revolutionary cadres as a prelude to future guerrilla activity in the *sierra*. Some officers acknowledged that if Indian recruits were treated badly and no attempt was made to integrate them into society after their military services ended, then they might emerge from two years of army service as future guerrillas.[26] Thus, satisfactory performance by Indian conscripts in literacy training was an important item on the new army Inspection Code enacted in 1960. Significantly, junior officers charged with the training of these recruits could be penalized for the failures of their charges to make adequate progress in their literacy training.[27] Although vocational training for army recruits was also actively initiated in April, 1962, with emphasis on the trades desperately needed throughout Peru. Plumbing, carpentry, electronics, mechanics, and basic building construction were stressed. By the mid-1960s, this vocational program involved the training of three thousand recruits in ten different trades.[28] Vocational training during a two-year military stint could not be expected completely to lift Indian conscripts out of their poverty-stricken life-styles, but it at least demonstrated the army's concern for their welfare as well as an anxiety regarding their future revolutionary potential.

Because of the motives delineated by Colonel Mercado Jarrín and discussed at the beginning of this chapter, the military's professional mission was further refined during the second Prado administration. Although it is not possible to quantify the influence this broadened professional perspective had within the officer corps, it is evident from the policies and public statements of armed forces personnel that their perception of the military as an agent for change was embraced by an increasing percentage of Peru's military men. Until July, 1962, however, when the military seized power from President Prado, civilian political rivalries kept the armed forces' command more involved in national politics than with charting development projects.

Until the electoral crisis of July, 1962, men in uniform conspired on only two occasions against the Prado government. With the important exception of the 18 July 1962 *coup d'état*, only one civil-military conspiracy and a police barracks revolt occurred during the Prado years. Moreover, military men held only the three armed forces portfolios during the Prado presidency, sharply contrasting with their deep involvement in the two previous administrations. This situation reflected markedly reduced dissension within the officer corps and the desire of military leaders to demonstrate a politically independent public image after their identification with the politics of the Odría regime. Through the first four years of his regime, Prado seemed satisfied with the low political profile adopted by the armed forces. In January, 1960 Prado told United States ambassador Theodore Achilles that he was sure that the armed forces were "completely loyal and democratically inclined."[29] Nevertheless, a civil-military conspiracy organized in February, 1958, and a police uprising that flared in July, 1959, were serious (if only brief) threats to the political stability of the period.

The lack of *Aprista* support for either the police rebellion or the earlier civil-military conspiracy reflected the strength of the APRA's adherence to the conditions of the *convivencia* with the Prado government. The party's position was explained by APRA secretary-general Ramiro Prialé in April, 1957.

Prialé claimed that the party's support of Prado in the 1956 election was a necessary tactical move dictated by the need for the APRA to gain legal status in order to be able to present its own candidates in the 1962 presidential election.[30] Prialé's comments and the *Aprista*'s abstention from subversive campaigns during the Prado administration demonstrated that APRA leaders knew they had little real chance to gain power by force. After the repeated failures of past revolutionary efforts (most notably the Callao revolt of 1948), Haya de la Torre and other top *Apristas* accepted the fact that the revolutionary tactics of the past no longer could produce political victory for the party.[31]

One of the most notable changes in the *Aprista* ideology was, as previously noted, the public shift in the international emphasis of the party from anti-imperialism to anticommunism and procapitalism. This policy change was made public after Haya de la Torre's release from the Colombian Embassy in Peru in 1954. The origins of this position can be traced to APRA policy during the first Prado administration, when Haya de la Torre modified APRA's anti-imperialist policy while he sought Washington's aid in having the party legalized. During the Bustamante presidency, as the Cold War became more intense, APRA's anticommunist position became increasingly strident. In keeping with this direction in policy, Haya de la Torre, Prialé, and Andres Townsend Ezcurra in April, 1961 had extensive conversations with President Kennedy's personal representative in Peru, Arthur Schlesigner, Jr. During these talks, Haya de la Torre brought up the matter of his long-standing proposal for the formulation of a national economic council designed to oversee Peru's economic development. The APRA chief insisted that foreign companies should be represented on the council, as he claimed such companies had the right to a voice in economic matters.[32] Regarding the volatile nationalist issue involving the status of the International Petroleum Company (a Standard Oil subsidiary that had dominated Peru's petroleum production since the 1920s), Haya de la Torre suggested that the solution might be the formation of a mixed state- and foreign-owned enterprise, with Peru controlling 50 percent of the IPC operation. He also added that IPC was worthy of praise for what it had done for its workers and that the company's labor policies should serve as a model for the rest of the nation's enterprises.[33]

In further conversations with United States ambassador James I. Loeb in January, 1962, Haya de la Torre and Prialé made a concerted effort to stress APRA's anticommunist position.[34] They argued that after thirty years of experience in fighting communism in Peru, APRA was best able to carry on the struggle against organized communist activity. Haya de la Torre rejected the idea that the armed forces should deal with the communists; he reasoned that military men could rely only on force and this, he insisted, was not an acceptable solution to the problem.[35]

Senior armed forces officers were not unaware of the more conservative ideological stance adopted by the APRA leadership. In March, 1961 the minister of war, General Alejandro Cuadra Ravines, commented that he was impressed with the "moderate and forward-looking" tone of the party's public pronouncements. Navy chief of staff, Vice Admiral Alfredo Sosa, although he considered himself a conservative, stated that he saw no connection between APRA and the Communist Party as other rightist officers had seen in the past. He said that he recognized the possibility of an APRA victory in the 1962 national elections and gave no indication that he thought the military would oppose an Aprista electoral victory.[36] Significantly, both of these officers cautioned that they did not speak for the rest of the armed forces when they made these statements. Their views, however, were certainly reflective of an understanding among some military men that APRA leaders had chosen a more conservative political course. Still, events in July, 1962 would demonstrate a continuing and pervasive anti-APRA feeling in the armed forces that would override the recognition of APRA's new conservatism.

The marked drift of Aprismo to the right caused serious divisions within the party. As already noted, many militants left the party after leading Apristas failed to support the Callao revolt of 1948. In 1959, another group of APRA activists rejected the party's new ideological position, and in November, 1960 they formed a political splinter group called APRA Rebelde (Rebel APRA). Led by Luis de la Puente Uceda, these former Apristas, who sympathized with the revolutionary objectives of the militants who led the Callao revolt of 1948, became increasingly committed to revolutionary action. They devoted most of their efforts after November, 1960 to espousing radical land reform.[37] In June, 1962, APRA Rebelde leaders decided to disassociate themselves completely from the parent party and changed the name of their organization to the Movimiento de Izquierda Revolucionaria (Movement of the Revolutionary Left, MIR) with de la Puente Uceda being named as secretary-general of the group. After establishing contact with the peasant organizer, Hugo Blanco, in October,

1962, the MIR began slowly preparing for the guerrilla campaign it would launch in 1965.[38]

The *APRA Rebelde* and later the MIR joined the Marxist *Movimiento Social Progresista* (Social Progressive Movement, MSP), the *Partido Socialista del Perú* (Peruvian Socialist Party, PSP), and the tiny *Frente de Liberación Nacional* (National Liberation Front, FLN) on the political left. All these groups failed to fill the void created by the swing of APRA to the right during the early 1950s. After this shift the political center was best represented by Fernando Belaúnde Terry's *Acción Popular* (Popular Action, AP) party and to a lesser extent by the *Partido Democrático Cristiano* (Christian Democratic Party, PDC), headed by Héctor Cornejo Chávez.

Belaúnde, along with a number of his close political colleagues, formed *Acción Popular* soon after his surprisingly strong showing in the 1956 elections.[39]   At *Acción Popular's* first party congress on 1 June 1957, Belaúnde set his party machinery in motion for a concerted bid for the presidency in the 1962 elections.[40]

The architect-turned-politician was easily the most dynamic political figure during the Prado regime. He traveled throughout Peru during these years "seeking the reality" of his nation and working to project an image of a technically oriented, nationalistic reformer.[41]   In keeping with his propensity for the flamboyant gesture, which he demonstrated during the 1956 elections, he fought a duel with his outspoken political critic, Senator Eduardo Watson Cisneros, in January, 1957.[42]   On another occasion, in May, 1959, Belaúnde served a few days in Peru's maximum security prison, *El Frontón*, after defying a government ban against political demonstrations. He was released soon after a bungled escape attempt drew even more national attention to his energetic campaign.[43]   In contrast to these impulsive actions, Belaúnde's careful efforts to court the support of armed forces officers displayed a shrewd understanding of the military's changing perspective.

Both Belaúnde's training as an architect and his proposals during the 1956 election campaign and after for the initiation of a broader range of armed forces-sponsored civic action projects contained a special appeal for Peru's military men.[44]   *La conquista del Perú por los Peruanos* (The Conquest of Peru by Peruvians), Belaúnde's first book, written in 1959, contained specific proposals for the military's participation in his development scheme for Peru. He suggested that badly needed mapping, sanitation, health, education, and construction projects could be conducted best by the armed forces.[45]   In a statement reminiscent of CAEM rhetoric, Belaúnde claimed that the "technical organizations of the military are well prepared to carry out a profound analysis of the national reality." He

noted that the armed forces training schools were centers for high-quality
scientific education and that the nation's universities could profit from the
work done at the military institutions. Belaúnde also made the key point
that other army officers (most notably Mercado Jarrín) had repeatedly
stressed that a military barracks can be considered a school—not just a
school to train men in the use of weapons, but a basic center in which
Indian youth are acculturated into the modern sector through military
training.[46] In July, 1960 United States ambassador Seldon Chapin noted
Belaúnde's efforts to enlist the support of military men for his coming
presidential candidacy.   Chapin indicated that Belaúnde was making
contacts with armed forces officers and was hoping for their support against
the APRA candidate.[47] The aspiring presidential candidate may have also
hoped that the identification of APRA with the conservative policies of the
Prado administration would also further alienate officers already inclined
to oppose an APRA presidential bid.

Despite Belaúnde's support within the armed forces, Prado served nearly
his entire presidential term in part because of relatively stable economic
conditions and his ability to maintain solidarity among his board-based
political coalition. The increase in the cost of living for the first five years
of the Prado government averaged a moderate 7.6 percent, and the food
and commodity shortages characteristic of Belaúnde's civilian regime did
not materialize.[48] Prado silenced his most vocal conservative political
critic, Pedro Beltrán, by shrewdly offering him the post of prime minister
in July, 1959. Through December, 1961 (when Beltrán resigned from the
cabinet) APRA leaders worked in relative harmony with a government
headed by two of the most powerful members of Peru's oligarchy. The
government's critics charged that this political détente was sustained by
mortgaging the future of Peru's impoverished sectors.[49] Prado's hollow
efforts in the area of agrarian reform certainly substantiate this criticism.

On 30 September 1960, the draft of a limited agrarian reform law was
submitted to Prado. Although the law was supposedly designed to "raise
the standard of living of the Peruvian campesino and secure the maximum
utilization of the land resources of Peru." The structure of the law made
it highly unlikely that land reform would be carried out with any vigor by
the government.[50] An Italian land reform expert, acting as an adviser to
the Prado administration, left Peru in December, 1961 after months of
frustration in dealing with his recalcitrant employers. He claimed that "this
government has no will for land reform."[51] The government's subsequent
inaction throughout the remaining seven months of the Prado regime
confirms this analysis. It should be recognized, however, that during the

first half of 1962, Prado's attention was turned more toward the national elections scheduled for 10 June 1962 than toward agrarian reform.

The 1962 national elections loomed as one of the most critical in Peru's history. For the first time, two parties with broad support, APRA and *Acción Popular*, would be contending for control of the presidency and the congress. Indications pointed to the candidacy of Haya de la Torre for only the second time since APRA entered the national political arena in 1930. Although their support was very limited, the remaining parties of the left gave progressives, Marxists, and socialists their best representation in any twentieth-century presidential election. Finally, the ultraright, as always, lacked a cohesive political organization. Pedro Beltrán solicited support for his presidential candidacy in late 1961, but his effort soon collapsed. But shortly after returning to Peru in March, 1961, former president Manuel Odría formed the *Union Nacional Odriísta* (National Odrist Union, UNO). Calling himself a "socialist of the right," Odría sought the support of the urban working classes, who were the prime beneficiaries of the social assistance programs of his administration. He was also endorsed by businessmen and industrialists who had profited handsomely from the general's public works programs.[52]

The first three months of 1962 witnessed intense political maneuvering by armed forces leaders and civilian presidential candidates in preparation for the June elections. The government party, the *Movimiento Democrático Pradista* (Pradist Democratic Movement, MDP), threw its support to Haya de la Torre and culminated the political arrangement of the *convivencia* that saw APRA support Prado's candidacy in 1956. APRA's newly conservative political position and his long-standing enmity toward Odría also persuaded Pedro Beltrán to support the APRA chief for the presidency. *Apristas* were thus placed in the totally unfamiliar position of having a government-sponsored candidate with strong conservative backing.[53] Even the normally cautious *Peruvian Times* ventured the opinion in January, 1962 that "in the three decades [since 1930] APRA has swung from a far left to a rightist or at least middle of the road position."[54]

The announcement of Haya de la Torre's candidacy with the official backing of the Prado government brought a quick reaction from the Belaúnde camp and senior officers of the armed forces. In talks with Adlai Stevenson during June, 1961 Belaúnde, possibly anticipating the Prado government's support for Haya de la Torre, expressed doubts that the 1962 elections would be free. He warned that if that event proved to be the case, there would be a revolution.[55] On 9 February 1962 Javier Alva Orlandini, a leading member of *Acción Popular*, charged that serious voter registration irregularities were being perpetuated by APRA and MDP leaders. Two weeks later, the National Election Jury (the body responsible for supervising the elections) admitted that some of Alva Orlandini's charges might have some justification.[56] More significant than these charges, however, was an initial warning given during early February to the United States ambassador that the armed forces' officer corps was not prepared to accept the presidential victory of Haya de la Torre.

The warning was made to Ambassador Loeb by the navy minister, Vice Admiral Tirado Lamb. Referring to the ideological shift of APRA during the Prado years, Tirado claimed that for APRA "no tactic is forbidden in their appetite for pretense; their apparent rectification of philosophies and methods does not bother them if that is the easiest way to attain their objectives."[57] Pursuing this point further, Tirado charged in an obvious reference to APRA that certain parties "which originally drank at communist fountains" have made changes in their political programs only because of expediency. Tirado Lamb cautioned Loeb against United States support for APRA and warned that if Washington backed only those parties it considered most popular, it could very well lead to the failure of United States policies in Latin America.[58]

By 2 March the armed forces' position on the candidacy of Haya de la Torre had been further clarified. Minister of War Aléjandro Caudra Ravines and General Juan Bossio Collas joined Tirado Lamb in voicing strong opposition to the APRA chief's presidential ambitions. General Cuadra Ravines claimed that an important factor motivating the military's antipathy to APRA was the belief of many officers that Haya de la Torre was a homosexual.[59] In further conversations with Loeb, Tirado Lamb also stressed the history of anti-APRA indoctrination in the armed forces and especially the hatred of Haya de la Torre. He said that it was too much to expect the armed forces to serve under the rule of such a party. Tirado claimed that he and General Cuadra Ravines had become broad-minded enough to work with APRA in the Prado government but he knew of no officer in the armed forces who would serve in an APRA cabinet. Finally, the navy minister insisted that if Haya de la Torre won the presidential election, the armed forces would prevent him from serving. Haya de la Torre's election would mean, according to Tirado, that the military would then have to suppress APRA, with the result that rebellious Apristas would probably turn to Castroism. Tirado Lamb told Loeb that he had expressed the same sentiments to APRA secretary-general Prialé and that the latter had merely listened without comment.[60]

Ambassador Loeb was instructed to reply to the armed forces leaders that the United States government would not support APRA or any other political group and that it had no intention of participating in the Peruvian political process. However, Loeb was informed that he should state that the United States was committed to the principles of representative democracy, which United States policymakers felt represented the views of the peoples of the Americas. Under these circumstances, Loeb told Tirado that the United States would find it very difficult to justify to the rest of the continent the granting of recognition or financial aid to any military regime that had overthrown an anticommunist democratic government.[61] This position was finalized after Loeb consulted with President Kennedy and other top administration officials in Washington in early March.[62] But the *coup d'état* in Argentina, deposing President Arturo Frondizi on 29 March, immediately put the United States policy to its first serious test. When the United States did not withhold recognition from the military-imposed interim government in Argentina, its position in opposing a similar military takeover in Peru was seriously undermined.[63]

During mid-April, APRA leaders Prialé and Haya de la Torre dismissed senior officers' threats to the *Aprista* chief's presidential candidacy. Prialé insisted that the rumors of a military intervention had no real foundation. He claimed that many officers had approached APRA to look for cabinet posts. Haya de la Torre offered the same evaluation of the military's position as Prialé did. According to the *Aprista* leader, the threats had no real substance. He even claimed that both Cuadra Ravines and General Odría had come to thank him for their promotions after the 1945 elections.[64] Despite his seemingly confident attitude, Haya de la Torre still sought to persuade Ambassador Loeb to notify all parties involved in the electoral process that the United States would not recognize any government imposed by force. Loeb and Chargé d'Affaires Douglas Henderson, however, refused to make such a blanket statement.[65] But as the elections drew near, the APRA leadership had greater reason for concern regarding the armed forces' action.

The involvement of the military in the 1962 election process was mandated under the Peruvian law. The supervision of election officials and voters at the polling booths was constitutionally delegated to the armed forces. Public statements by armed forces leaders indicated that they assumed the entire responsibility for the supervision of almost all phases of the election procedure.[66] This interpretation put the military at odds with the National Election Jury, which was dominated by Prado's appointees and supposedly had the final word in determining the outcome of any disputed election returns.[67] In April General Ricardo Pérez Godoy, chairman of the armed forces' joint command, referred to the military's broad interpretation of its electoral role as well as its ongoing investigation of alleged APRA and MDP registration irregularities. Speaking at the Escuela Superior de Guerra, Pérez Godoy emphasized that the constitutional responsibilities of the armed forces gave them the mandate to "confront all divisive and extremist forces which openly or covertly threaten the nation's institutions and to intervene in all situations which endanger the stability of democratic institutions and the ordered free and sovereign life of the republic."[68]

Pérez Godoy's comments were a prelude to the communiqué of the armed forces' joint command issued on 26 May, announcing that their investigation of voter registration lists had revealed that "the will to commit fraud is patent."[69] The joint command claimed that of the 3,697 male voter registration cards the armed forces had examined, 1,697 had been illegally issued, with most of the irregularities attributed to the APRA-Prado coalition.[70] Prior to the issuance of the communiqué, Belaúnde had charged fraud in the registration process, and on 20 May he threatened not to recognize the results of the coming elections unless the armed forces approved the final decision of the National Election Jury.[71]

It is evident that Belaúnde's preelection tactics reflected his own doubts about his ability to win the presidency without the aid of the armed forces. By demanding that the military review the election results and casting doubts upon their legitimacy, he lent support to the armed forces' campaign to block the election of Haya de la Torre. Admiral Tirado Lamb noted Belaúnde's tactic on 23 May when he told Ambassador Loeb that the leaders of Acción Popular cried fraud because they feared they would lose the election. Tirado Lamb reasoned that had they been sure of success they would have kept silent. In this same conversation, the admiral again insisted that the armed forces could not accept Haya de la Torre as president because many officers felt the APRA leader would "destroy the armed forces within three months."[72] This same attitude was expressed by General Julio Doig Sánchez, Peruvian military attaché in Washington, on 22 May. General Doig, who identified himself as strongly pro-Belaúnde, told his United States military hosts at a dinner party that APRA would try to cripple the armed forces if Haya de la Torre were elected. The military attaché said, however, that he was sure that the armed forces would intervene if APRA won, but only after the elections were over. General Doig also claimed that many officers felt that Odría was too old and "too old hat" for Peru.[73] Of even further significance was that General Nicolás Lindley López, commanding officer of the army and another supporter of Belaúnde, toured the nation's army installations during April and May to gauge the feeling of the armed forces on the question of the coming elections.[74] Lindley's efforts were apparently part of the armed forces' program to poll the officer corps several months before the elections to ascertain opinions on support for a *coup d'état*.[75] Clearly, the armed forces were prepared to abide by the results of the 10 June elections only so long as they met with their approval.

Haya de la Torre made some last-minute efforts during the first week of June to head off the increasingly evident armed forces opposition to his possible presidential victory. During a campaign address he claimed that APRA and the military were unified in their opposition to the common threat of communism. He also promised that the armed forces would be given "preferential attention" in the modernization of its military equipment.[76] While campaigning in Piura, the APRA chief placed a wreath at the monument to Miguel Grau, the Peruvian naval hero of the War of the Pacific.[77] These final efforts were made as six other presidential candidates made their final appeals to the electorate.

The seven candidates in the 1962 elections represented one of the largest fields of presidential aspirants in the history of Peru. Haya de la Torre ran under the banner of the *Alianza Democrática* (Democratic Alliance), a coalition of APRA and Prado backers. Joining him in the field were Belaúnde, Odría, Héctor Cornejo Chávez, representing the Christian Democrats, Luciano Castillo of the Socialist Party, army general (R) Cesar Pando Esgusquiza, standard-bearer of the National Liberation Front, and lawyer Alberto Ruiz Eldredge of the Social Progressive Party.[78] Belaúnde took an early lead in the balloting, and on 11 June he prematurely claimed victory while announcing in his colorful speaking style, "I lay down the sword and bestow on the outgoing government the laurels which it has earned for itself by the freedom of the election process."[79] Also praising the honesty of the election process the day after the elections was Colonel Roberto Gonzales Polar, chief of the department of civil military affairs in the Ministry of War. Colonel Gonzalez declared that "the elections have been conducted in all of the departments with complete order and all of the results were guarded by the armed forces."[80]

The vote counting proceeded very slowly, however, and a week after the elections, it became increasingly evident that Haya de la Torre and Odría were receiving sufficient support to prevent any candidate from gaining the constitutionally required 33.3 percent of the total vote to be named president. As the vote counting continued, it became apparent that the final decision regarding the presidency would have to be decided by the new National Congress.[81] Thus, the Prado government now faced its gravest political crisis.

When the final unofficial vote tabulation in late June showed Haya de la Torre with a slight lead over Belaúnde, the armed forces' leadership challenged the legality of the election process and again declared its opposition to the APRA leader.[82]   Prado tried to deal with the armed forces' opposition by attempting to transfer the anti-APRA commander of the air force, General Pedro Vargas Prada, to the Inter-American Defense Board in Washington, D.C. But the president withdrew his order when forty top air force officers, headed by Chief of Staff General Carlos Granthom Cardona, threatened to resign in protest. During the last week of June a joint armed forces committee took the initiative against Prado. Admiral Tirado and Generals Cuadra Ravines, Lindley López, and Salvador Noya Ferre presented Prado with a document proclaiming that Haya de la Torre was completely unacceptable to the armed forces as president. But Prado was not then willing to accede to these demands. The minister of development, Jorge Grieve, was informed by General Cuadra Ravines after the meeting with Prado that the joint committee was strongly influenced by the armed forces' poll, which indicated that both Haya de la Torre and Odría were not acceptable to the officer corps.[83]

The armed forces' leadership then brought its campaign against the election process into the open on 28 June when it issued a communiqué charging that fraudulent voting had occurred in seven of the nation's twenty-four departments. Singled out as especially dishonest were the returns from the *Aprista* strongholds of Cajamaraca, La Libertad, and Lambayeque.[84] On 3 July military leaders issued another ultimatum to Prado that stated that the armed forces would act if Haya de la Torre did not withdraw his candidacy within one week. This time Prado passed the ultimatum on to Haya de la Torre. Then on 4 July the APRA chief announced that the military had vetoed his candidacy. Haya de la Torre offered to renounce his candidacy for the good of the "constitutional order," but he insisted he was leaving the final decision up to the APRA leadership. Negotiations between the three leading candidates and government representatives then commenced with the aim of finding a solution to the election impasse, which was confirmed by the National Election Jury on 17 July.[85]

The final results released by the jury had Haya de la Torre leading Belaúnde by slightly less than thirteen thousand votes but gaining only 32.98 percent of the total ballots cast. Since the presidential decision was constitutionally mandated to the new congress, in which APRA controlled 40 percent of the seats, Belaúnde's or Odría's only chance for the presidency was an electoral pact with Haya de la Torre.[86] Belaúnde's talks with APRA broke down on 8 July. The *Acción Popular* candidate than left on 11 July for Arequipa, where he established barricades around his headquarters and declared that if the Prado regime did not overturn the election results "we will be obliged to overthrow the government and punish its crimes."[87] Belaúnde's movement quickly collapsed, however, when the armed forces' leadership disassociated itself from his radical actions. Nevertheless, senior officers in Lima gave Prado a final ultimatum on 14 July that coincided with Belaúnde's demand.

The senior commanders insisted that the entire election process be annulled and that Prado establish the framework for new elections. This path was the only way, the armed forces' leaders declared, that Prado could finish his constitutional term. The president held out against these demands and claimed that the National Election Jury was constitutionally independent and that he had no authority to annul the elections.

Meanwhile, with Belaúnde removed from the negotiations, Haya de la Torre and Odría worked to cement an agreement they hoped would prevent a military takeover and break the election deadlock. APRA leaders and the former president had been engaged in discussions since the first week of July in a relatively cordial manner.[88] On 14 July Odría, Haya de la Torre and General Pérez Godoy met together, and Peréz Godoy informed both men that because of the election fraud the armed forces could not accept an APRA president.

After the meeting of 14 July events moved swiftly, culminating in the coup d'état on 18 July. Prado's cabinet resigned en masse on 16 July in the face of the armed forces' demands that the elections be annulled. At the final cabinet meeting Admiral Tirado Lamb made public his own letter of resignation dated 12 July, in which he charged the National Election Jury with becoming the "complacent collaborator" of the APRA party. Tirado Lamb claimed that Peru was in grave danger of "political anarchy or fascist dictatorship" if the election crisis were not resolved.[89] The following day the joint command, without any mention of the service ministers, formally demanded that the president of the National Election Jury, José Enrique Belaúnde y Corzo, overturn the elections. A few hours later, Belaúnde y Corzo denied that the armed forces had the right to request the cancella-tion of the elections. He also asserted that the election irregularities claimed by the military were not serious enough to change the results of the elections.[90] In the late afternoon of 17 July events drew closer to a climax with the announcement by General Odría that he had finally reached an accord with the APRA. The agreement would give Odría the presidency. Aprista leader Manual Seoane would assume the first vice president's post, and APRA would become the dominant party in the National Congress.[91] Haya de la Torre later claimed that he contacted Pérez Godoy to inform him that APRA had reached an accord with Odría but that he was told by the chairman of the joint command that it was "too late."[92] The military then made its well-coordinated move to end the political deadlock on the terms of the officer corps.

At 3:20 A.M. on the morning of 18 July, tanks surrounded the National Palace while other troops were dispatched to various strategic sites in Lima. Colonel Gonzalo Briceño Zevallos, commanding the units around the palace, then ordered President Prado to surrender and claimed that he was authorized to destroy the building if the chief executive did not comply.[93] Only after eight tanks had pushed in the palace gate and entered the interior courtyard did Prado leave his residence. He was taken to a naval transport vessel, where he was detained briefly before being allowed to leave for Paris.[94] Military units also occupied the National Congress and the APRA headquarters, and by mid-morning on 18 July the joint command had established itself as the new *Junta de Gobierno* (government *Junta*) without loss of life and with only minor street disturbances. APRA leaders called a general strike in protest, but it failed completely.[95]

The 18 July movement differed significantly from past armed forces' *coups* in that the military acted as a unit and not as the instrument of a single *caudillo* such as Sánchez Cerro or Odría. The four members of the joint command, including its chairman, General Pérez Godoy, army commander general Nicholas Lindley López, air force chief general Pedro Vargas Prada, and navy commander vice admiral Juan Francisco Torres Matos, assumed posts as joint presidents of the new military government. The *Junta* quickly issued three decrees (cosigned by all four members) annulling the elections of 10 June 1962 and suspending constitutional guarantees for thirty days.[96] The armed forces' commanders then established a time limit of one year for their rule and General Pérez Godoy, in the government's first pronouncement, stressed that the *Junta* renounced any political ambitions of its own. He claimed that "none of us will be a candidate, nor offer himself as a candidate nor do anything to obtain a political post" as a result of their position in the military government. The general also insisted that when the *Junta*'s term expired, its members would return to their barracks in "silence and dignity."[97]

The new military government confronted minimal internal opposition following the *coup*. APRA leaders were relatively subdued, as was General Odría. The government kept order without press censorship or significant political repression.[98] Belaúnde praised the action of the armed forces and asserted that the *coup* was a "lesson" to those who "dare to commit fraud as a political method" and that such action could not be permitted in Peru without punishment.[99] The fact that many Peruvians expected some form of military action after the election impasse became apparent seems to have had an important effect upon their apathetic reaction to the *coup*.

Despite the absence of internal resistance, however, the new government was the target of sanctions from the United States government.

The United States broke diplomatic relations with the military government and suspended all but humanitarian assistance programs the same day the *coup* occurred.[100] Ambassador Loeb concluded that the overthrow of Prado represented "the sharpest case yet to express the United States determination to support democratic governments" in Latin America.[101] Nevertheless, the United States business community in Peru did not, for the most part, support its government's policy. Representatives of the leading United States corporations in Peru met with General Pérez Godoy on 19 July and pledged their support for the regime.[102] In their talks with the general, executives of the Grace Corporation, however, expressed concern that "young Nasserite colonels were ready for radical changes."[103] The *Junta's* position on the United States action was given by foreign minister Admiral Luis Edgardo Llosa on 20 July. He claimed that the United States suspension of recognition represented a "headstrong and unjustifiable attitude" and that Washington had moved without knowing the true reasons the armed forces had to act in "the defense of the constitution and the laws."[104] By the time the United States resumed diplomatic relations on 17 August, however, the military government gave indications that it would not follow the pattern of past authoritarian military regimes in Peru. It embarked on a cautious reformist path reflecting the military's growing recognition of the need to address Peru's problems of poverty and underdevelopment.

NOTES

1. Colonel (Later Division General) Edgardo Mercado Jarrín, "El ejército de hoy y un proyección en nuestra sociedad en periodo de transición," *Revista Militar del Perú*, 59, no. 685 (November-December, 1964), p. 1.

2. *Legislación Militar del Perú*, "Ley de Situación militar del oficiales del ejército, marina y fuerza aerea del Peru," 2 July 1956, p. 11; General Juan Mendoza R., "El ejército Peruano" in *Visión del Perú en el siglo XX*, 1, José Paraja Paz Soldán, (Lima: 1962), p. 324.

3. Vice Admiral Guillermo Tirado Lamb, *Sintesis expositiva de la gestión ministerial del Vice-Alimirante Guillermo Tirado Lamb*, Ministerio de la Marina, July, 1962.

4. Ibid.

5. Lieutenant Colonel Edgardo Mercado Jarrín, "La escuela de comando y estado mayor de Fort Leavenworth y algunas diferencias con nuestra, *Revista de la Escuela Superior de Guerra*, 5, no. 2 (April-May-June, 1958), pp. 15-35. This military journal will hereafter be cited as *RESG* with date and page number.

6. Personal interview with Vice Admiral (R) Luis M. Vargas Caballero, 6 May 1985, Lima, Peru.

7. Capitan Mario Lozada Uribe, El nuevo rol social de los institutos armados y fuerzás auxilares del ejército, marina, fuerza aerea, guardia civil y regimento guardia republicana (Lima: 1959), pp. 1-17.

8. Lieutenant Colonel Alejandro Medina, "La geografía economíca frente a la energía atomica," RMP, 52, no. 627 (March, 1956), pp. 49-61; Lieutenant Colonel Artemio García Vargas, "Programas de acción civica," RMP, 57, no. 608 (January-February, 1962), pp. 49-56.

9. Alfred Stepan and Jorge Rodríguez conducted a content analysis of the articles appearing in the RMP and RESG for the periods 1954-1957, 1958-1962, and 1963-1967. Defining "New Professionalism" as a primary orientation toward internal security and national development, these scholars found that for the era 1954-1957 only 1.7 percent of the articles fell into the New Professionalism category. This percentage dramatically increased to nearly 30 percent for the period 1958-1962 and over 50 percent for the years 1963-1967. Alfred Stepan, The State and Society: Peru in Comparative Perspective (Princeton: 1978) pp. 130-133.

10. Víctor Villanueva Valencia, El CAEM y la revolución de la fuerza armada (Lima: 1973), pp. 57, 221-224; José Z. García, "The Velasco Coup in Peru: Causes and Policy Consequences," Ph.D. diss., University of New Mexico, 1974, p. 52.

11. García, "The Velasco Coup," pp. 53-54.

12. Ibid., pp. 50, 57.

13. Ibid.

14. Interview with and personal papers of former Ambassador James I. Loeb, Cabin John, Maryland, 17 December 1973. Hereafter cited as Loeb interview and Loeb papers.

15. Luigi R. Einaudi and Alfred Stepan, Latin America Institutional Development: Changing Military Perspectives in Peru and Brazil (Santa Monica: 1974), p. 37. See also a summary of the A.D. Little proposal, Anonymous, "Programa de desarrollo nacional y regional para el Perú," RESG, 8, no. 2 (April-May-June, 1961), pp. 7-38.

16. U.S. Overseas Loans and Grants and Assistance from International Organizations, 1 July, 1945-30 June 1973, U.S. Agency for International Development, (Washington: D.C.: 1974), p. 57.

17. Tirado Lamb, Sintesis expositiva de la gestión ministerial del vice-almirante Guillermo Tirado Lamb (Lima: 1962), pp. 1-22; Peruvian Times, 8 February 1957, p. 2. The two cruisers were the former HMS Newfoundland and the HMS Ceylon. They were renamed the Almirante Grau and the Colonel Bolognesi, respectively. Jane's Fighting Ships, 1960-1961 (London: 1961), p. 241.

18. Peruvian Times, 3 February 1961, p. 2.

19. Willard F. Barber and C. Neale Ronning, Internal Security and Military Power: Counterinsurgency and Civic Action in Latin America (Columbus, Ohio: 1966), p. 65.

20. Ibid., p. 271.

21. Mercado Jarrín, "El ejército de hoy," pp. 9-11.

22. For a discussion of this study see David Scott Palmer, "The Impact of the Peruvian Army on Political Development in Rural Peru: A Preliminary Explanation," Cornell University, 1970.

23. See Chapter 1 for a discussion of Lyautey's and Gallieni's influence on Peruvian military theory.

24. Major Romulo Zanabria Zamudio, "Algo sobre, guerra de guerillas," RESG, 3, no. 1 (January-February-March, 1956), pp. 37-42.

25. Legislación Militar, 10 June 1959, p. 37.

26. Einaudi and Stepan, Changing Military Perspectives, p. 52.

27. Ibid.

28. Barber and Ronning, Internal Security, pp. 190-191.

29. Loeb papers.

30. Personal interview with Ramiro Prialé, 10 May 1985, Lima, Peru; The New York Times, 27 April 1957, p. 8.

31. Personal interview with Ramiro Prialé, 10 May 1985, Lima, Peru; The New York Times, 27 April 1957, p. 8.

32. Loeb papers. For a particularly good analysis of the changing ideological thrust of APRA during the Convivencia see Richard Clinton, "APRA: An Appraisal," Journal of Inter-American Studies and World Affairs, 12, no. 2 (April, 1970), pp. 280-297.

33. Loeb papers.

34. Ibid.

35. Ibid.

36. Ibid.

37. Epstein, "Motivational Bases of Loyalty in the Peruvian Aprista Party," Ph.D. diss., University of Illinois, 1970, pp. 38-59; Grant Hilliker, The Politics of Reform in Peru: The Aprista and Other Mass Parties in Latin America (Baltimore: 1971), pp. 88-89; Richard Gott, Guerilla Movements in Latin America (New York: 1972), pp. 336-351. See also "Libertad a las Apristas Rebeldes," Colección de Volantes, 1961 folder, a handbill calling for the release of two APRA Rebelde members who were arrested while doing organizational work in Cuzco and Puno.

38. Víctor Villanueva Valencia, Hugo Blanco y la rebelión campesina (Lima: 1967), p. 131.

39. Interview with Fernando Schwalb López Aldaña, Cabin John, Maryland, 14 March 1974. Schwalb was one of the founders of Acción Popular and was Belaúnde's first prime minister in 1963.

40. Ibid.; Arnold Payne, The Peruvian Coup d'Etat of 1962: The Overthrow of Manuel Prado (Washington, D.C.: 1968) p. 34.

41. Belaúnde visited some of the most remote villages in Peru during these travels, and in 1959 he published La conquista del Perú por los Peruanos (Lima: 1959), which was later translated as Peru's Own Conquest (Lima: 1964), containing a general outline of his proposed presidential programs.

42. Peruvian Times, 18 January 1957, p. 1. Both men were slightly injured (Belaúnde sustained a cut hand and Watson a nicked ear) before the duel was terminated by the combatants' seconds.

43. Peruvian Times, 29 May 1959, p. 2 and 2 June 1959, p. 1.

44. For Belaúnde's 1956 campaign platform see M. Guillermo Ramirez y Berrios, Examen espectral de los elecciones del 9 de Junio de 1963 (Lima: 1963), p. 40.

45. François Bourricaud, Power and Society in Contemporary Peru (New York: 1970), pp. 229-260, provides an excellent analysis of Belaúnde's political style and programs as they were outlined in La conquista del Perú por los Peruanos and during

his campaign. See also Víctor Villanueva Valencia, *Ejército Peruano: Del caudillaje anárquico al militarismo reformista* (Lima: 1973), p. 264.

46. Fernando Belaúnde Terry, *Peru's Own Conquest* (Lima: 1964), pp. 203-206.
47. Loeb papers.
48. *Peruvian Times*, 21 April 1961, p. 2.
49. Bourricaud, *Power and Society*, p. 273.
50. *Peruvian Times*, 7 October 1960, p. 1.
51. Loeb papers.
52. *Peruvian Times*, 31 March 1961, p. 2; "La Union Nacional Odrfista Viva!," *Colección de Volantes*, 18 May 1961.
53. Payne, *The Peruvian Coup d' Etat of 1962*, pp. 38-39.
54. *Peruvian Times*, 5 January 1962, p. 2; Ramírez y Berrios, *Examen espectral*, pp. 40-41.
55. Loeb papers.
56. *La Prensa*, 23 February 1962, p. 1.
57. Loeb papers.
58. Ibid.
59. Ibid. Fredrick Pike, in his biography of Haya de la Torre entitled *The Politics of the Miraculous in Peru: Haya de la Torre and the Spiritualist Tradition* (Lincoln, Nebraksa: 1986) discusses the issue of Haya de la Torre's alleged homosexuality.
60. Loeb papers.
61. Ibid.
62. Ibid. Loeb returned to Washington, D.C., in early March, 1962 for consultations regarding the armed forces' position on the candidacy of Haya de la Torre. His response to the position of the military was formulated at a meeting with President Kennedy that was also attended by Arthur Schlesinger, Jr., George Ball, and Richard Goodwin. (Loeb interview.)
63. The position of the Kennedy administration was explained by Arthur Schlesinger, Jr., in 1967, when he claimed that "Frondizi sank without a trace, therefore it was difficult to suppose that nonrecognition would accomplish anything" (Angela King Westwater, "Recognition of Latin American Military Regimes during the Kennedy Administration," Master's thesis, New York University, 1967, p. 34).
64. Loeb interview and Loeb papers.
65. Loeb interview and Loeb papers.
66. This attitude was reflective of the military's recognition of the broad powers granted to it under Article 213 of the Peruvian Constitution of 1933.
67. Payne, *The Peruvian Coup d'etat of 1962*, pp. 41-42.
68. Loeb papers.
69. *El Comercio*, 27 May 1962, p. 1; *Peruvian Times*, 1 June 1962, p. 1.
70. *Peruvian Times*, 1 June 1962, p. 1.
71. Enrique Chirinos Soto, *Cuenta y balance de las elecciones de 1962* (Lima: 1962), p. 63; *El Comercio*, 21 May 1962, p. 1.
72. Loeb interview and Loeb papers.
73. Loeb papers.
74. Loeb papers.
75. Víctor Villanueva Valencia, *El militarismo en el Perú*, (Lima: 1962), pp. 210-211.
76. Bourricaud, *Power and Society*, p. 285.

77. *La Tribuna*, 2 June 1962, p. 1.

78. Ibid.

79. The literature dealing with the 1962 elections is extensive. The best works are Chirinos Soto, *Cuente y balance*; Payne, *The Peruvian Coup d'Etat of 1962*; Bourricaud, *Power and Society* (especially, the chapter entitled "The Rules of the Game"); César Martín, *Dichos y hechos de la política Peruana* (Lima: 1963); and Richard Patch, "The Peruvian Elections of 1962 and Their Annulment" in *American Universities Field Staff Reports*, (New York: 1962).

80. Bourricaud, *Power and Society*, p. 295.

81. Martín, *Dichos y hechos*, p. 16.

82. The final unofficial vote tabulations, subject to the review of the National Election Jury, were as follows: Haya de la Torre (Alianza Democrática)---557,047; Belaúnde (AP)---544,180; Odría (UNO)---480,798; Cornejo (PDC)---48,792; Pando (FLN)---33,941; Castillo (PSP)---16,658; Ruiz (MSP)---9,202 (Payne, *The Peruvian Coup d'Etat of 1962*, p. 43). See the Peruvian armed forces, *La fuerzas armadas y el proceso electoral de 1962* (Lima: 1963) for the military version of the electoral fraud issue. The best interpretations of the 1962 elections concede that some vote fraud did take place, but as a whole, the voting was probably the cleanest in Peru's history. See Bourricaud, *Power and Society*, pp. 301-302.

83. Loeb papers.

84. *Peruvian Times*, 29 June 1962, p. 1.

85. Ibid., 20 July 1962, p. 2.

86. APRA controlled 109 of the 240 congressional seats, and *Acción Popular* only eighty-one. Odría's *UNO* was the swing party with forty-four elected congressmen.

87. Loeb papers; *The New York Times*, 13 July 1962, p. 7. Haya de la Torre claims he was in contact with Belaúnde in Arequipa and was attempting to continue the negotiations, but Belaúnde rejected this overture (Personal interview with Víctor Raúl Haya de la Torre, 14 July 1974, Lima, Peru).

88. *La Tribuna*, 4 July 1962, p. 1. APRA secretary-general Prialé held his discussions with Odría over cocktails at the fashionable Hotel Bolivar in Lima.

89. *The New York Times*, 17 July 1962, p. 1; Villanueva, *Ejército Peruano*, pp. 271-273, claims that the service ministers were displaced because the joint command considered them to be too closely linked with President Prado.

90. *The New York Times*, 17 July 1962, p. 1.

91. *El Comercio*, 17 July 1962, p. 2.; Martín, *Dichos y hechos*, pp. 35-36; Personal interview with Víctor Raúl Haya de la Torre, 14 July 1974, Lima, Peru.

92. Personal interview with Víctor Raúl Haya de la Torre, 14 July 1974, Lima, Peru.

93. *El Comercio*, 18 July 1962, p. 1. Much issue was made in the United States press that Colonel Briceño had been a student at the antiguerrilla ranger school at Fort Benning, Georgia.

94. Ibid.; *Peruvian Times*, 20 July 1962, p. 3.

95. *La Tribuna*, 21 July 1962, p. 1.

96. *Ordenes Generales de la Marina del Perú*, 31 July 1962, pp. 2-4.

97. Loeb interview.

98. Haya de la Torre and other APRA leaders were not arrested, and the party newspaper *La Tribuna* remained closed for only three days.

99. *The New York Times*, 19 July 1962, p. 1.

100. Loeb interview and Arthur Schlesinger, *A Thousand Days: John F. Kennedy in the White House* (Boston: 1965), p. 786.

101. Loeb interview.

102. Loeb papers.

103. Loeb papers.

104. *The New York Times,* 21 July 1962, p. 6.

8
The Generals as Presidents: 1962-1963

While the 1962-1963 military government was in power, it demonstrated the difficulty armed forces leaders confronted in translating their new professional ideology into government policy. A number of important reforms were enacted by decree in the first six months of the *Junta's* tenure, but no clear-cut rationale for the government's programs was articulated by the military leadership. As a result, the programs enacted lacked coherence, and some were even reversed when General Ricardo Pérez Godoy was ousted from the presidential palace by the other co-presidents, General Nicolás Lindley López, General Pedro Vargas Prada, and Admiral Juan Francisco Torres Matos in March, 1963. The vast majority of the armed forces' leadership was united, however, in the desire to return the government to civilian hands after the scheduled elections of 9 June 1963. This desire reflected their confidence in a Belaúnde victory and his proposed policies as well as the military's unwillingness, at this juncture, to remain in power for an extended period of time.

During its first four months in office, the military government effectively consolidated its political position and initiated measures dealing with election, housing, and agrarian reform. Due to the relative political tranquillity following the 18 July *coup*, the *Junta* ended the suspension of civil liberties only nine days after it seized power.[1] This action was in keeping with its policy of avoiding political repression, which would have strengthened the *Apristas* and probably further delayed diplomatic recognition by the United States. Peréz Godoy also met with United States business leaders and asked for their support on 24 July. He urged them to do everything possible to present the "facts" before the United States State Department regarding the *Junta's* position on the issue of United States recognition. In return, the general promised United States and other foreign business representatives that the new government would pose no threat to their interests.[2] United States investments in Peru totaled over $850 million in 1962, and this fact undoubtedly influenced the military government's carefully conciliatory policy toward United States capital.[3]

The Kennedy administration's policy of nonrecognition of the *Junta* was unquestionably undermined by its policy in the overthrow of Argentine president Arturo Frondizi. The young president remarked to Arthur Schlesinger on 1 August that neither the Latin American governments nor the Peruvian people had given Washington the support he had anticipated. The Chilean foreign minister had in fact warned Washington against "being more royalist than the King." Kennedy knew recognition of the *Junta* was thus inevitable, and he now sought to give the impression that Washington's condemnation of the *coup* was strong enough to force the *Junta* to make policy changes rendering the resumption of relations possible. To this end, United States Chargé d'Affaires Douglas Henderson conducted negotiations with the Peruvian government, and the *Junta* then sent representatives to the Council of the Organization of American States to promise the resumption of civil liberties and the holding of free elections as scheduled in June, 1963, with the further assurance of honoring the results. In response to these actions, the Kennedy administration resumed diplomatic relations on 17 August.[4] Economic assistance programs, with the important exception of military aid, were reinstated at the same time.[5] The United States recognition statement, however, contained a reference to internal political conditions in Peru. This document prompted the minister of foreign relations, Admiral Luis Edgardo Llosa, to release a strongly worded statement protesting the "improper tone" of the United States announcement. The stern attitude adopted by the *Junta* was praised as a "manifestation of dignity and independence" by the staunchly nationalist *El Comercio* on 19 August.[6] The military government had thus hurdled the last major barrier impeding the consolidation of its political control and had increased its prestige in the process. While the issue of United States recognition was being discussed during early August, the *Junta* made its first reform proposal public.

According to General Pérez Godoy, the *Junta* had clear objectives during his tenure as chief of the military government. The enactment of an election reform law was the government's highest priority. But also important were the regulation of the economy and the enactment of basic reforms in housing, national planning, taxation, and the agrarian sector.[7] During early August the first of these programs was put into motion when a commission was established to write a new election statute and Pérez

Godoy announced that the *Junta* was in the process of creating a National Planning Institute.[8] On 31 August the government issued a decree that began preparations for the establishment of an Institute of Agrarian Reform and Colonization. These measures, issued during the first six weeks after the *Junta* assumed power, provided the basis for the key reforms of the next four months.

The new election law was promulgated on 5 December. It contained important revisions of existing election regulations. The multiple ballot system, wherein each political party printed its own list of candidates for the national elections, was scrapped and replaced by a single ballot form. More significantly, the number of deputies and senators was reduced from 241 to 180 because the government stated that it wanted to avoid the splintering of political representation in congress. In the first draft of the reform, approved by the *Junta* in late September, the number of congress-men had been cut to 140, but the military leaders later restored forty-five seats. The measure also included tighter restrictions on voting and registration.[9]

In a special address to the nation on 20 October, Pérez Godoy announced the establishment of the *Instituto Nacional de Planificación* (National Planning Institute). The institute was founded in order to "stimulate the incentive and creative quality of the distinct sectors of the population and especially to assure the participation of the active forces of the economy."[10] The head of the institute was given the rank of cabinet minister, and its members were to be chosen from key sectors of the national economy. As the institute was designed to be the foundation for national development planning, it was given a permanent status. Pérez Godoy stressed, however, that the institute was to be an apolitical body and that its members would refrain from political activity beyond the scope of their specific government duties.[11] The creation of the National Planning Institute was a manifestation of the reformist orientation of the *Junta*. The integration of economic development planning in a permanent, cabinet-level body reflected the military government's recognition of the need for long-term economic policy. This type of organization had been advocated by the CAEM personnel before 1962. Nevertheless, Pérez Godoy later denied that the CAEM played any direct role in the creation of the institute or participated officially in the planning or programs of the military government from 18 July 1962 to 3 March 1963 (the period of Pérez Godoy's leadership).[12] Just as with the Velasco government after 1968, CAEM's influence was more ideological than administrative.

In conjunction with the creation of the National Planning Institute, the military government in late November unsuccessfully sought the services of the Belgian sociologist and economic development adviser, Frere L. J. Lebret. During the Prado regime Peruvian officers had sought the teaching services of Lebret, and they hoped the administration would heed some of his policy suggestions. The Prado government was opposed to the Lebret mission, however, and the military request was canceled.[13] The *Junta's* renewed efforts to obtain Lebret's talents in 1962 demonstrated its desire to enlist foreign economic advice on the subject of agrarian reform and thus displayed limited confidence in CAEM's administrative capabilities.

During November 1962, the *Junta* moved ahead in the areas of housing and agrarian reform. With the cooperation of the United States Agency for International Development (AID) the government announced plans to construct sixty thousand low-cost housing units in Lima and other areas throughout Peru. The cost of the project was set at one billion soles (thirty-seven million dollars), of which AID was to contribute 620 million soles.[14] Pérez Godoy also announced on 19 November the creation of a National Housing Bank. Financed in part by the funds provided through the Alliance for Progress, it was formed to extend credits for housing construction and the establishment of essential services such as light, power, and sewage.[15] These programs represented the first systematic effort by any Peruvian regime to deal with the dreadful living conditions of Lima's urban poor. During mid-November the *Junta* also established the platform for the first substantive agrarian reform program in Peru's history.

On 13 November the military government gave permanent legal status to the *Instituto de Reforma Agraria y Colonización* (Institute of Agrarian Reform and Colonization, *IRAC*), the organization charged with implementing agrarian reform. The *IRAC* originally was mandated to write an agrarian reform law for seven impoverished regions throughout Peru where rural unrest was most intense. It became quickly evident, however, that the government would attempt only a small-scale pilot project in the strife-ridden La Convención Valley. Assigned to administer the project was Lieutenant Colonel Enrique Gallegos Venero. As Coordinator General of the Socio-Economic Activities of La Convención and Lares, Gallegos Venero later wrote that when he arrived in the valley the *campesinos* were ripe for exploitation by communist agitators preying on "hate that had accumulated for centuries."[16] Significantly, Gallegos Venero was one of the original "radical colonels" who helped plan the 3 October 1968 *coup* and later became one of Velasco's inner circle of policy advisers during the subsequent military government.

The *campesinos* in the valley had, since early 1962, strengthened their position vis-à-vis the *hacendados* by initiating a nearly completely effective labor boycott. Although an April, 1962 decree by the Prado government abolished the feudalistic *condiciones*, it still insisted that the *campesinos* pay rent to the *hacendados* for the parcels they were farming. As part of the boycott, the *campesinos* refused to pay these rents. It was at this point that the *Junta* granted the *campesinos* control over the parcels they had been working for years on the stipulation that legal title to the land would be obtained upon payment to the government for the parcels. The *Junta* then would compensate the *hacendados* for the loss of the parcels.[17] Critics of the *Junta*'s agrarian reform policy charged that the government was merely recognizing the *campesinos*' de facto control of the parcels in an effort to diffuse the volatile political climate in the valley. General Lindley López, the premier and minister of war, responded to these critics by insisting that the *Junta* could not be expected to launch a full-scale program when it would remain in office for only one year.[18]

The actual details of the La Convención pilot project were not released until 28 March 1963, when the *Junta*'s minister of agriculture announced that about fourteen thousand *campesinos* would "become owners of the land they work."[19] Twenty-three haciendas in the Urubamba Valley in La Convención were earmarked for future acquisition by the government either by expropriation or by direct purchase for distribution among fourteen thousand landless residents of the region at an estimated cost of $1.1 million.[20] The land was to be taken by one of three separate measures outlined by the agrarian reform decree: (1) by direct expropriation; (2) by government purchase with a down payment of 15 percent in cash and the balance in eight to fifteen annual installments, with up to 8 percent interest on the balance outstanding; and (3) by direct purchase from the owners by the *campesinos* with the approval of the IRAC. The small farmers who purchased land under the pilot program were to repay the government at a low rate of interest over a period extending up to twenty years. As a part of the project an army engineer battalion was sent to the region to construct a through highway from Cuzco and feeder roads within the pilot area itself.[21] The first land put up for sale from the expropriated properties was made available on 12 June 1963, only one month before the *Junta* left office.[22] But under the provisions of the decree initiating the project, land redistribution was to continue for up to three years from the beginning of the agrarian reform.[23]

Notwithstanding the limited scope of the *Junta*'s agrarian reform project, it was the first attempt by any Peruvian government to begin the redistribution of land on a systematic basis. The creation of the IRAC demonstrated that the military leadership was committed to a broader agrarian reform program in the future. The selection of the La Convención and Lares region as the first site for the implementation of land redistribution was significant. It indicates that the armed forces clearly understood that agrarian reform was intricately linked to alleviating the conditions promoting rural unrest. Critics of the La Convención and Lares project argued that peasant land seizures of much of the property involved in the program, prior to the initiation of the pilot project, reduced the *Junta*'s agrarian reform to merely a recognition of the peasants' de facto control of the land they had seized.[24] Nevertheless, the relationship between social action projects and the armed forces' increasingly comprehensive definition of national defense (as it applied to the issue of internal subversion) was manifested in the agrarian reform project. Apart from the *Junta*'s efforts in the area of land redistribution, in late 1962 it introduced two other reform measures dealing with tax and education reform.

On 5 December 1962, the *Junta* issued a decree declaring 1963 "The Year of Literacy" and proposing an all-out effort to reduce illiteracy in the nation. The Ministry of Education proposed a plan for national literacy training, and the government encouraged other educational programs. But these initiatives were more of a commitment to educational reform rather than a manifestation of the government's intent to launch an ambitious program in its six remaining months in office. Thus, minimal progress was made before the *Junta* stepped down in July, 1963.[25]

On the issue of tax reform, however, more tangible efforts were made. At the end of 1962 the government decreed a tax of twenty-five soles per ton (about ninety-four cents) on the nation's fishing industry. In addition, a new graduated tax on incomes over 100,000 soles per year ($3,730) was put into effect on 1 January 1963.[26] These taxes, while not excessive, were unpopular with business interests and upper-income groups. The tax controversy was apparently one of a number of issues that prompted the removal of Pérez Godoy as president of the *Junta* by his more conservative military colleagues on 3 March 1963. Other cracks in the institutional solidarity of the military government were clearly evident, however, before Pérez Godoy's replacement by General Nicolás Lindley López in March, 1963.

The first indication of dissension within the military government came on 5 October 1962 with the resignation of the minister of government and police, General Juan Bossio Collas. General Bossio gave "health reasons" for his resignation, but according to Pérez Godoy, General Bossio renounced his cabinet post under intense pressure from General Lindley López.[27] The minister was the most progressive officer in the military government and had been a member of the activist junior army officer organization, CROE, during the early 1940s.[28] Before his resignation, General Bossio made a number of public statements that led to his removal from the cabinet. During September he engaged in a debate with the editors of La Prensa, who warned that the peasant unionizing and land seizures led by Hugo Blanco in La Convención and Lares might be the beginnings of a Castro-inspired guerrilla movement.   General Bossio discounted the importance of what he termed "paper guerrillas" and derided the "journalistic visions" of the La Prensa editors.[29] Far more serious, however, was his declaration in late September that the military government had immediate plans to nullify the long-standing and controversial contract of the International Petroleum Company.[30] The Junta was not prepared to take such action, and General Lindley López, in particular, viewed General Bossio's statement as a an attempt to embarrass the Junta.[31] Consequently, Lindley López secured the minister's resignation with the support of the other members of the Junta.[32] General Bossio's removal reflected the military government's sensitivity on the issues of foreign capital and rural unrest.

As General Pérez Godoy's statements to the foreign business community in July, 1962 prove, the Junta was committed to maintaining a friendly relationship with foreign investors. The Junta president took pride in the fact that the military government in the remaining months of 1962 was able to improve substantially Peru's balance of payments, oversee an increase in the nation's gross national product, and still realize a budget surplus in excess of 400 million soles.[33] It is obvious that the military government viewed immediate economic stability as closely linked with the continued presence of Peru's chief sources of foreign investment. On this key point, the senior officers in the government were at odds with military planners in the CAEM, who wrote in 1963: "The sad and desperate truth is that in Peru the real powers are not the Executive, the Legislative, the Judicial or the Electoral, but the latifundistas [owners of excessively large land holdings], the exporters, the bankers, and the American investors."[34] While not a dominant aspect of the armed forces' professional perspective before 1963, economic nationalism emerged as a key element in the military's ideology between 1963 and 1968.[35] But despite a lack of consensus on the issue of the role of foreign capital before 1963, military men were in accord in supporting the Junta's decisive actions against radical activists operating in Peru's central and southern regions.

The most charismatic and successful radical figure during the early 1960s was the peasant organizer Hugo Blanco.[36] This young Trotskyite began his work to unify various peasant groups in the Cuzco area in 1958.[37] By 1961 Blanco had created 148 individual peasant unions in the La Convención Valley and had led a number of successful strikes by the tenants of the large haciendas of the region.[38] Primarily because of ideological differences with Peru's leading Marxist groups, Blanco was unable to obtain the needed manpower or financial support for a campaign of peasant land seizures he attempted to lead during 1962.[39]   During late October, 1962 the government responded to the land seizures in the La Convención region by sending a large force of *Guardia Civil* units, under the command of Colonel Arturo Zapata Cesti, to dislodge the peasants. The *Guardia Civil* established headquarters in two key haciendas in La Convención and the valley of Lares.[40]   These units met with stubborn resistance from the peasants, and Blanco himself became a fugitive after allegedly killing a member of the *Guardia Civil* while attempting to seize arms for his movement on 13 November 1962.[41]

Blanco was not captured until late May, 1963, but his effectiveness as a peasant organizer ended after he was forced into hiding to avoid arrest.[42] During the last two months of 1962, however, disorder continued in the La Convención and Lares regions.   Violent confrontations between the *Guardia Civil* and peasants near the town of Chalhuay in December resulted in the deaths of forty-six tenant farmers.[43]   Only after the announcement of the *Junta*'s agrarian reform program for the La Convención region in March, 1963 did the land seizures and the unrest begin to subside. The activities of peasant unions in this area never went beyond the point of strikes and occupation of the large land-holdings. But Blanco's organizational success during his five years of work in the politically volatile La Convención and Lares region convinced military leaders of the potential for rebellion in the area. The fact that the *Junta*'s agrarian reform program contributed to the reduction of peasant unrest in this region had a profound impact upon the military's attitude toward the value of land reform in the years to come.[44]

In contrast to its approach toward unrest in the La Convención region, the *Junta* took stronger measures to deal with labor disorders in northern and central Peru during late 1962 and early 1963. In December, 1962 bloody riots at the copper mines at La Oroya in central Peru and the large commercial sugar plantations near the northern coastal town of Chiclayo resulted in the *Junta*'s mass roundup of communist labor leaders and other leftists during the first week of January, 1963. Prior to these arrests, the *Junta* had allowed communist labor organizers a relatively free hand in gaining new adherents. Pérez Godoy lent his support for these activities by attending a meeting of the communist-controlled port workers' union.[45] This policy was followed in an apparent effort to counteract APRA's strength in Peru's labor movement. Nevertheless, an abrupt reversal of this strategy was initiated after the outbreak of violence and sabotage at the end of 1962.

During the third week of December a strike by four thousand members of the metal workers' union at the United States-owned Cerro de Pasco Corporation complex at La Oroya erupted into rioting that caused one death and numerous injuries and resulted in four million dollars in damage to Cerro's facilities.[46]   The government attributed the rioting to the communist *Frente de Liberación Nacional* and sent the minister of government and police, General German Pagador Blondet, to deal personally with the disturbances.[47]

The rioting at La Oroya was followed on 2 January 1963 by even more violent clashes between workers and police at the *Hacienda Patapo* in the sugar area near Chiclayo. A series of fires set by the labor agitators caused over one million dollars in damage to the hacienda's buildings and crops. In the ensuing confrontations between *Guardia Civil* units and rioting workers, three persons were killed and twenty injured (including seven policemen).[48] According to Pérez Godoy the disturbances at La Oroya and Chiclayo were the work not only of "elements with communist tendencies" but also of *Apristas* and some members of the oligarchy who were trying to tarnish the image of the military government as the 1963 elections drew nearer.[49] In any event, the *Junta* arrested only a few APRA members in its sweeping crackdown on leftist groups launched on 4 January.

On the night of 4 January and throughout the following day, police and other government agents arrested over eight hundred known communists and members of other leftist groups in a carefully coordinated effort throughout Peru.[50] Over three hundred persons were arrested in Lima, including General (R) César Pando Esgusquiza, the FLN presidential candidate in the 1962 elections; Luis Alvarado, head of the bank employees' union; and Guillermo Sheen, chief of the commercial employees' union, both of which unions were communist-dominated.[51]

After the government suspended constitutional guarantees in the wake of the mass arrests on 5 January, General Pagador Blondet claimed that the *Junta* had acted to destroy a communist conspiracy that was directed through Havana with headquarters in Prague.[52] A government communiqué issued on 6 January claimed that the conspiracy involved a wide range of leftist groups that had planned to launch a series of hit-and-run raids between 15 and 20 January. These raids, the *Junta* claimed, would have involved the destruction of bridges, fuel storage areas, communications facilities, and military installations. Key military and police leaders were also said to have been targets for assassination.[53] The government's statement charged that the first phase of the conspirators' operation had already begun with the infiltration of the nation's labor movement and the initiation of a series of violent strikes like those at Cerro de Pasco and

Chiclayo. The day before the issuance of the communiqué, the government demonstrated its newly adopted hard line toward strikes by using tanks to suppress the seizure of a Callao shoe factory by its twelve hundred workers.[54]

Despite the gravity of the government's charges, less than two hundred of those originally arrested on 4 and 5 January were detained for an extended period. This group was taken to the *El Sepa* Penal Colony in the department of Loreto, where they were gradually released until only sixty remained to stand trial.[55] Eventually, none of the suspects was ever convicted due to lack of sufficient evidence, and the government was never able to validate its charges of a widespread communist conspiracy.[56] The *Junta*'s anticommunist campaign was a direct shift from its policy of maintaining an open political climate with the continuance of full constitutional liberties. Moreover, the government crackdown followed soon after the conservative press chided the *Junta* for allowing communist infiltration of the labor and student movements. *La Prensa* charged that the communists were using their new freedom to instigate violent attacks on policemen and soldiers and to promote the destruction of private property, such as occurred in the riots at La Oroya.[57] The thrust of the newspaper's argument was that by using communists to displace APRA elements in the nation's labor movement, the *Junta* was exposing soldiers and policemen to the risk of assassination by subversives whom the military leaders erroneously imagined they could control for their own benefit.[58] Whether the *Junta* acted in direct response to the charges of the conservative press is not certain. But military leaders clearly perceived the subversive potential of Peru's small cadres of communist, Trotskyite, and Castroite militants. With the arrest and detention of most of the nation's leftist leaders, the military government embarked on a more conservative political course that de-emphasized reform. This swing to the right reflected the same divisions within the ranks of the armed forces' senior leadership following the ouster of General Juan Velasco Alvarado by General Francisco Morales Bermúdez in 1975. The most important casualty of this policy shift was *Junta* president Pérez Godoy.

The first reports of dissension within the *Junta* appeared in January 1963 after the retirement dates of Pérez Godoy and Admiral Juan Francisco Torres Matos, had passed. Torres Matos was replaced as navy commander by Vice Admiral Florencio Texeira on 1 January, but both he and Pérez Godoy retained their positions in the military *Junta*.[59] At a news conference on 11 January, Pérez Godoy emphatically denied rumors of divisions within the military government and insisted that both his and Torres Matos's retirement would not have any effect upon their continued presence in the military government.[60] One week later, at another press conference, the *Junta* president raised the controversial issue of the International Petroleum Company's contract in the same manner that led to the removal of General Bossio from the government in October, 1962. He claimed that the military government considered the question of the IPC contract to be of national importance and insisted that plans existed to give the issue a "constitutional solution" before the *Junta* left office.[61]

As was the case when General Bossio announced an imminent settlement of the IPC question, after Pérez Godoy's pronouncement no further statement was made by the government. Instead, during early February the three other members of the *Junta* presented their colleague with a memorandum demanding that he adopt a more restricted role as president of the *Junta*. Specifically, they insisted that Pérez Godoy (1) abolish his monthly national television addresses and his frequent news conferences; (2) not make any decision of national importance without consulting the three other members of the *Junta*; (3) remove himself and his family from the National Palace as a place of residence; (4) cease issuing decree laws on matters that required prolonged study; and (5) help assure that the *Junta*'s full attention would be devoted to conducting the national elections as scheduled on 9 June, subsequently transferring the executive power to the newly elected president on 28 July.[62] The demands presented in the memorandum reflected the principal issues causing intense friction between Pérez Godoy and the other copresidents of the *Junta*. Generals Lindley López and Vargas Prada, along with Admiral Torres Matos, insisted that Pérez Godoy must immediately comply with these demands if he were to remain a member of the ruling *Junta*.[63] Throughout February, Pérez Godoy complied with all of these demands, with the exception of transferring his residence from the National Palace. He refrained from conducting press conferences and did not make important policy decisions.[64] Nevertheless, the serious split in the military leadership became public knowledge and the topic of gossip in the national press.

The news magazine *Caretas* in mid-February reported that the differences among the *Junta* members extended even to their wives. The wife of General Pedro Vargas Prada was said to be extremely upset that Pérez Godoy, in his post of president of the *Junta*, was receiving a larger salary than was her husband. Moreover, because of Pérez Godoy's position, his wife was given the directorship of a national charitable organization, and that caused even more hard feelings, according to the magazine.[65] This public airing of these squabbles undoubtedly heightened the tension among the copresidents. Less than three weeks after the article appeared, a confrontation between General Lindley López and Pérez Godoy resulted in the latter's removal from the military government.

Despite Pérez Godoy's compliance with nearly all the demands contained in the memorandum of early February, Lindley López provoked a showdown with the *Junta* president on 28 February by resigning from the government to protest what he considered Pérez Godoy's overly ambitious conduct in office.[66] In the two days following Lindley López's resignation, a series of meetings involving the *Junta*, the cabinet, and other members of the armed forces' high command was held to resolve the crisis. These meetings resulted in the decision to reject the resignation of Lindley López and instead to demand that Pérez Godoy renounce his post in military government.[67]

In the early morning hours of 3 March, Lindley López and the other two co-presidents in the *Junta* acted to assure Pérez Godoy's swift removal from office. The National Palace was surrounded by troops from the army's ranger unit. Then soldiers, armed with machine guns, accompanied air force general Carlos Silas Baroni and his army colleague, General Rodolfo Belaúnde, into the building and escorted Pérez Godoy and his family from the executive mansion at 6:30 A.M.[68] After the deposed *Junta* president was taken to his permanent residence in the Lima suburb of Miraflores, he made a brief statement denying the charges of *caudillismo* that had been used by the other *Junta* members as a justification for his removal from office. He also insisted that his former colleagues did not intend to deport him or make him a prisoner. *Guardia Civil* sentries were placed outside Pérez Godoy's residence, however, immediately following his arrival.[69]

After assuming Pérez Godoy's post in the military government, Lindley López claimed that the action was taken for purely institutional reasons. He said, "We did not overthrow the government last July to enthrone Pérez Godoy as a dictator."[70] Elaborating, Lindley López claimed that the personal way in which Pérez Godoy ran his office was contrary to the collective organization of the presidency.[71]

Other interpretations have been offered as to the exact reasons for Pérez Godoy's ouster besides those presented by Lindley López. According to *La Prensa*, Pérez Godoy's friendship with former president Manuel Odría prompted the ousted *Junta* member to favor Odría's interests over those of Belaúnde's in making government appointments. Lindley López's strong advocacy of Belaúnde's candidacy thus led to the crisis that toppled Pérez Godoy.[72] Similar to this version is Víctor Villanueva's suggestion that Pérez Godoy had actually attempted to cement a pact among Odría, Haya de la Torre, and himself to block the victory of Belaúnde in the coming elections. This pact was the main reason for his removal, according to Villanueva's interpretation.[73]

Pérez Godoy himself pointed to the unwillingness of the three co-presidents to continue the reforms initiated while he was *Junta* president as the main reason for his dismissal.[74] He correctly maintained that the tax reform measures initiated by the military government on 1 January 1963 were reversed soon after Lindley López replaced him. On 21 March the *Junta* issued a decree law that reduced corporate levies, eliminated the special government tax on fish tonnage, and lowered taxes on upper-income groups. Taxes on incomes ranging from one million to five million soles per year ($37,300 to $186,000) were reduced from 38 to 34 percent.[75] Pérez Godoy claimed that these tax reductions forced the *Junta* to order a comprehensive 4 percent cut in government spending for the remainder of its tenure in office.[76]

While it is true that the rollback of the tax increases initiated while Pérez Godoy was in office indicated that a more conservative fiscal policy was followed by the military government after 3 March, these measures did not foreshadow a complete abandonment of the reform programs begun earlier. The pilot agrarian reform project in La Convención was, of course, initiated less than a month after Pérez Godoy was deposed. On 29 March the *Junta* also announced that its housing construction program would continue; it released plans to build or improve twelve thousand homes for teachers at a cost of thirty-five million dollars (part of which would be funded by foreign assistance loans).[77] Additionally, the National Planning Institute and the National Housing Bank were encouraged to continue their operations during the final five months of the military government.[78] But because very few substantive reforms were begun during this period and because the tax measures of late March clearly benefited the wealthy, some critics charged that with the rise of Lindley López to the presidency of the *Junta*, the plutocracy was better served.[79] In the same vein, the new *Junta* chief's praise of the United States as the "Great Democracy of the North" during a press conference on 29 March also caused consternation among Peruvian nationalists who had earlier applauded the *Junta*'s firm public position toward Washington.[80] What Pérez Godoy's ouster definitely reflected was the ideological divisions within the high command that were characteristic of the armed forces' institutional makeup.

Despite the charges that Lindley López led the *Junta* away from the reforms initiated under Pérez Godoy, his comments after the 1963 elections offer evidence that he favored some selected measures enacted by the military government. On 15 June 1963, Lindley López proudly pointed to the reforms the *Junta* enacted. He claimed that the military government "had broken with a bad tradition. . . . In the last twelve months, the government had made much progress. . . . It has created a Housing Bank and set down the necessary platform for agrarian reform. We have created an Institute for Planning that has been well received."[81] These comments notwithstanding, Lindley López and his colleagues Torres Matos and Vargas Prado were still primarily political caretakers during the *Junta*'s last months in office.

Lindley López continued to insist in the face of much skepticism that the *Junta* was fully committed to leaving office on 28 July after a new president had been elected.[82] The ultimatum given to Pérez Godoy in early February, which in part demanded that the government's full attention be devoted to facilitating a smooth voting process in 1963, foreshadowed the goal of the military government after the dismissal of the first *Junta* president. Moreover, when Fernando Belaúnde Terry cemented a political alliance in February 1963 that greatly enhanced his presidential chances, the *Junta* was given an added incentive to hold the elections as scheduled.

In late February, 1963 Belaúnde's *Acción Popular* consummated an agreement with the *Partido Democrático Cristiano*. PDC leaders pledged their badly needed support in Lima and Arequipa.[83] Also aiding Belaúnde's cause was the absence of all but one candidate from the extreme left in the presidential field. The left had been dispersed and its key leaders imprisoned after the January, 1963 roundup by the *Junta*. Therefore, no candidates were presented by the *Partido Socialista*, the *Partido Social Progresista*, and the *Frente Liberación Nacional*, whose standard-bearers had garnered a total of nearly sixty thousand votes in the 1962 elections. Only a little-known candidate, Mario Samane Boggio, represented the "independent left" in the 1963 elections. Thus, Belaúnde was able to gain the vast majority of these votes as well as those of the *Partido Democrático Cristiano*.[84]

The armed forces' support for Belaúnde was also a critical factor in the 1963 elections. With the passage of the new election statute and the close supervision of the registration process by the *Junta* during 1963, the military assumed almost complete responsibility for the conduct of the elections. Yet, deposed *Junta* president Pérez Godoy later claimed that there were voting irregularities involving the use of blank ballots that favored Belaúnde in the *Aprista* strongholds of Cajamarca and Trujillo.[85] Although Haya de la Torre and Odría were again allowed to seek the presidency, both candidates were clearly unacceptable to the officer corps.[86] It seems likely that the military would have again intervened to prevent the victory of Haya de la Torre or Odría had either won the 1963 election.

Odría's last-minute pact with Haya de la Torre immediately before the *coup* of 18 July made him even more objectionable to many officers who considered him the symbol of intrigue and political reaction.[87] The military government decided to risk allowing Odría and Haya de la Torre to run again in 1963 because they controlled the electoral machinery, and Belaúnde's presidential chances appeared decidedly better than they had been before the 1962 elections. The armed forces' leaders also recognized that the cancellation of the candidacies of Odría and Haya de la Torre would have unquestionably weakened Belaúnde's legitimacy once he assumed the presidency.

In the elections held on 9 June 1963, Belaúnde emerged a decisive victor over both Haya de la Torre and Odría. The final vote tabulation showed Belaúnde with 708,931 or 39 percent, while Haya de la Torre tallied 623,532 or 34.3 percent, and Odría trailed 463,325 or 25.5 percent.[88] Of the three candidates, only Odría had fewer votes than in the previous election. Belaúnde's victory was attributable to his ability to gain votes of the far left, which had gone to three different candidates in 1962, and his alliance with the PDC, whose candidate had polled nearly fifty thousand votes in the previous election. In the 1963 balloting, Mario Samane Boggio attracted only a minuscule 1 percent of the total votes cast and opened the way for Belaúnde's electoral gains.[89] In the congressional balloting, however, Belaúnde's *Acción Popular* fell far short of gaining a majority in the senate or the Chamber of Deputies.[90]

In view of his party's minority position in the congress, Belaúnde tried to establish a modus operandi with APRA and the UNO in order to obtain a working legislative majority. After a series of conferences among Belaúnde, Odría, and Haya de la Torre during early July, however, the president-elect failed to reach an agreement. An important item preventing an accord was Belaúnde's proposed agrarian reform program, which neither the UNO or the APRA representatives were ready to support.[91] After Belaúnde's efforts to construct a legislative coalition fell through, APRA and the UNO arrived at an agreement on 26 July to control the election of congressional officers in the voting of the following day.[92] Thus, when Belaúnde took the oath of office on 28 July, he faced a presidential tenure with a hostile congress.

In accordance with the repeated promises of the *Junta* during 1962 and 1963, General Lindley López delivered the presidential sash to Belaúnde on 28 July. The *Junta* was obviously pleased with the results of the election; soon after Belaúnde declared victory, a representative called at his private residence to present the congratulations of the three copresidents of the military government.[93] When the armed forces officers returned to their barracks after restoring the presidency to civilian control, there was a strong current of opinion in the Lima press that the military, having witnessed the election of a candidate closely allied with their evolving nation-building mission, would not be satisfied to remain aloof from national affairs in the years to come. One observer noted, after Belaúnde's election, that the armed forces "expect much and they tend to be impatient. If Belaúnde is unable to resolve differences and undertake reforms by constitutional means, there remain officers who believe that the welfare of the country is above the constitution and bears no relationship to the observance of the democratic process."[94] These words would prove prophetic as the Belaúnde presidency, begun in a glow of confidence and idealism, would soon face political and economic controversy and the growing impatience of the new president's restive military allies.

NOTES

1. *Peruvian Times*, 27 July 1962, p. 1. The best study of the 1962-1963 military government is Víctor Villanueva Valencia, *Un año bajo el sable* (Lima: 1963).

2. *Peruvian Times*, 27 July 1962, p. 1.

3. Ibid., 3 August 1962, p. 1.

4. Arthur Schlesinger, Jr., *A Thousand Days: John F. Kennedy in the White House* (Boston: 1965), p. 787.

5. Ibid.; *Peruvian Times*, 22 August 1962, p. 1. Military aid was reinstated in early October.

6. Personal Papers of James I. Loeb; *El Comercio*, 19 August 1962, p. 1; François Bourricaud, *Power and Society in Contemporary Peru* (New York: 1970), p. 311.

7. Questionnaire completed by Division General (R) Ricardo Pérez Godoy, 1 August 1974, Lima, Peru.

8. *Peruvian Times*, 3 August 1962, p. 1; *La Prensa*, 3 August 1962, p. 1.

9. Richard Patch, "The Peruvian Elections of 1963," *American Universities Field Staff Reports* (New York, 1963), p. 6; *Peruvian Times*, 14 September 1962, p. 1, 28 September 1962, p. 1.

10. Ordenes Generales de Marina del Perú, 29 October 1962, pp. 1-7; *Peruvian Times*, 26 October 1962, p. 1.

11. *Peruvian Times*, 26 October 1962, p. 1.

12. Pérez Godoy questionnaire.

13. Luigi R. Einaudi and Alfred Stepan, *Latin American Institutional Development: Changing Perspectives in Peru and Brazil* (Santa Monica: 1971), p. 23; *El Comercio*, 21 November 1962, p. 1; *Legislación Militar del Perú*, 17 February 1959, pp. 129-130.

14. *El Peruano*, 10 November 1962, p. 1; *Peruvian Times*, 16 November 1962, p. 1.

15. Pérez Godoy questionnaire; *El Comercio*, 20 November 1962, p. 1.

16. Lieutenant Colonel Enrique Gallegos Venero, "Un combate victorioso en guerra contrarevolucionaria," *Revista Escuela Superior Geurra del Perú* 10 (July-September, 1963), pp. 7-26 as quoted in Alfred Stepan, *The State and Society: Peru in Comparative Perspective* (Princeton: 1978), p. 132.

17. Wesley W. Craig, Jr., "From Hacienda to Community: An Analysis of Solidarity and Social Change in Peru," Ph.D. diss., Cornell University, 1957, p. 45.

18. "Militares vs. Marxistas," *Caretas*, 9-21 November 1962, p. 15.

19. *El Comercio*, 30 March 1963, p. 1; *Peruvian Times*, 5 April 1963, p. 1.

20. *Peruvian Times*, 5 April 1963, p. 1.

21. Ibid.

22. Patch, "The Peruvian Elections of 1963," p. 5.

23. *Peruvian Times*, 5 April 1963, p. 1.

24. Héctor Béjar, *Peru 1965: Notes on a Guerrilla Experience* (New York: 1970), p. 56. Useful works on the Cuzco land seizures are Víctor Villanueva Valencia, *Hugo Blanco y la rebelión campesina* (Lima: 1967); Hugo Neira, *Cuzco: Tierra y muerte* (Lima: n.d.).

25. *El Comercio*, 6 December 1962, p. 1; Villanueva, *Un año bajo el sable*, pp. 151-157.

26. Pérez Godoy questionnaire, and Víctor Villanueva Valencia, *Ejército Peruano: Del caudillaje anárquico al militarismo reformista* (Lima: 1973), p. 292.

27. *El Comercio*, 6 October 1962, p. 1; Pérez Godoy questionnaire.

28. See Chapter 3 for the discussion of the CROE.

29. Bourricaud, *Power and Society*, p. 318.

30. Pérez Godoy questionnaire; Villanueva, *Ejército Peruano*, p. 286.

31. Pérez Godoy questionnaire.

32. Ibid. In an often-quoted statement Bossio was also reported to have said that the armed forces of 1962 were tired of being the "watchdogs of the oligarchy" in Peru.

33. Pérez Godoy questionnaire.

34. CAEM, *El estado y la politica general* (Chorrillos: 1963), p. 89, quoted in Einaudi and Stepan, *Latin American Institutional Development*, p. 18.

35. For a discussion of this point see Villanueva, *Ejército Peruano*, p. 321.

36. The best work dealing with Hugo Blanco is Villanueva, *Hugo Blanco*. See also Howard Handelman, *Struggle in the Andes: Peasant Political Mobilization in Peru* (Austin: 1975), pp. 79-83.

37. Villanueva, *Hugo Blanco*, p. 75.

38. Richard Gott, *Guerrilla Movements in Latin America* (New York: 1972), p. 319.

39. Villanueva, *Hugo Blanco*, pp. 102-134.

40. *El Comercio*, 23 October 1962, p. 13.

41. Ibid.; Gott, *Guerrilla Movements*, p. 328; Villanueva, *Hugo Blanco*, pp. 138-139.

42. Blanco was sentenced to twenty years in prison in 1963 for the murder of a member of the *Guardia Civil*; he was subsequently released in 1970.

43. Villanueva, *Un año bajo el sable*, p. 141.

44. Personal interview with Division General (R) Edgardo Mercado Jarrín, 10 May 1985, Lima, Peru.

45. *The New York Times*, 14 January 1963, p. 12.

46. *Peruvian Times*, 21 December 1962, p. 1.

47. Ibid.; Pérez Godoy questionnaire.
48. *El Comercio*, 3 January 1963, p. 1.
49. Pérez Godoy questionnaire.
50. *El Comercio*, 6 January 1963, p. 1; *Peruvian Times*, 11 January 1963, p. 1. Villanueva, *Ejército Peruano*, claims that the number arrested was actually fifteen hundred to two thousand.
51. *The New York Times*, 7 January 1963, p. 1.
52. *La Crónica*, 7 January 1963, p. 1.
53. *Peruvian Times*, 11 January 1963, p. 1.
54. Ibid.
55. *El Comercio*, 8 January 1963, p. 1; Villanueva, *Un año bajo el sable*, pp. 163-199.
56. Villanueva, *Ejército Peruano*, pp. 287-288.
57. *La Prensa*, 22 December 1962, p. 1.
58. Ibid.; *La Prensa*, 22 December 1962, p. 1; Bourricaud, *Power and Society*, p. 317.
59. *El Comercio*, 2 January 1963, p. 4.
60. Ibid., 12 January 1963, p. 1; *Peruvian Times*, 18 January 1963, p. 1.
61. *El Comercio*, 17 January 1963, p. 1; *Peruvian Times*, 18 January 1963, p. 1.
62. Villanueva, *Ejército Peruano*, p. 290.
63. Ibid.
64. Ibid.
65. *Caretas*, 1-15 February 1963, p. 10.
66. *El Comercio*, 3 March 1963, p. 1.
67. Ibid.
68. Ibid., 4 March 1963, pp. 1, 6.
69. Ibid., p. 4.
70. *The New York Times*, 4 March 1963, p. 1.
71. Ibid.
72. *La Prensa*, 10 March 1963, p. 1. See also Bourricaud, *Power and Society*, p. 319; Villanueva, *Ejército Peruano*, p. 291; Patch, "The Peruvian Elections of 1963," p. 6.
73. Villanueva, *Ejército Peruano*, p. 291.
74. Pérez Godoy questionnaire.
75. Ibid.; *Peruvian Times*, 29 March 1963, p. 1.
76. Pérez Godoy questionnaire.
77. *El Comercio*, 29 March 1963, p. 1.
78. Both of these institutions became important for national planning and urban housing programs during the Belaúnde administration and the military government that took office in 1968.
79. Villanueva, *Ejército Peruano*, p. 292.
80. *El Comercio*, 30 March 1963, p. 1.
81. Patch, "The Peruvian Elections of 1963," p. 5.
82. *El Comercio*, 4 March 1963, p. 1 and 30 March 1963, p. 1.
83. *Peruvian Times*, 1 March 1963, p. 1; Patch, "The Peruvian Elections of 1963," p. 11.
84. Patch, "The Peruvian Elections of 1963," pp. 9-11; Bourricaud, *Power and Society*, p. 320.
85. Pérez Godoy questionnaire.

86. Personal interview with Víctor Villanueva Valencia, 27 July 1974, Lima, Peru.

87. Bourricaud, *Power and Society*, p. 320.

88. Ibid.

89. Ibid.

90. *Peruvian Times*, 21 June 1963, p. 1.

91. Ibid., 12 July 1963, p. 1; 19 July 1963, p. 1; 2 August 1963, p. 1.

92. *Peruvian Times*, 2 August 1963, p. 1.

93. *El Comercio*, 3 July 1963, p. 1.

94. Patch, "The Peruvian Elections of 1963," p. 14.

9
Reform to Revolution: 1963-1968

With the election of Fernando Belaúnde Terry the armed forces gained their most ardent civilian presidential ally in the twentieth century.[1] Belaúnde, an architect and urban planner by training, shared a grand vision for Peru's future with the most ambitious reformers in the officer corps. Perhaps impressed with the public works projects of Brazilian president Juscelino Kubitschek, Peru's new president linked his nation's modernizaiton to a symbol similar to Kubitschek's Brasilia. Belaúnde's vision, the "Marginal Jungle Highway," a road-building program that would integrate the lightly inhabited *montaña* and *selva* with the rest of the nation by means of a main north-south highway and a complex system of feeder roads, mirrored the road-building and colonization schemes outlined by army visionaries as early as the 1920s.[2] This ideological partnership afforded Belaúnde the military's support as he struggled with a hostile congress and a steadily deteriorating economy throughout the bulk of his presidency. Only when the architect's reform programs began to falter in the face of *APRA* and *Odriísta* opposition in congress, the politically explosive International Petroleum Company controversy, and the political disintegration of *Acción Popular*, would his former military allies begin to abandon the beleagured president. The culmination of this disenchantment came when a small group of army officers, led by chief of staff, General Juan Velasco Alvarado, carried out the *golpe de estado* on 3 October 1968.

Belaúnde, an active force in Peruvian politics since 1956, was born in Lima on 7 October 1912 into a distinguished and publicly active family. He spent his teen and early adult years in Paris and Miami after his father was deported by Leguía in 1924. When his father accepted a diplomatic post in the Benavides administration in 1933, the future president enrolled in the School of Architecture at the University of Texas at Austin, graduating in 1935. Practicing both his profession and politics, Belaúnde joined the *Frente Democrática Nacional* in 1945 and was elected as a congressional deputy. The Odría *coup* ended his initial venture into politics, and in 1950 he became the dean of the School of Architecture at the *Escuela Nacional de Ingenieros*. With the approach of the 1956 elections, the aspiring political leader accepted the leadership of the *Frente de Juventudes Democráticas* and from then on became one of Peru's most prominent political leaders.[3] As already noted, the publication of his book, *La conquista del Perú por los Peruanos*, in 1959 seemed, in part, calculated to gain him increased support in the nation's military barracks. In words reminiscent of Morla Concha's 1933 article in the *Revista Militar*, Belaúnde wrote in 1959, "In a sense each barracks can be considered a school and the armed forces today more than ever constitute schools of scientific education."[4]

Belaúnde's perception of the military as a highly trained, technically oriented force was largely accurate. Indeed, Peruvian military men were some of the best educated in Latin America. Army officers, after four years of training at the *Escuela Militar de Chorrillos*, were required to take eighteen months of additional training before even being considered for promotion to captain. Advancement to the rank of major required that an officer pass a two-year, three thousand-hour training regimen at the *Escuela Superior de Guerra*.[5] Particularly after 1950, entrance into the ESG became highly competitive, and despite being permitted to apply up to four separate times for admission, fewer than half of the applicants were eventually successful.[6]

A few top graduates of the ESG were sent overseas to study and serve in administrative positions in the United States and Europe. For example, seven of the eleven original members of the 1962 to 1963 military government, including its four copresidents, trained for periods of up to eighteen months at United States air force installations in Texas, the Command and Staff School at Fort Leavenworth, Kansas, and the United States navy's Fleet Sonar School in Key West, Florida. Colonels Edgardo Mercado Jarrín, José Benavides, and Alfredo Arrisueño, who played prominent early roles in the Velasco government, studied at Fort Leavenworth, Fort Knox, and the Inter-American Defense College, respectively. Velasco himself served as the Peruvian army's delegate to the Inter-American Defense Board in Washington, D.C., during the early 1960s.[7]

Many graduates of the ESG and advanced foreign military training installations served as instructors at Peru's various military education centers upon the completion of their command training. With the military's commitment to education, it was possible for an officer, if he was one of the few to be selected to study at CAEM, to spend nearly one-third of his military career in a variety of service schools. Up to half of an officer's career could be involved in educational pursuits if he also served as an instructor or administrator in these schools. With this heavy emphasis on education, it is understandable that promotion was intimately tied to rank in the *Escuela Militar*'s graduating class. Between 1940 and 1965, 80 percent of the army officers attaining the army's highest rank of division general graduated in the top 25 percent of their military academy class. For brigade general the figure was nearly 54 percent. After 1950, without attendance at the *Escuela Militar*, it became nearly impossible to rise through the enlisted ranks to the grade of second lieutenant. Indeed, between 1951 and 1965 less than 4 percent of the officer corp's new members were promoted from the enlisted ranks. This figure contrasted sharply with the 27 percent figure for the fifteen years prior to 1950.[8] Family influence, political contacts, and other nonacademic or nonservice-related criteria continued to play a role in the promotion process throughout the 1960s. Yet armed forces officers perceived their institution to be more merit-oriented than other sectors of Peruvian society. With a self-perception such as this, Peru's men in uniform placed increasing pressure on Belaúnde to grant them a wider civic action role even while they retained their traditional distrust for the civilian-led democracy.

Aside from delegating to the military an active role in national planning, civic action, and public works projects, Belaúnde's initial presidential programs were an eclectic blend of liberal Catholic reformism, pre-Hispanic values, and state capitalism. During the 1963 campaign the new president had taken a nationalist position and boldly pledged to resolve the explosive IPC issue within thirty days. Although negotiations began almost immediately after Belaúnde took office, the unresolved IPC question would plague the president to the end of his presidency.[9] A combined public and private sector approach was employed by the president regarding national development projects. The new government quickly launched a road-building and public works program that was primarily carried out by army engineers and air force aerial mapping units. A detailed agrarian reform proposal was submitted to the congress only weeks after Belaúnde was inaugurated. The agrarian reform scheme was associated with the government's "Marginal Jungle Highway" and *selva* colonization project, which was really the focus of Belaúnde's development vision.

Underpinning the government's program at the national level was Popular Cooperation, a community-based development program combining the pre-Columbian communal spirit with the newly created Peace Corps. Tools, building materials, and technical advice, along with private volunteers (mostly university students), would be provided by the government for local projects ranging from road building to school construction.[10] The new regime also outlined ambitious public housing and education programs that would involve Popular Cooperation volunteers. Significantly, over the course of the Belaúnde administration these housing and literacy programs received the least opposition in congress and proved to be the most successful initiatives of the president's reform agenda.

Belaúnde's hopes for his reform package were quickly tempered by the Acción Popular-Christian Democratic minority alliance in congress. Controlling only twenty of the forty-five senate seats and fifty of the 140-member Chamber of Deputies positions, Belaúnde felt compelled to hold talks with Haya de la Torre and Odría just prior to taking office in the hope of arriving at a compromise that would give the APRA-UNO factions a few cabinet posts in exchange for their legislative support.[11] These talks failed, however, and on 19 August party representatives of the APRA and UNO announced a congressional alliance.[12] The initial explanation for the alliance was that it was cemented only to elect congressional officers, but La Coalición, as it came to be called, immediately began to impede Belaúnde's legislative program by countering it with its own proposals.

The formation of La Coalición represented the most drastic compromise of APRA's original liberal principles, but from a strictly political perspective, it was merely the culmination of a rapprochement between Haya de la Torre and Odría arrived at before the 18 July 1962 coup d'état that deposed President Prado. More than two decades later, long-time APRA leader Ramiro Prialé explained the party's rationale in forming La Coalición. He insisted that APRA was only safeguarding its legal position in congress by forming the alliance because the 1963 elections were fraudulent, and APRA was merely seeking political support against the illegal representatives of Acción Popular and the Christian Democrats. Prialé also argued that the responsibility for the failure of the July, 1963 talks between Belaúnde and Haya de la Torre rested with the president-elect, who Prialé claimed rejected an understanding with APRA.[13] Personal animosity between Belaúnde and Haya de la Torre may well have been another reason for the APRA leader's tactics. Haya de la Torre expressed contempt for Belaúnde as early as the 1956 elections, calling him a "furtive copy of his uncle" (Víctor Andres Belaúnde).[14] For his part, Belaúnde, during the often-bitter 1963 presidential campaign, derided the *APRA* leader as "Odría's bootlick."[15] When one considers Haya de la Torre's unwillingness to accept a Belaúnde presidency in 1962, the most important motivation for this agreement with Odría in forming *La Coalicíon* was clearly the protection of *APRA*'s traditional image as Peru's leading reformist party. If undercutting Belaúnde's promised wave of reformist legislation required cooperation with his former bitter enemy, then this was a compromise Haya de la Torre was prepared to make.

The formation of *La Coalicíon* had far-reaching implications for *APRA* and the Belaúnde administration. Many *Apristas*, including party leader Manual Seoane, openly denounced the pact. Seoane dramatized his protest by withdrawing from active party politics before his death in Washington, D.C., in September, 1964.[16] It is also probable that former *Aprista* militants serving in the ranks of the *Movimiento de Izquierda Revolucionaria* (MIR) were further radicalized by the *APRA* leadership's opposition to Belaúnde's agrarian reform program. Luis de la Puente Uceda, secretary general of the *MIR*, had long been interested in agrarian reform. For his degree at the University of Trujillo in 1957, he wrote a thesis dealing with land reform that was published in 1966 as *La reforma del agro Peruano*.[17] The slow pace of agrarian reform in the face of congressional opposition before 1965 probably helped persuade the MIR leader to establish a guerrilla *foco* in the southern *montaña* in June of that year, in the hope of enlisting the support of the disenchanted peasantry.

Peru's peasants had indeed demonstrated their militant spirit by launching one of the most massive series of land invasions in Latin American history on Belaúnde's inauguration day. Undoubtedly spurred on by the new president's campaign promise of major agrarian reform, approximately 300,000 peasants invaded between 350 and 400 haciendas and corporate holdings in the latter half of 1963 and early 1964.[18] Nearly every Peruvian department was involved, but the major incursions occurred in the Cuzco, Piura, and Cerro de Pasco regions. Belaúnde at first tolerated these invasions and even ordered his first vice president, Edgardo Seoane, to announce on 3 August the government's decision to use its authority under the agrarian reform law enacted by the 1962 to 1963 *Junta* to expropriate and distribute lands previously seized by the invaders.[19] This announcement only seemed to encourage further incursions, and in an obvious attempt to gain control of the situation through peaceful, legal means, Belaúnde submitted his agrarian reform proposal to congress on 12 August.

Containing 240 separate articles, the primary purpose of this highly complicated measure was to satisfy the traditional land hunger of Peru's peasantry while at the same time not seriously disrupting agricultural production. Expropriated holdings would be compensated in long-term bonds, with the properties to be subdivided into family-sized holdings to be purchased over a twenty-year period. Existing *minifundio* (very small holdings) were subject to concentration, and farm cooperatives were also to be created. Small landholders and members of cooperatives would be aided by government technical and financial assistance. Significantly, major concessions were made for the highly efficient, capital-intensive sugar estates of the north coast. These well-irrigated properties, owned in many instances by foreign capitalists and corporations, practiced reasonably progressive labor policies and under the provisions of the law were allowed to retain holdings of up to seven thousand acres.[20]

In conjunction with his agrarian reform proposal, the president announced on 20 August a colonization program for the *selva* region that would create *nucleos selváticos* or nuclear towns designed to be the population centers for the government's program of new land development.[21] The colonization program was intricately related to the "Marginal Jungle Highway" project and required more of the president's attention in the ensuing years than the agrarian reform program.

Congressional opposition to Belaúnde's agrarian reform and colonization programs was quickly forthcoming. Barely more than a week after the colonization program was made public, *UNO* congressional representatives introduced their own *selva* colonization project and called for a mixed civilian and military commission appointed by congress to administer the project.[22] Within the next month both *UNO* and *APRA* congressmen presented counterproposals to the government's agrarian reform package as well. The *UNO* bill stipulated cash payment prior to expropriation of properties, no restriction on *latifundio* (very large holdings), and priority support for its colonization project. The main feature of *APRA*'s agrarian legislation was the exclusion from expropriation of the large coastal sugar estates that were *Aprista* labor strongholds.[23] By the end of September *La Coalición* had effectively blocked Belaúnde's agrarian reform bill through its congressional tactics and attacks in the Lima press. For the next eight months a congressional committee wrangled over the details of compromise legislation until a final bill was passed and signed by the president.

Law 15037, enacted on 21 May 1964, was a complicated maze of bureaucratic detail that, in the words of Belaúnde's own prime minister, Oscar Trelles, "was born dead."[24] Responsibility for the implementation of the law was shared between the executive and congress, an arrangement assuring a lack of coordination in the conduct of the program. Funding was inadequate from the beginning as the large cash demands necessitated by the immediate indemnification procedures for expropriated properties left the agrarian reform agencies financially nearly bankrupt. APRA pressure in congress was responsible for the inclusion of Article 25, which excluded the commerical sugar estates of the north coast from expropriation. A jungle of legal detail placed dozens of procedures between the peasant and the final acquisition of his land title, and this situation was exacerbated by the lack of peasant representation at any level of the agrarian reform program.[25]

These failings were overlooked in the flush of excitement over the enactment of Peru's first comprehensive agrarian reform in its history. But over the course of the next four years only 873,000 acres of expropriated holdings were distributed to fewer than twelve thousand families.[26] When one considers that at the initiation of the agrarian reform program in 1964, 1 percent of the population owned 60 percent of the available land, these figures appear even less impressive. The peasants who had invaded haciendas and corporate lands during the first two years of the Belaúnde administration and were able to hold onto the land were, ironically, the primary de facto beneficiaries of the government's agrarian reform initiatives. This fact, along with the knowledge that former army enlisted men had directed some of these invasions, was clearly recognized by the armed forces' leadership.[27]

Agrarian reform failed during the Belaúnde administration not only because of congressional opposition, an unworkable law, bureaucratic inertia, and skillful landowner resistance but also because of the president's own priorities. Belaúnde's road-building and colonization master plan for the eastern highland jungle region of the so-called Ceja de Montaña was given priority in the government's reform scheme from the beginning. The president clearly stated this priority in the 1965 English edition of his 1959 book, La Conquista del Perú por los Peruanos, when he wrote, regarding agrarian reform, "The fastest and most economical solution to the problem is the incorporation of land in the Ceja de Montaña or high jungle into the national economy by means of access roads."[28] Unquestionably, to the architect-president, opening new agricultural lands to needy peasants by means of a massive public works project had distinct political and personal appeal. Belaúnde's "Marginal Jungle Highway" was more than a "pet project"; it so fascinated him that he clung to this scheme long after he was deposed in October, 1968.[29] Moreover, developing new land was certainly politically less painful than expropriating the holdings of well-entrenched hacendados and powerful foreign corporations. The armed forces played an integral role in the Ceja de Montana project, and Belaúnde obviously hoped this fact would help ensure military loyalty to his

government. Finally, foreign lending agencies were willing to offer financial
assistance to the colonization program but were less inclined to fund Peru's
agrarian reform.[30]

Belaúnde's *Ceja de Montaña* program helped divert national attention
away from the weakness of his agrarian reform program largely because of
its tremendous supposed potential for opening virgin lands for Peru's
impoverished peasants. Scheduled for completion in 1979, the "Marginal
Jungle Highway" would extend along nearly one thousand miles of Peru's
Amazon basin, connecting similar road-building projects in Colombia,
Ecuador, and Bolivia. Three main systems of feeder roads—the Olmos-
Chachapoyas, the Lima-Huanuco-Tingo Maria-Pucallpa, and the
Lima-Ica-Cuzco routes—would be the focus of the colonization effort, with
about five million acres of new land to be opened for approximately
500,000 colonists.[31] Army engineering and construction units were heavily
involved in the Olmos-Chachapoyas and the Lima-Ica-Cuzco projects from
the beginning of the Belaúnde administration. These teams were aided by
air force aerial mapping units, reflecting the military's heaviest involvement
in civic action projects in the history of the armed forces.[32] Given their
traditional advancement of such "nation-building" activities, military leaders
were distinctly proud of their role in Belaúnde's national development
scheme and often gave foreign military personnel guided tours of these
construction sites.[33]

Army leaders in particular were aware that the Johnson administration
had closely linked military aid to Latin American nations to "nation
building." This policy was outlined in a "National Security Action
Memorandum" in April, 1964 from McGeorge Bundy to Secretary of State
Dean Rusk and Secretary of Defense Robert McNamara. Of the six
criteria for determining military assistance to the Latin American nations,
the first priority stated, "Military expenditures by the host country must be
consistent with and proportionate to expenditures for social and economic
development." For his part, Belaúnde continued to praise the work of the
armed forces and noted in each of his presidential messages from 1963 to
1967 the progress of the military's civic action efforts.[34]

Clearly, the armed forces believed there was a direct link between "civic
action" and the elimination of the conditions promoting internal subversion. The system of feeder roads constructed in conjunction with the 1963
agrarian reform project in the La Convención Valley was cited by the
"Coordinator-General of the Socio-Economic Activities of La Convención
and Lares," Lieutenant Colonel Enrique Gallegos Venero, as one of the
reasons for the reduction of peasant unrest in the region. Gallegos Venero,
a graduate of the *Escuela Superior de Guerra*, CAEM, and the army's

Intelligence School, referred to the agrarian reform and civic action project in the valley of La Convencíon and in Lares as the army's "counter-offensive of democracy."[35]   Assessing the impact of the La Convencíon project, the military administrator asserted that "it is not enough to destroy or paralyze the Marxist enemy; it is [also] necessary to gain the support of the masses."[36]

The La Convención project and the subsequent *Ceja de Montaña* program were the first concrete examples of army officers' argument since the 1920s: not only were road building and colonization essential for cultural unity and economic development, but, more importantly, they were vital components of the army's concept of national defense.   Thus, Belaúnde's colonization program coincided neatly with the army's historical perspective on its expanding national defense mission and represented the first major commitment by a civilian president to act on the armed forces' view of their more sharply defined mission in national affairs.

If the military's civic action role fulfilled its conception of its proper national mission, this role did not prevent the emergence of a serious rural guerrilla movement in 1965.[37]   With the capture of Hugo Blanco in May, 1963, the Peruvian left was deprived of its most effective rural activist. An attempt was made to form a Peruvian revolutionary front, ostensibly aimed at supporting the activist peasants' organizing activities and land occupa- tions, but this effort failed. Reflective of the radical left's lack of ideological or strategic unity was the inability of Blanco and the MIR's Luis de la Puente Uceda to agree on a common campaign when the two met in October, 1962.[38]   These same differences prevented the lack of a coordinated guerrilla effort when three separate operations were initiated in the region of Junín, Cuzco, and Ayacucho in mid-1965. Long before these operations began, however, the Peruvian military had been preparing intellectually and tactically for counterinsurgency operations.

Army officers were studying and writing about guerrilla warfare well before their first major military confrontation with rural insurgents in 1965. As previously elaborated, the basis for the army's intellectual analysis was the work of the premier French colonial counterinsurgency tacticians, Gallieni and Lyautey. The army's intellectual concern grew more intense in the late 1950s, particularly after Castro's guerrilla victory in Cuba in January, 1959. One of the army's experts on the question of rural insurgency was the military administrator of the 1963 La Convención and Lares agrarian reform and road-building projects, Lieutenant Colonel Enrique Gallegos Venero. In 1964 the lieutenant colonel insisted that the rural guerrilla threat to Peru and all of Latin America was growing increasingly severe. Clearly referring to anticipated assistance from the

United States, Gallegos Venero argued that "the war against Communist subversion must be international in scope, it must be permanent, and it must be total."[39] "This will be long and difficult," Gallegos Venero warned, while noting that the principal means of combating rural insurgency was to "win the confidence of its people" through social and economic development in each locality of military operations.[40]

Colonel Luis Vera Cruzada was convinced that hemispheric guerrilla activity was guided and directed by Fidel Castro who, according to Vera Cruzada, was "obsessed" with spreading his guerrilla-based revolution to Venezuela, Colombia, Bolivia, and Peru. Castro's "obsession," according to Vera Cruzada, was largely a manifestation of his desire to please Moscow—the driving force, according to the colonel, behind guerrilla activity throughout the Third World. Vera Cruzada may have also been interested in maintaining a climate of cooperation with Washington with his assertion that the ultimate aim of Soviet-directed Third World guerrilla activity was to bring down the democratic systems of the United States and Western Europe.[41] The army's leading intellectual of the pre-Velasco years, Colonel Edgardo Mercado Jarrín, in his seminal article written in 1964, "El ejército de hoy y un proyección en nuestra sociedad en periodo de transición," placed the importance of counterinsurgency training in a clearer perspective when he argued that one of the most important factors stimulating modernization in the Peruvian army since the early 1940s was the challenge of confronting and successfully combating guerrilla warfare.[42]

Peruvian armed forces' officers prepared tactically for their antisubversive combat mission at the Escuela Superior de Guerra and the CAEM, and younger officers prepared at the United States military's School of the Americas in the Panama Canal Zone and the United States army's Special Warfare Center and School at Fort Bragg, North Carolina. Between its inception in 1949 and 1964, 805 Peruvian armed forces' officers trained at the School of the Americas, which changed its training emphasis in the early 1960s from hemispheric defense to internal security and counter-insurgency training. Officers taking the internal security course were enrolled in subjects that included counterinsurgency operations, military intelligence, military police operations, command and staff procedures, infantry, jungle operations, and airborne training. Civic action as a means of promoting economic growth and reducing rural unrest was also taught.[43] Created in 1956, the Special Warfare School and Center at Fort Bragg enrolled only a limited number of Peruvian officers through 1964 in courses designed to produce core trainees for special forces and psychological warfare units. In 1963, the United States assistant secretary of state

for Latin American affairs, Edwin M. Martin, summarized the purpose of
the training at the School of the Americas and Fort Bragg:

This assistance is being provided for the control of Communist-inspired civil
disturbances, for vigilance and control of movement and subversions inside the
countries and across their borders and for the maintenance of operations and
patrols of rural areas for detection and dispersion of guerrilla movements.[44]

Drawing upon the training at Peruvian and United States military
installations, the Peruvian army formed a counterinsurgency unit under the
command of Colonel Gonzalo Briceño Zevallos in the early 1960s to serve
as its primary reaction force against rural guerrilla activity.[45] The eagerness
of the Peruvian army to engage in counterinsurgency operations is
evidenced by the comments of Peruvian army officers to the United States
military attaché in Lima, Colonel James D. Aikens, during the mid-1960s.
Peruvian army officers repeatedly offered their moral support for the
Vietnam campaign, and some of these officers indulged in idle chatter
regarding the formation of a volunteer Peruvian army unit to assist the
United States military in its Southeast Asian campaign.[46] Then when the
MIR and the *Ejército de Liberación Nacional* (ELN), headed by Héctor
Béjar, began forming their campaign strategies in 1964 and early 1965, the
Peruvian armed forces were prepared and eager to meet them in the field.

Luis de la Puente Uceda, leader of the MIR, developed a clear ideological identification with Cuba after he attended the First National Agrarian
Reform Forum in Havana in July, 1959 while he was still a member of
APRA. Many other MIR militants traveled to Cuba in the early 1960s,
and by early 1964 the MIR leadership was prepared publicly to announce
its program. In a lengthy speech in Lima's Plaza San Martín on 7 February
and with the publication of MIR's major policy statement, *Nuestra posición
frente a la revolución mundial* (Our Position regarding the World Revolution), de la Puente Uceda emphatically stated the MIR's revolutionary
philosophy. He referred to the United States as the "Great Monster of the
North" and claimed only a revolution "with the arms in the hands of the
people" could succeed.[47] The MIR leaders' embryonic campaign strategy,
published in the *Monthly Review* in November, 1965, reflected Luis de la
Puente's idealism and lack of realistic objectives as the planning for the
guerrilla campaign entered its formative stage. "We envisage," he wrote,
"a people's war pushing outward from the Andes to the coast, from the
countryside to the cities, from the provinces to the capital."[48] The MIR
made its revolutionary objectives public, before establishing its guerrilla
focos in the Peruvian *sierra*, because its leaders believed that the revolution

must be led by a disciplined coalition political party with a large number of activists energetically working with the peasantry and the "progressive" middle class. This publicity, of course, exposed the MIR operations to Peruvian military intelligence and directly conflicted with the tactics employed by the second principal guerrilla organization, the ELN.

According to ELN leader Héctor Béjar, his revolutionary group was interested not in creating one more political party to add to the confusion of Peru's fragmented left, but in trying to build a disciplined military team at the same time as a "free association of coalitionists" was created. Ultimately the successful military campaign would mobilize the peasantry and the "proletarian agricultural, manufacturers and mining sectors," to forge the coalition party.[49] Béjar also argued that the differences between the MIR and the ELN were deeper than their tactical disagreements. He noted that the MIR was primarily an organization with Aprista roots and that the ELN was a revolutionary cadre with ties to the Communist Party. Since APRA and the Communist Party had been feuding since the late 1920s, these inherent differences were reflected in the ideological distrust between the two groups. Eventually, on 9 September 1965 the MIR and the ELN agreed to form a "National Coordinating Command," but this agreement occurred three months after the initial guerrilla operations and only forty-five days before the death of MIR leader de la Puente Uceda in his guerrilla headquarters on the Mesa Pelada Plateau near Cuzco.[50]

When the guerrillas began operations on 9 June 1965 with an attack on the Santa Rosa mine and the Runatullo hacienda near the village of Andamarca in the department of Junín, three main guerrilla focos had already been established. The 9 June attack was led by the Tupac Amaru faction of the MIR, which was led by Guillermo Lobatón and was based on the upper Andamarca River between the villages of Andamarca and Satipo. Luis de la Puente Uceda's and Ruben Tupayachi's Pachacutec group set up camp on the Mesa Pelada Plateau in the Eastern range of the Andes near the La Convención Valley in the department of Cuzco. The ELN, led by Béjar, operating under the title of the Javier Heraud front, (a Peruvian poet and guerrilla killed by army troops near Puerto Maldonado in 1963) established mobile camps in the province of La Mar in the department of Ayacucho.[51] Béjar's group, despite operating between the two MIR focos, never consolidated operations with de la Puente or Lobatón for the tactical and doctrinal differences previously described. Moreover, the Tupac Amaru front's attack on the Santa Rosa mine and neighboring hacienda apparently caught both Béjar and de la Puente still in the midst of final preparations for their opening assaults. Thus, Lobatón's Tupac Amaru group was the primary target of Guardia Civil operations.

Lobatón's second-in-command, Maximo Velando Gálvez, ambushed a *Guardia* column at Yahuarina on 27 June.[52] By the time another *Guardia* detachment was again attacked by the Tupac Amaru front on 14 July, Belaúnde was under enormous pressure from the armed forces to allow the military a free hand in suppressing the rural unrest.

In early July Belaúnde attempted publicly to belittle the initial guerrilla successes by referring to the insurgents as mere "cattle rustlers." Nevertheless, by a supreme decree issued on 2 July the armed forces' joint command was given responsibility for the supression of the guerrillas, and two days later another supreme decree suspended civil liberties for thirty days throughout Peru.[53] These measures were supplemented on 20 August by legislation that made the guerrillas subject to the code of military justice and charges for treason, with the ultimate penalty of death. Similar penalties were sanctioned for individuals convicted of aiding the guerrillas. A second law called for the establishment of a special fund of 200 million soles (eight million dollars) to provide resources for the armed forces and their auxiliaries in combating the guerrillas. The funds were to be raised by a bond issue to be designated the "Defense of the National Sovereignty." Significantly, the former arch-conservative prime minister during the Prado administration, Pedro Beltrán, made the dramatic public gesture of purchasing the first five million soles of the bond issue.[54]

The government measures of early July were apparently not enough of a mandate for armed forces' leaders, for on 14 July they presented Belaúnde with an ultimatum demanding total control over the antiguerrilla operations or the president would face an "institutional *coup*."[55] Now given a free hand, from mid-July onward the armed forces launched an aggressive campaign to eliminate the guerrilla threat throughout Peru. Initially concentrating on Lobatón's operations now centering in the forest area bordering on the Sanamora River, air force planes bombed villages of the Campas Indians, who supported the Tupac Amaru's operations in the region.[56] Army units continued to clash with the Lobatón column until it was finally destroyed in early January. In the interim, the focus of the antiguerrilla campaign shifted to the Cuzco region when the Pachucutec column of Luis de la Puente Uceda began operations. De la Puente issued a communiqué on 30 August to announce the beginning of his campaign. His forces had their first clash with government troops on 9 September. Under the command of General Alberto Maldonado, the Peruvian Fourth Army sent five army detachments against de la Puente's stronghold on the Mesa Pelada on 20 September. At the same time units of the Fourth Army built base camps and two roads leading to the Mesa Pelada to facilitate operations against the guerrillas.[57] When the guerrilla forces withdrew farther onto the plateau in the face of superior government forces, the air force began bombing raids employing conventional explosives as well as napalm in an attempt to destroy the guerrilla encampments.[58] The final assault by the army on the Pachacutec front's base camps was aided by detailed information provided by a defector from the guerrillas' camp, Albino Guzmán. Guzmán had been a member of the MIR's Regional Committee and was involved in the preparation for the establishment of the Mesa Pelada *foco*.[59] After an attempted breakout of their surrounded position on 23 October near Amaybamba, de la Puente and seven of his followers were eliminated by the army. De la Puente's exact cause of death is uncertain as his death was never officially announced by the armed forces. But since few prisoners were taken by Peruvian troops in the guerrilla campaign, it appears likely he was either killed in action or executed after his capture.[60]

Héctor Béjar's *ELN* forces, after initiating operations in Ayacucho on 24 September with an attack on the Chapi Hacienda, confronted little government resistance until troops were transferred from the Mesa Pelada operations in late November. Béjar's group eluded government troops until they were ambushed by an army detachment on 17 December at Tincoy. Béjar escaped, only to be later captured and sent to prison. Béjar later wrote an analysis of the guerrilla movement and went on to become an adviser to the Velasco government.[61]

With the suppression of the guerrillas in less than seven months, the armed forces demonstrated their capacity to combat a potentially serious internal insurrection. Nevertheless, the military exacted a costly price for its victory. Reliable statistics on the guerrilla campaign are unfortunately lacking, since the official armed forces' account makes no mention of civilian casualties, and newspaper correspondents were not allowed into the operational theaters. But unquestionably the cost in lives and material resources was quite high. The often-cited figures of Rogger Mercado list eight thousand peasants killed and nineteen thousand hectares burned, presumably by napalm.[62] The armed forces listed only thirty-two soldiers killed in the campaign, but Mercado disputes these figures and claimed fifty-six died.[63] Even if Mercado's figures are somewhat inflated, they still reflect a massive response to a relatively limited guerrilla threat. Then, too, the use of napalm, the policy of taking few prisoners, and the utilization of Central Intelligence Agency (CIA) operatives in the campaign demonstrate the military leadership's determination to prevent a Cuban-style guerrilla movement from gaining a foothold in Peru.

Regarding the CIA's involvement in the counterinsurgency campaign, evidence exists that a CIA mole infiltrated de la Puente Uceda's *foco* at the beginning stages of his campaign. CIA records contain a cable dated 12 February 1964 outlining detailed information about MIR's campaign plans, its expectation of receiving arms from Brazil and Chile, and directions for smuggling these arms into Peru and noting the receipt of a personal letter of support for de la Puente's offensive from Mao Zedong. The memorandum also claimed that MIR activists were being sent to train in North Korea and the People's Republic of China.[64]

Moreover, in their final summary of the military's operations against the guerrillas, the armed forces' official account displayed a marked anxiety regarding the reappearance of the guerrilla threat. The armed forces' official version warned that the threat of subversion was still "latent" and charged that the 1965 campaign was part of the Kremlin's efforts to aid the Third World revolutionary movement. The report insisted that the guerrillas were aided materially by Moscow and Peking and their *focos* were established after training in Cuba's *Sierra Maestra*.[65] It is quite apparent that the massive land invasions by the peasantry in 1963 to 1964 made the armed forces' leadership acutely aware of the militant potential of landless *campesinos* once they were properly trained and organized by guerrilla leaders. Thus the immediate elimination of the 1965 guerrilla *focos* was viewed as imperative by the high command before a guerrilla-*compesino* alliance could be forged. International considerations may have also prompted the armed forces to act as decisively as they did. The simultaneous escalation of the United States' military involvement in Vietnam, with the initiation of "Operation Rolling Thunder" coming in the midst of the Peruvian antiguerrilla campaign, possibly strengthened the armed forces' revolve to repress massively its own guerrilla threat and demonstrate their counterinsurgency expertise to their United States military mentors. Then, too, as has been discussed at length, the army officer corps had been analyzing the nature of guerrilla warfare for decades. The army was well aware of the guerrillas' potential for creating internal disorder, the ultimate collapse of government, and, most threatening of all to the officer corps, the dismantling of the armed forces and their replacement with a paraprofessional revolutionary army. The lessons of the Bolivian revolution of 1952 and of Cuba in 1959 must have been still fresh in the minds of the Peruvian officer corps.

The failure of the 1965 guerrilla offensive cannot be fully ascribed to a well-planned and executed military response. The ideological and tactical divisions preventing the MIR and ELN from effectively integrating their operations helped doom their movements. Support from the urban centers, vital to the success of the Cuban revolution, was never really forthcoming in Peru. There were isolated bombing incidents at the exclusive Club Nacional and Hotel Crillion in Lima and some bank robberies, which were apparently linked to the guerrilla operations in the *sierra*. Nonetheless, these incidents never created the climate of urban unrest engendered by student revolutionaries in Cuba prior to Castro's victory. This fact may be explained by the unwillingness of the Peruvian Communist Party to aid the guerrillas after the repression of the party by the Pérez Godoy government in January, 1963.[66] Moreover, as the guerrilla *focos* were being planned in early 1964, the *Guardia Civil* arrested twenty "communist agitators" near Cuzco and imprisoned them in the Sepa prison colony, while six communists "known to have been trained in Cuba" were arrested by the Peruvian Investigative Police in the Lima suburb of Miraflores with a cache of weapons and dynamite.[67] These arrests and subsequent jailings, along with the earlier repression of party members, undoubtedly undermined the willingness of Communist Party leaders to ally themselves with a guerrilla movement not ideologically in tune with party doctrine. To this situation must be added the split in the Communist Party ranks over the Sino-Soviet dispute in the early 1960s.

Organizational and tactical shortcomings and an obvious lack of internal security also contributed to the guerrillas' defeat. Unlike Hugo Blanco, none of the guerrilla leaders of 1965 spoke Quechua, and the language barrier was only one of many cultural impediments undermining their peasant recruiting effort. According to Béjar:

Despite friendship, language was always a barrier that separated the rebels from the natives. Peasants identify Spanish with the boss, especially in places like Ayacucho which has a very large Quechua population. For the guerrillas to gain the trust of the peasantry, they must be able to speak Quechua, and not just any Quechua, but the dialect spoken in the zone they are operating.[68]

Added to this problem was Luis de la Puente Uceda's decision publicly to announce the opening of his guerrilla campaign and establish a fixed base camp on the Mesa Pelada, both in violation of standard guerrilla procedure. These poor decisions led to the quick isolation and destruction of the MIR *foco*.

In the final analysis the lack of widespread peasant support for the guerrillas may be explained by the success of the earlier land invasion movement, the limited agrarian reform program initiated in the La Convención Valley in 1963, and the promise of more comprehensive agrarian reform by the Belaúnde administration. Peasants who distrusted middle-class revolutionaries from Lima were clearly unwilling to stake their lives on vague promises of revolutionary change while chances of peaceful reform remained on the horizon.

A central question emerging from the 1965 antiguerrilla campaign is what impact the suppression of the rebels had on the thinking of armed forces' leaders regarding their national mission. The military leaders believed, as the Belaúnde government announced on 8 July, that the guerrillas were operating with the "material assistance of Moscow, Havana, and Peking."[69] But at the same time it appears that some military leaders were troubled about the army's role in brutally suppressing the guerrilla uprising and were unconvinced of its success in eliminating the potential for future internal subversion. General Edgardo Mercado Jarrín, who assumed the post of director of military intelligence in 1967 helped plan the Velasco *coup* and then played an integral role in the subsequent military government, later claimed that the 1965 campaign convinced him of the need for "social justice" in the countryside as a means of alleviating the conditions promoting rural unrest.[70] Colonel Jorge Fernández Maldonado, who also was one of the Velasco plotters and later joined the government in 1969 as one of its most radical proponents of major reform, later argued that "the best manner to combat internal subversion is not with repression but by bringing about national change."[71] And General José Graham Hurtado, later a member of Velasco's Council of Ministers, commented in *La Prensa* in August, 1972 that the guerrilla campaign "rang the military's alarm bell" regarding the necessity of major social reforms in Peru's "unequal society."[72]

The assessments of Mercado Jarrín, Fernandez Maldonado, and Graham Hurtado must be judged within the context of the hyperbolic reformist rhetoric of the Velasco years. Yet they are strikingly similar to Gallegos Venero's ambitious claims for his "counter-offensive for democracy" in the valley of La Convención and Lares in 1963. Repression of a rural guerrilla threat clearly fell within the confines of the military's traditional internal security role, but at no time in this century, prior to the 1980s, had Peru experienced such large-scale rural unrest as it had in the period 1959-1965. Army writers for decades lamented the unequal nature of Peruvian society and called for the armed forces to help rectify this problem. For many armed forces' officers during the Belaúnde years, it became more urgent than ever that they begin to act on a nation-building mission, then only partially being met by the army's involvement in the civic action programs under the aegis of Belaúnde's *Ceja de Montaña* project.

The ultimatum given Belaúnde by the armed forces' high command in early July, 1965 demanding they be given a free hand in the suppression of the guerrillas, reflected the military's growing distrust of the president's ability to provide decisive leadership. This distrust would increase dramatically during Belaúnde's last three years in office as he faced a deteriorating economy, a crisis over foreign warplane purchases, the breakup of the alliance with the Christian Democrats, and the splintering of his own party *Acción Popular*. Most damaging of all, however, were a smuggling scandal involving top members of the government and the military and the president's explosively unpopular attempted settlement of the simmering IPC dispute.

During his first two years in office Belaúnde's administration enjoyed a stable economy that kept his congressional opponents reasonably subdued and the military satisfied with his economic performance.[73] As late as August, 1964, Peru boasted a $165 million trade reserve, a stable currency, labor peace, and an inflow of foreign investment totaling $130 million from July, 1963 to August, 1964.[74] Beginning in 1965, however, the government's policy of deficit spending on its development and social welfare projects, coupled with congressional refusal to raise taxes, prompted government indebtedness to increase at a rate of 90 percent per year from late 1964 to 1967. Moreover, the urban consumer price index rose an average of 14 percent during these years. Even more significant for Lima's burgeoning *barriada* population, the cost of food jumped 70 percent between 1964 and 1968.[75] Congressional refusal to raise the badly needed new taxes forced Belaúnde to turn to foreign lending agencies for assistance, but this tactic tended to increase inflationary pressures and raise Peru's debt-servicing charges as a share of its export earnings by 9 percent in the four years prior to Belaúnde's overthrow.[76] Even foreign financing was fraught with problems as the unresolved IPC controversy prompted Washington to freeze AID funds and curtail other sources of low-interest loans. This action was bitterly resented by Belaúnde, who later lamented that during the AID negotiations for the restoration of funds, "They always said maybe and asked for more feasibility studies. By the time we finished these, I was flying to Argentina."[77] The president's hard feelings might explain why, when his government was facing a serious balance of payments crisis in mid-1967, he refused two United States "program loans" totaling fifty-five million dollars ear marked for alleviating the trade deficit, with the argument that the austerity measures required as a condition for the loans were too restrictive for the "modest" sum involved.[78]

The government's economic problems, highlighted by the trade deficit, which averaged sixty million dollars per year during Belaúnde's last four years in office, called for decisive action. Specifically, some economic critics called for the devaluation of the *sol*, which, despite the inflation of the 1960s, remained pegged at 26.32 to the United States dollar since

1959. The equally vital refinancing of the foreign debt was also being called for, but the IPC dispute and another ongoing conflict with the United States-owned Southern Peru Copper Company prevented Belaúnde from making any progress in this area.[79] After unwisely claiming previously that to devalue the sol would be "treasonous," the president took this necessary but painful step on 1 September by devaluing the nation's monetary unit 40 percent. This move set off a wave of strikes as Peru's workers protested their reduced spending power.[80] Amidst rumors of a military *coup* prompted by the economic dilemma, the president was confronted with a military purchasing crisis, adding further to the instability of his regime.

In early 1967 the Belaúnde government sought to purchase Northrup F5A Freedom Fighters from the United States for the air force. This request was very likely prompted by the United States sale of twenty-five Skyhawk attack bombers to Argentina in 1966 and (more importantly for Peru's defense concerns) the purchase of twenty Hunter attack fighters by Chile in early 1967. Peru's request was strongly opposed in the United States Congress, where the opposition was led by Senator Morse of Oregon and Congressman Ryan of New York. Presenting a view that became characteristic of the Alliance for Progress philosophy, Congressman Ryan argued the F5A purchase would "retard the development our aid is supposed to promote and encourage militarism and international instability."[81] In the midst of the F5A dispute, Washington exacerbated the crisis by blocking the sale of six British Canberra bombers to Peru, invoking a clause in the terms of the Anglo-American leasing agreement dating from the Marshall Plan.[82] Clearly under pressure from the air force, Belaúnde then began talks with the French government for the purpose of buying twelve Mirage V fighters at a cost of 1.5 million dollars each. With this development, the United States State Department advocated the sale of the F5As and Carlos Saenz de Santamaría, representing the Inter-American Committee for the Alliance for Progress, visited Peru on several occasions to try to dissuade Belaúnde from making the Mirage purchases. But the president argued that he was unable to oppose the mounting pressure from military leaders to acquire the highly sophisticated supersonic Mirage Vs.[83] In a comment reflective of the troubled United States-Peruvian economic relationship during the Belaúnde years, Senator Morse lamented, after Peru's decision to buy the French fighters, "What we should have said [to Peru] is go and buy them [the Mirages] from France and get your aid from France too."[84] The Belaúnde administration eventually finalized the Mirage deal with the French government at a cost of over twenty million dollars. The controversy undermined United States-Peruvian military relations, which reached a low point during the Velasco administration with the expulsion of the United States military mission. It also reflected Belaúnde's willingness to bend to military pressure as his political legitimacy further weakened in early 1968 due to the continuing economic malaise and a smuggling scandal that reached into upper levels of the armed forces and Belaúnde's administration.

Revelations that contraband goods, unreported by senior officials of Peruvian customs, were being flown into Peru, led to the dismissal in March of the superintendent of customs, the commander of the Peruvian Investigative Police (PIP), and the head of the Fiscal Police.[85] Further inquiries led to the involvement of military personnel in the scandal—a navy transport and two destroyers were supplying navy PXs with the contraband material. The main focus of the illegal trade, however, was in automobiles smuggled into Peru to avoid the extremely high import tarriff, which could raise the price of a six thousand-dollar automobile on the open market to eighteen thousand dollars. Estimates placed the number of contraband cars at two thousand annually, thus representing a significant loss of revenue to a government in the throes of a serious economic crisis.[86]

The congress responded to the smuggling scandal by appointing an investigative commission headed by an *Aprista*. Belaúnde, feeling the pressure, went on television in late March to praise the work of his administration and the contributions of the armed forces, which he characterized as the "unknown collaborators [in the construction of] the highways of the Andes who will endanger their lives at times to save the lives of the peasants."[87] After offering this diversionary praise of his government and the military, Belaúnde announced the appointment of General Francisco Morales Bermúdez, an engineer, as the new minister of finance, with specific responsibilities of cleaning up the smuggling scandal. General Morales Bermúdez was also given a free hand in dealing with Peru's complex economic problems.[88] In a striking parallel to the policies of President Bustamante prior to the Odría *coup* of October, 1948, Belaúnde was now relying heavily on military support to fend off the growing civilian criticism of his regime, while at the same time hoping to co-opt the military backing for an increasingly likely *golpe de estado* spawned by the smuggling scandal.

General Morales Bermúdez's investigation did not prevent the Lima press and some congressmen from charging high-level armed forces involvement in the affair. Christian Democratic Congressman Carlos Vinetea alleged in mid-April that the scandal included military members of Belaúnde's government.[89] Minister of War General Julio Doig Sánchez heatedly denied these charges on 22 April, while announcing that an internal investigation conducted by the military concluded that the armed forces' officers under investigaton by the congressional commission were "completely uninvolved in illegal acts." General Doig Sánchez and other military officers in the Belaúnde government then met with the presidents of the senate and Chamber of Deputies. Soon afterward, congressional attacks on individual armed forces officers ended, and the public furor over the scandal faded.[90] Aprista congressmen who initially supported the investigation obviously lost their enthusiasm when it appeared that the armed forces' leadership was so threatened by inquiry that a possible coup might result. This unease may have motivated Haya de la Torre to issue a thinly veiled warning to the armed forces on 21 April when he announced that a "new veto against my possible candidacy [in the 1969 elections] at this time would be unacceptable and would frustrate the people's aspirations."[91] Clearly, Haya de la Torre was worried about a coup's preventing an APRA victory in the coming elections, and the fear of a coup prompted Aprista congressmen to back away from the smuggling scandal and end their crippling opposition to a badly weakened Belaúnde administration.

Belaúnde's political fortunes suffered even further when in an election on 12 November 1967, which was viewed as a mandate for the president's economic policy, the Acción Popular candidate was defeated in his effort to win a vacant seat in the Chamber of Deputies for the Lima district. Soon thereafter the Christian Democrats severed their ties with Acción Popular and claimed the government had abandoned the policies upon which the alliance was originally forged in 1964.[92] Vice President Edgardo Seoane, a critic of the Belaúnde administration policies since the passage of the agrarian reform legislation, then resigned his post as prime minister, to which the president had reluctantly appointed him during the devaluation crisis of September, 1967. Seoane's resignation touched off a bitter struggle within Acción Popular between Seoane's and Belaúnde's supporters that would reach a violent culmination after the president's unpopular effort to settle the IPC controversy in September, 1968.

With Belaúnde's political props collapsing under him, APRA clearly feared a military coup against an isolated president. The party then sought to shore up the faltering administration. Aprista congressmen, free to act after the breakup of the APRA-UNO alliance in early 1968, cooperated in granting the president broad fiscal powers to resolve the continuing economic crisis. Instituting austerity measures and new taxing powers, Belaúnde, during the first quarter of 1968, finally began to get the economy on a sounder footing. Negotiations were renewed to refinance

Peru's foreign debt, the trade deficit declined, and the rate of inflation was substantially curtailed. But it was a question of too little, too late for both Belaúnde and APRA as his belated economic successes were more than undermined by faltering efforts to resolve the IPC issue, which had plagued his administration from the beginning.

Belaúnde's inability to negotiate a final settlement with IPC throughout the first four years of his administration weakened his personal prestige, angered Peruvian nationalists, disrupted AID assistance, and engendered the animosity of elements of the armed forces. The IPC controversy was somewhat similar to the Mexican government's disputes with foreign oil companies in the aftermath of the Mexican revolution. Under the terms of Article 27 of the Mexican Constitution, the government controlled the subsoil rights of the nation and thus its petroleum reserves. Foreign companies disputed this control, and the issue was finally resolved when Mexican president Lázaro Cardenas expropriated most of the foreign petroleum companies in March, 1938. The Belaúnde administration made the same claims regarding subsoil rights, but unfortunately IPC's legal position was greatly strengthened by the terms of the original contract with the Leguía government in 1922, which made no mention of subsoil rights.[93] Moreover, IPC executives had developed a particular talent for resisting the efforts of Peruvian political leaders to restrict its operations in Peru.

The Sechura Desert negotiations during the Bustamante regime, for example, weakened the president's political position and demonstrated APRA's most striking reversal of its anti-imperialist principles. It also prompted the vitriolic opposition of such arch-conservative nationalists as Pedro Beltrán and the Miró-Quesada family, who subsequently lent their support to Bustamante's overthrow. After IPC threatened to cease drilling operations, President Manuel Prado, in July, 1959, allowed the company major price increases. These tactics prompted an attack on the terms of the 1922 contract by nationalist congressmen and the Miró-Quesada-owned newspaper, El Comercio. Thus, IPC's nationalization was continually raised as an issue during the last years of the second Prado administration. The company tried to head off military opposition prior to the 1960s by granting the air force land in its La Brea y Pariñas enclave in 1946 to build the "El Pato" air base, and in subsequent years the IPC provided housing for air force and army officers on its properties. In all of these instances, however, IPC required the armed forces to recognize the company's subsoil rights regarding the property it ceded to the military.[94] It is fair to assume that these conditions must have offended the sensibilities of some nationalist officers who understood that control of the nation's petroleum reserves was a critical component of national defense. Moreover, nationalist military men must have also appreciated the vulnerability of foreign petroleum companies in the face of the decisive actions of strong military leaders such as Cardenas and Bolivian president Colonel David Toro, who expropriated Standard Oil of New Jersey's holdings in 1937. Still, the military leadership was so divided over the IPC issue as late as the 1962-1963 military government that it was a factor in the resignations of Minister of Government General Juan Bossio Collas and President Ricardo Pérez Godoy.

When Belaúnde took office he could not ignore the intense feelings generated by IPC and he rashly promised a quick settlement to the company's status in Peru. But IPC's hold on the Peruvian economy was substantial, as it extracted nearly 85 percent of the nation's petroleum from its fields at La Brea y Pariñas and Lobitos. The company's Talara refinery also processed more than 60 percent of the nation's crude oil and—significantly, for the military's defense capability—all of Peru's aviation fuel.[95] Not suprisingly, a CAEM commission, headed by then Colonel Franciso Morales Bermúdez, studied the IPC issue one year after Belaúnde took office and concluded that the state should refuse any settlement with the company and nationalize the existing petroleum reserves. The commission also concluded that EPF (Empresa Petrolea Fisicales), Peru's state-controlled petroleum company, was capable of exploiting IPC's existing deposits.[96] Like previous CAEM proposals, these recommendations were not binding on the Belaúnde administration or the armed forces' high command. In fact, as will be subsequently discussed, Morales Bermúdez would later take a more favorable position toward IPC during the last months of the Belaúnde presidency, a position reflecting the military's sensitivities on this highly volatile nationalist issue.

Belaúnde's negotiations with IPC extended through his entire presidency and are too complex to be discussed here in detail.[97] The substance of the debate, however, centered on the company's payment of reparations for its operations on a tax-free basis under the original contract with the Peruvian government and the abrogation of subsoil rights under the same accord signed in 1922. The president's early antagonists in the debate proved to be not only IPC, but the avidly nationalist Miró-Quesada family, owners of the powerful conservative newspaper, El Comercio. The newspaper stridently demanded the company's nationalization. At the same time, the United States State Department, under the initiative of Under-Secretary of State Thomas Mann, kept pressure on the government by freezing all AID funds soon after President Lyndon B. Johnson took office in November, 1963.[98] United States aid was finally resumed after conversations between Belaúnde and Presidential Assistant Walt W. Rostow in March, 1966 determined that the Peruvian president had no intention of nationalizing the company. This aid was again suspended after the Mirage V purchases in 1967, the suspension thus clouding the IPC negotiations further.

Belaúnde's increasingly serious economic and political problems after 1965 undermined his bargaining position with the company, which was using all of its resources both in Peru and in the United States to prevent the eventual nationalization of its properties. The company sent its general manager, Fernando Espinoza, to argue IPC's main objective: a contract to continue operations in Peru after any final settlement with the Peruvian government was reached. But by mid-1967 Belaúnde faced overwhelming pressure from the congress, the press, and elements within his own party to nationalize the company. In late July, 1967 the president actually signed Law 149696, calling for the transfer of the company's La Brea y Pariñas properties to the state and declaring the 1922 contract null and void.[99] This "revindication" of Peru's national honor, however, was thwarted by a protracted appeals process, which once again postponed a final settlement. Rumors of a possible army *coup*, to be led by Chief of Staff General Julio Doig Sánchez, prompted Espinoza to meet with General Doig Sánchez and former finance minister Francisco Morales Bermúdez on several occasions during which, according to Espinoza, he was assured of the military leader's "favorable disposition" toward the company.[100] Morales Bermúdez's position is difficult to understand, given his chairman-ship of the 1964 CAEM commission recommending the company's nationalization. Perhaps Morales Bermúdez's intimate knowledge of the IPC negotiating process as Belaúnde's finance minister led him to adopt a more cautious approach. More likely, his conservative beliefs, made sharply evident after he assumed the presidency in 1975 upon General Velasco's overthrow, explained his later conciliatory attitude toward the company. Given the tough position of the Johnson administration during the negotiations, Morales Bermúdez and General Doig Sánchez might also have feared a curtailment of United States military assistance should the military overthrow Belaúnde and seize IPC's holdings.

When General Juan Velasco Alvarado became army chief of staff in March, 1968, the army's position hardened toward IPC. Velasco was born in Piura, not far from IPC's properties, and was intimately familiar with the company's inordinate power in the region. As an infantry captain just prior to the opening of hostilities with Ecuador in July, 1941, Velasco was assigned the duty of commandeering IPC vehicles at the Talara refinery to move his troops to the front. He was delayed twenty-four hours while an

IPC official asked for authority to grant Velasco's order. This incident reportedly infuriated the young captain and may very well have influenced his later highly negative attitude toward IPC.[101]

The new hard line of the army leadership was firmly supported by *El Comercio*, which sought to put further pressure on the company by carrying a story in late March of a military official of EPF who demanded that his organization take over IPC. The administrator backed his demand by claiming the armed forces' high command fully concurred in his decision.[102] By June events were moving beyond IPC's ability to resist a final solution to the long-delayed settlement. Belaúnde's negotiating position with IPC was weakened when Edgardo Seoane, a vitriolic critic of the company, was nominated as the presidential candidate of *Acción Popular* for the upcoming 1969 elections. Five weeks later Haya de la Torre announced his presidential candidacy on the APRA ticket, further weakening Belaúnde's bargaining position.

IPC officials responded to this situation by announcing three days before Belaúnde's scheduled 28 July Independence Day address to congress that it was willing to renounce its subsoil claims, transfer the La Brea y Pariñas properties to the government, and drop its insistence on a future operation contract. In return, IPC wanted all government debt claims against the company abandoned and Belaúnde's assurance that EPF would sell its petroleum product from La Brea y Pariñas to the North American firm in order that it could continue its refining and marketing operations at its Talara refinery.[103] What seemed to be the final terms of a settlement were debated for three weeks over a dispute involving EPF's selling price to IPC. This wrangle was finally resolved, and on 13 August 1968 the *Acta de Talara*, giving the government control over the La Brea y Pariñas oilfields, was finally signed.[104] The apparent victory for the Belaúnde administration soon turned into a crisis that toppled his government. Carlos Loret de Mola, who had previously resigned as president of EPF in September, charged in a television address that the eleventh page of the contract, which carried the highly controversial price of the petroleum EPF was to sell to IPC, was mysteriously missing. The Lima press immediately charged that fraud had been committed, and Loret de Mola began leading a public attack on the contract.[105] The *"pagina once"* scandal quickly lost Belaúnde his remaining congressional adherents when APRA congressmen dropped their support for the president and joined the chorus of critics of the Talara contract. An obviously bitter president then expelled Seoane from *Acción Popular* and ordered the party's reorganization. Party members quickly aligned themselves with the two warring leaders, and the struggle finally escalated into a violent confrontation for control of *Acción Popular* headquarters. This street battle of 24 September, which saw the president's own party members exchanging gunfire for the control of the party, surely convinced military leaders that Belaúnde was no longer capable of governing.[106]

In the midst of the page-eleven uproar, thirty-six generals under General Velasco's leadership convened to discuss the affair. They subsequently forwarded their opposition to the accord to the president and asked that their views be passed on to congress. Velasco promised a public communiqué by the armed forces' joint command on the matter, but the chiefs of the navy and air force chose to remain silent on the issue.[107] When Belaúnde's loyal minister of war, General José Gagliardi, made a public statement supporting the president, Velasco claimed Gagliardi's statement had "no validity."[108] Velasco, who was organizing a *coup d'état* well before the final IPC crisis, now began laying final plans for Belaúnde's overthrow and the establishment of a military government under his leadership.[109]

Velasco was born in Castilla, near Piura, on 16 June 1910 into a family of eleven children, headed by a father who worked as a medical assistant. His early childhood, spent in the schools of his native city, was characterized as one of "dignified poverty, working as a shoeshine boy in Piura." His short stature, his dark-skinned mestizo appearance, and his unpolished personal mannerisms later reminded many of the previous military president from Piura, Sánchez Cerro. In fact, his army colleagues and the Peruvian public called him "El Chino" and "El Negro" in reference to his Indian features.

Apparently having no influential military contacts, Velasco stowed away on a ship to Lima, falsified his age, and entered the army as a private on 5 April 1929. He then reportedly took a competitive exam for entrance into the *Escuela Militar de Chorrillos* and finished first among all applicants. Upon graduation from the *Escuela Militar*, with high honors and at the head of his class, Velasco's rise through the army's ranks was unspectacular but completely on schedule. He attained the rank of captain in 1940, major in 1945, lieutenant colonel in 1949, colonel in 1951, brigade general in 1955, and division general in 1965. Except for his brief involvement in the 1941 Ecuador war already described, Velasco boasted no substantial combat experience, but this lack can be explained by Peru's military inactivity during the future military president's later career. Velasco was not a scholar, as were many of his colleagues in the post-1968 military government. A careful review of the main Peruvian military journals finds nothing written by Velasco during his rise through the ranks. This lack of intellectual activity seems to bear out the estimates of those who claim that Velasco was not a man of keen intelligence but rather a competent soldier with an uncanny ability to judge the abilities, political proclivities, and, most of all, the loyalty of his fellow soldiers. These qualities apparently prompted his appointment to every important army command prior to his selection as chief of staff. His impressive career duties included instructor at the *Escuela Oficiales*, chief of the Battalion of Cadets, instructor at the *Escuela Superior de Guerra*, commander of the Infantry Battalion Twenty-nine, director of the *Escuela Militar de Chorrillos*, director of the Infantry School, chief of the general staff of the *Centro de Instrucción Militar del Perú*, commander of the army's Second Division, military attaché to France, chief of staff of Peru's First Military Region, inspector general of the army, Peru's delegate to the Inter-American Defense Board, and finally chief of staff of the army.[110]

What is significantly lacking from Velasco's career is a stint at the CAEM. If he was to have been selected for CAEM's class of colonels, he would have been named during the Prado years when the center's influence was increasing within the officer corps. Clearly, despite CAEM's growing importance, it still was not a mandatory requirement for a top command position. Furthermore, CAEM was not, as has already been argued, the exclusive agency for the promotion of a social reformist position for the armed forces.

Velasco's political views prior to 1968 seem to defy easy classification. He was the son-in-law of a prominent *Aprista* but also maintained close social connections with the Prado family. The general became an ardent admirer of De Gaulle while serving as Peru's military attaché in France, but he also got along well with United States army chief of staff Harold Johnson and became his fishing partner while he was serving on the Inter-American Defense Board in Washington, D.C.[111] Despite these apparent inconsistencies, Velasco was an officer of deep social sensibilities. Vice Admiral Luis Vargas Caballero, an officer with decidedly more conservative views than Velasco regarding the armed forces' social reform mandate, credits Velasco with seeking to "end the many injustices in our society" while he headed the "Revolutionary Government of the Armed Forces."[112] United States army colonel James T. Aikens, Washington's military attaché in Peru throughout most of Belaúnde's last three years in office, described Velasco as a man who was "highly competent and dedicated to his job" and who frequently expressed dislike for Peru's landed oligarchy and often mentioned the need for effective agrarian reform.[113] Finally, Velasco's prime minister, General Edgardo Mercado Jarrín, characterized the general as a "man of truth with a clear sense of social justice because of his modest background."[114]

Since Velasco planned and executed the 3 October *coup d'état* with the knowledge and assistance of only a dozen other army officers and without the consent of the navy or air force, the issue must be raised whether his movement was merely a traditional *golpe* in the Sánchez Cerro or Odría mold. The *Comando Conjunto* in 1962 took careful precautions to assure the full cooperation of the officer corps in their *coup d'état*, while later seeking to maintain a unified armed forces' command during their year in office. Velasco would become the unquestioned *jefe* of the post-1968 government and would not allow a joint command structure in the style of the 1962 *Junta*. Moreover, Velasco clearly enjoyed his role of army chief of staff and president of the joint command prior to the *coup*. His activist role is reflected in the high profile he adopted during the IPC crisis and his consistent socializing with foreign dignitaries such as the French ambassador to Peru, Guy Dorgel, who decorated the general with the French Legion of Merit for his services as Peru's military attaché to France. That same month, Velasco played host to United States army general John D. Henry, heading a delegation from the Inter-American Defense Board.[115] In July, 1968 Velasco was given a red-carpet reception by his Argentine military hosts on an official visit to that country.[116] Clearly, during the years prior to the *coup* Velasco became accustomed to the highest positions of power in the Peruvian army and all the amenities that accompanied these positions. When one considers that Velasco was scheduled to retire from the army in early 1969, the issue of personal motivations for the *coup* looms even larger. The problem of Velasco's retirement was resolved less than a week after the 3 October *golpe* when he was placed in a special "reserve" status as president of the republic by "Army General Order Number Four."[117] Velasco issued this order despite the fact that when a poll was taken regarding the general's retirement among the heads of the armed services, the vote was deadlocked.[118] Finally, it is safe to assume that a soldier who rises through the ranks from private to army chief of staff is a man of ambition and direction. If not a *caudillo* in the traditional sense, who used the armed forces for his personal aggrandizement, Velasco appears to have been a man who relished power and sought a place in history by commanding the armed forces in revolutionary new directions.

There is little question that the movement Velasco and his twelve coconspirators headed was not supported by the armed forces as a unit. The secretive nature of the *coup* planning process and the protracted period required to consolidate Velasco's radical ideological position within the officer corps after the *golpe* are clear evidence of this fact. Thus, an analysis of the *coup* and its perpetrators will help place the position of the entire officer corps in a clearer perspective.

Throughout the formative phase of the *coup* planning, Velasco's principal co-conspirator was General Edgardo Mercado Jarrín, director of the *Centro de Instrucción Militar del Perú* at the time of the *golpe* but commander of the army Intelligence Service during the plot's early stages. Mercado Jarrín was joined by General Alfredo Arrisueño, commander of the Armored Division; General Alberto Maldonado, commander of Lima's Second Military Region; and General Ernesto Montagne Sánchez, inspector general of the army. Seven colonels commanding key units were also included in the plot: Jorge Fernández Maldonado, Leonidas Rodríguez Figueroa, Enrique Gallegos Venero, Rafael Hoyos Rubio, Pedro Richter Prada, Miguel Angel de la Flor, and Leoncio Pérez Tenaud.[119] Colonel Gallegos Venero, who headed the army Intelligence Service at the time of the *coup*, it will be recalled, was the administrator of the La Convención and Lares civic action project in 1962. His subdirector of army Intelligence Service, Colonel Leonidas Figueroa, and Gallegos Venero appear to have been involved in the very early planning stages of the plot. The other colonels, especially Colonel Hoyos Rubio, commander of the army's Special Forces Unit, were selected by Velasco for both their strategic command positions and their avowed reformist ideologies.[120] As later interviews with a number of officers involved in the *coup* have borne out, the Intelligence Service was heavily involved in the conspiracy, and CAEM's influence was negligible. Colonel (later General) Jorge Fernández Maldonado later claimed that the comprehensive information gathered by the Intelligence Service in the 1960s was far more valuable in gaining an insight into Peru's national problems than were the theories learned at the CAEM. Fernández Maldonado concluded, "Graduates of the Intelligence School came to see the urgent need for national change in order to end a system of social injustice, exploitation and dependency."[121] Fernández Maldonado's views on social reform were shared by Colonel Rodríguez Figueroa, who, as a prominent member of Velasco's government, claimed, "The central, profound, permanent and substantive goal of the government was raising mass living standards."[122] As these views indicate, Velasco surrounded himself with officers who were in accord with his ambition of enacting profound changes in Peruvian society, a society that witnessed the beleaguered Belaúnde administration nearly completely paralyzed during the last days before the 3 October *coup*. In a futile effort to save his government, Belaúnde appointed a new cabinet only fourteen hours before the *coup* was executed. The president asked Velasco to serve as the minister of war, but he refused.[123]

Belaúnde's overthrow was carried out in a carefully coordinated and bloodless movement conducted in the early morning hours of 3 October.

Key elements in the military action were General Arrisueño's armored units, headquartered in Lima's Rimac District directly adjacent to the National Palace, and Colonel Hoyos Rubio's Special Forces Unit, which carried out the president's arrest. The National Congress, the Prefecture of Police, the Central Telephone Exchange, and the nearby air force base at Las Palmas were occupied while Lima's downtown district was sealed off prior to the capture of the National Palace. Thirty tanks then encircled the National Palace, and Colonel Hoyos Rubio's troops entered the building at approximately 2:30 A.M. and escorted the loudly protesting Belaúnde into a waiting jeep. He was then driven to Jorge Chávez Airport and placed upon a waiting airplane bound for Buenos Aires. The commander of the air force, General Alberto López Causillas, and the navy commander, Vice Admiral Mario Castro de Mendoza, were then informed that "the army is in control of the nation." Both men were then asked for their support for the movement. General López Causillas accepted the fait accompli and was named minister of aviation in the new government. Admiral Mendoza refused to support the *coup* and resigned, whereupon he was immediately replaced by Vice Admiral Raul Riós Pardo de Zela, who was then named navy minister in Velasco's all-military cabinet. By mid-afternoon, military commanders throughout the country were informed of the *coup*, and their support was received. Two officers opposing the *coup*, General José Gagliardi, Belaúnde's former minister of war, and General Alejandro Sánchez Salazar, chief of the army's general staff and Velasco's designated successor as army commander, were placed under temporary house arrest while the *coup* was being consolidated.[124]

The manifesto released by the Velasco government following the *coup* foreshadowed the unprecedented reforms to be undertaken during the next six years and justified the overthrow of Belaúnde in harsh terms:

The armed forces of Peru, conscious of the desires of its citizens and of the unprecedented need to put an end to the financial chaos, administrative immobility, improvisation, surrender of the national wealth and its exploitation in the benefit of the privileged few as well as the loss of the principle of authority and the incapacity to carry out the structural reforms for the well-being of the Peruvian people and the development of the country, assume the responsibility for the management of the state in order to guide it definitively toward the attainment of national objectives.[125]

As foreign observers surmised, the Velasco government had every intention of establishing long-term rule.[126] Indeed the varied and complex motives for the *coup* assured that Peru's men in uniform would rule the nation longer than any twentieth-century military regime.

The question of why the army seized power in October, 1968 has no single answer. Certainly the inherent distrust of civilian politicians, manifested by the military since the violent civil-military confrontations of the 1930s, reached its apex during the final troubled years of the Belaúnde administration. Officers who felt qualified to administer the nation in the mid-1960s saw the architect Belaúnde as an acceptable alternative because of his enthusiastic support for the expansion of the military's role and because of his own technocratic vision for a new Peru. When Belaúnde's legitimacy as a reform president was undermined by an antagonistic congress, an obstructionist United States foreign policy, and his own limitations as a political leader, officers such as General Velasco were convinced that not even the most qualified civilian could govern the nation and bring about reform through the democratic process. This notion is quite apparent in the wording of the "Revolutionary Manifesto" of 3 October, which charged the government with "incapacity" in its responsiblity to enact the "structural reforms" necessary for the "well-being" of the nation.

When the officer corps looked ahead to the 1969 elections, they saw an even more foreboding scenario. With *Acción Popular* in shambles and the Christian Democrats not a self-sustaining party, no moderate, reformist, civilian alternative to APRA was left. Haya de la Torre, at seventy-three, now headed a party of aging and conservative leaders who demonstrated their political partisanship to an unparalleled degree in their congressional alliance with the *Odríistas*, which resulted in the sabotage of Belaúnde's agrarian reform program. Moreover, the military's apprehension of APRA's still-militant capabilities were confirmed when party leader Armando Villanueva del Campo called for a "counterrevolution" soon after Belaúnde was deposed. Thus, it was no coincidence that APRA's radio station was closed down at the time of the *coup*. In testimony to Peru's complex political process, the APRA of the 1930s was unacceptable to the military's high command because of its revolutionary ideology. *Apristas* of the late 1960s were objectionable to the officer corps because of their apparent disdain for legitimate reform. Finally, APRA remained Peru's only coherent and disciplined political party. It had been capable of vast ideological shifts in the past, and military leaders could not predict what the party would do once it attained power. APRA still retained significant populist appeal, and it might well begin to enact the reforms that the military had now come to believe were their sanctioned mission. Indeed, Haya de la Torre insisted in 1974 that "the Velasco government has simply stolen our program," with a conviction that was difficult completely to dismiss.[127]

The Velasco *coup* can also be viewed as an effort to co-opt the latent revolutionary tendencies of a society long denied the social justice it so desperately required. The unprecedented peasant activism of the late 1950s and early 1960s, and the guerrilla uprising of 1965 indeed "rang the bell of the military's consciousness" regarding the need for reform. Nevertheless, the Velasco government's program for change was to be a reform program that the military would administer, without the broad popular participation of the Peruvian masses. These reforms were the military's attempt to attain *bienestar* (national well-being) as well as assure the solidarity of the armed forces as an institution. The lesson of Castro's revolution and the liquidation of Cuba's national army must have been still fresh in the minds of Peru's military men in 1968. The future fortunes of the armed forces and the nation were always intertwined in the minds of the nation's military men. If reform brought about social justice while at the same time assuring the security of the military establishment, all the better.

Ultimately, the Velasco *coup* can be interpreted as the culmination of the armed forces' search for a meaningful national mission. Since the early 1900s, Peru's military men boasted an egocentric form of patriotism often interpreted to mean that only the armed forces could save Peru. Yet prior to the 1960s, with the exception of the Ecuadoran war, the Peruvian military reality was defeat on the battlefield and limited activity in the field of reform. Military men were nation builders only in their own minds or in the pages of their military journals. The limited utility and redundancy of the armed forces became even more evident in the post—World War II nuclear age, which saw the United States adopt the primary responsibility for hemispheric security as well as an integral role in the internal security of the Latin American nations after 1960. Seeking to rationalize its limited conventional warfare contributions to the nation, the military's answer was a more sophisticated and comprehensive definition of its national defense mission. As expressed by an increasing number of officers after World War II, national defense now meant more than protecting the nation's borders or eradicating internal subversion; it became any activity that contributed to the national well-being. Thus, Peru's soldiers could argue, as many did during the Velasco years, that they were, above all, enacting reforms not only to bring about social justice but also to safeguard the future security of the nation as well. International corporations and landed oligarchs now became the targets of Peru's soldiers, not the Ecuadoran, Colombian, and Chilean soldiers of past conflicts. As the incredibly ambitious programs of the Velasco regime demonstrated, Peru's soldiers at last assumed a mission worthy of justifying to themselves and their countrymen their value to the nation.

NOTES

1. Belaúnde claimed the support of the officer corps in the 1962 and 1963 elections while boasting powerful allies such as General Lindley López. Belaúnde retained this popularity until well into the third year of his regime according to Colonel (R) James T. Aikens, U.S. military attaché to Peru, 1965-1968. Personal interview with Colonel Aikens, 28 June 1985, Hampton, Virginia.

2. Fernando Belaúnde Terry, *Peru's Own Conquest* (Lima: 1965), pp. 14-16. See, for example, the article by Colonel Vidal C. Panzio, "La ley de conscripción vial y la defensa del país," *Revista Círculo del Militar del Perú* (April, 1926), pp. 339-341, cited in Frederick Nunn, *Yesterday's Soldiers: European Military Professionalism in South America: 1890-1940* (Lincoln: Nebraska: 1983), p. 278. Panzio foresaw Belaúnde's ambitious goals for his highway project in claiming that roads would transmit Western culture to the Peruvian interior.

3. Belaúnde, *Peru's Own Conquest*, pp. 14-16.

4. Ibid., pp. 202-203.

5. Personal interview with Víctor Villanueva Valencia, 27 July 1974, Lima, Peru; Carlos Astiz and José García, "The Peruvian Military: Achievement Orientation, Training and Political Tendencies," *Western Political Quarterly* 25, no. 4 (December, 1972), pp. 667-681.

6. Ibid.

7. *United States Congressional Record*, 108, Part 2, Senate, 1962, p. 15423; Anonymous, "Nuevas autoridades en el ejército," *Actualidad Militar* 119, no. 4 (30 September 1957), pp. 26-38.

8. Astiz and García, "The Peruvian Military," p. 673; Luigi Einaudi, *The Peruvian Military: A Summary Political Analysis* (Santa Monica: 1969), p. 7.

9. The best history of the IPC controversy is Adalberto Pinelo, *The Multinational Corporation as a Force in Latin American Politics: A Case Study of the International Petroleum Company in Peru* (New York: 1973). See also Augusto Zimmerman Zavala, *La historia secreta del petróleo* (Lima: 1968) and Richard Goodwin, "Letter from Peru: Takeover of the International Petroleum Co.," *New Yorker* 45, 17 May 1969, pp. 41-109.

10. For Belaúnde's views on Popular Cooperation see his *Peru's Own Conquest*, pp. 97-104.

11. *The New York Times*, 7 July 1963, p. 20.

12. *La Prensa*, 20 August 1963, p. 1.

13. Personal interview with Ramiro Prialé, 10 May 1985, Lima, Peru.

14. Donald C. Henderson and Grace R. Pérez, *Literature and Politics in Latin America: An Annotated Calendar of Luis Alberto Sánchez Correspondence, 1919-1980* (University Park, Pennsylvania: 1982), Document 1098, p. 270.

15. David Werlich, *Peru: A Short History* (Carbondale, Illinois: 1978), p. 280.

16. *La Prensa*, 11 September 1964, p. 1.

17. Richard Gott, *Guerrilla Movements in Latin America* (New York: 1973), p. 337.

18. Howard Handelman, *Struggle in the Andes: Peasant Political Mobilization in Peru* (Austin, Texas: 1975), p. 121.

19. *La Prensa*, 4 August 1963, p. 1.

20. For a discussion of the agrarian debate in congress and an analysis of the legislation see François Bourricaud, *Power and Society in Contemporary Peru* (New York: 1970), pp. 335-342; *La Prensa*, September, 1963, pp. 6-7; Richard Patch, "Peru's New President and Agrarian Reform," *American Universities Field Staff Reports*, 10, no. 2. (August, 1963); Richard N. Patch, "The Peruvian Agrarian Reform Bill: Legislation for an Ideal," *American Universities Field Staff Reports*, 2, no. 3 (1964). James R. Petras and Robert La Porte, Jr., *Cultivating Revolution: The United States and Agrarian Reform in Latin America* (New York: 1971), pp. 33-123, offers a comprehensive discussion of Belaúnde's agrarian reform proposal and its subsequent problems.

21. *La Prensa*, 21 August 1963, p. 1. See *Ordenes Generales del Ejército* no. 23, June, 1965, for the army's general directive on this project.

22. *La Prensa*, 29 August 1963, p. 1.

23. Petras and La Porte, *Cultivating Revolution*, p. 53.

24. Ibid., p. 54.

25. Ibid., pp. 53-97, passim; Werlich, *Peru*, p. 285.

26. Petras and La Porte, *Cultivating Revolution*, p. 100; Handelman, *Struggle in the Andes*, p. 121. The Velasco government disputed the figures of the Belaúnde administration and claimed only 783,000 acres were expropriated to the benefit of 7,224 families.

27. Henry Dobyns and Paul Doughty, *Peru: A Cultural History* (New York: 1976), p. 236. The authors note that former army conscripts led the land invasions for the Indian community of San Pedro de Cajas in the department of Junín and in the occupation of lands owned by the Cerro de Pasco Corporation.

28. Belaúnde, *Peru's Own Conquest*, p. 156.

29. Belaúnde continued to promote his road-building scheme during his second presidential administration (1980-1985), with little substantive results.

30. Less than two months into Belaúnde's term, *La Prensa* announced a $40 million Export-Import Bank loan to finance a section of the "Marginal Jungle Highway." *La Prensa*, 14 September 1963, p. 1.

31. Emilio Romero, *Geografía económica del Perú* (Lima: 1968), pp. 90-97; Werlich, *Peru*, p. 283.

32. *La Prensa*, 23 September 1963, pp. 26-30 carries a detailed review of the beginning of armed forces' involvement in the *Ceja de Montaña* project.

33. United States military personnel were among those favored by the Peruvian army with such tours (personal interview with Colonel (R) James Aikens, 28 June 1985, Hampton, Virginia).

34. Memo from McGeorge Bundy to the secretaries of state and defense and director of AID, National Security File (Subject File) Box no. 1, 22, April 1964, Lyndon B. Johnson Presidential Library, Austin, Texas; see *El Perú Contstruye, Mensajes del presidente constitucional de la republica, Fernando Belaúnde Terry, 1963-1967* (Lima: 1968). Belaúnde's 1967 message is particularly useful for details of the colonization project. See Belaúnde's, *Mensajes*, 1967, p. 853.

35. Lieutenant Colonel Enrique Gallegos Venero, "Un combate victorioso en guerra contra revolucionaria," *Revista Escuela Superior de Guerra* 10, no. 3 (July-September 1963), p. 19.

36. Ibid., p. 23.

37. A study of the 1965 guerrilla movement should begin with Leon Campbell, "The Historiography of the Peruvian Guerrilla Movement, 1960-1965," *Latin American Research Review* 8, no. 1 (Spring, 1973), pp. 45-70. For the military's official history of the guerrilla campaign see, Perú, Ministerio de Guerra, *Las guerrillas en el Perú y su represión* (Lima: 1966). Other valuable studies are Gott, *Guerrilla Movements*, pp. 307-397, Rogger Mercado, *Las guerrillas del Perú* (Lima: 1967). Héctor Béjar, *Perú 1965: Notes on a Guerrilla Experience* (New York: 1969); Brian Loveman and Thomas M. Davies, eds., *Guerrilla Warfare* (Lincoln, Nebraska: 1985).

38. Gott, *Guerrilla Movements*, p. 342.

39. Lieutenant Colonel Enrique Gallegos Venero, "Problemas de la guerra contra revolucionaria," *RESG* 11, no. 2 (April-May-June, 1964), pp. 98-99.

40. Ibid., p. 100.

41. Colonel Luis Vera Cruzada, "La guerra revolucionaria a guerra subversiva y la guerra de guerrilla," *Revista Militar del Perú* 63, no. 704 (May-June, 1968), pp. 54-55.

42. Colonel Edgardo Mercado Jarrín, "El ejército de hoy y su proyección en nuestra sociedad en el período de transición, *RMP* 59, no. 685 (November-December, 1964), p. 17.

43. William F. Barber and D. Neale Ronning, *Internal Security and Military Power: Counterinsurgency and Civic Action in Latin America* (Columbus, Ohio: 1966), pp. 144-147; *Peruvian Times*, 21 May 1985, p. 16; "U.S. Army School of the Americas," in Brian Loveman and Thomas M. Davies Jr., *The Politics of Anti-Politics: The Military in Latin America* (Lincoln, Nebraska: 1978).

44. Barber and Ronning, *Internal Security and Military Power*, p. 149.

45. Ibid., p. 150.

46. Personal interviews with Colonels (R) James Aikens and Bernard Big, 28 June 1985, Hampton, Virginia. Colonel Aikens also completed a questionnaire. Colonel Big, who was the U.S. army's airborne adviser to the Peruvian army from 1965 through 1968, and Colonel Aikens noted that Peruvian army officers' support for the U.S. Vietnam War effort soured when they became disillusioned with the conduct of the war. The concurrent success of the Israeli army in the Six-Day War against Egypt was offered as a sharp contrast to the Vietnam campaign by the Peruvians, according to Aikens and Big.

47. Gott, *Guerrilla Movements*, pp. 337-346, passim.

48. Luis de la Puente Uceda, "The Peruvian Revolution: Concepts and Perspectives," *Monthly Review*, 17, no. 6 (November, 1965), pp. 12-28. For an example of the MIR's propaganda campaign, see "Abajo la represión contra EL MIR," 8 January 1964, *Colección de Volantes*, 1964 folder.

49. Héctor Béjar, *Perú 1965*, (New York: 1970), p. 70.

50. Ibid., p. 66.

51. Ibid., p. 74.

52. Mercado, *Las guerrillas*, pp. 151-156; Béjar, *Perú 1965*, p. 88; Perú, Ministerio de Guerra, *Las guerrillas*, pp. 35-53; *Peruvian Times*, 25 June 1965, p. 2; *The New York Times*, 13 June 1965, p. 38. A third guerrilla *foco* led by Gonzalo Fernandez

Gasco and Elio Portocarrero was to be established in the department of Piura, but it never went into action.

53. *Peruvian Times*, 2 July 1965, p. 1; Gott, *Guerrilla Movements*, pp. 358-359; Mercado, *Las guerrillas*, pp. 157-158.

54. *Peruvian Times*, 9 July 1965, p. 1 and 27 August 1965, p. 2; *Ordenes Generales del Ejército*, no. 27, 21 July 1965, p. 3.

55. Versions of this incident can be found in Víctor Villanueva Valencia, *Ejército Peruano: Del caudillaje anárquico al militarismo reformista* (Lima: 1973), p. 302; Jane Jacquette, "The Politics of Development in Peru," Ph.D. diss., Cornell University, 1973; Carlos Astiz, *Pressure Groups and Power Elites in Peruvian Politics* (Ithaca: 1969), p. 157.

56. *The New York Times*, 14 August 1965, pp. 4-5.

57. Gott, *Guerrilla Movements*, p. 370; *The New York Times*, 28 September 1965, p. 43; Perú, Ministerio de Guerra, *Las guerrillas del Perú*, pp. 65-66.

58. The use of napalm in the Mesa Pelada campaign was reported in *The New York Times*, 11 October 1965, p. 14. Villanueva, *Ejército Peruano*, p. 302, claims the napalm was manufactured by the International Petroleum Company. Mercado, *Las guerrillas*, p. 186, states that saturation bombing with both conventional bombs and napalm "burned the plateau and massacred peasants." Mercado also cites incidents of torture during the interrogation of prisoners by the Peruvian Investigative Police, p. 172. See also "Respondes al terror militar con un amplio frente democrático" Communicado de La Juventud de Comunista Peruano, 23 August 1965, *Collectión de Volantes*. This flier specifically attacks the military's use of napalm against the "Liberation columns of the Sierra."

59. For discussions of Albino Guzmán's role in the suppression of the Mesa Pelada *foco*, see Anonymous, "Acontecimientos en la sierra central y sureste y país," *Actualidad Militar* 4, no. 80 (30 September 1965), pp. 2-3; Béjar, *Perú 1965*, p. 80; Gott, *Guerrilla Movements*, p. 371.

60. *The New York Times*, 25 October 1965, p. 17, reported De la Puente's death and the demise of his seven guerrilla comrades. Gott, *Guerrilla Movements*, surmises he was either killed in action or executed after his capture. The government's official history, Perú, Ministerio de Guerra, *Las guerrillas del Perú*, p. 67, claims that Puente Uceda and two companions were killed in action. It makes no mention of the other four guerrillas whom *The New York Times* reported killed.

61. Béjar, *Perú 1965*, p. 109. Béjar's account of his guerrilla activities was written while he was in Lima's *El Frontón* prison for his actions against the government. The book later won the *Casa de las Americas* Literary Prize. The Velasco government released Béjar as they did Hugo Blanco. Blanco refused to serve in any capacity in the post-1968 military government.

62. Mercado, *Las guerrillas*, p. 231; Perú, Ministero de Guerra, *Las guerrillas del Perú*, p. 70, makes no mention of civilian casualties in its general summary of the campaign.

63. Mercado, *Las guerrillas*, p. 231.

64. The CIA's involvement in the campaign is vaguely discussed in Victor Marchetti and John D. Marks, *The CIA and the Cult of Intelligence* (New York: 1974), pp. 124-125. More definitive evidence is offered by Colonel (R) Bernard Big, who claimed a member of the "Company" was assigned as an adviser to *Guardia Civil* troops operating against the guerrillas (personal interview with Colonel Big, 28 June 1985, Hampton, Virginia). Colonel Big also noted that

members of Peru's "Special Forces" antiguerrilla units bragged about their efficiency in gaining information quickly from their captors and were "euphoric" after the campaign. Allegations of torture of prisoners during interrogation was made by the MIR in "Comunicado #3 del Comando Revolucionario Nacional del MIR, 'El Guerrillero,'" 26 September 1965, *Colección de Volantes* and in Mercado, *Las guerrillas*, p. 186. See also Central Intelligence Agency, Intelligence Information Cable (Peru), 10 February 1964, Plans of the MIR for Revolutionary Action," National Security File, Lyndon B. Johnson Presidential Library.

65. Perú, Ministerio de Guerra, *Las guerrillas del Perú*, pp. 76-82.
66. See Chapter 8 for a discussion of this incident.
67. *Peruvian Times*, 7 February 1964, p. 1 and 14 February 1964, p. 1.
68. Béjar, *Perú 1965*, p. 110.
69. *The New York Times*, 5 July 1965, p. 3 and 9 July, 1965, p. 8.
70. Personal interview with Division General (R) Edgardo Mercado Jarrín, 10 May 1985, Lima, Peru.
71. Maria del Pilar Tello, *Golpe o revolución: Hablan los militares del 68* (Lima: 1983), p. 123.
72. *La Prensa*, 27 August 1974, quoted in Villanueva, *Ejército Peruano*, p. 303.
73. The best accounts of the Belaúnde administration's economic policies are Pedro Pablo Kuczynski, *The Peruvian Democracy under Economic Stress: An Account of the Belaúnde Administration* (Princeton: 1977); E.V.K. Fitzgerald, *The Political Economy of Peru, 1956-1978* (Cambridge, England: 1979); Rosemary Thorp and Geoffrey Bertram, *Peru, 1890-1977: Growth and Policy in an Open Economy* (New York: 1978); Jane Jacquette, "The Politics of Development in Peru."
74. Jacquette, "The Politics of Development," pp. 98-150; Thorp and Bertram, *Peru, 1890-1977*, p. 277; Fitzgerald, *The Political Economy of Peru*, pp. 225-226.
75. Jacquette, "The Politics of Development," p. 151.
76. Ibid.
77. See Goodwin, "Letter from Peru," pp. 41-109 for a detailed discussion of Belaúnde's economic travails with Washington. Belaúnde's comments were made in a speech at Cornell University soon after he was deposed and are reported in Jacquette, "The Politics of Development," p. 151.
78. *The New York Times*, 13 August 1967, p. 29.
79. Jacquette, "The Politics of Development," p. 152.
80. *The New York Times*, 26 October 1967, p. 3.
81. *United States Congressional Record*, 113, Part 22, Senate, 1967, p. 29581.
82. *The New York Times*, 13 August 1967, p. 29.
83. Ibid., 8 October 1967, p. 19.
84. *United States Congressional Record*, 113, Part 22, Senate, 1967, p. 30278.
85. Jacquette, "The Politics of Development," p. 166.
86. Ibid.; telephone interview with Colonel (R) Bernard Big, 16 July 1985. The involvement of Peruvian armed forces pesonnel in smuggling activities was confirmed by a senior armed forces officer in a confidential interview with the author in May, 1990 in Callao, Peru.
87. *La Prensa*, 22 April 1968, p. 1; Jacquette, "The Politics of Development," p. 169.
88. *El Comercio*, 22 March 1968, p. 1; Jacquette, "The Politics of Development," p. 168.

89. Jacquette, "The Politics of Development," p. 168; *La Prensa*, 20 April 1968, p. 1.

90. Jacquette, "The Politics of Development," p. 169; Víctor Villanueva Valencia, *Nueva mentalidad militar en el Perú* (Lima: 1969), p.134.

91. *La Prensa*, 22 April 1968, p. 1; Jacquette, "The Politics of Development," p. 169.

92. *La Prensa*, 13 November 1967, p. 1.

93. The terms of the March 1922 contract were extremely favorable to the company. According to Thorp and Bertram, "IPC was assured of security in control of its entire oil field, and was obliged to pay normal surface tax only on those claims in active production. Idle claims were subject to a virtually negligible special tax. The company was exempted from payment of royalties on its production, and its export tax liability was frozen for fifty years" (Thorp and Bertram, *Peru, 1890-1977*, p. 110).

94. Pinelo, *The Multinational Corporation*, p. 96.

95. Werlich, *Peru*, p. 271.

96. George Philip, *The Rise and Fall of the Peruvian Military Radicals, 1968-1976* (London; 1978), p. 72.

97. The tortuous course of these negotiations is discussed in Pinelo, *The Multinational Corporation*, pp. 110-144.

98. Goodwin, "Letter from Peru," p. 60.

99. Pinelo, *The Multinational Corporation*, p. 134.

100. Ibid., p. 137. The assessment was made by Pinelo on the basis of an interview with Espinosa in 1971.

101. Ibid. Pinelo lists a "confidential" source as the basis for this account.

102. *El Comercio*, 28 March 1968, p. 1; Pinelo, *The Multinational Corporation*, pp. 137 and 147.

103. Pinelo, *The Multinational Corporation*, p. 139.

104. Ibid., p. 148.

105. Ibid., pp. 140-144. The "missing" page 11 will probably remain a mystery. Richard Goodwin's explanation that it was most likely lost when the contract was being handled by intermediaries seems plausible. See Goodwin, "Letter from Peru," pp. 82-86. Loret de Mola's resignation may also have been prompted by his animosity over Belaúnde's failure to reappoint him as president of EPF.

106. *La Prensa*, 25 September 1968, p. 1; *Peruvian Times*, 27 September 1968, p. 2.

107. Pinelo, *The Multinational Corporation*, p. 143; *El Comercio*, 13 September 1968, p. 1; *La Prensa*, 16 September 1968, p. 1.

108. *La Prensa*, 21 September 1968, p. 1, and 22 September 1968, p. 1.

109. Estimates of how long the Velasco *coup* was in the planning stage vary. Zimmerman Zavala claims that Velasco and Colonels Gallegos Venero and Rodríguez Figueroa began the process in late April, 1968. Augusto Zimmerman Zavala, *El Plan Inca: Objetivo revolución Peruana* (Lima: 1974), p. 36. Division General (R) Edgardo Mercado Jarrín, who was one of the conspirators, suggests the process was shorter (personal interview with Mercado Jarrín, 10 May 1985, Lima, Peru).

110. This biographical sketch of General Velasco is drawn from the following: Anonymous, "Nuevas autoridades en el ejército," *Actualidad Militar*, 7, no. 119 (30 September 1967), pp. 26-38; personal interview with Division General (R) Edgardo

Mercado Jarrín, 10 May 1985, Lima, Peru; personal interview with Vice Admiral (R) Luis Vargas Caballero; questionnaire response from Vargas Caballero, 6 May 1985, Lima, Peru; personal interview and questionnaire response from Colonel (R) James Aikens, 28 June 1985, Hampton, Virginia; Philip, *The Rise and Fall of the Peruvian Military Radicals*, pp. 76-77; Zimmerman Zavala, *El Plan Inca*, passim; Werlich, *Peru*, p. 304.

111. Philip, *The Rise and Fall of the Peruvian Military Radicals*, p. 76; *The New York Times*, 4 October 1968, p. 3.

112. Response to questionnaire submitted to Vice Admiral (R) Luis Vargas Caballero, 13 May 1985, Lima, Peru.

113. Response to questionnaire submitted to Colonel (R) James T. Aikens, 8 July 1985, Hampton, Virginia.

114. Personal interview with Division General (R) Edgardo Mercado Jarrín, 10 May 1985, Lima, Peru.

115. Anonymous and untitled, *Actualidad Militar* 7, no. 125 (March, 1968), pp. 20-27.

116. Anonymous, "Viaje de los jefes del ejército," *Actualidad Militar* 7, no. 129 (July, 1968), pp. 18-19.

117. *Ordenes Generales del Ejército*, no. 44, 10 October 1968, p. 2; Anonymous, "Generales del ejército pasan al retiro," *Actualidad Militar* 8, no. 2 (15 February 1969), pp. 22-25.

118. Personal interview with Vice Admiral (R) Luis E. Vargas Caballero, 6 May 1985, Lima, Peru.

119. This list is composed from interviews with General Mercado Jarrín and Admiral Vargas Caballero; Zimmerman Zavala, *El Plan Inca*, pp. 93-150, passim; José Z. García, "The Velasco Coup in Peru: Causes and Policy Consequences," Ph.D. diss., University of New Mexico, 1974, p. 183. García places two other officers in the group of conspirators: Colonels José Graham Hurtado and Anibal Meza Cuadra.

120. Zimmerman Zavala, *El Plan Inca*, p. 36.

121. Del Pilar Tello, *Golpe o revolución*, p. 122.

122. Liisa North and Tanya Korokovin, *The Peruvian Revolution and the Officers in Power 1967-1976* (Montreal: 1981), p. 53.

123. *Peruvian Times*, 20 September 1964, p. 1.

124. This account is composed from the following: personal interview with Colonel (R) James Aikens, 28 June 1985, Hampton, Virginia (who was familiar with the exact location of the armored division); personal interview with General (R) Edgardo Mercado Jarrín, 10 May 1985, Lima Peru, and Vice Admiral (R) Luis Vargas Caballero, 6 May 1985, Lima, Peru; Zimmerman Zavala, *El Plan Inca*, pp. 130-138; *Peruvian Times*, 3 October 1968, p. 1; *La Prensa*, 3 October 1968, p. 1; *El Comercio*, 3 October 1968, p. 1; *The New York Times*, 4 October 1968, pp. 1-2.

125. *Ordenes Generales del Ejército*, no. 44, 10 October 1968, pp. 1-2. The manifesto constituted the first decree law of the military government and was widely published in the Lima press.

126. *The New York Times*, 4 October 1968, p. 2.

127. Personal interview with Víctor Raúl Haya de la Torre, 13 July 1974, Lima, Peru.

10
The Unfulfilled Mission:
The Velasco Revolution and its Legacy

"A few years ago they were buying Mirage jets; now they aren't able to buy boots for their troops."[1] This assessment of the Peruvian armed forces' material condition, made in September, 1989 by an observer with more than a decade of direct contact with Peru's military establishment, was confirmed in the same year when the navy's commanding officer announced in his annual message that the mission of the navy during the year was its mere survival.[2] The armed forces' deep malaise as Peru entered the 1990s mirrored the nation's more comprehensive problems of an inflation-wracked economy, a decade-long terror campaign by *Sendero Luminoso*, and a national infrastructure being progressively destroyed by years of civil war and neglect.[3] Considering Peru's present vast problems, one would find it easy to dismiss the reforms of the military government of Juan Velasco Alvarado as a failure. Yet, the issue is far more complex, and from a historian's perspective, a precise assessment of the *Docenio* or twelve years of military rule under Velasco and his successor, General Franciso Morales Bermúdez, is still not possible. Nevertheless, armed forces' personnel, both active and retired, are now beginning to voice their views on the Velasco years and their legacy for contemporary Peru. Based on interviews with Peruvian armed forces' personnel and drawing on the voluminous literature on the Velasco reforms, this study will close with an overview of the armed forces during military rule and troubled decade of the 1980s.

Beginning with the expropriation of the International Petroleum Company's holdings in Peru less than a week after the 3 October 1968 *golpe de estado*, the Velasco government during the next seven years initiated more than forty-two hundred laws and 150,000 executive decisions aimed at substantially altering Peruvian society and the country's relations with the international community.[4] Obviously, no attempt can be made comprehensively to analyze these programs here, but the motivations of the armed forces' officers who governed Peru for twelve years after the Velasco *golpe* will be discussed in some detail. A brief overview of the Velasco reforms will also help clarify the reformist orientation of Peru's "Revolutionary Government of the Armed Forces."

The 1968-1980 military government was the longest continuous rule by any twentieth-century Peruvian regime. But to be precise, the period must be viewed as two distinct governments, the *Septenato* (seven-year rule) of the Velasco regime and the five-year transition back to traditional policies and civilian rule under Velasco's successor, General Franciso Morales Bermúdez Cerutti. In broadly categorizing the Velasco reforms, Stephen Gorman noted that they fell into four main policy objectives: (1) social justice, (2) popular participation, (3) national independence, and (4) economic development.[5] Within the framework of these goals, the Velasco regime decreed one of the most far-reaching agrarian reforms in Latin American history nine months after taking power. As the regime progressed, it sought to restructure labor-management relations, the production and distribution of products, the scope and function of foreign corporations in Peru's economy, the role of the state in the national economy, and Peru's relations with the international community. Peru's educational system was modified to allow greater access by the popular sectors. Literacy requirements for voting were eased, thus significantly expanding the national electorate. And the role of the Indian in society was given at least tacit acceptance with the recognition of Quechua as an official national language. Nearly three years into the Velasco regime, an attempt was made officially to mobilize popular support for the government with the creation of the *Sistema Nacional de Apoyo a la Movilización Social* (National Social Mobilization Support System, SINAMOS). And as the revolutionary government of the armed forces was faltering in May, 1974, the most creative and controversial measure of the Velasco era was decreed with the creation of the Social Property Enterprises (EPS). The social property legislation was designed to grant Peruvian labor a greater share of the nation's productive capacity by grafting a Yugoslavian model on Peru's basically free-market economy.

In this discussion, closer attention will be given to the agrarian reform program, SINAMOS, and Peru's foreign policy initiatives during the Velasco era. But it is useful to note here that the unparalleled scope, diversity, ideological pluralism, and often clear inconsistency of the Velasco reforms can be attributed to the idealism, administrative inexperience, and policy differences within the armed forces' leadership. In 1968, few armed forces' officers questioned the capability of the military successfully to reform Peruvian society. Of the four principal figures of the Velasco government interviewed for this study—Generals Francisco Morales Bermúdez, Jorge Fernández Maldonado Solari, Edgardo Mercado Jarrín, and Admiral Luis M. Vargas Caballero—three felt the armed forces were capable and qualified to initiate major structural change in Peru. Admiral Vargas Caballero believed that it was not the proper function of the armed forces totally to direct this change but rather to aid in the process within the constitutional framework. The army's "nation-building mission," consistently expressed since the 1930s, was most emphatically articulated by Generals Mercado Jarrín and Fernández Maldonado.[6]

Despite their idealism and confidence, only General Morales Bermúdez brought any substantive government experience to the Velasco government. As Belaúnde's minister of economy, Morales Bermúdez was the exceptional Peruvian armed forces officer, with significant policy-making experience in a sensitive government position. Unlike their Argentine and Brazilian counterparts, who had been administering state corporations since the 1940s, Peru's military leaders stayed on the periphery of policy planning as Peru's economy remained largely free of state-run enterprises. The Velasco regime's increasing reliance upon civilian advisers and the visionary nature of many of its programs were a clear manifestation of the inexperience of its military administrators. The improvisational nature of the Velasco reforms calls to mind the rough analogy of Franklin D. Roosevelt's initial New Deal measures. Indeed, both governments strove to restructure economic systems they perceived to be in profound crisis. Significantly, neither was unwilling to abandon capitalism in the process. The New Deal, however, was operating in a democracy and was powered by the engine of popular consensus. Further, many New Deal leaders drew upon experience in economic planning and government. Both these essential characteristics were lacking in the Velasco government.

A final factor contributing to the uneven nature of the Velasco program was the ideological differences within the government. Any institution as complex as an armed forces' establishment will, of course, harbor a wide range of political opinion. These differences are only partially restrained by military discipline and the command structure. Some attempts—most notably by Guido Chirinos Lizares and Enrique Chirinos Soto in El Septenato, 1968-1975; George Philip in The Rise and Fall of the Peruvian Military Radicals, 1968-1976; Liisa North and Tanya Korovkin in The Peruvian Revolution and the Officers in Power, 1967-1976, and Henry Pease García in El ocaso del poder oligárquico—have been made to detail the decision-making process within the officer corps during the Velasco years.[7] When one sets aside the personal loyalties, family connections, and individual ambitions that these authors discuss as components of the policy-making process, however, three distinct ideological groups emerge: conservatives, state modernizers, and progressives.

A conservative element encompassing most of the navy's senior leadership and smaller elements within the army and air force, best represented by Admiral Luis M. Vargas Caballero and, ultimately, General Franciso Morales Bermúdez, favored only a limited role for the armed forces in restructuring Peruvian society. The conservatives sought economic development through a partnership with the private sector and emphasized increased savings and investment and limited controls on foreign capital. Recalling the goals of his government while in retirement, Morales Bermúdez argued that he tried to establish "a pluralistic economy and political climate, while rejecting an extreme statist position that would negate the presence of the private sector."[8] Admiral Vargas Caballero was even more emphatic in his insistence that the armed forces restrict their activities to a more traditional military role. When asked in 1985 if the armed forces were prepared to initiate the reforms of the Velasco era, Vargas Caballero responded, "I believe no group is so prepared for such sweeping reforms in such a short time. The armed forces are not prepared for political action; it should help the government but within its own field."[9] Vargas Caballero's views were shared by most of the navy's senior commanders. And when he openly challenged Velasco's decision to expropriate Peru's newspapers in May 1974, he precipitated the most serious internal crisis of Velasco's government until his overthrow in August, 1975. Vargas Caballero recalled:

My most difficult moment was when I decided to resign [over the expropriation issue]. It was with a great deal of effort that I was able to convince my fellow officers that my resignation was the only way to avoid a useless conflict with the army and air force, which would be contrary to the navy and probably cost many lives.[10]

At the height of this crisis over the Velasco government's policy toward the media, the navy was put on full alert with the fleet ready to sail, and marines were detached to defend the Callao naval base.[11] Conservatives within the navy were clearly ready to defend aggressively their limited view of the armed forces' mandate after six years of Velasco's rule. The state modernizers had, by this time, increased their influence within the armed forces' establishment.

The armed forces' professional mandate, to promote Peru's development, was viewed as much more expansive by the second primary interest group in the armed forces: the modernizers or moderates. Clearly, representing the majority of the army officer corps during the Velasco years, these officers visualized their mission as it had been outlined in their service journals for seven decades. They would be active agents in every aspect of the development process. Their primary objectives were greater national security and enhanced *bienestar*, to be achieved by removing the structural weaknesses of Peruvian society by reforms initiated and largely implemented by the armed forces. The widely recognized spokesman of the modernizers was General Edgardo Mercado Jarrín. As director of the Intelligence School at the time of the Velasco *coup* and an intellectual in the tradition of Manuel Morla Concha, José del Carmen Marín, and Marcial Romero Pardo, Mercado Jarrín achieved a professional stature far exceeding that of his predecessors. One measure of the increased acceptance of the modernizer's doctrine in the army during the Velasco era was Mercado Jarrín's administrative prominence. Throughout the Velasco regime, Mercado Jarrín held the posts of minister of foreign relations, prime minister, and minister of war. During Velasco's grave illness in 1975, Mercado Jarrín held the temporary post as Peru's military chief executive before Velasco reasserted his authority and resumed power. The dramatic shift in Peru's foreign policy; its cooperative relations with the Soviet Union, the People's Republic of China, and Cuba; the expulsion of the United States army's military mission; and the expropriation of the Internal Petroleum Company all occurred while Mercado Jarrín held the foreign minister's portfolio. This reform policy, which will be discussed in greater substance later, was given great emphasis by Mercado Jarrín in May, 1985. He argued that with the 3 October revolution the Peruvian military attempted to chart a "Third Position" to attain national well-being. Their mission rejected the extremes of capitalism and communism and recognized that the latent threat of insurgency was the armed forces' primary concern in maintaining national defense. Mercado Jarrín insisted that the suppression of "human rights" as a fundamental by-product of Latin American counterinsurgency policy since World War II had only exacerbated the threat.[12] Peru's solution was, of course, to have the military take the lead in restructuring society to eliminate the causes of social injustice and, thereby, ensure national security. Basic structural reforms, such as the agrarian reform law, were enthusiastically supported by the modernizers as essential for Peru's security and national well-being. The modernizers differed with their progressive colleagues in the Velasco government over the issues of national mobilization and the extent to which structural

reforms should be slowed in favor of programs designed primarily to
promote social justice. Here, the debate of the Social Property Legislation
of May, 1974 drew modernizers and progressives apart.

The progressive element of the officer corps during the Velasco era has
drawn the most attention from scholars in their effort to explain the
uniquely reformist outlook of the military regime. Most progressives were
colonels at the time of the 3 October *coup*, with backgrounds in the
Intelligence Service. They formed a firm cadre around Velasco in defense
of an increasingly radical program of change. The military president
appointed a number of these officers to key command positions in the
armed forces, but their consistent power base was the *Comité de
Asesoramiento de la Presidencia* (COAP) or Advisory Committee to the
Presidency. Among the most active members of this group were army
generals Leonidas Rodríguez Figueroa, Enrique Gallegos Venero, Rafael
Hoyos Rubio, Jorge Fernandez Maldonado, Miguel Angel de la Flor, and
Anibal Meza Cuadra. Later, army general José Graham Hurtado and
General Rolando Gilardi (air force) would play significant roles in the
progressive coalition.

Succinctly, as distinct from the conservatives and modernizers the
progressives emphasized an agenda of radical change through programs
stressing social justice to be achieved through agrarian reform, worker
participation, economic nationalism, and, to a lesser degree, popular
mobilization. In retrospect, General Fernández Maldonado saw the Velasco
revolution in decidedly more class-oriented terms than did his moderate
colleagues. He decried the military's role before the early 1960s as "faithful
watchdogs of the oligarchy," while insisting that his progressive colleagues
were united by the "recognition of the necessity and urgency for radical
change."[13]

Significantly, this generation of army officers was the first to be come
under both French and United States military influence. Velasco
graduated from Chorillos in 1934, but most of the army officers serving in
his government received their commissions in the mid- to late-1940s. The
social activism of the French school was thus fused with the cold war
perspective taught to these officers at Fort Leavenworth and Fort Bragg in
the United States.

Most of the primary reforms of the Velasco era carry the imprint of the
progressives' ideology. They were particularly significant in the formulation
of the agrarian reform program, the Industrial Law, nationalization of major
foreign properties, and the implementation of the social property concept.
They were least effective in the generation of popular support for the
government's reforms, and this failing ultimately led to their downfall in

the power struggle within the armed forces. There is one central question that must be asked regarding the progressives' ideology: What prompted them to take a fundamentally different outlook from many of their own colleagues and, certainly, from the repressive policies of their military contemporaries throughout South America?

One common link drawing the progressives together is the influence of General Alfredo Rodríguez Martínez, who, as director of the *Escuela Superior de Guerra* and later the chief of the General Staff, exerted a "profound humanizing influence" upon many of these progressive officers. General Fernández Maldonado referred to Rodríguez Martínez as "my teacher and my guide," who imparted to his students "an immense love for Peru and an authentic spirit of social justice."[14] General Rodríguez Martínez counted among his students most of the officers listed above. What also served as a catalyst for the progressive perspective among these officers was their experience in the Intelligence Service. General Fernández Maldonado, the leading spokesman of the progressives within the Velasco government, explained his intelligence background and its impact on his reformist viewpoint in a 1983 interview.

I was privileged to work with Generals Rodríguez Martínez and Juan Bossio Collas in the creation and improvement of a system of Intelligence which included the Army's Intelligence School, its Intelligence Service, and the National Intelligence Service. . . . The intelligence activity opened our eyes and made us see the urgency for change in our country in order to put an end to social injustice, exploitation, and dependency.[15]

A number of these progressive officers with Intelligence Service backgrounds also served in the La Convención theater of operations during the 1965 antiguerrilla campaign. One officer in particular, General Enrique Gallegos Venero, stands out as the "model" Peruvian army progressive of the Velasco era. Author of a number of articles in the *Revista de Escuela Superior de Guerra* in the early 1960s on countersubversive operations, Gallegos Venero worked on the pilot agrarian reform project in La Convención in the period 1962-1963 before his involvement in the Velasco coup. As a member of Velasco's inner circle, Gallegos Venero was appointed director of army intelligence and commander of Lima's armored brigade before assuming the administration of Peru's agrarian reform program as minister of agriculture from November, 1974 to July, 1976.[16]

Holding this diverse coalition of armed forces' factions together, until a grave illness weakened his grip on power after 1974, was General Velasco Alvarado. Described by Fernández Maldonado as "*muy soldado*" (very much the soldier), Velasco unquestionably directed the course of the revolution through its most critical stages. Velasco saw himself as a soldier first and a social reformer thereafter. As such, he had little tolerance for dissent within his government and once reportedly ran a cabinet meeting with his revolver on the table in front of him. In an earlier time, he would have dominated the armed forces as a *caudillo* like Sánchez Cerro or Odría, but the institutional mechanics of the modern Peruvian armed forces prevented this throwback. Ultimately, Velasco's lack of personal charisma and ambition precluded him from building a political power base independent of the armed forces. Clearly, he was no Perón, and he apparently had no desire to be another Odría. Fernández Maldonado, who is perpetuating the Velasco legacy in Peru today as the leader of a small political party advocating a return to *Velasquista* reformism, saw him as a "socialist" with a clear vision of Peru's fundamental problems.[17] Velasco's own political views during the revolution were never precisely clear, but in an interview with *Caretas* magazine shortly before his death in 1977, he was quite revealing regarding his personal views. Articulating the traditional nation-building rhetoric, Velasco argued that the objective of his government was "to make Peru an independent nation and to bring about structural changes promoting economic development." He boasted that "the oligarchy is now dead" in Peru as a result of his reforms. Reflecting his strong antipolitical views, the retired general added that "civilians had been governing Peru for 150 years, but it took the armed forces to make a revolution." When asked by investigative journalist Cesar Hildebrandt to state precisely his political preferences, Velasco replied, "I have clear sympathy with Christian Democracy and its principles. It is a unique party with precise and concrete points of view."[18] Velasco's identification with Christian Democratic ideals was evident during his regime when he brought the leader of Peru's Christian Democratic Party, Héctor Cornejo Chávez, into his government as one of his closest advisers.

Velasco was not alone in his embrace of Christian Democracy as a framework for his reform. A number of the key members of his government claimed to be committed Roman Catholics. General Fernández Maldonado often spoke of the importance of Christian idealism as one of the ideological pillars of the revolution. Fernández Maldonado, along with Generals Leonidas Rodríguez Figueroa and Alfredo Carpio Becerra, completed the intensive Christian retreats known as the *Curisillo de Cristianidad* prior to the revolution. Moreover, Generals Mercado Jarrín and Morales Bermúdez were graduates of schools run by religious orders before they entered the military.[19]

The humanistic and largely nonideological appeal of Christian Democracy was plainly evident in much of the rhetoric and programs of the Velasco government. The "Third Position" between capitalism and communism was strikingly similar to the position adopted at the 1968 Latin American Bishop's Conference in Medellín, Colombia. The CELAM document, issued at the conference, warned that Latin America found itself in "a situation of injustice which could be termed one of institutional violence, because current structures violate fundamental rights, creating a situation which demands global, bold, urgent, and profoundly renovating transformation."[20]

Coinciding exactly with the birth of the "Liberation Theology" movement in Latin America actively espoused by Peru's articulate reformist priest, Father Gustavo Gutiérrez, the Velasco reforms were applauded by Peru's Cardinal Juan Landázuri Ricketts. The Education Reform package was even reviewed by Peru's bishops, who were instrumental in the final wording, which stated that Peruvian education sought "the integral formation of the human person in his immanent and transcendental projections."[21] For their part, armed forces officers raised as either "cultural Catholics" or committed Christians found the disciplined humanism of Christian Democratic reform a nonthreatening framework for change. The humanism seemed to blunt the hard edges of their barracks revolution, and it certainly contrasted, for example, with the rigid Catholicism espoused by their Argentine military contemporaries.

Given the ideological pluralism of the Velasco government's reform agenda, a key question comes to mind. To what extent did CAEM doctrine shape the military's perspective? Every leader and policymaker of the Velasco government interviewed for this study downplayed CAEM's influence. Mercado Jarrín and Vargas Caballero described the center's impact as "marginal." Mercado Jarrín further insisted that CAEM doctrine did not sufficiently consider the issue of "social justice" he claimed was critical to the Velasco government's programs. George Philip and José Z. García have noted the increasing conservatism of the CAEM prior to the Velasco *coup*, and this conservatism may well explain why the center was virtually excluded from participation in the Velasco regime's reform initiatives.[22] More than twenty years after the Velasco *coup*, CAEM spokesmen have reinforced these interpretations. They now term the theory that CAEM doctrine underlay the Velasco reforms as "fantasy," while claiming that Velasco largely ignored the center throughout his entire regime. A professor of geopolitics at the CAEM accused the Velasco government of being "anti-intellectual" and "infiltrated with leftists" and noted that the center has drawn more heavily on national defense doctrine from the Inter-American Defense College in Washington, D.C., and Brazilian military institutions in recent years. Alberto E. Bolívar

Ocampo, professor of geopolitics at the CAEM, further insisted that the center was never really a "think tank" for the Peruvian military but more a "laboratory" to examine long-range planning perspectives for Peru's future.[23]

The limited impact of the CAEM thus leaves the distinct impression that the highly pluralistic nature of the Velasco regime's programs was anchored to two ideological foundations: the long-held "civilizing mission" articulated by army officers since the early twentieth century and the Christian humanist doctrine of Latin America's emerging "Liberation Theology," which meshed perfectly with the timing and outlook of the Velasco government. The Velasco government's readiness to enlist a wide array of foreign agencies and Peruvian civilian advisers in formulating its reform initiatives reflected both its anxiety concerning its own lack of administrative experience and its unwillingness to entrust policy formulation to agencies such as the CAEM, which military progressives, at least, felt had lost touch with Peruvian reality.

Unquestionably, the scope of the Velasco regime's reforms went far beyond what CAEM administrators and nearly all Peruvians originally envisioned. The agrarian reform, its attempt at popular mobilization, and its foreign policy manifested best the regime's intensive effort to promote change and its inability to maintain this course. Consequently, these three aspects of the Velasco government will be analyzed as part of this overview.

From its inception on 24 June 1969, when General Velasco, using the words of Túpac Amaru II, proclaimed "Peasant, the landlord will no longer eat from your poverty," the agrarian reform program became the cornerstone of the military government's agenda for change. An authority on rural unrest in Peru, Howard Handelman, noted, "More than any other program initiated by the Velasco government, Agrarian Reform Decree Law 17716 expressed the 'radical reformist' modernizing ideology of the military's more progressive sector."[24] Over the nine years of reform, the governments of Velasco and Morales Bermúdez transferred more than 9.5 million hectares of land to more than 370,000 Peruvian families.[25] The Velasco regime originally regarded agrarian reform in highly technical terms and envisioned it as a way of modernizing the rural sector, increasing productivity and purchasing power, and re-allocating economic resources from the agrarian to the urban industrial sector.[26] The military government had even more ambitious sociopolitical aims. In the words of the more radical members of the military government, it sought to "break the back" of Peru's rural landed oligarchy. With the swift expropriation of the north coast communal agricultural estates, the military also aimed to eliminate or substantially reduce the political influence of APRA-dominated labor unions among the permanent wage laborers of the coastal enterprises.

Ranking in scope with the Mexican and Cuban agrarian reforms of this century, Peru's program created three types of benefactors: family-sized agricultural units, indigenous communities, and, most particularly, agricultural cooperatives known as *Sociedad Agricolas de Interés Social* or *SAIS* (Agrarian Social Interest Societies) and *Cooperativas Agrarias de Producción* or *CAPS* (Agrarian Production Cooperatives). Fearing unproductive fragmentation of the newly expropriated large estates, the military government redistributed a significant majority of the expropriated land into cooperatives. The concepts underlying these cooperatives were quite eclectic, like many of the Velasco government's reforms. The Christian Democracy ideal of communal property, the Marxist concept of collectivized agriculture, and the centuries-old Andean traditions of the *ayllu* (clan of communal land-holding units) were the conceptual pillars of the agrarian reform. Idealism aside, however, these cooperatives, which ignored the land hunger of the *eventuales* (north coast seasonal labors) and often infringed on traditional claims of *sierra* Indian communities, aroused intense resentment from many of the rural Peruvians who received no land under the agrarian reform program.[27]

Reform in Peru's agriculture sector, while sweeping and quite systematic, highlighted the hard reality that not enough land was available to those in desperate need. At the completion of the agrarian reform in the late 1970s, only 0.18 hectares of crop land per person were available in Peru. These figures rank Peru with India as one of the worst in the world. One estimate of the final results of the agrarian reform thus concluded that significantly less than one-third of the agrarian population benefited directly from the program.[28]

With all of its inadequacies, the agrarian reform still eliminated *latifundia*, something that only Bolivia, among the South American nations, has been able to achieve in this century. When in 1973 the military government abolished the *Sociedad Nacional Agraria* (National Agrarian Society), the symbol of Peru's landed oligarchy, it signaled an end to the almost complete dominance of the patrón over the *campesinos* in the *sierra* that had endured since the late sixteenth century. These *campesinos* then became more politically conscious and, in the words of a Maryknoll priest who worked for more than a decade in the Puno region following the reform, "gave them some reason to hope for a better future."[29]

Sendero Luminoso's dominance of the central *sierra* departments since the mid-1980s has made it vitally clear, however, that agrarian reform did not defuse the "latent insurgency" threat in Peru's highland regions as the military government had hoped. The Ayacucho region, the poorest in Peru, did not significantly benefit from the agrarian reform, and *Sendero Luminoso* used the area's desperate poverty to its advantage during its initial recruiting efforts. Now, as Peru enters the 1990s, the legacy of the agrarian reform is becoming more evident. Most expropriated land was redistributed not to Indian communities but rather to the former tenants of seized haciendas, which were subsequently converted to cooperatives. Land invasions, dissolution, and bankruptcy have undermined many of these original cooperatives while traditional Indian communities have become stronger. This process has increased unrest and violence in the *sierra*, but as Indian communities respond to this instability, their defensive mechanisms have resulted in stronger community bonds. As in centuries past, the foundation of *sierra* agriculture depends on the ability of these communities to defend their interests against yet another powerful threat, *Sendero Luminoso*.[30]

If the agrarian reform was the Velasco regime's most notable accomplishment, the regime's greatest failing was its inability to generate popular support for its reform program. In a confidential interview with Norman Gall in 1971, an army general explained the Velasco government's dilemma:

One of our greatest defects is the military habit of ordering and expecting to be blindly obeyed. This just doesn't happen in society at large. We deeply want to transfer power to the people, but we have not been able to find a way of doing this. To call elections without first carrying out our structural reforms, without first putting real power in the people's hands through the agrarian reform and the industrial community, would just bring us back to the political farces of the past without any real improvement in Peruvian society. We admit that our greatest political problem is to give a real role to the people in this process that is going on now.[31]

Fearing a loss of control of the revolutionary process and painfully sensitive to criticism, the Velasco regime tried to administer the government as if it were a barracks. Armed forces officers held all top administrative positions in the government until the first civilian was appointed in 1975. Admiral Vargas Caballero's dismissal and the subsequent expropriation of Peru's newspapers in July, 1974 are further evidence of this mentality. But this thinking is not surprising. While Velasco was muzzling the press and purging dissident military commanders, the Argentine armed forces were beginning to prosecute their "Dirty War" in earnest, and the Pinochet regime in Chile was violating its countrymen's human rights to an extent now only beginning to be fully revealed.

The peaceful "transmission belts" designed to shift popular participation at a pace acceptable to the Velasco regime were SINAMOS, the "tactical support" of the pro-Soviet Communist Party and a newly organized labor and agrarian sector. A group of intellectuals, led by anthropologist Carlos Delgado, assumed by mid-1971 a powerful advisory function within the Velasco government. Regarding the question of popular mobilization, the Delgado cadre played an instrumental role in the creation of SINAMOS and also advised against the establishment of a military political party that would have institutionalized the armed forces' leadership function.[32] The military was unwilling to share political power with civilians in an "Institutional Revolutionary Party," as that would have involved openly shared decision making, which was contrary to the armed forces' self-image.

On the other hand, an exclusively military political party would have sharply alienated conservatives such as Admiral Vargas Caballero very early during the Velasco government. More fundamentally, such a political party would have created a parallel power structure within the armed forces and undermined the promotion process, military discipline, and the chain of command. This phenomenon was occurring in a de facto fashion anyway, as Velasco rewarded his loyal followers with promotions and key troop commands. To have institutionalized this political partisanship within the officer corps would have reversed the professional progress of the armed forces since the Odría years and reawakened fears of caudillismo under Velasco.

SINAMOS was the military government's effort to mobilize controlled support for its program without risking the creation of a mass-based political party. Its primary purpose included "the training, orientation and organization of the national population, the development of social interest entities, and communication and particularly dialogue between the government and the national population."[33] The Velasco regime wanted to avoid the emergence of a popular interest group that would dictate the course of its revolutionary program through sheer pressure on the government. Indeed, when Committees for the Defense of the Revolution (CDR), similar to those in Cuba and Sandinista Nicaragua, appeared spontaneously in the Lima pueblos jóvenes in early 1969, these groups were quickly discouraged by the government. Despite the regime's efforts, "block groups," based on a variety of ethnic and community ties, still dominate the communities today.

The immediate stimulus for the establishment of SINAMOS was the massive land invasion in April, 1971 at Pamplona on property adjoining the Jesuit-owned College of the Immaculate Virgin outside of Lima. Previous efforts by the government to control smaller invasions had failed, and SINAMOS was designed to be the agency to channel this emerging urban mobilization along lines dictated by the military.[34] Soon SINAMOS was responding to growing political unrest in the recently expropriated north coast sugar estates and in other rural areas as the uneven nature of the government's reforms provoked increasing discontent.

SINAMOS never fulfilled its original function and, in the end, generated the most intense opposition of any of the Velasco reforms. As David Scott Palmer concluded in his study of popular mobilization during the Velasco years, "Citizens saw SINAMOS as an attempt by the central government to control their local organizations . . . as a result many new agency headquarters became 'lightning rods' for local opposition against the regime."[35] Civilian political foes of the Velasco regime and conservative opponents within the military also bitterly opposed SINAMOS because they perceived it to be what it was not: the forerunner of an institutional party of the revolution. SINAMOS was effectively dissolved after its Lima headquarters was burned during the riots inspired by a police strike in February, 1975. Other efforts of the Velasco regime to monitor labor and agrarian mobilization were equally unsuccessful for largely the same reason.

Seeking to undermine APRA influence in Peru's labor movement and create a more "reliable" union structure in late 1972, Velasco established the Confederación Trabajadores de Revolucionario del Perú (Confederation of Workers of the Peruvian Revolution, CTRP). Never really a serious challenge to the established unions, the CTRP aroused the same fears in the labor sector that SINAMOS inspired, and, ultimately, the Velasco and Morales Bermúdez regimes were confronted with labor unrest unsurpassed in Peru's history.

The agrarian equivalent to the CTRP, the Confederación Nacional Agraria (National Agrarian Federation, CNA) inspired similar violent opposition from the militant peasant leagues organized during the land invasions predating the Velasco government. Indian communities, whose land claims against adjoining haciendas were often ignored with the creation of state cooperatives, saw the CNA as further proof that the Velasco regime was seeking their demobilization.

Just as the Odría and Pérez Godoy governments used Peru's pro-Soviet Communist Party as a political lever against APRA, the Velasco regime enlisted the same tactic. Velasco's press secretary and adviser, Augusto Zimmerman Zavala, acknowledged during a 1976 interview in Panama, that "the Communists were our tactical allies, but we would not say so."[36] Unlike Odría and the 1962-1963 military Junta, however, the Velasco regime's clandestine alliance with the Communist Party was a poor bargain. Luis Pásara observed:

The Communists did act as a counterweight to opposition from conservative groups and APRA. . . . But the Communists gained many advantages through their tactic of critical support thanks to the fact that they had their own political organizations and others under their control as well. Moreover, the Communists did not fight labor demands but sparked them and channelled them. . . . The Communist Party thus profits politically, increasing its own ranks.[37]

As Peru developed close diplomatic ties with the Soviet Union after 1970, its "tactical alliance" with the Communist Party meshed with its new foreign policy initiatives. Still, the wave of strikes, many of them communist-inspired, that helped bring about Velasco's overthrow in August, 1975 was the most dramatic evidence that the regime's popular mobilization campaign was a failure.

The Velasco regime's warm relations with the Soviet Union, begun when Peru opened diplomatic relations with Moscow in February, 1969, were the centerpiece of a stridently nationalist foreign policy with the following objectives: (1) lessened dependence on United States economic and military assistance, (2) expansion of relations with the socialist bloc nations, (3) vigorous participation in Third World multilateral diplomacy, (4) regional economic integration with the Andean Pact (established in 1969), and (5) a broad defense of Peru's economic sovereignty, particularly in relation to its two hundred-mile territorial sea claims.[38] This foreign policy had broad support within the military and was ably administered by General Edgardo Mercado Jarrín as Velasco's first foreign minister. With its emphasis on lessened dependency, diplomatic pluralism, and heightened nationalism, Peru's international policy decidedly reflected the extremely comprehensive national defense doctrine articulated by armed forces' officers since the 1950s. Peru's navy, for example, actively enforced this defense of its two hundred-mile territorial sea claims by seizing dozens of tuna vessels of the United States and other nations throughout the early years of the Velasco regime.

Peru's tense relations with the United States during the Velasco era must be viewed in the context of the expropriation of the International Petroleum Company and, more fundamentally, the war in Vietnam. The Velasco government refused to compensate IPC after the seizure on 9 October 1968 and argued that the initial contract between the company and the Peruvian government was invalid, and, therefore, no compensation was justified. This position was the only politically acceptable one that the Velasco government could assume, given the nationalistic implications of the controversy. While the Nixon administration never implemented the automatic suspension of economic aid called for by the Hickenlooper

Amendment, United States aid of all types remained suspended until the last year of the Velasco regime.

Peru's military relations with the United States reached a low ebb in February, 1969 after a particularly controversial incident in the "Tuna War" prompted Washington to invoke the Pelly Amendment, suspending all United States military aid to Peru. The Velasco regime responded by expelling the United States military missions. Thus, nearly a quarter of a century of cooperation between the army and air force and nearly fifty years of partnership between the navies of these two nations came to an end. Velasco's decision manifested not only the independent nationalism of his regime but also the United States military's performance in Vietnam. Prior to the 3 October 1968 *coup*, United States military personnel in Peru were criticized by Peruvian army officers for what they termed Washington's "no win" policy in Southeast Asia. The inevitable contrast between Israel's stunning performance in the 1967 Middle East War and the Vietnam campaign was also made.[39] At this very low point in United States military prestige, Peru began to explore other options for military assistance, and the Soviet Union became an increasingly attractive possibility.

The Velasco regime's anti-imperialist rhetoric and its policies of economic nationalism drew praise and interest from Moscow. Soviet analysts viewed these policies as politically encouraging and capable of shifting the balance of power in favor of the Soviet Union. The Soviet Union gained significant goodwill after a devastating earthquake in the Callejón de Huaylas, near Chimbote in northern Peru, killed seventy thousand people and left 500,000 homeless on 31 May 1970. Soviet medical teams gave valuable assistance to the injured and loaned Mi-8 helicopters to be used in relief efforts. Seventy Soviet medical personnel lost their lives in this operation when their plane crashed in the North Sea while en route to Peru[40].

After Peru established diplomatic ties with the Soviet Union and other Eastern bloc nations in late 1968, favorable trade terms with Moscow, including attractive lines of credit and other financial incentives, produced an increase in trade from twenty-three million dollars in 1968 to $283 million in 1975.[41] Beginning in 1974, the USSR and other socialist nations began offering scholarships to Peruvian students for both undergraduate and postgraduate training in the particularly critical areas of engineering, medicine, and the natural sciences. These trade and cultural ties, while significant, were secondary to the massive weapons purchases that would draw the Soviet military and the Peruvian army and air force into a level of technical cooperation second only to Cuba in the Western Hemisphere.[42]

Before negotiating an arms package with the Soviet Union in mid-1973, the Peruvian army and air force did approach the United States, France, and Israel, but Washington refused to respond and French and Israeli prices were deemed too expensive. Exact terms of the initial weapons purchase in 1973 have never been made public, but it is known that Soviet arms were sold at low prices, under extended credit, with low-interest terms and long grace periods. In a second round of arms sales, during the Morales Bermúdez regime in December, 1976, for example, thirty-six Sukhoi SU-22 fighter bombers were purchased for $250 million with a ten-year payment period. The initial purchases of Soviet weapons in 1973-1974 included Soviet medium-sized T-54 and T-55 tanks, 122 and 130mm tank transporters, radio controlled antiaircraft guns, artillery, rocket launchers, and Mi-6 and Mi-8 helicopters.

Francisco Morales Bermúdez later insisted that these initial arms purchases were "strictly a business deal without ideological implications."[43] This view was also shared by his more progressive colleague in the Velasco government, Jorge Fernández Maldonado, who stressed the high quality and low cost of the Soviet equipment.[44] Further major purchases of Soviet Mi-8 helicopters, surface-to-air SA-3 and SA-7 missiles, Sukhoi SU-22 fighter bombers, and AN-26 F Antonov airplanes, established a substantial Soviet technical assistance presence in Peru.

Despite these denials of any ideological significance to Peru's weapon's liaison with the Soviet Union since 1973, it must be noted that the bulk of the army's two armored brigades (350 T-54 and T-55 tanks) are Soviet weapons. Moreover, the core of the air force's aircraft (52 SU-22 Sukhoi fighter bombers) are also Soviet-made. For most of the late 1970s and early 1980s, at least one hundred Soviet technical advisers remained in Peru to assist in training and maintenance for these weapon systems. More importantly, more than eight hundred army and air force personnel have trained at Soviet military institutions since the mid-1970s.[45] The implications of these ties with the Soviet military establishment are not yet clear. Only a few minor examples of Soviet influence have surfaced in Peru's army service journals.[46] Some consequences are now becoming evident. The navy's decision to refuse Soviet arms and instead purchase frigates and submarines from Italy and West Germany, respectively, has increased interservice tensions. Additionally, as Peru's economy has deteriorated, the ability of the army and air force to sustain the high maintenance demands of their Soviet weapons has been badly strained. As the Soviet economy undergoes dramatic change with Gorbachev's reforms, the willingness and ability of the Soviets to supply spare parts to Peru will become questionable.[47]

The decision of the Velasco and Morales Bermúdez regimes to engage in long-term arms agreements with the Soviet Union has been the most lasting and potentially significant aspect of the military government's foreign policy during the *Docenio*. Other initiatives, such as Peru's leading role in the Andean Pact and its involvement in the Third World multilateral diplomacy, have been de-emphasized. The Velasco regime sharply raised the profile of Peru's international presence. But after Velasco's government was replaced by Morales Bermúdez and during the subsequent civilian regime of Fernando Belaúnde Terry, Peru returned to a more traditional foreign policy.

The agrarian reform, SINAMOS, and Peru's innovative foreign policy were but a portion of the most ambitious program for change in Peruvian history. Yet, as Peter Cleaves and Martin Scurrah have observed, the Velasco reforms were decreed "against the opposition or apathy of major forces in society . . . and in favor of groups that could offer no immediate support."[48] It is conceivable that the desperate poor in Lima's *pueblos jóvenes* and the *sierra's* more politically conscious *campesinos* might have sustained a popular base for the revolution had the military government been willing aggressively to seek their allegiance. The progressives within the Velasco regime seemed to be moving in this direction in mid-1974 with the introduction of the social property initiatives, which were the most drastic economic redistribution measures ever considered in Peru. But at this juncture, a wide array of developments had weakened both Velasco and his progressive cadre within his government. The regime never recovered from this crisis, and Velasco was eased from power on 29 August 1975 by his prime minister, General Francisco Morales Bermúdez.

Writing more than twenty years later, Morales Bermúdez claimed his *golpe de estado* of 29 August, announced from Tacna, in the midst of the fifth meeting of the Non-Aligned Nations being held in Lima, was precipitated by Velasco's progressive inability to perform his presidential duties as a result of his declining health.[49] After he suffered an abdominal aneurism in early 1973 and the subsequent amputation of a leg, Velasco's performance became increasingly erratic. Morales Bermúdez, after quietly surveying the armed forces' leadership, was able to gain the acquiescence of even Velasco's progressive colleagues for his removal from office. Nonetheless, Velasco's illness was only the catalyst for his government's downfall. Peru's declining economy, increasing armed forces' factionalism, and mounting conservative opposition to the government were the most decisive developments bringing Morales Bermúdez to power.

Benefiting from high prices for copper, sugar, and other principal exports and borrowing heavily from international lenders, partially in expectation of major oil revenues that never materialized, the Velasco regime enjoyed an economic "honeymoon," lasting its first five years in office. The world recession, coinciding with OPEC's oil embargo, however, generated an economic crisis in Peru, which exposed the structural weaknesses of the military government's economic program. Heavy dependence upon the import of foodstuffs (including even potatoes) and industrial goods, a refusal to reform the tax structure, an inconsistent manufacturing policy,   • and limitations on export expansion weakened an economy already made vulnerable by a sharp decline in the world price of copper and sugar and poor yields in the once-booming fishing industry. The major expenditures for Soviet arms exacerbated the crisis after 1973. By early 1975, international banks were reversing their once-liberal lending policies to Peru, and the Velasco regime was in deep economic trouble. The crisis sparked labor unrest and generally undermined public confidence in the military government.

More fundamentally, by the end of the Velasco regime in August, 1975, it was starkly evident that the military government had lost its opportunity to accomplish its two major socioeconomic objectives: to reduce Peruvian economic dependency while promoting social justice. According to Thorp and Bertram, this failure resulted from the government's inability to adopt a consistent economic strategy. These economic analysts concluded:

By refusing to move to the left the military lost their opportunity to mobilize mass support among the traditional-sector labor force, and to use major redistributive policies to promote a more inward-directive development strategy. At the same time, by attacking business interests and the Right, the military lost the confidence and support of local capitalists and alienated foreign interests.[50]

While the Velasco government was experiencing its final economic crisis, military factionalism and conservative opposition to the regime significantly increased. The crisis, prompted by Admiral Vargas Caballero's forced resignation, effectively ended the navy's institutional support for the regime after May, 1974. Moreover, the navy again confronted the prospect of open conflict with the government in April, 1975 over the removal of Vargas Caballero's successor, the outspokenly proregime navy minister, Admiral Guillermo Faura.[51]

The alienation of the navy coincided with the appearance of a hard-line faction within the army calling itself "La Misión" (the mission). Pitting itself against the army's progressive wing, La Misión, led by General Javier Tantaleán Vanini, emphasized traditional military values of order and discipline and opposed further efforts to enlist popular participation for government reforms. Appealing to Velasco's soldier instincts, Tantaleán Vanini joined the president's inner circle. With this intensive factionalism emerging, armed forces unity was largely eroded by late 1974. These divisions encouraged conservative opposition to the Velasco government, which became particularly strong after the expropriation of the nation's newspapers in July, 1974.[52]

The expropriation of the conservative newspaper *El Comercio*, in particular, sparked protests in Lima's affluent suburbs of San Isidro and Miraflores. These relatively mild disturbances, however, were only a prelude for much more violent actions against the government during the last years of Velasco's tenure. On 2 December 1974 the first assault on members of the Velasco government occurred when two gunmen fired on Generals Javier Tantaleán Vanini, Edgardo Mercado Jarrín, and Guillermo Arbulú from a passing car in Lima and slightly wounded Tantaleán Vanini and Arbulú.[53]

Little more than two months later, one of the worst urban riots in the Lima area erupted in the midst of a strike by the *Guardia Civil*. After an assault by army tanks on the *Guardia Civil* headquarters, demonstrations, widespread arson, and looting occurred, with military facilities and the SINAMOS headquarters being particular targets. Eighty-six people died in these riots, with 155 wounded.[54] The disturbances marked the first serious attempt by elements of APRA to use violence to bring down the government since the October, 1948 Callao revolt. Haya de la Torre hinted at APRA's antigovernment intentions in a July, 1974 interview when he boasted that Chile's anticommunist strongman, General Augusto Pinochet, had recently claimed that Chile needed "a strongly anti-Communist Party like Peru's APRA to counter its Marxist elements."[55] Haya de la Torre later admitted APRA's involvement in the riots. With an explanation that was strikingly similar to the circumstances of the 1948 Callao revolt, he claimed that young *Aprista* militants, protesting economic conditions and the failure of the government to call free elections, had initiated the rioting, and the party leadership did not intervene to stop them. Party leader Armando Villanueva, as had Manuel Seoane, after the 1948 Callao revolt, blamed young *Aprista* "hotheads" for the riots.[56] APRA's ideological position may have shifted dramatically to the right since the Callao revolt, but its political tactics appeared to have remained basically the same.

If the explanations of the APRA leaders are true regarding the circumstances of the February, 1975 riots, then Haya de la Torre learned from the Callao fiasco the political dangers of undercutting *Aprista* militants.

More probably, however, it seems likely APRA leaders used the *Guardia Civil* strike, growing conservative opposition to the government, and the public divisions within the armed forces' leadership to weaken the Velasco regime further. In sharp contrast to Callao, APRA's use of violence in February, 1975 achieved its tactical objectives. Less than eight months later, Velasco was deposed, and a more conservative military government under General Francisco Morales Bermúdez gave APRA much greater political freedom.

When Morales Bermúdez became military president on 29 August 1975, he promised not to vary "one millimeter" off course from Velasco's reforms.[57] But under pressure from conservatives, the World Bank, and the International Monetary Fund, he soon opted for orthodox economic policies that were designed to ease foreign credit restrictions and increase the sharply reduced levels of foreign investment. Sacrificed with this policy were the social goals of the Velasco years. Fernández Maldonado, who, along with other military progressives, would leave the government within a year, later characterized the Morales Bermúdez government as a "counter-revolution."[58]

Indeed, by 1977 the most controversial aspects of Velasco's economic policies, the Industrial Community and Social Property legislation, were abandoned. Yet the Morales Bermúdez government's international credit standing had not significantly improved. After Peru was granted a $340 million loan by various international banks, on the promise of imposing a strict austerity program, the government's decision to purchase the Sukhoi SU-22 fighter bombers from the Soviet Union for $250 million generated a credit freeze. IMF negotiators then insisted on further drastic austerity measures involving a major reduction in public expenditures to reduce inflation, elimination of subsidies on gasoline and food items, and regular devaluation of the sol.[59] Even the partial imposition of this "shock therapy" caused a wave of labor unrest, including the largest coordinated general strike in Peru's history on 19 July 1977.

In a May, 1990 interview, Morales Bermúdez justified his policies by arguing they were necessary to reduce the pervasive role of the military in the governing process, to encourage private sector activity, and to reopen Peru's economy to international markets.[60] While he was implementing these policies, Morales Bermúdez at least tried to maintain a rhetorical facade commensurate with the Velasco years. On 4 October 1977 the government announced the *Plan de Gobierno Túpac Amaru* (Government Plan of Túpac Amaru), designed to "replace" the Velasco's government's *Plan Inca*. Publicly, the *Plan Túpac Amaru* was announced as a blueprint to "complete and readjust the structural reforms" begun under Velasco to achieve "social democracy and full national participation." These rhetorical exercises were implemented while Morales Bermúdez adopted two primary political tactics to generate support for his beleaguered government.[61]

The first approach was a *rapprochement* with APRA, which Morales Bermúdez initiated during a speaking tour of Trujillo in April and early May, 1976, when he urged citizens of these original *Aprista* strongholds to overcome the legacy of the Trujillo massacres of July, 1932 and reach a "dialogue" with the government. As the son of an army colonel whose father was killed by *Apristas* in Trujillo in 1939, Morales Bermúdez's plea for a dialogue carried particular significance.[62] Haya de la Torre responded favorably to Morales Bermúdez's overtures, and APRA political fortunes improved to the extent that the party dominated the elections for the Constitutional Assembly in June, 1978, with the APRA leader elected president of that political body. This was the first and only time Haya de la Torre was elected to any national political office during nearly half a century of political activity in Peru.

Morales Bermúdez's efforts to make peace between the army and APRA aroused intense opposition from General Fernández Maldonado and other remaining progressives in the Morales Bermúdez government, to the extent that they violated orders and staged the traditional commemoration of the army's victims of the Trujillo uprising on 7 July 1976.[63] This open protest against the Morales Bermúdez policy undoubtedly hastened the resignation from the government that same month of Fernández Maldonado, along with his progressive colleagues, Generals Enríque Gallegos Venero, Miguel Angel de la Flor, and Leonidas Rodriguez Figueroa.

These resignations did not end armed forces' factionalism. Within a year, two power groups in the army command emerged to test the "institutionalists," who sought a smooth transition to civilian rule, thereby assuring armed forces unity and professionalism. These factions, known as the *Duros* (hard-liners) and *Blandos* (moderates), differed sharply over the issue of government suppression of public disorders and strikes occasioned by the economic policy of the Morales Bermúdez government. In early 1978, the minister of the interior, General Luis Cisneros Vizquerra, leader of the *Duros*, confronted the *Blandos*, who sympathized with the ideals of the Velasco government, on the question of leftist political participation in the proposed Constitutional Assembly. Morales Bermúdez was able sufficiently to quiet this professional bickering to allow APRA to assume a leading role in the assembly without further internal armed forces turmoil.[64]

These divisions within the officer corps and the increasing unpopularity of the regime's economic programs prompted the Morales Bermúdez government to pursue a second tactic, designed to promote greater military and national unity. After negotiations among Peru, Bolivia, and Chile regarding granting land-locked Bolivia a corridor to the sea broke down in 1976, Peru adopted a hard-line position toward Chile and, later, Ecuador. Emboldened by its newly acquired Soviet tanks and fighter bombers, the Morales Bermúdez government de-emphasized the progressive Third World diplomacy of the Velasco era in favor of a more traditional military policy favoring military readiness and national sovereignty.[65] A "War Scare" was initiated in mid-1976, with a media campaign that warned a Chilean invasion was imminent. In the Cuzco region, for example, young women (ages seventeen and eighteen) were actually briefly "drafted," provided with ill-fitting uniforms, and taught the rudiments of parade drill before they were eventually allowed to return quietly to civilian life. Heightened tensions with Chile and Ecuador also, of course, helped justify Peru's major arms purchases in a time of economic crisis.[66]

Interestingly, this hard-line foreign policy was implemented even after Morales Bermúdez met with Bolivian and Chilean military commanders before his 29 August 1975 coup, in an attempt to defuse rising tensions. As late as April, 1977 there remained a strong belief within the Chilean high command that Peru would invade their nation before the one-hundredth anniversary of the outbreak of the War of the Pacific in 1979.[67]

The September 1973 Pinochet coup in Chile and heightened tensions with the right-wing Hugo-Banzer government in Bolivia justified, in some measure, Peru's more traditional "border defense" mentality throughout the Morales Bermúdez administration. Fundamentally, it was also an understandable position for the armed forces to adopt after the "civilizing mission" of the Velasco years had been largely abandoned. If they had not succeeded in restructuring Peruvian society, then the armed forces' leadership felt it was, at least, necessary fully to equip and modernize the military while they were in a position to do so.

Notwithstanding its aggressive foreign policy initiative, with its emphasis on national sovereignty, by 1978 Peru's military establishment was psychologically exhausted and ready to return political power to civilians. Morales Bermúdez, reflecting later on his tenure as military president, continually referred to his desire to remove the armed forces from politics.[68] Perhaps the most damaging aspect of a decade of military rule was institutional corruption. One high-ranking armed forces officer, who held a variety of positions in the Velasco and Morales Bermúdez governments, later claimed, "Twelve years of military rule produced one of the biggest cartels of immoral behavior in the armed forces." This officer cited kickbacks on the major weapons purchases of the Docenio as the principal source of corruption during the twelve years of military rule.[69] General Javier Tantaleán Vanini's administration of the ministry of fisheries under Velasco, for example, was so scandalous that he was arrested and briefly detained after Morales Bermúdez assumed power.[70]

The Peruvian army's close ties with its Argentine counterparts reinforced the view that long-term military rule could be terribly divisive and damaging to the military's national image. By 1978, the Brazilian military's process of political "decompression," or return to civilian rule, was well along after fourteen years in power. Peru's own version of political "decompression" was the Constitutional Assembly, convened soon after the June, 1978 elections. APRA delegates played a leading role in the Constitutional Assembly, whose president, Haya de la Torre, now eighty-three years old and ill with cancer, demonstrated a degree of statesmanship unmatched in his long political career. The assembly was widely viewed as a body elected not only to codify the basic reforms of the military government but also to serve as the transition to civilian rule. When the assembly promulgated the new constitution on 12 July 1979, all Peruvians eighteen years of age or older were granted suffrage without previous literacy restrictions. The military government's education, labor, and agrarian reforms were also incorporated in the national charter, along with judicial reform and measures to grant greater regional autonomy to the nation's departmental governments. The term of Peru's president was shortened from six to five years, with no immediate reelection. The most significant indication that the military government was sincere about returning power to civilians was evident in Articles 273 and 278, which defined the armed forces' role as simply "to guarantee the independence, sovereignty, and territorial integrity of the Republic."[71] This limited mandate contrasts significantly with the military's charge in the 1933 constitution to "guarantee the Constitution and laws of the Republic and to maintain public order." The military *coups* of 1948, 1962, and 1968 were all justified under this provision of the 1933 constitution. After more than a decade of military rule, the armed forces were now prepared legally to limit their political mandate. With the work of the Constitutional Assembly now complete, the Morales Bermúdez government allowed Peru's political parties to renew full political activity as a prelude to the 1980 national elections.

Haya de la Torre's death in August, 1979 soon resulted in an intense power struggle within the APRA leadership between the left of center, Armando Villanueva del Campo, and a minority faction headed by the more conservative Andrés Townsend. From this power struggle, the youthful protegé of Haya de la Torre, Alan García Pérez, would eventually emerge as a compromise secretary-general of APRA by 1982. *Aprista* disunity in the absence of Haya de la Torre, however, aided the candidacy of former President Fernando Belaúnde Terry as the leader of the revitalized *Acción Popular*. Belaúnde, who spent most of the *Docenio* teaching in Washington, D.C., appeared to benefit from his long absence from Peruvian politics and a sympathy vote as the victim of Velasco's 1968 *coup*.

Belaúnde's election, with 45 percent of the vote among a large field of fifteen candidates, at first seemed to manifest the continuity of Peru's civilian political process after extended military rule. The former architect campaigned on many of the same issues he raised in his successful 1963 presidential effort. He emphasized Peru's need to return to a neoliberal free-market economy and even revived his "Marginal Jungle Highway" development scheme abandoned during his first administration. Peruvian society was vastly different in 1980, however, from the nation Belaúnde first administered in 1963.

While the military programs of the *Docenio* stopped far short of initiating a social revolution, these reforms did significantly alter existing political patterns, mobilized the labor sector, democratized the university system, and encouraged the emergence of an industrial middle class. Rather than the dismantling of Peru's existing political party structures, the *Docenio* witnessed the maturation of the nation's previously weak parties of the left. Former political prisoners Héctor Béjar and Hugo Blanco, for example, became prominent political actors after they were released by the Velasco regime. More importantly, Peru's first viable leftist coalition, *Izquierda Unida* (United Left), benefiting from its support in Lima's *pueblos jóvenes*, elected the city's first Marxist mayor, Alfonso Barrantes, in 1983. Some observers see this phenomenon as the emergence of a new form of urban populism and compare it to the populist politics of the 1930s that gave rise to APRA's national prominence. Indeed, Alan García Pérez, as APRA's youthful successor to Haya de la Torre, returned to the party's populist and antiimperialist roots during his successful 1985 presidential campaign.[72] Ultimately, however, the strength and volatility of Peru's new mass electorate were not fully clear until the surprising victory of Alberto Fujimori in the 1990 elections. Campaigning almost exclusively in Lima's impoverished *pueblos jóvenes*, this son of Japanese immigrants made pointed racial and social contrasts between himself and his urbane political opponent, the renowned novelist Mario Vargas Llosa, as he surged from virtual anonymity to a decisive political victory.

The nation's more militant labor movement had already begun to assert its new strength throughout the last years of the military government.

During the continued economic crisis of the 1980s, labor unrest became endemic. The 1980s saw Peru experience an average of 670 strikes and 18.5 million lost "man hours" per year.[73] Of course, this massive labor unrest reflects Peru's desperate economic conditions, but it also surely demonstrates a newly energized labor sector emerging from the years of military rule.

Jeffrey L. Klaiber, S. J., a professor of history at Lima's Catholic University, views the Velasco regime's education reform as instrumental in opening the doors of Peru's universities to the poor for the first time.[74] Ultimately, this reform may be one of the most profoundly positive initiatives of the military government, but throughout the 1980s, it has generated heightened political activism and allowed *Sendero Luminoso* to employ Peru's universities and high schools as recruiting grounds for revolutionary movement. Below the university level, the military government's education reform seems to have infused an activist spirit among the nation's teachers that was not present prior to the Velasco years. Whether striking or protesting for better pay or better conditions in the nation's schools, the teachers have been some of the most militant elements of the newly aggressive labor force.

From a social class perspective, the *Docenio* coincided with and clearly enhanced the growth of an urban-industrial middle class. As Aníbal Quijano argued very early in the Velasco years, the military government was seeking to "consolidate the trend that was already under way toward the conversion of the urban-industrial sector into the dominant sector of the Peruvian economy as a whole."[75] Employing traditional national defense doctrine, the Velasco regime did not attempt to eliminate or even discourage the heavy involvement of foreign capital in Peru's principal extractive industries. Rather, through its nationalization of such key foreign firms as IPC, Cerro de Pasco, and Marcona Mining Corporation, while encouraging new foreign investment in petroleum exploration in the *oriente*, the military tried to alter the terms of foreign economic involvement in its favor. It was hoped that Peru's industrial independence and national defense capabilities would thereby be enhanced. While this process was occurring, the military government ambitiously sought to reconcile the inevitable conflict between the emerging urban-industrial middle class and the more militant labor sector with the Industrial and Social Property legislation. But these simultaneous goals of modernization and social justice were directly at cross purposes, and neither was attained. What did unquestionably succeed was the Velasco government's attempt to break the remaining hold of the traditional oligarchy in favor of what Velasco termed the "national bourgeoisie" or "small and medium industrialists."[76] As this emerging urban middle class entered the 1980s, however, it confronted an economy during the Belaúnde (1980-1985) and García (1985-1990) governments that tested its very ability to survive, much less exert its newly acquired economic and political influence.

Seeking to accelerate the Morales Bermúdez administration's break with the highly statist economic program of the Velasco administration, President Belaúnde initiated a neoliberal, laissez-faire economic policy formulated by newly prominent "manager technocrats" and middle-class entrepreneurs serving in his Council of Ministers and in *Acción Popular*'s congressional delegation.[77] The enthusiasm of these economic planners was soon dampened, however, by low prices for Peru's exports, severe inflation, and growing pressure from the ever-present IMF. Throughout Belaúnde's five years as president, this scenario changed very little. As Belaúnde went through one finance minister after another, with some publicly challenging his economic program, Peru's economy continued its decline. By mid-1984, Belaúnde's unwillingness to devalue the *sol* by 20 percent, as the IMF demanded as part of its basic requirements for refinancing Peru's thirteen billion-dollar foreign debt loan, resulted in a massive teachers' and state workers' strike, which the Belaúnde administration met with a thirty-day state of emergency.

The president of Peru's Central Bank, Richard Webb, in a public break with both the administration and the IMF in late June, 1984, criticized the Belaúnde government for ending the public workers' strike with pay increases and continued subsidies on food and gasoline and thus dooming any possible IMF agreements. On the other hand, Webb decried the IMF debt service schedule as "intolerable" and noted that well over half of Peru's projected export income for the period 1985-1989 (nine to ten billion dollars) would be required for interest on Peru's foreign debt.[78] Understandably, the foreign debt issue became one of the central planks of Alan García's 1985 presidential campaign. García's pledge to limit debt service payments to 10 percent of Peru's export earnings prompted an enthusiastic response from the economically beleaguered Peruvian electorate.

Belaúnde's economic difficulties fueled continual speculation that he would again fall victim to a military *coup*. He was clearly aware of this possibility and thus sought the working accord with the armed forces' leadership that he had never been able to achieve during his first administration. His relations with the military were helped immeasurably by his highly vocal support of Peru's brief border confrontation with Ecuador in the Cordillera del Condor region in northeastern Peru during late January and early February, 1981. The clash began on 28 January, when a Peruvian helicopter fired on Ecuadoran border units that, the Peruvians claimed, had established a military base in Peruvian territory. The seventy-eight-kilometer Peru-Ecuador border in the Cordillera del Condor area, eight hundred miles northeast of Lima, had not been accurately fixed even by the 1942 Rio Protocol, which ended the 1941 Zarumilla-Marañon conflict.[79] Ecuador subsequently denounced the 1942 protocol anyway and claimed it had been imposed under duress. The January, 1981 border conflict, the most serious since 1941, saw Peruvian helicopter, air force, and commando units push Ecuadoran forces back from their original positions in five days of fighting. Exact casualty figures were not announced, but as many as two hundred may have died in the short but intense border clash.[80]

Like President Prado forty years before, Belaúnde quickly journeyed to the scene of hostilities to pose with Peruvian troops for photographs, while he described the Ecuadoran operation as a "macabre masquerade" that would be met with "grave consequences" if it did not cease. When the hostilities concluded, Belaúnde returned to cheering crowds in Lima with a Peruvian flag that had been raised over a recaptured Ecuadoran outpost.[81] The president's posturing led The New York Times to conclude that the victorious clash with Ecuador "had erased Belaúnde's touchy relations with the military."[82] This successful military operation, like the Prado administration's secret bank loan to the armed forces in the 1940s (see Chapter 3), strengthened the modus vivendi between Belaúnde and the armed forces' high command reached during the first months of his presidency. The agreement, negotiated with the president by army commander General Rafael Hoyos Rubio, who represented the last institutional link with the Velasco regime, guaranteed the armed forces "complete independence on internal and professional matters" and immunity from "misdeeds" during the Docenio. In exchange, the armed forces' command promised to confine its activities to strictly professional matters.[83] In effect, this agreement validated the 1979 constitution, limiting the political role of the armed forces in Peruvian politics. Belaúnde's "understanding" with the armed forces clearly went beyond their political role, as the massive weapons purchases indicate.

Peru's arms purchases during the Belaúnde administration approached, in dollar value, those of the Docenio. The expensive focus of these purchases was the highly sophisticated Mirage-2000 interceptors bought from France in December, 1983. Bought at a very high rate of interest, compared to the Soviet weapons purchases of the Docenio, the Mirage sales were made amid circumstances strikingly similar to those of Belaúnde's first administration. The Mirage 2000s were bought after Peru was denied less expensive General Dynamics F-16 fighters by Washington in early 1983. With the Mirage sales and other purchases of Soviet Mi-24 Hind helicopters for the air force, in addition to large quantities of automatic rifles and night vision equipment for the army, the military and police share of the budget reached nearly 30 percent, almost twice the publicly announced figure.[84] Pressure on the Belaúnde government by the military to make additional weapons expenditures continued during 1984 as the air force sought to replace fourteen Mirage jets reportedly loaned to Argentina during the 1982 Falklands/Malvinas War. The army also wanted to acquire spare parts for eighty T-55 Soviet tanks idled by Moscow's refusal to service these weapons until further payment was made on Peru's one billion-dollar arms debt.[85]

Critics of these arms purchases argued the expenditures were exacerbating Peru's international credit problems and were only marginally responsive to Peru's primary national security threat: Sendero Luminoso's escalating campaign of violence. Few mentioned, however, that Peru's main police agency, the Guardia Civil, which had assumed the primary role of combating Sendero Luminoso until late 1983, was virtually ignored by the Belaúnde administration. By 1985, Peru's police, among the most poorly paid in Latin America, had seen 175 of their ranks assassinated by Sendero gunmen.[86] Poor pay and the threat from Sendero Luminoso were only two of the many problems confronting Peru's corrupt and faction-ridden police agencies. When the APRA candidate, Alan García, prevailed over Alfonso Barrantes, a member of Izquierda Unida and the candidate of a divided Acción Popular in the 1985 presidential elections, García redirected the government's attention away from the armed forces to focus more on Peru's beleaguered police units.

The thirty-six-year-old Alan García assumed the presidency in July, 1985 amid renewed optimism that the charismatic APRA leader would bring new energy and ideas to the struggle against terrorism and chronic economic problems. Handpicked by Haya de la Torre to head a group of twelve promising young party members, García and the "Bureau of Conjunctions," as the group was called, became the bridge between APRA's Old Guard and its youth movement. Upon completing advanced studies in Paris and Spain, García was named national secretary of party organization and, by 1982, became the badly divided party's compromise choice for APRA's secretary-general.[87] During his 1985 presidential campaign, García projected a moderate, moralistic image, rejecting the party's traditional slogan, "Only APRA Can Save Peru," for his own promise to be "President of all Peruvians."

García's election in May, 1985 brought the first *Aprista* to the Pizarro Palace in the party's history and was achieved without significant armed forces' opposition. Morales Bermúdez's agreement with APRA and the military's preference for the seemingly more moderate García over the Marxist candidate of *Izquierda Unida*, Alfonso Barrantes, explain the armed forces' tolerance of García's electoral victory after more than a half century of opposition. Moreover, García's early foreign policy pronouncements pointed to a sharp break with Belaúnde's low-profile, pro—United States posture and appealed to the nationalist sentiments of armed forces' leaders. Indeed, when García announced, soon after taking office in July, 1985, that he would limit Peru's foreign debt payments to 10 percent of the country's export earnings and then began reactivating Peru's involvement in the Non-Aligned Movement, he was returning to the basic outlines of the Velasco regime's foreign policy. In September, 1985, García's foreign minister, Allan Wagner, at a Non-Aligned Movement meeting in Angola, emphasized Peru's need to stress "non-alliance with the international centers of power," similar to Velasco's "Third Position" during the 1970s.[88]

From another perspective, García's foreign policy, stressing anti-imperialism and confrontation over the debt issue, amounted to a return to APRA's anti-imperialist doctrinal roots. Announced with great fanfare, with speeches at the United Nations and at the inauguration of the *Sandinista* Constitution in Nicaragua, García proclaimed to a Managuan audience in January, 1987, in words reminiscent of the young Haya de la Torre, that he had come "to take in my hands together with you the anti-imperialism banner, which is the banner of all our continent."[89] Besides cultivating his own international image, García clearly hoped his stance on the debt issue and anti-imperialism would bond the still-weakened APRA-party structure more firmly together. Anti-imperialism had served this function for the beleaguered APRA until World War II, but, like most of García's programs, within two years of his inauguration, his foreign policy was floundering badly.

Through March, 1987 García's economic programs produced an artificial prosperity, resulting in an 8.5 percent GNP growth rate for 1986 (the highest in Latin America). Near-record economic growth was occurring, however, as Peru's economy confronted triple-digit inflation and the increasingly troubling question of the nation's isolation from international credit sources. Within six months, the "economic bubble had burst," and García responded by initiating an effort to expropriate Peru's largest domestic commercial banks in October, 1987. This highly unpopular tactic set off an economic decline unprecedented in Peruvian history. In February, 1988 the García government was forced to dip into its gold reserves to meet its financial obligations. By June, 1990 Peru still had not resolved the rescheduling of payments on its seventeen billion-dollar foreign debt, and inflation, by some estimates, had reached a cumulative 1 million percent during García's five years as president.[90] This economic crisis devastated all sectors of the economy, but, unlike the Belaúnde administration, the military did not remain immune from the country's economic travails.

Risking his early understanding with the armed forces, García broke with Belaúnde's nearly "blank check" approach to the military's arms purchases and cut by half the Belaúnde administration's purchase of twenty-six Mirage-2000 fighters in September, 1985.[91] This decision set the air force against García, who successfully thwarted a *coup* attempt by one of its commanders, General Luis Abram Cavallerino, in April, 1987. Abram Cavallerino's abortive effort to overthrow García was briefly supported by other senior air force officers who served the air base at Las Palmas. While the other services aided García in isolating the Abram Cavallerino movement, their commanders expressed discontent with the president's economic policies and, particularly, with the creation of a single Ministry of Defense in April, 1987.[92] Not since the creation of the *Comando Conjunto* (joint command) in 1957 had there been a further attempt to consolidate the armed forces' high command. As armed forces' factionalism during the Velasco administration indicated, the *Comando Conjunto* was a very fragile, consultative body. The three armed services still maintained their individual political influence through their respective ministers in the cabinet, and they correctly viewed García's attempt to appoint a single minister of defense to represent their combined interests as a measure designed to reduce their collective political role in his civilian government. The fact that the position of minister of defense could be held by a civilian further threatened armed forces' autonomy.

García's program to consolidate and reform Peru's police agencies generated further ill will within the armed forces. The cornerstone of his police reform was the Organic Law of the Police Forces, passed in February, 1986, providing for the eventual unification of Peru's main police agencies, the *Guardia Civil*, *Guardia Republicana*, and *Policía de Investigaciones del Perú* (Peruvian Investigative Police, Peru's FBI), into a single national police force. Wracked by corruption, poor discipline, and widespread criminal activity, Peru's police agencies were badly in need of reform measures. By mid-1987, more than eighteen hundred policemen had been purged from the ranks by the García administration and charged with a variety of infractions. A new unified police academy was proposed, commands of the three police agencies were combined, and new weapons

for the police were purchased from North Korea. These reforms prompted
the fired commander of the *Guardia Civil* to accuse the García administration of trying to "create a police force docile to the party."[93] Police
resistance to García's measure culminated in a two-day *Guardia Civil* strike
in May, 1987, forcing army and navy units to maintain order. Perhaps
remembering the damage to the Velasco regime prompted by the bloody
suppression of the February, 1975 police strike, García ordered the armed
forces units to exercise restraint against the striking members of the
Guardia Civil. The use of navy and army units as a temporary constabu-
lary and subsequent major salary increases for the police and other
concessions further increased armed forces' resentment against the García
government.[94] The police reform was viewed by the military as an attempt
by the president to build a loyal political base within the national police
agencies.   Significantly, García's police programs were the first major
initiatives to reform these agencies since President Augusto Leguía's
contracting of a Spanish *Guardia Civil* mission in the early 1920s (see
Chapter 1). Leguía's efforts provoked armed forces' opposition then, and
García's policies were arousing the same response as his administration
came to a close.

García's escalating problems with the armed forces and police occurred
in the context of his government's increasingly unsuccessful campaign
against terrorism. By the late 1980s, two guerrilla movements, *Sendero
Luminoso* and the *Movimiento Revolucionario Túpac Amaru* (Túpac Amaru
Revolutionary Movement, MRTA), had plunged Peru into civil war.
MRTA, primarily an urban-based terrorist group with ties to communist
Cuba and the M-19 movement of Colombia, was clearly overshadowed by
Senderista revolutionary activity throughout Peru. The scope of this study
will not permit a detailed analysis of MRTA's operations during the past
decade. On the other hand, a basic understanding of Peru's present crisis
requires a discussion of *Sendero Luminoso* and the military's response to its
declared "fifty-year war" against the Peruvian state.

One must try to understand the *Partido Comunista del Perú en el Sendero
Luminoso de José Carlos Mariátegui* (Peruvian Communist Party in the
Shining Path of José Carlos Mariátegui, its official name) in the historical
context of Andean resistance movements since the Spanish conquest.[95]
Only the widespread revolt of Túpac Amaru II, in the early 1780s, can
compare with the scale of *Sendero Luminoso*'s military campaign two
centuries later. By mid-1980, *Senderistas* were operating in all of Peru's
administrative departments, and their military columns dominated *sierra*
and *selva* provinces, containing nearly half of the nation's population.
Sendero Luminoso's self-styled "people's war" has cost a minimum of

seventeen thousand lives and at least twelve billion dollars in property damage and brought an already badly faltering economy to the point of collapse.[96] Like no other previous resistance movement, *Sendero Luminoso* has successfully exploited the glaring vulnerabilities of Peruvian society to its revolutionary advantage. The ignorance and neglect of Peru's poorest *sierra* provinces by the nation's modern coastal sector, the cultural dualism of a long-divided social fabric, and, most of all, the lack of hope of young Peruvians for a better future have fueled *Sendero Luminoso's* unprecedented success during the past decade. *Sendero Luminoso* is no longer a rural-based guerrilla movement attacking isolated *Guardia Civil* outposts, as it appeared to be in the early 1980s. Now it is a fundamental reality of Peruvian society with no foreseeable end to the war *Senderistas* initiated when they burned ballot boxes in the small Andean market town of Chuschi on 17 May 1980.

With its messiah-like leader, its secretive and rigidly disciplined organization, and its single-minded conviction that only *Sendero Luminoso* can save Peru, this revolutionary front mirrors these aspects of the early APRA. *Sendero Luminoso* is often referred to as Maoist, but this description does not accurately reflect its complex ideological orientation. The founder and presently unquestioned leader of *Sendero Luminoso*, Abimael Guzmán Reynoso, declares that his movement is an amalgam of the socialist communal teachings of José Carlos Mariátegui, the basic precepts of Marxism-Leninism, the guiding theoretical and tactical doctrines of Mao Zedong, and his own reinterpretation of these principles as applied to contemporary Peruvian reality.[97] Significantly, although his followers are seeking to enhance the cult of leadership surrounding their Presidente Gonzalo (his nom de guerre) with the Quechua reference to Guzmán as *Puka Inti* (Red Sun), in his only published interview, in July, 1988, he made few references to Andean traditions as a component of his revolutionary philosophy. Moreover, Guzmán reserved as much praise for the "great Marxist" Josef Stalin as he did for the seeming ideological inspiration for *Sendero Luminoso*, Mariátegui.[98] A brief look at Guzmán and the evolution of *Sendero Luminoso* prior to 1980 will help clarify the complex ideological orientation of *Sendero* and place its present "people's war" in clearer perspective.

The original Peruvian Communist Party (PCP) was founded in 1930 by Eudocio Ravines and some of the same individuals who aided José Carlos Mariátegui to form the Peruvian Socialist Party (PSP) two years earlier. Mariátegui's premature death in 1930 left the PCP without a dynamic leader, and it suffered a number of doctrinal crises throughout the next four decades as it also faced repression from most Peruvian governments.

Sendero Luminoso's beginnings can be traced to 1964, when the Sino-Soviet rivalry prompted the pro-Chinese faction of the PCP to break with the pro-Soviet majority wing and form PCP—*Bandera Roja* (Red Flag). *Bandera Roja* favored the continual commitment to the armed struggle, while the pro-Soviet faction, led by Jorge del Prado, accepted Moscow's party line and abandoned revolutionary violence. In the midst of this national party struggle, Abimael Guzmán, then a philosophy professor at the University of San Cristóbal de Huamanga in Ayacucho, embraced *Bandera Roja* and used his position as secretary of the Regional Committee of the splinter faction in Ayacucho to become the second-ranking member of the party.[99]

Born out of wedlock in the southern city of Mollendo in 1934, Guzmán was sent to Arequipa at fourteen for a Catholic high school education. Described as a "priest's dream" by a former classmate, Guzmán nevertheless later recalled how the 1948 Callao revolt and the 1950 Arequipa uprising against the Odría dictatorship profoundly influenced his social consciousness. At the Universidad San Agustín in Arequipa, Guzmán earned simultaneous degrees in philosophy and law; he completed his philosophy thesis, *Acerca de la teoría kantiana del espacio* (About the Kantian Theory of Space), in January, 1961 and his Bachelor of Law thesis, *El estado democrático-burgués* (The Bourgeois-Democratic State), later that same year. His intellectual mentor at San Agustín, Dr. Miguel Angel Rodríguez Rivas, described him as "a theorist of the highest level."[100] Already a member of the Communist Party at the university in Arequipa, Guzmán brought his well-defined Marxist views to San Cristóbal de Huamanga when he joined the philosophy faculty of the recently reopened university in 1962. A former member of the anthropology faculty at San Cristóbal de Huamanga and a close friend of Guzmán's wife, Augusta La Torre, recalls that he arrived at a time when Marxist discussion groups were already active at the university. This former colleague knew him as an intellectual with a charisma that soon attracted a loyal student following.[101]

During the early 1960s, Guzmán began to dominate the university discussion groups, which then included students, professors, and local residents of Ayacucho. At these meetings, Guzmán and his growing following preached a revolutionary restructuring of Peruvian society while claiming with conviction that they could "redeem" Peru.[102] Guzmán acted on his convictions and organized party cells and peasant land invasions in the Ayacucho region, while he also traveled twice to China for extended military and political training. The revolutionary's visits to China shaped his views on the nature of the armed struggle and supplied him with practical training in organizational techniques, tactics, and the use of explosives.[103]   After returning from China in 1965, he confronted a factionalized *Bandera Roja*, which soon split into four competing groups. Guzmán, after gaining control of San Cristóbal de Huamanga in university elections, and using as its base the school of education and high school extension programs operating in the departments of Ayacucho, Huancavelica, and Apurímac, formed the *Partido Comunista del Perú en el Sendero Luminoso de Mariátegui* in February, 1970. The declared leader of *Sendero Luminoso*'s political position was soon strengthened when he was named personnel director of San Cristóbal de Huamanga, giving him control over hiring for an institution of fifteen thousand students, 70 to 75 percent of whom were of Indian origin.[104]

Throughout the 1970s, *Sendero Luminoso*, through careful planning and organizing, created the party's cell structure and developed its "generated organisms" (groups separate from the party but allied with its general principles). These "generated organisms" included students' and women's groups, trade unions, teachers, and the *Movimiento de Campesinos Pobres* (Movement of Poor Peasants, MCP). According to *Sendero Luminoso*, these organizations were created as part of a "broad mobilization to get deep into the heart of the masses, to agitate, to open the party and help prepare for the beginning of the people's war." After nearly two decades of organizational work, Guzmán chose May, 1980 to launch the "peoples' war" because the national elections held in May marked the imminent conclusion of the *Docenio*. This moment was opportune, according to Guzmán, because "with the military leaving after twelve years they could not readily undertake a struggle against us right away; nor could the military immediately retake the helm of State because they were politically exhausted and discredited."[105] With these calculations *Sendero Luminoso* began to apply the theories of Maoist revolution to warfare in the Peruvian *sierra*.

Like Mao Zedong's protracted revolutionary war in China, Guzmán envisioned *Sendero Luminoso*'s campaign in Peru to require as long as fifty years. Reinterpreting the Chinese leaders' three-stage strategy of extended revolutionary struggle, *Sendero Luminoso* has announced a five-stage formula for the "peoples' war." Originating in the *sierra* and spreading throughout highland Peru, the "peoples' war" would eventually surround and "strangle" the cities. The timetable would include (1) agitation and armed propaganda, (2) sabotage against Peru's socioeconomic system, (3) the generalization of the peoples' war, 4) the conquest and expansion of the revolution's support base and the strengthening of the guerrilla army, and (5) general civil war, the siege of the cities, and the final collapse of state power.[106] By 1990, *Sendero Luminoso* announced it had achieved the fourth phase of its revolutionary program, and its own assessment appeared to be accurate.

From a tactical perspective *Sendero Luminoso's* success has been achieved through careful preparation and intelligence, cautious recruitment practices, and secure internal cell structure, which has so far thwarted efforts at widespread penetration by the military's intelligence services. *Sendero Luminoso* rarely initiates operations in an area without a protracted presence and intelligence gathering by its operatives. An exception was the guerrilla group's initial campaign in the Puno region in the mid-1980s where the independent Aymara people resisted *Sendero Luminoso's* penetration and helped the military locate and destroy key *Senderista* columns. *Sendero Luminoso* has since returned to the Puno area after more rigorous preparation and recruitment.[107]

Sendero Luminoso attracts its recruits from the increasingly large body of unemployed, the dispossessed *sierra* population, university and high school students, and since 1986, from the ranks of organized labor. The actual process of integrating a recruit into *Sendero's* permanent rank and file may take as long as three years, with the potential *Senderista* generally required to complete a series of progressively difficult and dangerous tasks designed to test his or her loyalty and commitment to the cause. In urban areas, recruitment is generally finalized when the aspiring revolutionary kills a policeman and returns with his weapon. In the *sierra*, young recruits often are initiated after slaying a captured member of the local *rondas campesinas* (peasant defense brigade), either by decapitation or stoning.[108] *Sendero Luminoso* has made a consistent practice of recruiting very young members for its ranks. Peruvian marines have captured *Senderistas* as young as eight years old. Women also compose a significant portion of the organization's membership. These recruiting practices have a decided advantage for *Sendero Luminoso*. Young recruits are often impressionable and eager for adventure in their otherwise despairing lives. *Sendero Luminoso* provides a means of venting their frustration and anger against conditions they feel are overwhelming them. Membership soon bonds these preteens and teenagers to the revolutionary cause well into adulthood. According to *Sendero Luminoso*, children, as the "orphans of the Revolution," must be encouraged to fight in the "people's war." Teens and preteens, with few political convictions, are reportedly being "educated" in special camps in order to be made aware of the teachings of Presidente Gonzalo and to educate others.[109] As a CAEM staff member noted recently, *Sendero Luminoso* recruitment of the very young also has frustrated the military's attempt to infiltrate the organization. "The Intelligence Service simply doesn't employ young teenagers," he concluded, acknowledging the

obvious.[110]   The enlisting of women produces the same benefits while
broadening the base of the organization.   Young female *Senderistas* have
also reportedly been used to infiltrate military households as domestic
servants to gather information prior to the assassination of high-ranking
armed forces' officers.

Clearly learning from the mistakes of the 1965 guerrilla campaign,
Sendero Luminoso's active membership is organized through a highly
secretive and so far reasonably secure cell structure.   Originally numbering
about two hundred cells in 1981, the organization clearly contained many
more by the end of the decade.   Generally numbering only five members,
each cell has a *responsable político* (political officer), who may have been
trained in China, North Korea, or Cuba in tactics and the use of
explosives.   Other cell members are charged with logistic, physical fitness,
self-defense training, "political education," and basic medical care.
Communication with other cells is done only through the commander to
maintain internal security.[111]   This procedure has proven highly effective
in preventing the infiltration of *Sendero Luminoso* but has also impeded
large-scale operations and easy vertical communication from the organization's command.   The commanders apparently feel this cell structure can
be modified only when military conditions permit full-scale operations.

Adhering to its five-stage revolutionary timetable, *Sendero Luminoso*
created the military arm of its revolutionary organization, the *Ejército
Guerrillero Popular* (Popular Guerrilla Army, EGP) in 1983.   While relying
on newly created *Bases de Apoyo* (Base of Support) established throughout
the southern *sierra* and western *selva* regions, *Sendero* gradually expanded
its operation after overcoming initial setbacks when the Peruvian army and
the marines entered the war in earnest in 1983.   The Belaúnde administration and the army's high command refused to acknowledge the severity of
Sendero Luminoso's threat in the central *sierra* prior to late 1982.   Mirroring
his early response to *MIR*'s 1965 guerrilla campaign, Belaúnde downplayed
Sendero Luminoso's rebellion in Ayacucho and left the antiguerrilla
campaign largely in the hands of the *Guardia Civil*'s brutally repressive
counterterrorism force known as the *Sinchis*.   After Peru's regular military
forces replaced the ineffectual *Sinchis*, they greatly increased the scale of
operations in the Ayacucho region, while at the same time attempting to
enlist the *rondas campesinas* against *Sendero Luminoso*.[112]   Initially, the
armed forces sought to parlay traditional village rivalries over water and
land disputes to swell the ranks of the *ronderos* and to encourage
anti—*Sendero soplones* (informers).   The military met with little success in
the central and southern *sierra*, and their campaign frequently resulted in
brutal reprisals by *Sendero Luminoso* against entire villages that had

cooperated with the armed forces. *Sendero Luminoso* has been more effective in exploiting these village rivalries and internal village animosities with its *juicios populares* (people's trial). After one such trial, eight unknown, hooded *Senderistas* executed two cattle thieves and publicly whipped three others during August, 1981, in the village plaza of Chuschi in the province of Cangallo in Ayacucho Department. Significantly, the cattle thieves were from a neighboring village, that had been feuding with Chuschinos since the sixteenth century over village boundaries.[113]

Sendero Luminoso's "moralization" program and popular anger against the military's antiterrorist campaign enabled the organization to withstand the armed forces' initial offensive in the period 1983-1984 and expand its operations throughout the central *sierra* and into Lima by 1985. One observer, familiar with conditions in the Ayacucho region at this time, claimed that the military's anti-*Sendero* campaign "had turned meek people into lions."[114] If one believes *Sendero Luminoso*'s own accounts, its EGP had grown to include fourteen thousand fighters, while its popular committees controlled 405 towns and villages by June, 1987.[115] This war had also spread to Lima with a vengeance during this same year, as *Sendero Luminoso*'s sabotage campaign caused numerous blackouts. Additionally, by May, 1986 *Senderistas*, through a Lima offensive involving bombings and selected assassinations of public officials, police, and high-ranking armed forces' officers, drove the military leadership to demand that President García declare Lima an emergency zone. Already exercising nearly total political autonomy over a dozen provinces in the central *sierra*, the military was clearly responding to increased labor strife and the assassination of Admiral Carlos Ponce Canessa in early May. The García administration rejected this request, which it claimed would mean "the virtual abdication of the democratic government."[116] This pressure on García may well explain, however, the administration's tacit approval of the violent suppression of *Senderista* insurrections in the Lurigancho and El Frontón prisons on 19 June 1986.[117] More than three hundred prisoners died during the military's operation against the prisons. Moreover, one of *Sendero Luminoso*'s leading strategists, Antonio Díaz Martínez, died in the suppression of the Lurigancho prison uprising. *Sendero Luminoso*'s activity in Lima was drastically scaled back after its worst tactical setback since the guerrilla organization was founded.

The prison massacres, MRTA's increased activity in Lima, and the increasing suffering of Lima's poor as a result of the deteriorating economy and the civil war may have also convinced *Sendero Luminoso* to reduce its military operations in Lima after 1986 in favor of more aggressive political organizing among trade union members and university students.

Sendero Luminoso's operations in highland Peru and in the coca-producing upper Huallaga Valley three hundred miles northeast of Lima, however, have accelerated.   By protecting Quechan-speaking coca-producing peasants, who migrated to the upper Huallaga Valley in the late 1960s and 1970s, against both the narco-traffickers' *sicarios* (hired gunmen) and the Peruvian government's antinarcotics campaign, *Sendero Luminoso* has assured itself a foothold in the valley and a substantial source of revenue.[118]   The presence of the United States government's Drug Enforcement Administration (DEA) in the upper Huallaga Valley at Santa Lucia since 1988 has not disrupted *Sendero Luminoso's* modus vivendi with Peru's drug traffickers.   Moreover, the Bush Administration's thirty-five million-dollar program, announced in May, 1990 to aid the military's operations in the upper Huallaga Valley, has since been rejected by the Fujimori administration.[119]

Now, after more than ten years of civil war and nearly two decades of *Sendero Luminoso's* organizational activity, it is still not precisely clear to what degree the organization has attracted a peasant base.   Clearly, conditions in the Ayacucho region throughout the *Docenio* provided fertile ground for *Senderista* organizers.   Cynthia McClintock notes the drastic decline in living standards of the Ayacucho peasantry throughout the 1970s and early 1980s despite the national agrarian reform program, which barely touched this poverty-stricken region.[120]   Expectations were raised by the Velasco regime's rhetoric and then dashed by the government's neglect of Ayacucho. The situation was made even worse by the Belaúnde policy of maintaining low prices for agricultural products, which affected Ayacucho's limited market economy in an especially devastating way. As previously stated, the armed forces' campaign against *Sendero Luminoso* has unquestionably driven young Indian peasants into the terrorist group in significant numbers. Yet the question remains: Does *Sendero Luminoso's* image of a Maoist state, tailored to Peruvian realities, conform to the cultural outlook of the Quechua and Aymara people of highland Peru? Carlos Íван Degregori, one of the Peru's leading authorities on *Sendero Luminoso*, rejects the peasant link and argues that *Sendero Luminoso* is primarily a movement of intellectuals and "young people without hope."[121] Evidence gathered by a United States anthropologist in the Chuschi region during the mid-1980s seems to support this view. Commenting on *Sendero Luminoso's* attempt to impose a structure for communal planting based on localized residential barrios in 1982, the anthropologist concluded that the effort failed miserably. Noting that *Senderistas* were apparently ignorant of the complex network of reciprocity, kinship, and moiety structures in the village governing agricultural production for centuries, the scholar concluded *Sendero Luminoso* was as ill informed as Velasco's agrarian reform planners during the previous decade.[122]

Sendero Luminoso has appealed to the Andean mythology and the tradition of resistance dating from the pan-Andean *Taki Ongoy* movement of the 1560s. But will the complex and dynamic reciprocal relationships of Andean peasant societies accommodate the Marxist/Maoist dogma of *Sendero Luminoso?* The terrorist group's operations and resulting military repression left the Chuschinos, in the words of one resident, "between the sword and the wall." By 1983, the people of Chuschi requested that a *Guardia Civil* post be established in their village for the first time.[123] The experience of the *Chuschinos* may tell us something about the future of *Sendero Luminoso*'s campaign to win over the peasantry, but Peru's civil war has witnessed violent retaliation against entire villages and the forced relocation of others by the armed forces. It is on the military campaign against *Sendero Luminoso* that the issue of peasant participation may very well rest.

After more than a decade of conflict with *Sendero Luminoso*, the Peruvian armed forces have not yet demonstrated a capability of defeating the insurgency. Some within the armed forces' leadership argue that restraints imposed upon them by the García administration, in particular, have impeded the war effort. Uncertainty over the incoming García government's policy toward the armed forces' operations in Ayacucho, for example, did force the marine units to reduce their patrols by more than 50 percent in early 1985.[124] Armed forces' commanders in the emergency zones, however, do exercise extraordinary latitude in conducting their operations. Constitutional guarantees are suspended in the zones, and press coverage of the military operations is severely restricted. The many reports of human rights violations by the police and the armed forces since the war began in 1980 have been only partially investigated by international agencies. Abuse of the local population has unquestionably aided recruitment by *Sendero Luminoso* and undermined the willingness of the *sierra* population to assist the military in the war effort.[125] General (R) Edgardo Mercado Jarrín addressed this very issue when he sharply criticized the military campaign in a June, 1983 BBC broadcast, declaring that the Belaúnde administration had not sought a dialogue with *Sendero Luminoso* as it should have. Mercado Jarrín charged that the armed forces were being employed as "agents of repression" in the war effort, without any accompanying "positive action" in the emergency zones. The former commander of the armed forces during the Velasco government stressed the importance of "respecting human rights" and warned against the "Argentinization" of the war effort.[126] Ironically, the army's commander in the Ayacucho region fully appreciated Mercado Jarrín's criticism and the fundamental reality of the war against *Sendero Luminoso*. After a year in Ayacucho, General Adrian Huaman Centeno concluded:

Here the solution is not military, because if it had been military, I would have resolved it in minutes. If it were a question of destroying Ayacucho, it would not have existed for half an hour. . . . But that is not the answer. What is happening is that we are talking about human beings from the forgotten *pueblos* who have been crying out for 160 years and no one has paid any attention to them. Now we are reaping the result.[127]

As of late 1990, the human rights problem in Peru had not improved. A report issued by Peru's National Coordinator of Human Rights concluded "Violations of human rights in Peru are a permanent and systematic practice." Soldiers and marines confronted by an elusive and highly dangerous enemy are clearly acting out of frustration in a war which has no rules. But the issue of whether human rights abuses are a result of the armed forces' leadership's decision to "Argentinize" the war or rather are the results of poorly disciplined regional commanders acting on their own is not clear. What is becoming increasingly evident is that a tour of duty combating *Sendero Luminoso* is not career enhancing. The war against this sinister enemy is still not a top priority in the Peruvian military's national defense perspective.[128]

That the defeat of the *Sendero Luminoso* insurgency has primarily a social, not a military, solution is clearly recognized by veterans of the Ayacucho campaign in other branches of the armed forces. Yet military officers holding such views run the risk of being ostracized for their social consciousness. Since the high-profile social activism of the Velasco years and its diversive impact upon armed forces' unity, there has emerged a backlash against armed forces' officers who voice similar progressive views. They are now seen as politically ambitious by their colleagues and as threatening by civilian politicians.

In another profoundly significant sense, there now exists a strategic reaction to the comprehensive "national defense" activism of the Velasco years. Since the increasing border tensions with Chile and, particularly, since the Cordillera del Condor conflict with Ecuador in early 1981, a "border defense mentality" has pervaded the Peruvian army. In large measure, the armed forces delayed nearly three years before committing their forces in significant numbers to the Ayacucho emergency zone because of the perceived "threat" from Ecuador and Chile. At the end of the past decade, 60 to 70 percent of the military's deployable combat capability was located on or near the northern and southern frontiers.[129]

What is more, the vast majority of the weapons purchased during the Belaúnde administration had no relation to the escalating conflict with *Sendero Luminoso*. As late as September, 1989, a United States military officer, long familiar with the Peruvian military, stated that Peru's armed forces had only begun fully to recognize and respond to *Sendero Luminoso* as the nation's primary security threat.[130] The army's journal literature of the 1980s reflects this change in mentality. Formerly rich in discussions of countersubversive strategy and "nation-building" theory in the 1960s and early 1970s, Peru's army journals, now published only intermittently because of budget restraints, have surprisingly few articles of this type. No substantive discussions of *Sendero Luminoso* are evident. One article in particular, published in the army's journal, *Actualidad Militar*, in February, 1988 epitomized the army's border defense mentality. Entitled "Fuerte Arica: Un bastión de seguridad" (Fortress Arica: A Bastion of Security), the article featured a picture of a Soviet T-55 tank and its crew with the caption "Guarding the territorial integrity of our country."[131] Nearly half a century after the last French soldiers departed Peruvian soil, the "Maginot line mentality," bolstered by continued border tensions with Chile and Ecuador, seems to pervade the thinking of Peru's contemporary army commanders. Whether this attitude is really a legacy of the war of the Pacific and French military training, or is better explained as a narrowing of the military's perceived national defense mission since the Velasco years will be determined only by the future conduct of the war against *Sendero Luminoso*.

From 1983 onward, the Peruvian army looked not to its French traditions for a counterinsurgency strategy against *Sendero Luminoso* but rather to the United States army's "strategic hamlet" campaign plan employed in Vietnam. Despite the criticism of the United States army's Indochina campaign in the 1960s, the Peruvian armed forces seem to be following a similar strategy.[132] This policy, coupled with the establishment of regional detention centers, has exacerbated rural poverty and enabled *Sendero Luminoso* to exploit the resulting socioeconomic dislocation to its advantage. Such a strategy was effectively utilized by the British army in fighting Malaysian guerrillas during the 1950s. A highly developed "intelligence apparatus" was a critical component of the British army's overall countersubversive operation. Self-sustaining small-unit operations also served the British well in their campaign.

Perhaps the greatest single failure of the armed forces' campaign against *Sendero Luminoso* is the inadequacy of its military intelligence. The very existence of *Sendero Luminoso*, according to a CAEM staff member in May, 1990, is evidence of the inadequacy of military intelligence agencies during the *Docenio*.[133] Yet ten years after *Sendero Luminoso* began its "people's war," the armed forces are reluctant to share intelligence information, and intelligence data are not systematically circulated within the army regarding *Sendero Luminoso* operations. Army intelligence reports of engagements with *Senderistas* are often generalized to the point of being of marginal value.[134] The decline of Peruvian military intelligence since the mid-1960s may well be due to a de-emphasis on the role of the intelligence services within the military command structure. The inordinate influence of the army intelligence service within Velasco's inner circle of advisers is widely known to have caused long-lasting resentments after the his regime ended. Exacerbating the intelligence problem is the Peruvian army's lack of experience in small-unit operations. Army patrols have not been able to maintain operations for extended periods away from their well-fortified base camps. This problem has limited their effectiveness in engaging *Sendero Luminoso* columns and allowed *Senderistas* to retain control of the countryside.

Just as *Sendero Luminoso* has exploited the vulnerabilities of Peruvian society, it has also starkly exposed the weaknesses of the nation's armed forces. The military appears most vulnerable among the rank and file. A lack of data and accessibility to enlisted personnel hinders efforts to examine such issues as the impact of military service, the relations between officers and the Indian rank and file, and the attitudes of active enlisted personnel regarding military service. It is clear that the army's methods of acquiring soldiers has changed little in the past five decades. Males, eighteen years old and above, are subject to two years of military service. They are often "drafted" when army units roll into *sierra* villages, check the identity papers of the community's young men, and drive away with the required quota of recruits. During the Velasco era, starting salaries for army recruits were attracting *sierra* Indians to army service. The García years, however, have witnessed a drastic decline in the quality of life for the army's foot soldiers. The army is now having difficulty feeding, clothing, and providing medical care for its soldiers. It also confronts the increasing threat of *Sendero Luminoso*'s infiltration of the enlisted ranks. APRA's success in subverting enlisted men from the early 1930s to the 1948 Callao revolt has already been emulated on a smaller scale by *Sendero Luminoso*. In 1987, a *Senderista* cell within the army assassinated a ranking officer in Huancayo.[135] How much progress *Sendero Luminoso* has made in winning over army troops is open to speculation. It is clear that *Sendero Luminoso*'s control of many *sierra* provinces will make army recruiting extremely difficult in the immediate future. Even greater problems impeding the army's effort against *Sendero Luminoso* are the language barrier between Spanish-speaking officers and their Quechua foot soldiers and the lack of a well-trained noncommissioned officer class to train army recruits. A core of career noncommissioned officers could provide more stability and, perhaps, temper the often harsh discipline of army officers.[136] The Peruvian army's fifty-two thousand conscripts, many of them Indians or residents of Lima's expanding *pueblos jóvenes*, will determine the future of the military's effort to defeat *Sendero Luminoso*. How military service affects the political attitudes and social status of the army's draftees will also be a crucial issue for Peru's future.

Only two studies, both now more than twenty years old, have addressed the question of the impact of military service on army draftees. Luigi Einaudi in the mid-1960s and David Scott Palmer in 1969 made some preliminary conclusions on the issue of military service and army veterans' attitudes. Einaudi, while stating that the "effect of modern military service is virtually impossible to judge," did note that army service offered the Indian literacy training and the opportunity to learn Spanish and, in some cases, provided useful technical skills. Einaudi also concluded that there is "evidence to suggest that Indian peasants who serve in the army do in significant numbers cease to be peasants."[137] Palmer, citing a survey of 825 men (144 of whom had military service) residing in eighteen Peruvian communities in 1967, concluded that military service heightened their political awareness and participation. This conclusion was especially true if they were drafted from less developed and more traditional Indian communities. The survey also concluded, although less emphatically, that army service tended to affect their socioeconomic status positively.[138]

Anecdotal evidence gathered by the author of this study is more mixed. A marine officer who served in the Ayacucho region in the mid-1980s commented on the significant number of army veterans holding leadership positions in the villages in his zone of operations.[139] On the other hand, a Maryknoll priest with more than a decade of service near Puno during the 1980s downplayed the benefits of military service for local veterans. In stark contrast to Edgardo Mercado Jarrín's claim in a 1960s article that army service produced "permanent vehicles for Peru's modernization," the priest saw few veterans returning with technical skills. He also commented that, if anything, military service seemed to teach the previously hardworking peasants "how to be lazy."[140]

On the question of relations between officers and enlisted men, data are also very limited. One young naval officer with experience in the United States navy did concede that the social gulf between officers and the ranks was wide. Interviewed in May, 1990, the naval officer claimed it was possible for officers and enlisted men to develop friendships in the United

States navy, but not in its Peruvian counterpart.[141] Another more senior member of the naval officer corps acknowledged that Peru needed to develop a system that encouraged career-oriented recruits.   Noting Argentina's unhappy experience with its newly drafted foot soldiers in the Falklands/Malvinas War, he declared Peru must improve pay and service conditions to retain talented personnel.[142]

This dilemma and the armed forces' other problems must be resolved in the midst of the military's worst crisis since the War of the Pacific. A naval officer candidly admitted that as the García administration drew to a close, his institution was "at the breaking point" as a result of the service budget restraints prompted by Peru's devastated economy.[143]   These conditions sparked the inevitable speculation about a *coup d'état*, but armed forces' leaders are aware of the consequences of ending the longest, continuous period of genuine democratic government in Peru's history. They are also reluctant to risk the internal factionalism a military government would surely stimulate in an already beleaguered military establishment. Just as important, insightful military leaders are aware that *Sendero Luminoso* welcomes a military dictatorship and widespread repression to, in the words of Abimael Guzmán, "irrigate the revolution" with the blood of its victims. Yet, as two scholars have recently argued, Peru is a democracy without peace, a society that is immersed in diffuse violence. Héctor Béjar, veteran of the failed 1965 guerrilla offensive, offers a chilling description of Peru's present state of cultural violence:

Certainly those in the armed struggle know why they are fighting, but I doubt if they know for what. . . . What we have today is a confusing mix of guerrilla fighting, sabotage and terrorism, propaganda and intimidation, clean fighting and dirty war, revolution and vengeance, over social resentment.[144]

With these conditions, it is very difficult to predict what lies ahead for the armed forces and the Peruvian people. Nonetheless, some conclusions regarding the Peruvian armed forces of today can be made. The search for a clearly defined national mission, seemingly embodied in the Velasco government's reforms, must now continue. The army has turned away from the comprehensive national defense doctrine underpinning the structural changes of the Velasco years in favor of a more narrowly defined and traditional border defense mission. Partly as a reaction to the intense military factionalism of the *Docenio*, but also as a reflection of a lessened confidence in their own abilities to resolve Peru's fundamental problems, the armed forces were reluctant to engage the *Sendero Luminoso* insurgency for nearly three years after it began. This situation contrasts directly with the immediate response to the far less threatening 1965 guerrilla operation during the first Belaúnde administration.

From another perspective, the army's own self-identity may have become even more muddled since the mid-1970s. The severing of its formal ties with the United States military establishment and the initiation of its technical and training liaison with the Soviet Union add yet another layer on the eclectic mix of military ideologies shaping the mentality of Peru's army officers. In succeeding generations of army leaders since the 1940s, the army has been trained by French, United States, and Soviet officers. Like the complex mix of United States, Soviet, and French equipment, which is often difficult to repair and mobilize, the army officer corps itself may soon have a greater difficulty in standardizing its thinking about a future mission. One ramification of Soviet influence in the army is now clear; it has intensified already-pronounced differences with the navy.

Even with these problems, there are, nevertheless, reasons for hope. Unlike any other military establishment in Latin America, elements of the Peruvian armed forces have demonstrated an ability to recognize and resolve the nation's fundamental social problems. While the Argentine, Brazilian, and Chilean military establishments rejected social reform in favor of repression in the post-World War II era, the Peruvian military enacted a program of change comparable in scope only to the revolutionary agendas of Mexico, Cuba, and Nicaragua. The lack of success of the Velasco regime testifies as much to the magnitude of the country's problems as it does to the military's inability to assist in resolving them. Many contemporary armed forces' officers are keenly sensitive to Peru's deep social divisions and the internal problems of their institutions. There is, for instance, an initiative to incorporate philosophy and ethics as a primary component of the curriculum at the naval war college.[145] And even the conservative Francisco Morales Bermúdez insists that the armed forces should maintain an active social role during this new decade.[146] The armed forces, particularly the army, are still widely regarded as one of the main avenues of social mobility in Peruvian society. A visitor to the army's academy at Chorrillos will be impressed today by the number of cadets of Indian origin in attendance. Even among the ranks of the more conservative and competitive naval officer corps, there are those who speak with admiration regarding the army's function as a socializing agency in Peruvian society.

Peru, now more than ever, needs a stable and progressive armed forces' establishment to defeat the Sendero Luminoso insurgency and help rebuild the nation's shattered infrastructure once the war is over. Not since 1879 has the Peruvian military faced as great a challenge as it confronts at present. If a negotiated settlement cannot be achieved, and this prospect does not appear immediately likely, then border conflicts with Chile and Ecuador must be resolved, and the extremely costly weapon systems, purchased since the 1970s, must be gradually "mothballed." Peru's present economic crisis has rendered many of these weapons nonserviceable, anyway. With a renewed emphasis on counterinsurgency, without the repression characterizing the first decade of the military's campaign against *Sendero Luminoso*, the armed forces may have a reasonable chance of defeating the insurgency.

The Fujimori government, during its first six months in office, has demonstrated a willingness to work more closely with the military in combating *Sendero Luminoso* and MRTA than the previous administration. In December, 1990, for example, President Fujimori proposed a law that would give military courts jurisdiction in prosecuting cases of terrorism. It is unmistakably clear, however, that the war can be waged only in the context of a more comprehensive effort to resolve the social ills that have fueled *Sendero Luminoso*'s rebellion for the past two decades. The armed forces do, indeed, still have both a military and social role to play if the Peruvian government and its military leaders will again recognize and act on these dual missions.

Many of the same challenges facing the Peruvian military in the 1990s confront the armed forces of other South American nations. Regional security must be sharply redefined in the aftermath of the Cold War and in view of limited economic means. Extremely expensive high-technology weapon systems cannot be purchased in sufficient numbers to guarantee national security against a formidable military foe without United States assistance. Argentina's experience in the Falklands/Malvinas War is clear evidence of this. Moreover, these sophisticated weapons systems can barely be maintained by troubled nations struggling to recover from the most economically damaging decade since the 1930s. The growing domestic arms-producing capability of Chile, Argentina, and especially Brazil can be oriented toward combating terrorism and supplying the Andean nations with the helicopters, light aircraft, and small arms necessary to confront their own internal security needs.

Equally important, the restoration of democratic governments through-out South America in the 1980s has not dramatically diminished the political role of the armed forces. The armies of Argentina, Brazil, and Chile are tenaciously guarding their control over institutional military concerns. Continued military unrest in Argentina and the defiant statement of Chile's former dictator and armed forces' commander General Augusto Pinochet in January, 1991 that "constitutionally, nobody can ask for my resignation" are clear indicators of this trend. The decision of Argentina's president Carlos Menem to pardon the military and police commanders sentenced to long prison terms for their roles in the "Dirty War" illustrates how desperately Menem is seeking to "make peace" with the nation's military.

Six decades have passed since the professional armed forces of Argentina, Brazil, Chile, and Peru emerged as powerful arbiters of their nations' destinies. Yet their missions and their constitutional mandate within a democracy still remain ill defined. Achieving a meaningful clarification of these roles will be the most important priority of Latin America's military establishments as this century draws to a close.

Peru's immediate future is as uncertain as that of any Latin American nation. But the resolve of its people in confronting and adapting to the challenges of their daily lives offers the greatest hope for the years ahead. Whether in Lima's teeming *pueblos jóvenes* or the harsh highland environments of the *sierra*, Peru's people are demonstrating a remarkable ability to cope. Villages in the Ayacucho region, abandoned during the early years in the war against *Sendero Luminoso*, are being repopulated. If Peru's leaders can tap the innate strength of their people in ways far more positive than they have in the past, then Peruvians will survive the present crisis and begin building the moral and material foundations for a better future.

NOTES

1. Confidential interview with a U.S. army officer, 10 September 1989, Washington, D.C.

2. Confidential interview with a Peruvian naval officer, 26 May 1990, Lima, Peru.

3. By the Peruvian government's count, *Sendero Luminoso*, between 1980 and 1988, destroyed 989 high-tension power transmission towers and 165 bridges in its campaign of sabotage. See Comisión Especial, Senado de la Republica, *Violencia y Pacificación*, Anexo 1, Julio de 1988, cited in Philip Mauceri, *Militares: Insurgencia y democratizacion en el Perú, 1980-1988* (Lima: 1989), p. 28.

4. Hernando De Soto, *The Other Path: The Invisible Revolution in the Third World* (New York: 1988), p. 197.

5. Stephen Gorman, *Post-Revolutionary Peru: The Politics of Transformation* (Boulder: 1982), pp. 1-32. The best analysis of the Velasco regime's programs is Abraham Lowenthal, ed., *The Peruvian Experiment: Continuity and Change under Military Rule* (Princeton: 1975). For a recent statistical analysis of the Velasco programs see Amílcar Vargas Gavilano, *La revolución de Velasco en cifras* (Lima: 1989).

The Unfulfilled Mission   291

6. These four individuals were interviewed in Lima during research visits to Peru in 1985 and 1990. Specific dates of each interview will be provided when the interviewee is cited in the text.

7. The North and Korovkin work is particularly useful since it is based on interviews with fifty-nine armed forces officers serving in the military government from 1968 to 1976. See Liisa North and Tanya Korovkin, *The Peruvian Revolution and the Officers in Power, 1967-1976* (Montreal: 1981). See also Dirk Kruijt, *La revolución por decreto* (Lima: 1988).

8. Personal interview with General (R) Francisco Morales Bermúdez Cerrutti, 29 May 1990, Lima, Peru. See also Francisco Morales Bermúdez Cerrutti, Apuntes sobre autoritarismo y democracia (Lima: 1989), pp. 275-283.

9. Questionnaire response from Vice Admiral (R) Luis Vargas Caballero, 13 May 1985, Lima, Peru.

10. Ibid.

11. Confidential interview with a Peruvian naval officer, 29 May 1990, Lima, Peru.

12. Personal interview with General (R) Edgardo Mercado Jarrín, 10 May 1985, Lima, Peru.

13. Maria del Pilar Tello, *Golpe o revolución: Hablan los militares del 68* (Lima: 1983), 1, pp. 120-124.

14. Ibid., p. 122.

15. Ibid.

16. George Philip, *The Rise and Fall of the Peruvian Military Radicals, 1968-1976* (London: 1978), pp. 78, 110-111.

17. Personal interview with General (R) Jorge Fernández Maldonado Solari, 29 May 1990, Lima, Peru.

18. "Velasco: Se Confiesa," *Caretas*, 3 February 1977, pp. 29-35.

19. Personal interview with Jeffrey L. Klaiber, S.J., 26 May 1990, Lima, Peru; Jeffrey Klaiber, *Religion and Revolution in Peru, 1824-1976* (Notre Dame: 1977), p. 178. While Fernández Maldonado was serving in the Velasco government, he wrote about the relationship of Christian democracy and the government's reforms in his article, "Fuerza armada, cristianismo y revolución en el Perú," *Participación*, Lima (August, 1973), pp. 4-13. In the dedication to his 1989 book, *Apuntes sobre autoritarismo*, Morales Bermúdez praises his early education at the Colegio de la Immaculada, where he claimed he "learned to become a man and a Christian."

20. CELAM (Consejo Episicipal Latinamericano), Documento Final de la Comisión, no. 1, Subcomité II, Sección III (Bogatá, Colombia, 1968), quoted in Alfred Stepan, *The State and Society: Peru in Comparative Perspective* (Princeton: 1978), p. 34.

21. Klaiber, *Religion and Revolution in Peru*, p. 176.

22. Philip, *The Rise and Fall of the Peruvian Military Radicals*, pp. 78-79; José Z. García, "The Velasco Coup in Peru: Causes and Policy Consequences," Ph.D. diss., University of New Mexico, 1974, passim.

23. Personal interviews with General Armando Llosa Alvarez, CAEM's subdirector; Rear Admiral Manuel Reyna, director of education and programs at CAEM; and Alberto E. Bolívar Ocampo, professor of geopolitics at the center, 30 May 1990, Chorrillos, Peru. For examples of contemporary doctrine see the CAEM's journal, *Defensa Nacional.* This journal has been published since 1981.

24. Howard Handelman, "Peasants, Landlords and Bureaucrats: The Politics of Agrarian Reform in Peru," *American Universities Field Staff Reports*, no. 1, 1981, p. 6.

25. Ibid., p. 13.

26. Ibid., p. 7; Peter Cleaves and Martin J. Scurrah, *Agriculture, Bureaucracy and Military Government in Peru* (Ithaca, New York: 1980), passim.; Anibal Quijano, "Nationalism and Capitalism in Peru," *Monthly Review*, 23, no. 3 (July-August, 1971), pp. 1-22.

27. Norman Gall, "The Master Is Dead," *Dissent*, 18 (1971), pp. 303-304. On the problems of the agrarian reform's implementation see Douglas Earl Horton, "Haciendas and Cooperatives: A Study of Estate Organization, Land Reform, and New Reform Enterprises in Peru," Ph.D. diss., Cornell University, 1976; Enrique Mayer and Marisol de la Cadena, *Cooperación y conflicto en la comunidad andina: Zonas de producción y organización social* (Lima: 1989).

28. Handelman, "Peasants," p. 16.

29. Telephone interview with Father Robert Hoffman, 22 June 1989. Father Hoffman did missionary work in the Puno region for more than a decade, beginning in the mid-1970s.

30. For a study of conflict and change in the Ayacucho region during the 1980s, see Billie Jean Isbell, "The Emerging Patterns of Peasants' Responses to *Sendero Luminoso*," Department of Anthropology, Cornell University, 1988.

31. Gall, "The Master Is Dead," p. 303.

32. Luis Pásara, "When the Military Dreams," in Cynthia McClintock and Abraham Lowenthal, eds., *The Peruvian Revolution Reconsidered* (Princeton: 1983), pp. 328-329; Carlos Delgado, *El proceso revolucionario Peruano: Testimonio de lucha* (Buenos Aires: 1972), pp. 43-46, 62-65. "Transmission belts" was the military's own term for social participatory agencies like SINAMOS.

33. Decree Law #18896 (22 June 1971), Article 2, quoted in David Scott Palmer, *Peru: The Authoritarian Tradition* (New York: 1980), p. 13.

34. Stepan, *The State and Society*, pp. 184-186; De Soto, *The Other Path*, pp. 45-47.

35. Palmer, *Peru: The Authoritarian Tradition*, p. 113. See also David Scott Palmer, *Revolution from Above: Military Government and Popular Participation in Peru, 1968-1972* (Ithaca, New York: 1973), passim.; Julio Cotler, "The New Mode of Political Domination in Peru," Lowenthal, ed., *The Peruvian Experiment*, pp. 44-78.

36. Pásara, "When the Military Dreams," p. 328.

37. Ibid., p. 328.

38. Stephen M. Gorman, "Geopolitics and Peruvian Foreign Policy," *Inter-American Economy Affairs*, 36, no. 2 (Autumn, 1982), p. 79.

39. Personal interview with Colonel (R) James Aikens, 28 June 1990, Hampston, Virginia.

40. For a moving account of this incident see Barbara Bode, *No Bell to Toll: Destruction and Creation in the Andes* (New York: 1989).

41. Ruben Berrios, "Relations between Peru and the Socialist Countries," *Eastern European Quarterly*, 21, no. 1 (March, 1987), pp. 99-100.

42. Ibid. Peruvian students in the Soviet Union frequently complained of racial discrimination during the 1970s.

43. Personal interview with Francisco Morales Bermúdez, 29 May 1990, Lima, Peru.

44. Personal interview with Jorge Fernández Maldonado, 30 May 1990, Lima, Peru. See also Berrios, "Relations between Peru and the Socialist Countries," p. 112; The New York Times, 31 December 1976, p. 1.

45. Confidential interview with a former U.S. army officer in the army's Southern Command, 25 April 1990, Annapolis, Maryland; Berrios, "Relations between Peru and the Socialist Countries," pp. 112-113. For a review of Peru's Soviet weapons inventory see U.S. Arms Control and Disarmament Agency, World Military Expenditures and Arms Transfers, 1971-1980 (Washington, D.C.: 1983); SIPRI Handbook, (Washington, D.C.: 1989). See also the computer program "Milfacts" for current Peruvian weapons inventories. As of early 1991 approximately fifty Soviet technical advisers remained in Peru.

46. See, for example, General de División Víctor López Mendoza's article on the World War II Soviet campaign against Germany, "Cobertura de fronteras Enseñanzas de la guerra Sovietica-Alemana," Revista Militar del Perú, 85, no. 727 (May-August, 1988), pp. 5-9. Prior to the 1980s, articles on the Soviet army were extremely rare in Peruvian army journals.

47. Soviet tanks are notorious for their maintenance problems, and Peru was reportedly required to ship entire tanks back to the Soviet Union in the mid-1980s for repairs. For a discussion of the problems of Soviet weaponry see Andrew Cockburn, The Threat: Inside the Soviet Military Machine (New York: 1983).

48. Cleaves and Scurrah, Agriculture and Bureaucracy, pp. 276-277.

49. Morales Bermúdez, Apuntes sobre autoritarismo, p. 153.

50. Rosemary Thorp and Geoffrey Bertram, Peru, 1890-1977: Growth and Policy in an Open Economy (New York: 1978), p. 319.

51. For Admiral Faura's version of these events see Del Pilar Tello, Golpe o revolución, pp. 97-116.

52. Henry Pease García, El ocaso del poder oligárquico (Lima: 1977), p. 148; Philip, The Rise and Fall of the Peruvian Military Radicals, p. 152.

53. The New York Times, 3 December 1974, p. 12.

54. Morales Bermúdez, Apuntes sobre autoritarismo, p. 268; Philip, The Rise and Fall of the Peruvian Military Radicals, p. 156; The New York Times, 7 February 1975, p. 3.

55. Personal interview with Víctor Raúl Haya de la Torre, 14 July 1974, Lima, Peru.

56. See Caretas, 6 March 1975; Morales Bermúdez, Apuntes sobre autoritarismo, p. 268; Philip, The Rise and Fall of the Peruvian Military Radicals, p. 156. In an effort to verify charges of CIA involvement in these riots, an unsuccessful attempt was made to review the National Security files at the Gerald R. Ford Presidential Library in Ann Arbor, Michigan. These files were closed as of July, 1990.

57. See Daniel M. Masterson, "Peru's New Leader," The Christian Century, 112, no. 40 (3 December 1975), pp. 1112-1113.

58. Personal interview with Jorge Fernández Maldonado, 30 May 1990, Lima, Peru.

59. Thomas Sanders, "The Politics of Transition in Peru," American Universities Field Staff Reports, 24, no. 2 (December, 1977), pp 11-12.

60. Personal Interview with Francisco Morales Bermúdez, 29 May 1990, Lima, Peru.

61. Morales Bermúdez, *Apuntes sobre autoritarismo*, p. 275.

62. Ibid., p. 273; Klaiber, *Religion and Revolution*, p. 192. See Chapter 3 for discussion of this incident.

63. Philip, *The Rise and Fall of the Peruvian Military Radicals*, p. 157.

64. Mauceri, *Militares*, pp. 18-21.

65. Gorman, "Geopolitics and Peruvian Foreign Policy," p. 80.

66. Personal interview with Susan Niles, 25 June 1990, Ithaca, New York. Niles, an archaeologist, was doing research in the Cuzco region during the mid-1970s.

67. Confidential interview with a U.S. army officer who had recently returned from service in Chile, 15 April 1978, Washington, D.C.

68. Personal interview with Francisco Morales Bermúdez, 29 May 1990, Lima, Peru.

69. Confidential interview with a senior-grade armed forces officer, 29 May 1990, Callao, Peru.

70. Philip, *The Rise and Fall of the Peruvian Military Radicals*, p. 152.

71. Mauceri, *Militares*, p. 22.

72. See Alan García Pérez, *El futuro diferente: La tarea histórico del APRA* (Lima: 1982).

73. *El Comercio*, 25 May 1990, p. 7.

74. Personal interview with Jeffrey L. Klaiber, 26 May 1990, Lima, Peru. For a less positive interpretation of the Velasco government's education reform, see Robert S. Drysdale and Robert G. Myers, "Continuity and Change in Peruvian Education," in Lowenthal, ed., *The Peruvian Experiment*, pp. 254-301.

75. Anibal Quijano, *Nationalism and Capitalism*, p. 70.

76. See Denis Gilbert, "The Oligarchy and the Old Regime in Peru," Ph.D. diss., Cornell University, 1977.

77. See David Becker, *The New Bourgeoisie and the Limits of Dependency: Mining, Class, and Power in "Revolutionary" Peru* (Princeton: 1983); Elizabeth Dore, *The Peruvian Mining Industry: Growth, Stagnation and Crisis* (Boulder: 1988).

78. *Latin American Weekly Report* hereafter cited as *LAWR*, 29 June 1984, p. 9.

79. Jack Child, *Geopolitics and Conflict in South America* (New York: 1985), pp. 96-97.

80. Ibid.

81. *The New York Times*, 30 January 1981, p. 6; 1 February 1981, p. 3; 2 February 1981, p. 1; 10 February 1981, p. 2.

82. Ibid., 10 February 1981, p. 2.

83. *LAWR*, 26 June 1981, p. 6-7.

84. Ibid., 14 October 1983, pp. 1-2.

85. Ibid., 13 January 1984, pp. 6-7.

86. Jeffrey L. Klaiber, "Reform Politics in Peru: Alan García's Crusade against Corruption," *Corruption and Reform*, 2 (1987), p. 158.

87. Ibid., pp. 155-156.

88. *LAWR*, 27 September 1985, pp. 6-7.

89. Raymond Bonner, "Peru's War," *New Yorker*, 4 January 1988, p. 50.

90. *The New York Times*, 4 July 1990, p. 4.

91. Shortly after halving the Mirage purchases, García announced Peru would not pay for $300 million in repairs for the navy's flag ship, *Almirante Grau*, then being serviced in Holland. The Dutch government then threatened to seize and sell the

ship to Chile if Peru did not meet its obligations. The issue was eventually resolved.

92. *LAWR*, 16 April 1987, p. 9.

93. Klaiber, "Reform Politics in Peru," pp. 157-159.

94. *LAWR*, 29 May 1987, p. 11.

95. See, for example, Steve J. Stern, ed., *Resistance, Rebellion, and Consciousness in the Andean World, 18th to 20th Centuries* (Madison: 1987). The literature on *Sendero Luminoso* is becoming quite extensive. One should begin, if possible, with Luis Arce Borja, ed., *Guerra popular en el Perú: El pensamiento Gonzalo* (Brussels: 1989). These are the collected thoughts of *Sendero Luminoso*'s leader, Abimael Guzmán Reynoso. Guzmán's interview with Arce Borja in the 26 July 1988 edition of *El Diario* (the author's copy is a transcript) is quite insightful. Other studies of particular value are Carlos Ivan Degregori, *Sendero Luminoso: Los hondos y mortales desencuentros*, (parte 1, Lima: 1985); *Sendero Luminoso: Lucha armada y utopia autoritaria* (parte 2, Lima: 1986). Alberto Flores Galindo and Nelson Manrique, *Violencia y Campesinado* (Lima: 1986); Gabriela Tarazona-Sevillaño, *Sendero Luminoso and the Threat of Narcoterrorism*, (Washington, D.C.: 1990); David Scott Palmer, "The *Sendero Luminoso* Rebellion in Peru," in *Latin American Insurgencies*, George Fauriol, ed. (Washington, D.C.: 1985), pp. 67-96; Cynthia McClintock, "*Sendero Luminoso*: Peru's Maoist Guerrillas," *Problems of Communism* 32, no. 5 (1983), pp. 19-34; Cynthia McClintock, "Why Peasants Rebel: The Case of Peru's *Sendero Luminoso*," *World Politics*, 37 (1984), pp. 48-84; Gordon H. McCormick, *The Shining Path and the Future of Peru*, Rand Corporation (R-3781), March, 1990; Philip Mauceri, *Militares*. Three unpublished manuscripts were of particular value for this study. They are James M. Greene, "Peru's *Sendero Luminoso*: Ideology and Practice," senior honor's thesis, U.S. Naval Academy, Annapolis, Maryland, May, 1990; Isbell, "The Emerging Patterns of Peasants' Responses to *Sendero Luminoso*," Cornell University; Lewis Taylor, "Maoism in the Andes: *Sendero Luminoso* and the Contemporary Guerrilla Movement in Peru," Center for Latin American Studies, University of Cambridge, 1983. These sources were supplemented by interviews in Peru and in the United States on the *Sendero Luminoso* insurgency. Many of the interviewees must remain anonymous. Some Peruvian military intelligence documents regarding *Sendero Luminoso* were also reviewed.

96. "Report of Peru's Human Rights Commission, Peru, 1989-1990;" McCormick, *The Shining Path*, p. 1.

97. Arce Borja, Guerra popular en el Perú; Guzmán interview, *El Diario*, 24 July 1988 (author's transcribed copy).

98. Guzmán interview, *El Diario*, 24 July 1988, (transcript copy, p. 41).

99. Eudocio Ravines, *The Yenan Way* (New York: 1951), pp. 76-93; McCormick, *The Shining Path*, pp. 3-5; Greene, "Peru's *Sendero Luminoso*," pp. 19-28; Palmer, "The *Sendero Luminoso* Rebellion," pp. 67-71.

100. Bonner, "Peru's War," p. 35; Greene, "Peru's *Sendero Luminoso*," pp. 20-25; Gustavo Gorriti, "The War of the Philosopher King," *The New Republic*, 202 (18 June 1990), pp. 16-20. Gorriti is now completing a three-volume study of *Sendero Luminoso*.

101. Confidential interview, 11 July 1990, Ithaca, New York. This scholar, now teaching in the United States, taught at San Cristóbal de Huamanga intermittently throughout the 1960s.

102. Ibid.

103. Gorriti, "The War of the Philosopher King," p. 18; Palmer, "The *Sendero Luminoso* Rebellion," p. 69; Peruvian Military Intelligence Documents, quoted in Greene, "Peru's *Sendero Luminoso,* pp. 26-27.

104. Bonner, "Peru's War," p. 35; Palmer, "The *Sendero Luminoso* Rebellion," pp. 83-85.

105. McCormick, *The Shining Path,* pp. 11-12; Guzmán interview, *El Diario,* 26 July 1988 (transcript copy, p. 18).

106. *Sendero Luminoso's* five-stage revolutionary timetable is well known in Peru today.

107. Telephone interview with Father Robert Hoffman, 22 June 1989, Chicago, Illinois; McCormick, *The Shining Path,* p. 10.

108. McCormick, *The Shining Path,* pp. 11-14; confidential interview with a Peruvian Marine, 26 May 1990, Lima, Peru.

109. McCormick, *The Shining Path,* p. 13.

110. Confidential interview with a member of the CAEM staff, 30 May 1990, Chorrillos, Peru.

111. Taylor, "Maoism in the Andes," pp. 13-14; confidential interview with a Peruvian Marine, 26 May 1990, Lima, Peru; McCormick, *The Shining Path,* pp. 48-49.

112. For a discussion of the army's initial operations in the Ayacucho region see General Roberto C. Noel Moral, *Ayacucho: Testimonio de un soldado* (Lima: 1989). General Noel Moral was the highly controversial commander of the army's limited campaign during the early 1980s.

113. Isbell, "The Emerging Patterns of Peasants' Responses," pp. 10-11.

114. Confidential interview with a former Cristóbal de Huamanga professor, 11 July 1990, Ithaca, New York.

115. Captured *Sendero Luminoso* document, Peruvian Military Intelligence, cited in Greene, "Peru's *Sendero Luminoso,*" p. 33.

116. *LAWR,* 30 May 1986, p. 10.

117. The Peruvian army suppressed the Lurigancho uprising, in which more than 120 *Senderistas* were allegedly killed after their surrender. After shelling El Frontón (located on San Lorenzo Island off Callao), the navy and marine infantry put down the riot in that prison. A smaller insurrection was quickly ended when women *Senderista* prisoners surrendered after a few hours at the Santa Barbara women's prison in Callao. For the Peruvian government's official investigation of the prison incidents see Senador Rolando Ames, Presidente de la Comisión Investigadora, *Informe al congreso sobre los sucesos de los penales* (Lima: 1988). A day-by-day catalog of incidents of political violence in Peru from 1980 to 1988 is found in *Violencia política en el Perú* (2 vols.), published by the Centro de Estudios y Promoción del Desarrollo (DESCO). The prison riots are reviewed on pages 146-148 (vol. 2).

118. Robert B. Davis, "*Sendero Luminoso* and Peru's Struggle for Survival," *Military Review,* 70, no. 1 (January, 1990), p. 82; McCormick, *The Shining Path,* pp. 21-23. *Sendero Luminoso's* links with narcotics traffickers is discussed in Tarazona-Sevillaño, *Sendero Luminoso.*

119. According to one U.S. military source close to the Peruvian army, the thirty-five million dollars might have been used to address the armed forces' severe supply problems rather than to fund a coordinated antidrug operation (confidential interview, 30 May 1990, Lima, Peru).

120. McClintock, "Why Peasants Rebel," pp. 64-72; Palmer, "The *Sendero Luminoso* Rebellion," pp. 76-87.

121. See interview with Degregori in *Caretas*, 14 September 1987, pp. 34-37.

122. Isbell, "The Emerging Patterns of Peasants' Responses," p. 11.

123. Ibid., p. 12.

124. Confidential interview with a Peruvian Marine, 25 May 1990, Lima, Peru.

125. Amnesty International has increasingly cited Peru for human rights violations since the war against *Sendero Luminoso* began in 1980. Among a number of investigations conducted by Peruvian and international officials concerned with the issues of human rights violations was that carried out by the Latin American Federation of Associations of Relatives of Detained and Missing Persons (FEDEFAM). In a January, 1984, visit to Ayachucho, the FEDEFAM heard reports of 192 cases of detentions and disappearances by the security forces. See *LAWR*, 3 February 1984, p. 7.

126. *LAWR*, 10 June 1983. p. 2.

127. Quote in Susan C. Bourque and Kay B. Warren, "Democracy without Peace: The Cultural Politics of Terror in Peru," *Latin American Research Review* 24, no. 1 (1989), p. 26. This excellent article offers an insightful analysis of Peru's endemic violence during the past decade. General Huaman Centeno was subsequently relieved of his Ayacucho command.

128. "Report of Peru's Human Rights Commission, Peru, 1989-1990," National Coordinator of Human Rights; confidential interview, Washington, D.C., 8 January, 1991.

129. McCormick, *The Shining Path*, p. 35.

130. Confidential interview with a U.S. armed forces officer, September, 1989, Washington, D.C.

131. Fernando D. Solomon Campos, "Fuerte Arica: Un bastión de sequiridad," *Actualidad Militar* 25, no. 349 (February, 1988), pp. 6-9. The navy's journal, *Revista de Marina*, is continuing regular publication and offers high-quality articles on the *Sendero Luminoso* insurgency.

132. Davis, "*Sendero Luminoso* and Peru's Struggle," p. 84.

133. Confidential interview with CAEM staff member, 30 May 1990, Chorrillos, Peru.

134. Background intelligence on *Sendero Luminoso* organizational work is generally reasonably good. The intelligence services seem to be most wanting in the day-to-day intelligence gathering on *Sendero Luminoso*'s military operations. This assessment is based on a review of selected military documents and discussions with U.S. military personnel familiar with the Peruvian army's counterinsurgency operations.

135. McCormick, *The Shining Path*, p. 35.

136. Confidential interview with a U.S. military officer, 30 May 1990, Lima, Peru; McCormick, *The Shining Path*, p. 35.

137. Luigi Einaudi and Alfred Stepan, *Latin American Institutional Development: Changing Military Perspectives in Peru and Brazil* (Santa Monica: 1971), pp. 52-53.

138. David Scott Palmer, "The Impact of the Peruvian Army on Political Development in Rural Peru: A Preliminary Exploration," Cornell University, 1970.

139. Confidential interview with a Peruvian Marine, 26 May 1990, Lima, Peru.

140. Telephone interview with Father Robert Hoffman, 27 June 1989. For an insightful look at life in a Peruvian army barracks, see the interview with Jaime

Flores in José Matos Mar, *Taquile en Lima* (Lima: 1986). Jaime, who served in the armored division barracks in Rimac during the early 1980s, paints a starkly negative picture of army life. A similar view of life in a military prep school is presented in Mario Vargas Llosa, *La ciudad y los perros* (Barcelona: 1985). For a brief discussion of Peru's enlisted ranks see Robert Wesson, ed., *The Latin American Military Institution* (New York: 1986), pp. 10-11.

141. Confidential interview with a junior-grade Peruvian naval officer, 31 May 1990, Lima, Peru.

142. Confidential interview with a Peruvian naval officer, 27 May 1990, Lima, Peru.

143. Confidential interview with a Peruvian naval officer, 29 May 1990, Lima, Peru.

144. Héctor Béjar, quoted in Bourque and Warren, "Democracy without Peace," p. 13.

145. Interview with Admiral Jorge Hesse Ramírez, general director of naval instruction, 29 May 1990, Callao, Peru.

146. Personal interview with Francisco Morales Bermúdez, 29 May 1990, Lima, Peru.

Chronology

1824   The Spanish viceroy capitulates after independence forces are victorious at the Battle of Ayacucho.

1845-1862   The era of General Ramón Castilla is marked by relative political tranquility and economic progress based on guano and nitrate exports.

1872   The first civilian president, Manuel Pardo, is elected.

1879-1883   The War of the Pacific with Chile results in the permanent loss of Peru's southern provinces of Tarapacá and Arica.

1895   A bloody civil insurrection brings José Nicolás de Piérola to power.

1896   The first French army mission is contracted by Peru.

1914   General Oscar R. Benavides leads the first military coup d'état of the twentieth century.

1919-1930   The *Oncenio* of Augusto B. Leguía is characterized by heavy foreign investment, sharply curtailed civilian political activity, and the manipulation of armed forces by the dictator.

1920   The first United States naval mission to Peru is established.

1924	The *Alianza Popular Revolucionaria Americana*, APRA party is founded in Mexico City by Víctor Raúl Haya de la Torre.
1930-1933	Lieutenant Colonel Luis M. Sánchez Cerro dominates Peruvian politics after deposing Leguía.
1931	Sánchez Cerro defeats Haya de la Torre in presidential elections.
1932	The failed Trujillo revolt in July results in the deaths of hundreds of *Apristas* and long-lasting enmity between APRA and the armed forces.
1932-1933	The Leticia border dispute with Colombia nearly leads to war.
1933-1939	General Benavides rules Peru after Sánchez Cerro's assassination by a young *Aprista* in April, 1933.
1936	Presidential elections are annulled by Benavides after a APRA-supported candidate appears victorious.
1937-1939	Benavides solicits German and Italian support for Peru's army and air force.
1939-1945	Manuel Prado y Ugarteche serves as president after being hand-picked by Benavides.
1941	The July border conflict with Ecuador in the Zaumilla-Marañon region marks the high point of Peru's military operations in this century.
1943-1945	United States military influence in Peru increases substantially during World War II.
1945-1948	José Bustamante y Rivero is elected with *Aprista* support and confronts a civil-military unrest throughout his brief regime.

1948   3 October Callao naval revolt weakens Bustamante and enables General Manuel A. Odría to lead a successful coup d'état on 27 October.

1948-1956   General Odría autocratically rules while reluctantly permitting armed forces institutional reform. APRA is once again outlawed.

1950   The *Centro de Altos Estudios Militares* is founded.

1956-1962   Prado y Ugarteche is again elected, this time with open support of the APRA after a *convivencia* agreement is reached. Internal reforms within the armed forces are continued.

1957   An armed forces Joint Command is established.

1962   Prado is deposed by the armed forces Joint Command on 18 July after the presidential elections prove inconclusive.

1962-1963   An armed forces junta composed of the three service chiefs rules Peru initiating limited social and economic reforms.

1963-1968   Fernando Belaúnde Terry, elected with the enthusiastic backing of the armed forces, is unable to enact meaningful economic development.

1965   The Peruvian armed forces violently suppress three guerrilla *focos* in Peru's *sierra*.

1968-1975   After deposing Belaúnde in a 3 October 1968 coup d'état, General Juan Velasco Alvarado directs a program of social and economic reform unprecedented in Peruvian history.

1969   A comprehensive agrarian reform program is begun in October.

1971   SINAMOS, the unsuccessful effort to create a popular base for the Velasco reforms, is established.

1975   A bloody strike by Peru's police agencies in February further weakens the faltering Velasco regime and leads to the successful *golpe de estado* of General Francisco Morales Bermúdez on 29 August.

1975-1980   General Morales Bermúdez dismantles many of Velasco's reforms while leading the transition to civilian rule.

1980-1985   Fernando Belaúnde Terry is again elected and faces economic instability and the beginning of *Sendero Luminoso*'s "Peoples' War."

1985-1990   The first *APRA* president in Peru's history, Alan García Pérez, serves amidst continuing economic decline and the steadily increasing threat from *Sendero Luminoso*.

1990-1991   Alberto Fujimori is the surprise winner of the presidential elections and quickly enacts severe economic austerity measures while cooperating closely with the army in the campaign against *Sendero Luminoso*.

Glossary

AP

Acción Popular (Popular Action Party). The political party organized by Fernando Belaúnde Terry in the early 1960s as a vehicle for his bid for the presidency. Competing with APRA's constituency, it has been successful only with Belaúnde as its presidential candidate.

APRA

Alianza Popular Revolucionaria Americana (American Popular Revolutionary Alliance). Peru's most viable twentieth century political party. Founded in Mexico City in 1924 by the student leader, Víctor Raúl Haya de la Torre, the party originally espoused a radical antiimperialist doctrine. After World War II, APRA became increasingly more conservative, replacing its original antiimperialist rhetoric with anticommunism. The party's first successful presidential candidate, Alan García Pérez (1985-1990), returned to APRA's early antiimperialist doctrine in an effort to unify the party and gain international support for his programs. APRA's party members are known as *Apristas* and the movement itself as *Aprismo*.

CAEM

Centro de Altos Estudios Militares (Center of Higher Military Studies). Founded by the Peruvian army in 1950, with General José del Carmen Marín as its first director, CAEM became the armed forces' most advanced staff school. With civilian and military instructors and a student body composed of army and air force colonels and navy captains, as well as civilian technocrats, CAEM became a clearinghouse for civil-military developmentalist theory. It was largely ignored by the administration of

General Juan Velasco Alvarado (1968-1975) because the center was perceived as too conservative by the progressive Velasco administration.

CAPS

Cooperativas Agrarias de Producción (Agrarian Production Cooperatives). Agricultural cooperatives established by the Velasco regime in conjunction with its agrarian reform. CAPS, supposedly to be run by the workers on the large, expropriated estates, were often dominated instead by the state administrators (*técnicos*) appointed to aid in their administration.

COAP

Comité de Asesoramiento de la Presidencia (Presidential Advisory Council). General Juan Velasco Alvarado's inner circle of military advisers. This group was composed of many of the young progressive army officers who planned the 3 October 1968 *golpe de estado* led by Velasco. COAP is credited with generating much of the progressive reforms of the Velasco administration.

CROE

Comité Revolucionario de Oficiales del Ejército (Revolutionary Committee of Army Officers). Created in 1944, this underground organization of junior army officers sought to promote armed forces institutional reform through militant agitation.

CTP

Confederación de Trabajadores del Perú (Confederation of Peruvian Workers). One of Peru's largest labor organizations dominated by the APRA party.

CTRP

Confederación de Trabajadores de la Revolución Peruana (Confederation of Workers of the Peruvian Revolution). Established by the Velasco regime to create an official labor organization and counter APRA's labor influence; it is largely independent of the government today.

EGP

Ejército Guerrillero Popular (Popular Guerrilla Army). The military arm of *Sendero Luminoso's* (Shining Path's) insurgency. Founded in 1983, it is manned by young fighters, often in their teens and preteens, and is based on *Sendero Luminoso*'s political cell structure, generally containing five to seven members.

ELN
Ejército de Liberación Nacional (National Liberation Army). Led by the guerrilla fighter Héctor Béjar, the ELN began an offensive in the Ayacucho region in September, 1965. Béjar's movement, along with two other guerrilla fronts, was defeated by the Peruvian army in less than six months.

FDN
Frente Democrático Nacional (National Democratic Front). A tenuous political alliance forged in 1945 between the APRA and the moderate lawyer José Bustamante y Rivero. APRA supported Bustamante's successful bid for the presidency in 1945 and later pressed him for greater political power until his overthrow by General Manuel A. Odría in October, 1948.

IPC
International Petroleum Company. A Peruvian subsidiary of Standard Oil of New Jersey (Exxon) which dominated Peruvian petroleum production from the early 1920s until its expropriation by the Velasco regime within days after the military seized power in October, 1968. IPC's inordinate economic and political influence is considered to be one of the military's prime justifications for overthrowing Fernando Belaúnde Terry.

IU
Izquierda Unida (United Left). A coalition of Peru's leftist political parties originally formed by former members of the Velasco regime's "radical" inner circle of advisers. Since 1983, when he was elected mayor of Lima, Marxist Alfonso Barrantes has dominated IU.

La Misión (The Mission)
A hard-line, rightist faction in the Peruvian army emerging during the administration of General Francisco Morales Bermúdez (1975-1980). Advocating a return to strict military discipline and constitutional unity, La Missión also favored a crackdown on labor unrest and civilian protest. Its chief spokesman was General Javier Tantaleán Vanini. During the early 1980s, General Luis Cisneros Vizquerra assumed the leadership of the army's right wing, advocating particularly tough measures.

PCP-SL

Partido Comunista de Perú en el Sendero Luminoso de José Carlos Mariátegui (Communist Party of Peru in the Shining Path of José Carlos Mariátegui).   Commonly known as Sendero Luminoso, this guerrilla insurgency was founded by Abimael Guzmán Reynoso as a splinter faction of the Soviet-oriented Peruvian Communist Party in February, 1970. Since 1980, Sendero Luminoso has waged a savage war against the Peruvian state, a war costing thousands of lives and billions of dollars in property damage.

PUR

Partido Union Revolucionario (Revolutionary Union Party). Founded in 1931 to foster the presidential candidacy of Colonel Luis M. Sánchez Cerro, the PUR attracted extreme right-wing supporters well after Sánchez Cerro's assassination in April, 1933.

SAIS

Sociedades Agricolas de Interés Social (Agrarian Social Interest Societies).   Basically similar to the CAPS instituted in Peru's coastal regions, these agrarian reform cooperatives were established largely in the Peruvian sierra. Many have now gone into bankruptcy or have been seized by Indians from nearby traditional Indian communities.

SINAMOS

Sistema Nacional de Apoyo a la Movilización Social (National System of Support to Social Mobilization). Established by the Velasco government in June, 1971 as the official agency for mobilizing popular support for the military government's reforms, SINAMOS quickly sparked opposition by a wide array of special interest groups threatened by the military regime's programs.   SINAMOS was dismantled by the government of General Francisco Morales Bermúdez.

UNO

Union Nacional Odriísta (National Union of Odría Supporters). Formed in the early 1960s, as the personalist political party of former military dictator Manuel Odría (1948-1956), the UNO drew its support from the Lima shantytowns (pueblos jóvenes). The UNO allied with the Apristas to oppose the reforms of Fernando Belaúnde Terry's first administration (1963-1968).

Bibliography

Archives and Libraries

Adalai Stevenson Institute, Chicago, Illinois
Archivo Histórico de Marina del Perú, Lima, Peru
Centro de Altos Estudios Militares, Chorrillos, Peru
Centro de Estudios Histórico-Militares del Peru, Lima, Peru
Cornell University Libraries, Ithaca, New York
Escuela Superior de la Marina, Callao, Peru
Federal Records Center, Suitland, Maryland
Franklin D. Roosevelt Library, Hyde Park, New York
Gerald R. Ford Library, Ann Arbor, Michigan
Hemeroteca; Biblioteca Nacional, Lima, Peru
Hoover Institution, Stanford, California
Instituto de Estudios Histórico-Marítimos, Lima, Peru
Library of Congress, Washington, D.C.
Lyndon B. Johnson Library, Austin, Texas
Michigan State University Library, East Lansing, Michigan
National Archives, Washington, D.C.
Nimitz Library, U.S. Naval Academy, Annapolis, Maryland
Sala de Investigaciones; Biblioteca Nacional, Lima, Peru
Stanford University Library, Stanford, California
University of Illinois Library, Champaign, Illinois

Interviews

The following individuals were interviewed at the locations indicated. The dates of the interviews are given in the text notes. Some of these individuals were interviewed on numerous occasions. A number of individuals, who were interviewed both in Peru and in the United States, must remain anonymous.

Capitan de Fragata Alfonso Aguero Moras (director of the Peruvian Naval Museum), Lima, Peru

Colonel (R) James Aikens, Hampton, Virginia

Alberto E. Bolivar Ocampo (professor of geopolitics at CAEM), Chorrillos, Peru

Colonel (R) Bernard Big, Hampton, Virginia

Captain Jack D. Clay (former U.S. naval attaché to Peru), Lima, Peru

General (R) Jorge Fernandez Maldonado (former minister in the Velasco and Moralez Bermúdez governments and now a senator), Lima, Peru.

Capitan de Navio Fernando Grau Umlauff (former Subdirector Escuela Naval del Peru)

Víctor Raúl Haya de la Torre, Lima, Peru

Almirante Jorge Hesse, Lima, Peru

Father Robert Hoffman, Chicago, Illinois (telephone interview), Chorrillos, Peru

Colonel Julio Hinotosa Rubio, Peruvian army (assistant to the director of CAEM), Chorrillos, Peru

Father Jeffrey Klaiber, S. J., Catholic University of Peru, Lima, Peru

Major General Peruvian air force Armando Llosa Alvarez (subdirector of CAEM), Chorrillos, Peru

Ambassador (R) James I. Loeb, Cabin John, Maryland

Fernando Schwalb López Aldaña, Cabin John, Maryland

Contralmirante Daniel J. Mariscal Galiano, Lima, Peru

John V. Murra, Ithaca, New York

Susan Niles, Ithaca, New York

Ambassador (R) R. Henry Norweb, Cleveland, Ohio

Capitan de Fragata Jorge Ortíz Sotelo, Lima, Peru

Ramiro Prialé, Lima, Peru

General De Brigada Jorge Rabanal Portillo, Lima, Peru

Almirante Manuel Reyna (director of education and programs at CAEM), Chorrillos, Peru

Captain (R) Jack Roudebush, U.S. navy, Monterey, California (telephone interview)

Contralmirante (R) Federico Salmón de la Jarra, Lima, Peru
Captain (R) Roy Campbell Smith III, Annapolis, Maryland
Vice Almirante (R) Luis Vargas Caballero, Lima, Peru
Armando Villanueva del Campo, Lima, Peru
Víctor Villanueva Valencia, Lima, Peru
Capitan de Fragata (R) Luis Felipe Villena Gutierrez, Lima, Peru
General (R) Fred Woerner (former commanding general U.S. Southern
    Command, Panama), Annapolis, Maryland

Questionnaires

The following individuals completed detailed questionnaires submitted by the
author:

Colonel James Aikens
Division General (R) Ricardo Pérez Godoy
Robert S. McNamara (former secretary of defense)
Vice Almirante Luis M. Vargas Caballero

Documentary Collections

Colección del Volantes y Hoyas Sueltas in the Sala de Investigaciones of
    the Biblioteca Nacional del Perú
Conflicto con Colombia; Legajo de radios interceptados, 1933-1936 in the
    Centro de Estudios Histórico-Militares del Perú
Documentacion de la compaña militar con Colombia 1933, Diario de
    marchas y operaciones de la Va Division, 1932-1936 in the Centro
    de Estudios Histórico-Militares del Perú
Documentos relación con los sucesos de Trujillo (1932), Ministerio de
    Guerra, Division Comandancia in the Centro de Estudios Histó-
    rico-Militares del Perú
Exposición de Coronel Víctor Ramos sobre las operaciones en el conflicto
    con Colombia, 1932, 1933, Ministerio de Guerra (Reservada) in
    the Centro de Estudios Histórico-Militares del Perú
Ralación nominal de los oficiales, clases y soldados muertos en las acciones
    de armas en las fronteras del norte y nor-oriente en el conflicto
    con Ecuador en 1941; in the Centro de Estudios Histórico
    Militares del Perú

Rebelión Escuadra - Informe. Estado Mayor General de Marina, Coman-
    dante General de Escuadra. October, 1948. Archivo Histórico de
    la Marina.
Records of the Department of State Relating to the Internal Affairs of
    Peru, Record Group 59, Serial File 823.00 (Political Affairs),
    723.00 (Political Affairs), and 823.00 (Military Affairs), in the
    National Archives, Washington, D.C.
Records of the Military Intelligence Division General Staff Reports, Record
    Groups 165 and 319, in the National Archives, Washington, D.C.,
    and the Federal Records Center, Suitland, Maryland
Records of the Office of Naval Intelligence (ONI), Record Group 38, in
    the Natioanl Archives, Washington, D.C.
Records of the Office of Strategic Services (OSS), Record Group 226, in
    the National Archives, Washington, D.C.

Personal Papers and Correspondence

Personal Papers and Correspondence of Ambassador James I. Loeb
Correspondence of Víctor Villanueva Valencia
Personal Papers of Harry H. Hopkins
Personal Papers of Lyndon B. Johnson
Personal Papers of John Wesley Jones
Personal Papers of William A. Moffett (U.S. Navy)
Personal Papers of Henry Morgenthau
Personal Papers of Franklin D. Roosevelt
Personal Papers of Luis Alberto Sánchez
Personal Papers of Henry A. Wallace

Newspapers and Periodicals

Atlantic Monthly
El Callao
Caretas
El Comercio
La Croníca
Defensa Nacional
El Diario
Expresso

Gente
Internacional Revista Mundial
La Jornada
Life
Monthly Review
The New York Times
The New Yorker
Noticias
Oiga
El Peruano
Peruvian Times
La Prensa
Revista Diplomatica Peruana
La Tribuna
Ultima Hora
Variedades

Published Government Records

Comandancia General del Ejército, Lista Protocolar del Ejército del Perú Lima: Dirección de Inteligencia, Marzo, 1968

Diarios de los debates de las camaras de senadores y diputados, 1945-1948, in the Sala de Investigaciones of the Biblioteca Nacional del Perú

Diarios de los debates del senado; Legislativa extraordinaria de 1946, Sala de Investigaciones of the Biblioteca Nacional del Perú

El Perú Construye: Mensajes presentado al congeso nacional por el presidente constitucional de la republica del Perú, Fernando Belaúnde Terry, 1963-1967, Ministerio de Goberno, Lima, Perú

Escalafón General del Ejército in the Centro de Estudios Histórico-Militares del Perú, Ministerio de Guerra del Perú

La Fuerza Armada y el proceso electoral de 1962 (Lima: Imprenta de la Feurza Armada, 1963)

Legislación Militar del Perú in the Centro de Estudios Histórico-Militares de Perú, Ministerio de Guerra del Perú

Manuel A. Odría, "Mensaje presentado al congreso nacional 1955," in the Sala de Investigaciones of the Biblioteca Nacional del Perú

Manuel A. Odría, "Principios y postulados del movimiento de Arequipa; Extractos de Discursos y mensajes de General Don Manuel A.

Odría," in the Sala de Investigaciones of the Biblioteca Nacional del Perú

Memorias anual presentada por el señor Contralmirante Mariano H. Melgar, Ministro de Marina, 1947-1948, in the Sala de Investigaciones of the Biblioteca Nacional del Perú

Mensaje presentado al congreso por Doctor Manuel Prado, Presidente constitucional del Perú, 1959, in the Instituto de Estudios Histórico-Marítimos del Perú

Mensaje presentado al congreso por Doctor Manuel Prado, Presidente constitucional del Perú, 1960, in the Instituto de Estudios Histórico-Marítimos del Perú

Ordenes Generales de Aeronautica in the Centro de Estudios Histórico-Militares del Perú

Ordenes Generales del Ejército in the Centro de Estudios Histórico-Militares del Perú

Ordenes Generales de Guardia Civil y Policía in the Centro de Estudios Histórico-Militares del Perú

Ordenes Generales de Marina in the Centro de Estudios Histórico-Militares del Perú

Perú, Instituto Nacional de Planificación, *Analisis de la realidad socio-economica del Perú*, Lima: 1963

Plan de Estudios é Investigación del Curso de Defensa Nacional (Chorrillos: Centro de Altos Estudios Militares, 1990)

Perú, Ministerio de Guerra, *Las guerrillas de al Perú y su Represión* (Lima: Ministerio de Guerra, 1966)

Perú, Ley situación militar de la realidad socio-económica del Perú (Lima: Ministerio de Guerra, 1956)

Reforma Agraria, Decreto Ley No. 17716 (Lima: Distribuidor Inca, S.A. 1968)

Published Government Records and Personal Historical Accounts

Anuario de estadistico del Perú, 1948-1949, 1962 in the Sala de Investigaciones of the Biblioteca Nacional del Perú

Henderson, Donald C. and Pérez, Grace R., eds., *Literature and Politics in Latin America: An Annotated Calendar of Luis Alberto Sánchez Correspondence, 1919-1980* (University Park, Pa: The Pennsylvania State University Libraries, 1982).

Montagne Marckholtz, Ernesto, *Memorias de General de Brigada, E.P. Ernesto Montagne Marckholtz* (Lima: 1962)

Béjar, Hector, *Peru, 1965: Notes on a Guerrilla Experience* (New York: Monthly Review Press, 1970)

Historia de la Escuela Militar del Perú (Lima: Reprografica, 1962)

Papers Relating to the Foreign Relations of the United States, 1936-1959 (Washington, D.C.: U.S. Government Printing Office)

United States Congressional Record, 1950-1968 (Washington, D.C.: U.S. Government Printing Office)

Villanueva Valencia, Víctor, *La sublevación aprista del 48: La tragedia de un pueblo y un partido* (Lima: Milles Batres, 1973)

International Agency Reports

Comité Interamericano de Desarrollo Agricola, *Tecnocracia de la Tierra y desarrollo socio-economico del sector agrícola, Perú* (Washington, D.C.: Secretaria General de la organizacion de los Estados Americanos, 1966)

Peruvian Military Journals and Periodicals

Actualidad Militar
Defensa Nacional: Publicación del Centro de Altos Estudios Militares
Revista del Centro de Estudios Histórico-Militares del Perú
Revista del Centro de Instrucción Militar del Perú
Revista Escuela Militar de Chorrillos
Revista Escuela Superior de Guerra
Revista de la Marina
Revista Militar del Perú

Declassified Peruvian Military Intelligence Documents

"Antecedentes y Constitución del Partido, (1963-1979)". (This is a background study of the formation of *Sendero Luminoso*.) Listed under the classification of "Secret."

"Ubicación de los efectivos de las FFOO el día del ataque." (This is a general summary of one army operation against *Sendero Luminoso*.)

Doctoral Dissertations and Theses

Craig, Wesley W., Jr., "From Hacienda to Community: An Analysis of Solidarity and Social Change in Peru," Ph.D. diss., Cornell University, 1967.

Epstein, Edward C., "Motivational Bases of Loyalty in the Peruvian *Aprista* Party," Ph.D. diss., University of Illinois, 1970.

García, José Z., "The Velasco Coup in Peru: Causes and Policy Consequences," Ph.D. diss., University of New Mexico, 1974.

Gerlach, Allen, "Civil-Military Relations in Peru, 1914-1945," Ph.D. diss., University of New Mexico, 1973.

Gilbert, Dennis, "The Oligarchy and the Old Regime in Peru," Ph.D. diss., Cornell University, 1977.

Horton, Douglas Earl, "Haciendas and Cooperatives: A Study of Estate Organizations, Land Reform, and New Reform Enterprises in Peru," Ph.D. diss., Cornell University, 1976.

Jacquette, Jane, "The Politics of Development in Peru," Ph.D. diss., Cornell University, 1971.

Karno, Howard, "Augusto B. Leguía: The Oligarchy and the Modernization of Peru, 1870-1930," Ph.D. diss., University of California, 1970.

Munholland, Kim, "The Emergence of the Colonial Military in France, 1880-1905," Ph.D. diss., Princeton University, 1964.

Palmer, David Scott, "Revolution from Above: Military Government and Popular Participation in Peru, 1968-1972," Ph.D. diss., Cornell University, 1973.

Pope, Sharon S., "Harold B. Grow and the Establishment of Aviation in Peru, 1923-1930," master's thesis, University of West Florida, 1973.

Ortíz Sotelo, Jorge, "Sucesos en bordo de B.A.P. *Almirante Grau* con motivo de la caida de Laguia," Universidad Católica del Perú, Programa Letras y Ciencias Humanas, 1983.

Osberg, James A., "Centro de Altos Estudios Militares: Education for Change in the Peruvian Military, 1950-1973," Ph.D. diss., Southern Illinois University, 1975.

Westwater, Angela King, "Recognition of Latin American Military Regimes During the Kennedy Administration," master's thesis, New York University, 1967.

Unpublished Manuscripts

Greene, James M., "Peru's Sendero Luminoso: Ideology and Practice," Department of Political Science, U.S. Naval Academy, 1990.
Isbell, Billie Jean, "The Emerging Patterns of Peasants' Responses to Sendero Luminoso," Department of Anthropology, Cornell University, 1988.
Palmer, David Scott, "The Impact of the Peruvian Army on Political Development in Rural Peru: A Preliminary Explanation," Cornell University, 1970.
Taylor, Lewis, "Maoism in the Andes: Sendero Luminoso and the Contemporary Guerrilla Movement in Peru," Center for Latin American Studies, Cambridge University, 1983.

Books

Alcaza, Morela Luis, Historia Militar del Perú (Lima: Ministerio de Guerra, 1941).
Alexander, Robert J., Aprismo: The Ideas and Writings of Victor Raúl Haya de la Torre (Kent, Ohio: Kent State University Press, 1973).
Alexander, Robert J., Latin American Political Parties (New York: Praeger, 1963).
Alisky, Marvin, Peruvian Political Perspective 2d ed., (Tempe: Arizona State University Center for Latin American Studies, 1975).
Ambler, John Stewart, The French Army in Politics, 1945-1962 (Columbus: Ohio State University Press, 1966).
Arce Borja, Luis, ed., Guerra popular en el Perú: El pensamineto Gonzalo (Brussels: N.P. 1989).
Astiz, Carlos A., Pressure Groups and Power Elites in Peruvian Politics (Ithaca: Cornell University Press, 1969).
Baines, John M., Revolution in Peru: Mariatequi and the Myth (Tuscaloosa: University of Alabama Press, 1972).
Barber, Willard F., and Ronning, C. Neale, Internal Security and Military Power: Counterinsurgency and Civic Action in Latin America (Columbus: Ohio State University Press, 1966).
De la Barra, Felipe, Objetivo: Palacio de gobierno (Lima: Juan Meija Baca, 1967).
Basadre, Jorge, Historia de la republica del Perú, 12 vols., 5th ed. (Lima: Historia, 1966).

Becker, David, *The New Bourgeoisie and the Limits of Dependency: Mining, Class, and Power in "Revolutionary" Peru,* (Princeton: Princeton University Press, 1983).

Béjar, Héctor, *Peru 1965: Notes on a Guerrilla Experience* (New York: Monthly Review Press, 1970).

Belaúnde Terry, Fernando, *La conquista del Perú por los Peruanos* (Lima: Imprenta Minerva, 1959).

Belaúnde Terry, Fernando, *Peru's Own Conquest* (Lima: American Studies Press, S.A., 1965).

Blanco, Hugo, *Land or Death: The Peasant Struggle in Peru* (New York: Pathfinder Press, 1972).

Bode, Barbara, *No Bells to Toll: Destruction and Creation in the Andes* (New York: Charles Scribner, 1989).

Booth, David, and Sorj, Bernardo, eds., *Military Reformism and Social Class: The Peruvian Experience, 1968-1980* (New York: St. Martins Press, 1983).

Bourricaud, François, ed., *La oligarquía en el Perú* (Lima: Francisco Moncloa, 1969).

Bourricaud, François, *Power and Society in Contemporary Peru* (New York: Praeger, 1970).

Bueno Tovar, Oscar, *Las Fuerzas armadas y el Apra* (Lima: N.P., 1963).

Bustamante y Rivero, José Luis, *Tres años de la lucha por la democracia en el Perú* (Buenos Aires: Graficos Bartolome U. Chiesino, 1949).

Camino Brent, Armando, *Progresos del Perú, 1933-1939 durante el gobierno del presidente de la republica, General Oscar R. Benavides* (Buenos Aires: Editorial Guillermo Kraft, 1945).

Campbell, Leon G., *The Military and Society in Colonial Peru, 1750-1810,* (Philadelphia: American Philosophical Society, 1978).

Capuney, Manuel A., *Leguía: Vida y obra del constructador del gran Perú* (Lima: N.P., 1951).

Carey, James, *Peru and the United States, 1900-1962* (Notre Dame: Notre Dame University Press, 1964).

Chang-Rodriguez and Hullman, Ronald, eds., *APRA and the Democratic Challenge in Peru* (New York: The Bildner Center, 1988).

Chaplin, David, ed., *Peruvian Nationalism: A Corporatist Revolution* (Princeton: Transaction Books, 1976).

Chavarría, Jesus, *José Carlos Mariátegui and the Rise of Modern Peru, 1890-1930* (Albuquerque: University of New Mexico Press, 1979).

Chirinos Soto, Enrique, *Cuento y balance de los elecciones de 1962* (Lima: Villanueva, 1962).

Chirinos Soto, Enrique, *El Perú frente a junio de 1962* (Lima: Imprento Litografica, 1962).

Chirinos Lizares, Guido, and Chirinos Soto, Enrique, *El Septenato, 1968-1975* (Lima: 2d. ed. Editorial Alfa, 1977.

Cobas, Efrain, *Fuerza armada: Misiones militares y dependencia en el Perú* (Lima: Editorial Horizonte, 1982).

Cockburn, Andrew, *The Threat: Inside the Soviet Military Machine,* (New York: Random House, 1983).

Collier, David, *Squatters and Oligarchs: Authoritarian Rule and Policy Change in Peru* (Baltimore: Johns Hopkins University Press, 1976).

Corbett, Charles D., *The Latin American Military as a Socio-Political Force: Case Studies of Bolivia and Argentina* (Miami: Center for Advanced International Studies, 1972).

Cornejo Chávez, Héctor, *Nuevo principios por un nuevo Perú* (Lima: El Condor, 1960).

Cossio del Pomar, Felipe, *Haya de la Torre, el indoamericano* (Lima: Editorial Nuevo Pia, 1946).

Cotler, Julio, *Crisis politica y populismo militar en el Perú* (Lima: Instituto de Estudios Peruanos, 1969).

Cotler, Julio, *El populismo militar como modelo de desarrollo nacional: El caso peruano* (Lima: Instituto de Estudios Peruanos, 1969).

Craig, Gordon A., *The Politics of the Prussian Army, 1640-1945* (Oxford: Clarendon Press, 1955).

Davies, Thomas M., Jr., *Indian Integration in Peru: A Half Century of Experience, 1900-1948* (Lincoln: University of Nebraska Press, 1973).

Davies, Thomas M., Jr., and Víctor Villanueva Valencia, eds., *300 Documentos para la historia del APRA* (Lima: Editorial Horizonte, 1978).

Davies, Thomas M., Jr., and Víctor Villanueva Valencia, eds., *Secretos electorales del APRA: Corespondencia y documentos de 1939* (Lima: Editorial Horizonte, 1982).

Delgado, Carlos, *El proceso revolucionario peruano: Testimonio de lucha* (Buenos Aires: Siglo XXI Editores, 1972).

Delgado, Luis Humberto, *El militarismo en el Perú, 1821-1930* (Lima: Imprenta Gil, 1930).

Dellipiane, Carlos, *Historia militar del Perú.* 5th ed. (Lima: Ministerio de Guerra, 1964).

Deniz, José, *La revolución por la fuerza armada de Perú, 1968-1977* (Salamanca: Ediciones Segume, 1978).

Dew, Edward, *Politics in the Altiplano: The Dynamics of Change in Rural Peru* (Austin: University of Texas Press, 1969).

Dobyns, Henry, and Doughty, Paul, *Peru: A Cultural History* (New York: Oxford University Press, 1976).

Dore, Elizabeth, *The Peruvian Mining Industry: Growth, Stagnation and Crisis* (Boulder: Westview Press, 1988).

Earle, Edward Mead, ed., *The Makers of Modern Strategy: Military Thought from Machiavelli to Hitler* (New York: Antheneum, 1966).

Einaudi, Luigi R., *The Peruvian Military: A Summary Political Analysis* (Santa Monica: Rand Corporation, 1969).

Einaudi, Luigi R., and Stepan, Alfred, III, *Latin American Institutional Development: Changing Perspectives in Peru and Brazil* (Santa Monica: Rand Corporation, 1971).

Epstein, Fritz T., *European Military Influences in Latin America* (Washington, D.C.: N.P., 1941).

Finer, Samuel, *The Man on Horseback* (London: Pall Mall, 1960).

Fitzgerald, E.V.K., *The Political Economy of Peru, 1956-1978* (Cambridge, England: Cambridge University Press, 1979).

Fitzgerald, E.V.K., *The State and Economic Development: Peru Since 1968* (Cambridge England: Cambridge University Press, 1976).

Fitzgibbon, Russell H., ed., *The Constitutions of the Americas* (Chicago: University of Chicago Press, 1948).

García, Pérez Alan, *El futuro diferente: La tarea história del APRA* (Lima: Editorial DESA, 1983).

García, Rosell Cesar, *Historia de los cuerpos de tropa del ejército* (Lima: Servico de Prensa y Propaganda y Publicaciones Militares, 1951).

Gilbert, Dennis, *La oligarguía peruana: Historia de tres familias* (Lima: Editorial Horizonte, 1982).

Goodsell, Charles T., *American Corporations and Peruvian Politics* (Cambridge: Harvard University Press, 1974).

De la Gorce, Paul Marie, *The French Army: A Political Military History* (New York: George Brazille, 1963). Trans. by Kenneth Douglas.

Gott, Richard, *Guerrilla Movements in Latin America* (London: Nelson, 1970).

Hamill, Hugh, ed., *Dictatorship in Spanish America* (New York: Alfred A. Knopf, 1965).

Handelman, Howard, *Struggle in the Andes: Peasant Political Mobilization in Peru* (Austin: University of Texas Press, 1972).

Haya de la Torre, Víctor Raúl, *A donde va indoamerica?*, 2d ed., (Santiago: Ediciones Ercilla, 1935).

Haya de la Torre, Víctor Raúl, *El antiimperialismo y el APRA*. 3d ed., (Lima: Editorial Amuata, 1970).

Haya de la Torre, Víctor Raúl, *La defensa continental*, 4th ed., (Lima: Editorial Imprenta Amuata, 1967).

Haya de la Torre, Víctor Raúl, *Obras completas*, 6 vols., (Lima: Juan Meija Baca, 1976).

Haya de la Torre, Víctor Raúl, *Pensamiento politico de Haya de la Torre*, 5 vols., (Lima: Ediciones Pueblo, 1962).

Haya de la Torre, Víctor Raúl, *Trienta años de Aprismo* (Mexico, D.F.: Fondo de Cultura Economico, 1956).

Heare, Gertrude E., *Trends in Latin American Military Expenditures* (Washington, D.C.: U.S. Government Printing Office, 1971).

Hilliker, Grant, *The Politics of Reform in Peru: The Aprista and Other Mass Parties of Latin America* (Baltimore: Johns Hopkins University Press, 1971).

Hopkins, Jack, *The Government Executive of Modern Peru* (Gainesville: University of Florida Press, 1967).

Ingram, George, *Expropriation of U.S. Property in South America: Nationalization of Oil and Copper Companies in Peru, Bolivia and Chile* (New York: Praeger, 1974).

Janowitz, Morris, *The Military in the Political Development of New Nations* (Chicago: University of Chicago Press, 1964).

Johnson, John J., *The Military and Society in Latin America* (Stanford: Stanford University Press, 1964).

Johnson, John J., ed., *The Role of the Military in Underdeveloped Countries* (Princeton: Princeton University Press, 1962).

Kantor, Harry, *The Ideology and Program of the Peruvian Aprista Party* (Washington, D.C.: Saville Books, 1966).

Klaiber, Jeffrey C. *Religión y revolución en el Perú, 1824-1976* (Lima: Universidad del Pacificio, 1980).

Klarén, Peter, *Modernization, Dislocation and Aprismo: Origins of the Peruvian Aprista Party 1870-1932* (Austin: University of Texas Press, 1973).

Kruijt, Dirk, *La revolución por decreto* (Lima: Mosca Azul, 1988).

Kuczynski, Pedro Pablo, *Peruvian Democracy Under Economic Stress: An Account of the Belaúnde Administration* (Princeton: Princeton University Press, 1977).

Lambert, Jacques, *Latin American Social Structures and Political Institutions* (Berkeley: University of California Press, 1967).

Lieuwin, Edwin, *Arms and Politics in Latin America* (New York: Praeger, 1961).

Lieuwin, Edwin, *Generals vs. Presidents: Neomilitarism in Latin America* (New York: Praeger, 1964).

Loftus, Joseph, *Latin American Defense Expenditures, 1938-1965* (Santa Monica: Rand Corporation, 1968).

Loveman, Brian and Davies, Thomas M., Jr., eds., *The Politics of Anti-Politics: The Military in Latin America* (Lincoln: University of Nebraska Press, 1989).

Lowenthal, Abraham, ed., *Armies and Politics in Latin America* (New York: Holmes and Meier, 1976).

Lowenthal, Abraham, ed., *The Peruvian Experiment: Continuity and Change Under Military Rule* (Princeton: Princeton University Press, 1975).

Lowenthal, Abraham, and McClintock, Cynthia, eds., *The Peruvian Experiment Reconsidered* (Princeton: Princeton University Press, 1983).

Lyautey, Luis Hubert Gonzalve, *Lettres du Tonkin et de Madagasgar*, 2d ed., (Paris: Colin, 1921).

McAlister, Lyle, *The "Fuero Militar" in New Spain, 1765-1800*, (Gainesville: University of Florida Press, 1957).

McAlister, Lyle, Maingot, Anthony P., and Potash, Robert A., *The Military in Latin American Socio-Political Evolution: Four Case Studies* (Washington, D.C.: Department of Commerce, 1970).

McClintock, Cynthia, *Peasant Cooperatives and Political Change in Peru* (Princeton: Princeton University Press, 1981).

McCormick, Gordon A., *The Shining Path and the Future of Peru* (Santa Monica: Rand Corp., 1990).

Malloy, James M., *Authoritarianism, Corporatism and Mobilization in Peru* (Pittsburgh: University of Pittsburgh Press, 1973).

Marchetti, Victor and Marks, John D., *The CIA and the Cult of Intelligence* (New York: Alfred A. Knopf, 1974).

Marett, Robert, *Peru* (New York: Praeger, 1969).

Mariátegui, José Carlos, *Seven Interpretative Essays on Peruvian Reality*, 10th ed., (Austin: University of Texas Press, 1971). Trans. by Marjory Urquidi.

Martín, César, *Dichos y hechos de la politica peruana* (Lima: Santa Rosa, 1963).

Matos Mar, José, *Taquile en Lima* (Lima: Fundo Internacional Para la Promoción de las Culturas: 1986).

Mauceri, Philip, *Militares: Insurgencia y democratización en el Perú, 1980-1988* (Lima: I.E.P., 1989).

Mercado, Jarrín Edgardo, *Politica y defensa nacional* (Lima: Comisión Nacional de Plan de Gobierno, 1982).

Mercado, Jarrín Edgardo, *Un sistema de seguridad y defensa sudamericana* (Lima: Centro Peruano de Estudios Internacionales, 1989).

Mercado, Rogger, *Las guerrillas del Perú* (Lima: Fondo de Cultura Popular, 1967).

Mercado, Rogger, *La revolución de Trujillo* (Lima: Fondo de Cultura Popular, 1966).

Miró-Quesada Laos, Carlos, *Sánchez Cerro y su tiempo* (Buenos Aires: Liberta El Anteneo Editorial, 1947).

Montagne, Marckholtz, Ernesto, *Memorias del General de Brigada E.P. Ernesto Montagne Marckholtz* (Lima: N.P., 1963).

Moral, Roberto C. Noel, *Ayacucho: testimonio de un Soldado* (Lima: Publinor, 1989).

Morales Bermúdez Cerruti, Francisco, *Apuntes sobre autoritarianismo y democracia* (Lima: Ibesa, 1989).

Morales Bermúdez Cerruti, Francisco, *El projecto nacional* (Lima: Centro de Documentacion y Informacion Andina, 1982).

Morner, Magnus, *The Andean Past: Land, Societies and Conflicts* (New York: Columbia University Press, 1985).

Niera, Hugo, *El golpe de estado: Perú, 1968* (Madrid: Editorial ZYX, 1969).

Noel Moral, Roberto C. General, *Ayacucho: Testimonio de un soldado* (Lima: Publinor, 1989).

North, Liisa, *Civil-Military Relations in Argentina, Chile and Peru* (Berkeley: University of California Institute of Latin American Studies, 1966).

North, Liisa, and Korovkin, Tanya, *The Peruvian Revolution and the Officers in Power, 1967-1976* (Montreal: Center for Developing Area Studies, McGill University, 1981).

Nunn, Frederick M., *Chilean Politics, 1920-1931: The Honorable Mission of the Armed Forces* (Albuqerque: University of New Mexico Press, 1970).

Nunn, Frederick M., *The Military in Chilean History* (Albuquerque: University of New Mexico Press, 1976).

Nunn, Frederick M., *Yesterday's Soldiers: European Military Professionalism in South America, 1890-1940* (Lincoln: University of Nebraska Press, 1983).

Owens, Ronald Jerome, *Peru* (New York: Oxford University Press, 1963).

Ortíz, Sotelo, Jorge, *Escuela naval del Perú historia illustrada* (Callao: Escuela Naval del Perú, 1981).

Ortíz, Sotelo, Jorge, *Ex cadetes navales del Perú* (Lima: Asociación de Ex Cadetes Navales del Perú, 1981).

Palmer, David Scott, *Peru: The Authoritarian Tradition* (New York: Praeger, 1980).

Pareja, Paz-Soldán, José, ed., *Visión del Perú en el siglo XX*, 2 vols. (Lima: Libreria Stadium, 1962 and 1963).

Paret, Peter, ed., *Makers of Modern Strategy: From Machiavelli to the Nuclear Age* (Princeton: Princeton University Press, 1986).

Payne, Arnold, *The Peruvian Coup d' État of 1962: The Overthrow of Manuel Prado* (Washington: The Institute for Comparative Political Systems, 1965).

Payne, James, *Labor and Politics in Peru: The System of Political Bargaining* (New Haven: Yale University Press, 1965).

Pease, García Henry, *El ocaso del poder oligárquico: Lucha politica en la escena oficial, 1968-1975* (Lima: DESCO, 1977).

Perlmutter, Amos, *The Military and Politics in Modern Times* (New Haven: Yale University Press, 1977).

Philip, George, *The Rise and Fall of the Peruvian Military Radical, 1968-1976* (London: Anthlone Press, 1978).

Pike, Fredrick B., *The Modern History of Peru* (New York: Praeger, 1967).

Pike, Fredrick B., *The Politics of the Miraculous in Peru: Haya de la Torre and the Spiritualist Tradition* (Lincoln: University of Nebraska Press, 1986).

Pike, Fredrick B., *The United States and the Andean Republics, Peru, Bolivia, and Ecuador* (Cambridge: Harvard University Press, 1977).

Del Pilar Tello, Maria, *Golpe o revolución: Hablan los militares del 68* (Lima: Ediciones SAGASA, 1983).

Pinelo, Adalberto, *The Multinational Corporation as a Force in Latin American Politics: A Case Study of the International Petroleum Company in Peru* (New York: Praeger, 1973).

Pion-Berlin, David, *The Ideology of State Terror: Economic Doctrine and Political Repression in Argentina and Peru* (Boulder: Lynne Rienner Publishers, 1989).

Potash, Robert, *The Army and Politics in Argentina, 1928-1945: Yrigoyen to Perón* (Stanford: Stanford University Press, 1969).

Potash, Robert, *The Army and Politics in Argentina, 1945-1963: Perón to Frondizi* (Stanford: Stanford University Press, 1981).

Quijano, Anibal, *Nationalism and Capitalism in Peru: A Study in Neo-Imperialism* (New York: Monthly Review Press, 1971).

Ramírez y Berrios, Guillermo M., *Grandezas y miserias de un proceso electoral en el Perú* (Lima: Talleras Graficas, P.L. Villanueva, 1957).

Ravines, Eudocio, *The Yenan Way* (New York: Charles Scribner, 1951).

Rios, Pagaso Carlos, *Historia de la Escuela Militar del Perú* (Lima: Tallares Reprofgrafica, 1967).

Robinson, David A., *Peru in Four Dimensions* (Lima: American Studies Press, S.A., 1964).

Rodríguez Beruff, Jorge, *Los militares y el poder: Un ensayo sobre la doctrina militar en el Perú, 1948-1968* (Lima: Mosca Azul Editores, 1983).

Rodríguez, Luis A., *La verdad sobre la agresión peruana* (Quito: N.P., 1966).

Romero, Emilio, *Geografía economica del Perú* (Lima: Editorial Grafica Pacifica, Saba Raul, 1968).

Rouquié, Alain, *The Military and the State in Latin America* (Berkeley: University of California Press, 1987). Trans. by Paul E. Sigmund.

Salazar Larrain, Arturo, *La herencia de Velasco, 1968-1975* (Lima: Desa, 1977).

Sánchez, Luis Alberto, *Haya de la Torre el politico*, 2d ed., (Santiago de Chile: Editorial Ercilla, 1936).

Sánchez, Luis Alberto, *Haya de la Torre el Apra* (Santiago, Chile: Editorial, Pacifico, 1955).

Sánchez, Luis Alberto, *Testimonio personal: Memorias de un peruano del siglo XX*, 3 vols., (Lima: Ediciones Vilasan, 1969).

Scham, Alan, *Lyautey in Morocco, Protectorate Administration, 1912-1925* (Berkeley: University of California Press, 1970).

Scheina, Robert L., *Latin America: A Naval History, 1810-1987* (Annapolis: Naval Institute Press, 1987).

Schlesinger, Arthur, *A Thousand Days: John F. Kennedy in the White House* (Boston: Houghton Mifflin, 1965).

Scullard, Howard, *The Roman Republic: From the Gracchi to Nero* (New York: Praeger, 1959).

Sharp, Daniel A., ed., *U.S. Foreign Policy and Peru* (Austin: University of Texas Press, 1972).

Simon, Sheldon, ed., *The Military and Society in the Third World: Domestic and International Impacts* (Boulder: Westview Press, 1978).

Skidmore, Thomas E., *The Politics of Military Rule in Brazil, 1964-1985* (New York: Oxford University Press, 1988).

Stephens, Richard H., *Wealth and Power in Peru* (Metuchen, New Jersey: Scarecrow Press, 1971).

Stein, Steve, *Populism in Peru: The Emergence of the Masses and the Politics of Social Control* (Madison: University of Wisconsin Press, 1980).

Szulc, Tad, *Twilight of the Tyrants* (New York: Henry Holt, 1959).

Thorndike, Guillermo, *El año de la barbarie: Perú, 1932* (Lima: Nueva America, 1968).

Thorndike, Guillermo, *No mi general* (Lima: Mosca Azul Editores, 1976).

Thorp, Rosemary, and Bertram, Geoffrey, *Peru, 1890-1977: Growth and Policy in an Open Economy* (New York: Columbia University Press, 1978).

Tullis, La Mond, *Lord and Peasant in Peru: A Paradigm of Political and Social Change* (Cambridge: Harvard University Press, 1970).

Ureta, Eloy G., *Apuntes sobres una compaña, 1941* (Madrid: Editorial "Antorcha," 1953).

Vargas Gavilano, Amílicar, *La revolución de Velasco en cifras* (Lima: Ediciones INPET, 1989).

Vargas Llosa, Mario, *La ciudad y los perros* (Barcelona: Seix Barial, 1985).

Velasco Alvarado, Juan, *La voz de la revolucíon: Discursos de General de Division Juan Velasco Alvarado* (Lima: Editorial Ausonia, 1972).

Villanueva Valencia, Víctor, *El militarismo en el Perú* (Lima: Empresa Grafica T. Scheuch, S.A. 1962).

Villanueva Valencia, Víctor, *La sublevación aprista del 48: Tragedia de un pueblo y un partido* (Lima: Millas Batres, 1973).

Villanueva Valencia, Víctor, *100 años del ejército peruano: Frustraciones y cambios* (Lima: Juan Meija Baca, 1971).

Villanueva Valencia, Víctor, *Nueva mentalidad militar en el Perú* (Lima: Juan Meija Baca, 1969).

Villanueva Valencia, Víctor, *Un año bajo el sable* (Lima: Empresa Grafica T. Scheuch, S.A., 1963).

Villanueva Valencia, Víctor, *Hugo Blanco y la rebelión campesina* (Lima: Juan Meija Baca, 1967).

Villanueva Valencia, Víctor, *El CAEM y la revolución de la fuerza armada* (Lima: Instituto de Estudios Peruanos, 1973).

Villanueva Valencia, Víctor, *El APRA en busca del poder* (Lima: Editorial Horizonte, 1975).

Villanueva Valencia, Víctor, *Ejército Peruano: Del caudillaje anarquíco al militarismo reformista* (Lima: Juan Meija Baca, 1973).

Villanueva Valencia, Víctor, *El APRA y el ejército, 1940-1950* (Lima: Editorial Horizonte, 1977).

Villanueva Valencia, Víctor, *Asi Cayo Leguía* (Lima: Editorial Retuma, 1977).

Weil, Thomas., et al., *Area Handbook for Peru* (Washington, D.C.: U. S. Government Printing Office, 1972).

Werlich, David, *Peru: A Short History* (Carbondale: Southern Illinois University Press, 1978).

Wesson, Robert, ed., *The Latin American Military Institution* (New York: Praeger, 1986).

Wood, Bryce, *The United States and Latin American Wars, 1932-1942* (New York: Columbia University Press, 1966).

Wood, David, *The Armed Forces in Central and South America* (London: Adelphi Papers #34, Institute for Strategic Studies, 1967).

Zárate Lescano, José, *El mariscal Benavides: Su Vida y su Obra*, 2 vols. (Lima: Editorial Atlanida, 1976).

Zegarre de la Flor, Ricardo, *El gobierno del presidente constitucional de la república, General de División, Don Manuel A. Odría y el progreso del Perú* (Lima: N.P., 1952).

Zimmerman Zavala, Augusto, *La historia secreta del petroleo* (Lima: Editorial Gráfica Labor, 1968).

Zimmerman Zavala, Augusto, *El Plan Inca: Objetivo revolucíon Peruana* (Lima: Editorial del Diario Oficial Peruano, 1974).

Zook, David H., Jr., *Zarumilla-Marañón: The Ecuador-Peru Border Dispute* (New York: Brookman Associates, 1964).

Articles

Anonymous, "Accion Civica," *Actualidad Militar*, (30 April 1967), 1-16.

Anonymous, "Ascenso a Mariscal del Perú, General de Division, Eloy G. Ureta, *Revista Militar del Perú* 1 (Enero de 1946), 5-8.

Anonymous, "Colaboración del ejército en el desarollo del plan vial nacional," *Actualidad Militar* (15 August 1962), 1-16.

Anonymous, "A contecimientos en la Sierra central y sureste del Perú," *Actualidad Militar* (30 September 1968), 2-3.

Anonymous, "Ejército y subversión," *Actualidad Militar*, (31 January 1967), 32-36.

Anonymous, "Las escuelas superiores del ejército norte-americano," *Revista Militar del Perú* 8 (August, 1947), 319-322.

Anonymous, "Generales del ejército pasan al retiro," *Actualidad Militar* (15 February 1969), 22-25.

Anonymous, "Necrología: Mariscal del Perú, Oscar R. Benavides," *Revista Militar del Perú* 7 (July, 1945), 9-12.

Anonymous, "Nuevas autoridades en el ejército," *Actualidad Militar* (30 September 1967), 26-38.

Anonymous, "Peru: Partial Recovery," *Latin America* 7, no. 11 (16 March 1973), 85-86.

Anonymous, "Pasos preliminares para la colonización del Alto Marañon," *Actualidad Militar*, (15 July 1965), 6.

Anonymous, "El presidente de la republica recibe la insignia unica de gratitud nacional," *Revista Militar del Perú* 7 (Julio, 1942), 4-5.

Anonymous, "Resumen de programa de desarrollo industrial y regional para Perú, por Arthur D. Little Inc., *Revista Escuela Superior de Guerra* 2 (May-June, 1961), 1-18.

Anonymous, "Viaje del commandante general y del jefe de Estado Mayor General del ejército de Argentina," *Actualidad Militar*, (30 July 1968), 18-19.

Arce, Victor E., "La fuerza aérea del Perú en el siglo XX," in José Pareja Paz-Soldán, *Visión del Perú en el siglo XX*, vol. 2, 393-443.

Astiz, Carlos, and García José, "The Peruvian Military: Achievement Orientation, Training and Political Tendencies," *Western Political Quarterly* 25, no. 4 (December, 1972), 667-685.

Avery, William P. "Origins and Consequences of the Border Dispute Between Ecuador and Peru," *Inter-American Economic Affairs* 38 (Summer, 1979), 65-77.

Barnes, John M., "U.S. Military Assistance to Latin America: An Assess ment," *Journal of Inter-American Studies and World Affairs* 14, no. 4 (November, 1972), 469-488.

Barbís, D. M., "El ejército y la colonización de montaña," *Revista Militar del Perú* 12 (December, 1933), 1239-1242.

Benavides, Oscar, "Discurso pronuciado por el Presidente de la República en el día del ejército," *Revista Militar del Perú* 12 (December, 1935), 2243-2248.

Bonner, Raymond, "A Reporter at Large: Peru's War," *The New Yorker*, 4 January 1988, 31-58.

Bourque, Susan C., and Warren, Kay, "Democracy Without Peace: The Cultural Politics of Terror in Peru," *Latin American Research Review*, 24, no. 1 (1989), 7-34.

Bourricaud, François, "Los militares por que y para que," *Aportes*, 9 (April, 1970), 13-55.

Campbell, Leon, "The Historiography of the Peruvian Guerrilla Movement, 1960-1965," *Latin American Research Review* 8, no. 1 (Spring, 1973), 45-70.

Carey, James, "Peru's Encouraging New Spirit," *Current History* 49 (December, 1965), 321-327.

Del Carmen Marín, José, "Conocimientó de la ingeñería como arma," *Revista Militar de Perú* 4 (April, 1936), 625-642.

Del Carmen Marín, José, "El Perú y la defensa hemisférica, *Revista Militar del Perú* 628 (June, 1955), 200-213.

Davis, Robert B., "Sendero Luminoso and Peru's Struggle for Survival," *Military Review*, 70, no. 1 (January, 1990), 79-88.

Degregori, Carlos Ívan, "Sendero Luminoso: Los hondos y mortales desencuentros," (parte 1, Lima, LEP 1985).

Degregori, Carlos Ívan, "Sendero Luminoso: Lucha armada y utopia autoritaria," (parte 2, Lima, LEP 1986).

Castillo Pizarro, Arturo, "El Perú como nación—nacionalismo y conciencia nacional," *Revista Militar del Perú* 613 (January-February-March, 1955), 87-101.

Chaplin, David, "La Convención Valley and the 1962-1965 Guerrilla Uprising," in David Chaplin, ed., *Peruvian Nationalism: A Corporatist Revolution* (New Brunswick, New Jersey: Transaction Books, 1976), 277-290.

Chaplin, David, "The Revolutionary Challenge and Peruvian Militarism," in David Chaplin, *Peruvian Nationalism: A Corporatist Revolution* (New Brunswick, New Jersey: Transaction Books, 1976), 3-34.

Cleaves, Peter, and Pease Garcia, Henry, "State Autonomy and Military Policymaking," in Cynthia McClintock and Abraham Lowenthal, *The Peruvian Experiment Reconsidered* (Princeton: Princeton University Press, 1983), 209-244.

Clinton, Richard C., "APRA: An Appraisal," *Journal of Inter-American Studies and World Affairs*, 12, no. 2 (April, 1970), 280-297.

Clinton, Richard C., "The Modernizing Military: The Case of Peru," *Inter-American Economic Affairs*, 24, no. 4 (Spring, 1971), 43-62.

Colina, Leonicio R., "La industria y la defensa nacional," *Revista Militar del Perú* 1 (January, 1985), 37-59.

Cotler, Julio, "Political Crisis and Military Populism," *Studies in Comparative International Development*, 6, no. 5 (Spring, 1971), 95-113.

Cotler, Julio, "The Mechanics of Internal Domination and Social Change in Peru," in David Chaplin, ed., *Peruvian Nationalism: A Corporatist Revolution* (New Brunswick, New Jersey: Transaction Books, 1976) 35-74.

Craig, Gordon, "The Political Leader as Strategist," in Peter Paret, ed., *Makers of Modern Strategy: From Machiavelli to the Nuclear Age*, 481-509.

Cruzada, Luis Vera, "La guerra revolucionaria, la guerra subversiva y la guerra de guerrilla," *Revista Militar del Perú* 63, no. 704 (May-June, 1965), 52-66.

Davies, M. Thomas, Jr., "The Indigenismo of the Peruvian *Aprista* Party," *Hispanic American Historical Review* 51, no. 4 (November, 1971), 626-695.

Dickson, Thomas I., "An Approach to the Study of the Latin American Military," *Journal of Inter-American Studies and World Affairs* 14, no. 4 (November, 1972), 455-468.

Einaudi, Luigi R. "Revolution from Within? Military Rule in Peru Since 1968," in David Chaplin, ed., *Peruvian Nationalism: A Corporatist Revolution* (New Brunswick, New Jersey: Transaction Books, 1976), 401-427.

Figueroa Arévalo, Marcial, "El oficial de ejército y la integración del indigena a la nacionalidad," *Revista Militar del Perú* 52, 621 (July-August-September, 1955), 104-108.

Frankman, Myron, "Sectoral Policy References of the Peruvian Government, 1946-1968," *Journal of Latin American Studies* 6, no. 2 (June, 1974), 289-300.

Gall, Norman, "Peru: The Master Is Dead," *Dissent* 18, (1971), 280-320.

Gallardo, Echeverría Andres, "Las Visperas del 3 Octubre 1948," *Oiga* 8, no. 393 (2 October 1970), 37-38.

Gallardo, Echeverría Andres, "El Cuartelazo de Odría," *Oiga* 8, no. 397 (30 October 1970), 24-25, 46.

Gallegos Rendón, Jorge, "El ejército y la información pública," *Revista Escuela Superior de Guerra* 9, no. 2 (April-May-June, 1962), 83-92.

Gallegos Venero, Enrique, "Un combate victorioso en guerra contra revolucionaria," *Revista Escuela Superior de Guerra* 10, no. 3 (July-August-September, 1963), 7-27.

Gallegos Venero, Enrique, "El estudios de situaciones en guerra subversiva, *Revista Escuela Superior de Guerra* 9, no. 4 (October-November-December, 1962), 74-84.

Gallegos Venero, Enrique, "Inteligencia y Guerra no Convencional," *Revista Escuela Superior de Guerra* 13, no. 3 (July-August-September, 1966), 7-18.

Gallegos Venero, Enrique, "Problemas de guerra contra revolucionaria," *Revista Escuela Superior de Guerra* 11, no. 2 (April-May-June, 1964), 92-107.

Gilbert, Felix, "Machiavelli: The Renaissance of the Art of War," in Peter Paret, ed., *Makers of Modern Strategy: From Machiavelli to the Nuclear Age* (Princeton: Princeton University Press, 1986), 11-33.

Goodsell, Charles, "That Confounding Revolution in Peru," *Current History* 68 (January, 1975), 20-23.

Goodwin, Richard W., "Letter from Peru: Takeover of the International Petroleum Co.," *The New Yorker* 45 (17 May 1969), 41-109.

Gorriti, Gustavo, "The War of the Philosopher King," *The New Republic*, 202 (18 June 1990), 15-22.

Gottman, Jean, "Bugeaud, Gallieni, Lyautey: The Development of French Colonial Warfare," in Edward Mead Earle, ed., *Makers of Modern Strategy: Military Thought from Machiavelli to Hitler* (New York: Antheneum, 1966), 239-260.

Grayson, George W., "Peru's Military Government," *Current History* 58, no. 342 (February, 1970), 65-90.

Guerlac, Henry, "Vauban: The Impact of Science on War," in Peter Paret, *Makers of Modern Strategy: From Machiavelli to the Nuclear Age*, (Princeton: Princeton University Press, 1986), 69-90.

Guzmán, Reynoso, Abimael, *El Diario*, [Interview] with Luis Arce Borja, (24 July 1988), 1-22.

Harding, Colin, "Land Reform and Social Conflict in Peru," in Abraham Lowenthal, ed., *The Peruvian Experiment: Continuity and Change Under Military Rule* (Princeton: Princeton University Press, 1975), 220-253.

Haya de la Torre, Víctor Raul, "My Five Year Exile in My Own Country," *Life*, 38 (3 May 3, 1959), 152-164.

Ibánez, O'Brien, Gaston, "El Congreso y la fuerza armada," *Revista Escuela Superior de Guerra*, 12, no. 2 (April-May-June, 1965), 33-42.

Jaquette, Jane S. "Belaúnde and Velasco: On the Limits of Ideological Politics," in Abraham Lowenthal, ed., *The Peruvian Experiment: Continuity and Change Under Military Rule* (Princeton: Princeton University Press, 1975), 402-438.

Jaquette, Jane S. "Revolution by Fiat: The Context of Policy Making in Peru," *Western Political Quarterly* 25 (December, 1972), 648-666.

Klaiber, Jeffrey L., S. J., "Reform Politics in Peru: Alan García's Crusade Against Corruption," *Corruption and Reform* 2 (1987), 149-168.

Kossok, Manfred, "The Armed Forces in Latin America: Potential for Changes in Political and Social Functions," *Journal of Inter-American Studies and World Affairs* 14, no. 4 (November, 1972), 275-298.

Langley, Lester P., "Military Commitments in Latin America 1960-1968," *Current History* 56, no. 334 (June, 1969), 346-351, 367.

Lowenthal, Abraham, "Peru's Ambiguous Revolution," in Abraham Lowenthal, ed., *The Peruvian Experiment: Continuity and Change Under Military Rule* (Princeton: Princeton University Press, 1975), 3-43.

Lowenthal, Abraham, "The Peruvian Experiment Reconsidered," in Cynthia McClintock and Abraham Lowenthal, eds., *The Peruvian Experiment Reconsidered* (Princeton: Princeton University Press, 1983), 415-430.

330   Bibliography

Lyautey Gonsalve Hubert Louís, "Du rôle colonial de l'armee," *Revue Des Deux Mondes* (15 January 1900), 300-329.

Lyautey, Gonsalve Hubert Louís, "Du rôle social de l'officer," *Revue Des Duex Mondes*, 104, (15 March 1891), 443-459.

McAlister, Lyle N. "Peru," in Lyle N. McAlister, Anthony P. Maingot, and Robert Potash, *The Military in Latin American Socio-Political Evolution: Four Case Studies* (Washington, D.C.: Department of Commerce, 1970), 21-69.

McAlister, Lyle N., "Recent Research and Writings on the Role of the Military in Latin America," *Latin American Research Review* 11, no. 1 (Fall, 1966), 5-36.

McClintock, Cynthia, "Sendero Luminoso: Peru's Maoist Guerrillas," *Problems of Communism* 32, no. 5 (1983), 19-34.

McClintock, Cynthia, "Velasco, Officers and Citizens: The Politics of Stealth," in Cynthia McClintock and Abraham Lowenthal, eds., *The Peruvian Experiment Reconsidered* (Princeton: Princeton University Press, 1983), 275-308.

McClintock, Cynthia, "Why Peasants Rebel: The Case of Peru's *Sendero Luminoso*," *World Politics* 37 (1984), 48-84.

McNicoll, Robert E., "Intellectual Origins of *Aprismo*," *Hispanic American Historical Review* 23, no. 3 (August, 1943), 424-440.

Malloy, James, "Authoritorism, Corporatism and Mobilization in Peru," *Review of Politics* 36, no. 1 (Spring, 1974), 52-84.

Malloy, James M., "Peru Before and After the Coup of 1968," *Journal of Inter-American Studies and World Affairs* 4 (November, 1972), 437-454.

Masterson, Daniel M., "Peru's New Leader," *The Christian Century* 112, no. 40 (December, 1975), 1112-1114.

Masterson, Daniel M., "Soldiers, Sailors, and *Apristas*: Conspiracy and Power Politics in Peru, 1932-1948, in John F. Bratzel and Daniel M. Masterson, eds., *The Underside of Latin American History* (East Lansing: Center for Latin American Studies, Michigan State University, 1977), 24-42.

Masterson, Daniel M., "Field Research on the Modern Peruvian Military: A Selective Guide," in John TePaske, ed., *Research Guide to Andean History: Bolivia, Chile, Ecuador, and Peru* (Durham: Duke University Press, 1981), 253-256.

Masterson, Daniel M., "*Caudillismo* and Institutional Change: Manuel Odría and the Peruvian Armed Forces, 1948-1956," *The Americas*, 40, no. 4 (April, 1984), 479-489.

Masterson, Daniel M., "From *Caudillos* to Professional Soldiers: The Origins of Peru's Modern Armed Forces, 1895-1930," *Red River Valley Historical Journal* 5, no. 3 (Spring, 1981), 220-232.

Masterson, Daniel M., "Peru's Military Junta at the Crossroads," *The Christian Century* 41, no. 41 (November, 1974), 1127-1128.

Masterson, Daniel M., "The Changing Focus of *Aprismo*: Haya de la Torre, Alan García and the Anti-Imperialist Tradition in Peru," *Journal of Third World Studies* 7, no. 2, (Fall, 1990).

Medina V., Alejandro, "La geografía económica frente a la energía atómica," *Revista Militar del Perú* 52, no. 627 (January-February-March, 1956), 49-61.

Medina V., Alejandro, "Geografía social y humana," *Revista Militar del Perú* 51, no. 624 (October-November-December, 1955), 41-45.

Mendoza Rodríguez, Juan, "El Ejército Peruano, en el siglo XX," in José Pareja Paz-Soldán, *Visión del Perú en el siglo XX*, vol. 1, (Lima: Libreria Stadium, 1962) 291-349.

Mendoza Rodríguez, Juan, "Potencia del Perú en la junta inter-americana de defensa," *Revista Escuela Superior Guerra*, 8, no. 2 (April-June, 1961), 112-114.

Mercado Jarrín, Edgardo, "La política y la estratégia militar en el sistema interamericano," *Revista Militar del Perú* 706 (September-October, 1968), 5-19.

Mercado Jarrín, Edgardo, "La escuela de comando de estado mayor de Fort Leavenworth y algunas diferencias con nuestra," *Revista Escuela Superior de Guerra* 5, no. 2 (April-May-June, 1958), 15-35.

Mercado Jarrín, Edgardo, "El ejército de hoy y una proyección en nuestra sociedad en periodo de transición," *Revista Militar del Perú* 59, no. 685, (November-December, 1964), 1-20.

Mercado Jarrín, Edgardo, "La politica y la estrategia militar en la guerra contra subersiva en America Latina," *Revista Escuela Superior de Guerra* 11, no. 4 (October-November-December, 1964), 77-104.

Mercado Jarrín, Edgardo, "La politica de seguridad integral," *Revista Escuela Superior de Guerra* 11, no. 4 (October-November-December, 1964), 83-113.

Mercado Jarrín, Edgardo, "Las relaciones entre la política y la estratégia militar," *Revista Escuela Superior de Guerra* 12, no. 3 (July-August-September, 1965), 37-60.

Millington, Thomas, M., "The Latin American Military Elite," *Current History* 56, no. 334 (June, 1969), 352-354, 364.

Miró-Quesada Oscar, "La patria y el ejército," *Revista Militar del Perú* 6 (June, 1941), 29-52.

Morales Bermúdez, Francisco, "Planamiento Estratégico," *Revista Escuela Superior de Guerra* 10, no. 1 (January-February-March, 1963), 7-13.

Morla Concha, Manuel, "Función social del ejército Peruano en la organización de la nacionalidad," *Revista Militar del Perú* 30, no. 10 (October, 1933), 843-872.

Needler, Martin C., "Political Development and Military Intervention in Latin America," *American Political Science Review* 60, no. 3 (September, 1966), 616-626.

North, Liisa, "Ideological Orientations of Peru's Military Leaders," in Cynthia McClintock and Abraham Lowenthal, eds., *The Peruvian Experiment Reconsidered* (Princeton: Princeton University Press, 1983), 245-274.

Nun, José, "A Latin American Phenomenon: The Middle Class Military Coup," *Trends in Social Science Research in Latin America. A Conference Report* (Berkeley: University of California Press, 1965), 55-91.

Nunn, Frederick M., "Effects of European Military Training in Latin America: The Origins and Nature of Professional Militarism in Argentina, Brazil, Chile, and Peru, 1890-1940," *Military Affairs*, 39, no. 1 (February, 1975), 1-20.

Nunn, Frederick M., "Notes on the 'Junta Phenomenon' and the 'Military Regime' in Latin America with Special Reference to Peru, 1968-1972," *The Americas* 31, no. 3 (January, 1975), 237-252.

Nunn, Frederick M., "Professional Militarism in Twentieth-Century Peru: Historical and Theoretical Background to the *Golpe de Estado* of 1968," *Hispanic American Historical Review* 59, no. 3 (August, 1979), 391-417.

Palmer, David Scott, "The Sendero Luminoso Rebellion in Rural Peru," in Georges Fauriol, ed., *Latin American Insurgencies*, (Washington, D.C.: The Georgetown University Center for Strategic and International Studies and the National Defence University, 1985), 67-97.

Palmer, David Scott, and Middlebrook, Kevin Jay, "Corporatist Participation Under Military Rule in Peru," in David Chaplin, ed., *Peruvian Nationalism: A Corporatist Revolution*, (New Brunswick, New Jersey: Transaction Books, 1976), 428-453.

Pando Esguisquiza, César A., "El ejército, es improductivo?" *Revista Militar del Perú* 48, no. 8 (August, 1946), 371-387.

Pando Esguisquiza, César H., "Las misiones militares francesas y el ejército de Perú, *Revista Militar del Perú* 11 (November, 1946), 95-107.

Paret, Peter, "Clausewitz" in Peter Paret, ed., *The Makers of Modern Strategy: From Machiavelli to the Nuclear Age*, (Princeton: Princeton University Press, 1986), 186-216.

Pásara, Luis, "When the Military Dreams," in Cynthia McClintock and Abraham Lowenthal, eds., *The Peruvian Experiment Reconsidered* (Princeton: Princeton University Press, 1983), 309-346.

Patch, Richard, "Life in a Peruvian Indian Community," *American Universities Field Staff Reports Service* 9, no. 1, (1962), 1-29.

Patch, Richard, "Peru's New President and Agrarian Reform," *American Universities Field Staff Reports Service* 10, no. 2 (August, 1963), 1-10.

Patch, Richard, "The Peruvian Elections of 1962 and Their Annulment," *American Universities Field Staff Reports Service* 9, no. 6 (September, 1962), 1-13.

Patch, Richard, "The Peruvian Elections of 1963," *American Universities Field Staff Reports Service* 10, no. 1 (July, 1963) 1-14.

Patch, Richard W., "The Peruvian Agrarian Reform Bill: Legislation for an Ideal," *American Universities Field Staff Reports Service* 11, no. 3 (1964), 1-12.

Payne, Arnold, "Peru: Latin America's Silent Revolution," *Inter-American Economic Affairs* 20, no. 6 (Winter, 1966), 69-78.

Pérez Godoy, Ricardo, "La guerra moderna," *Revista Militar del Perú* 50, no. 5 (May, 1948), 87-91.

Pérez Godoy, Ricardo, "Un trabajo de historia militar a domicilio," *Revista Militar del Perú* 39, no. 11 (November, 1937), 427-437.

Pike, Fredrick B., "The Old and New APRA in Peru: Myth and Reality," *Inter-American Economic Affairs* 18, no. 2 (Autumn, 1964), 3-45.

Porch, Douglas, "Bugeaud, Galliéni, Lyautey: The Development of French Colonial Warfare," in Peter Paret, ed., *Makers of Modern Strategy: From Machiavelli to the Nuclear Age*, (Princeton: Princeton University Press, 1986), 367-407.

Rankin, Richard C., "The Expanding Institutional Concerns of the Latin American Military Establishments: A Review Article", *Latin American Research Review*, 9, (1977), 81-109.

Rozman, Stephen L., "The Evolution of the Political Role of the Peruvian Military," *Journal of Inter-American Studies and World Affairs* 12 (October, 1970), 539-569.

Sánchez Marín, Víctor, "El departmento de mobilización integral de la nación, elemento básico del ministro de defensa nacional," *Revista Escuela Superior de Guerra* 3 (July-August-September, 1955), 30-53.

Sanders, Thomas G., "The Politics of Transition in Peru," *American University Field Staff Reports Service* 24, no. 2, (December, 1977), 1-15.

Thorp, Rosemary, "The Evolution of Peru's Economy," in Cynthia McClintock and Abraham Lowenthal, eds., *The Peruvian Experiment Reconsidered* (Princeton: Princeton University Press, 1983), 39-64.

Torres, Oscar N., "La instrucción militar en las universidades y escuelas superiores," *Revista Militar del Perú* 42, no. 7 (July, 1940), 369-402.

Valdez Pallette, Luis, "Antecedentes de la nueva orientación de las fuerzas armadas en el Perú," *Aportes* 10, no. 17 (January, 1971), 163-181.

Valdizan Gamio, José, "La marina de guerra peruana en el siglo XX," in José Pareja Paz-Soldán, ed., *Visión del Perú en el siglo XX*, vol. 1, (Lima: Libreria Stadium, 1962), 351-392.

Velarde, Cesar A., "La instrucción civil en el ejército," *Revista Militar del Perú* 37, no. 11 (November, 1935), 2119-2121.

Webb, Richard, "Government Policy and the Distribution of Income in Peru, 1963-1973," in Abraham Lowenthal, ed., *The Peruvian Experiment: Continuity and Change Under Military Rule* (Princeton: Princeton University Press, 1975), 79-127.

Whyte, William F., "Rural Peru: Peasants as Activists," in David Chaplin, ed., *Peruvian Nationalism: A Corporatist Revolution* (New Brunswick, New Jersey: Transaction Books, 1976), 241-251.

Index

344   Index

1930 coup, 34; coup unleashes
new social forces, 40; early career
reviewed, 43; political philosophy,
43; policy toward armed forces and
police, 43-44; rivalry with APRA,
45-52; wins presidency 1931, 47;
suppresses Callao mutiny, 48;
defeats Trujillo revolt, 49-51; in
Leticia conflict, 51-52; assassinated by an *Aprista*, 52, 59
Sánchez-Cerrista Faction, 53-59 passim. See also *Partido Union Revolucionario*
San Cristóbal de Huamanga, University of, 7, 267
Santisteban Silva, Gen. Antonio, 72,
74
San Martín, José de, 11, 24
Scheina, Robert, *Latin America: A
Naval History, 1810-1987*, 15
Schlesinger, Arthur, Jr., 165, 180
n.63, 184
School of the Americas (Panama),
212
Sedan, French defeat at, 12
Senate Boycott (Peru 194), 102
Sendero Luminoso (Shining Path): 4,
6; in narcotics trafficking, 8, 281;
illustrates limits of military, 14;
evolution of, 274-282; similarity to
early APRA, 275; five-stage timetable, 277-278; recruiting practices, 277-278; role of women in,
279; revolutionary tactics, 279-
280; impact of prison riots, 280-
281; role of peasantry in, 281-282;
armed forces strategy against, 282-
285; welcomes military repression,
287; mission of military against,
288. See also Communist Party
(Peru) and Abimael Guzmán
Reynoso
Seoane, Manuel, 55, 96, 112, 119,
143, 207
Siete Partidas, 10, 20 n.17
SINAMOS (*Sistema Nacional de*

Apoyo de Movilizacion Social), 244,
255-256, 306
Sinchis, 279
Smuggling Scandal (Armed Forces),
222-223
Social Property Enterprises (EPS),
244, 263
Sociedad Nacional Agraria (National
Agrarian Society), 253
Soviet Union, Influence of in Peru,
257, 258-263
State Modernizers (Velasco govern-
ment), 247-248
Stein, Steve, 132
Sukhoi SU-22 fighter bombers, 259,
263

Tacna, Province of, 4, 25
Tacna-Arica dispute, 33
Taki Ongoy Movement, 282
Tanks (Soviet T-54 and T-55), 259,
271
Tantaleán Vannini, Gen. Javier,
261-262, 266
Tarapaca, Province of, 25
Tax Reform, 188, 195
"Third Position" of Velasco govern-
ment, 247, 251
Thorp, Rosemary (and Bertram,
Geoffrey), *Peru, 1890-1977: Growth
and Policy in an Open Economy*, 8,
261
Tiahuanaco, 4
Tirado Lamb, Adm. Guillermo, 160-
161, 170, 172, 175
Toro, David, 55-56, 225
Torre, Augusta, 276
Torres, Gen. Oscar, 92-93, 137
Torres Matos, Adm. José, 176, 192
Trafalgar, legacy of, 13
La Tribuna (Lima), 72-73, 95, 120
Trujillo Jail Massacre, 50
Trujillo Revolt (1932), 49-51
Túpac Amaru II, 1, 6, 252. See also
José Gabriel Condorconqui

About the Author

DANIEL M. MASTERSON is an Associate Professor of History at the United States Naval Academy, Annapolis, Maryland. Specializing in modern Latin American history and Latin American militarism, he has edited *The Underside of Latin American History* and *Naval History: The Papers of the Sixth Naval History Symposium*.